DANGEROUS THOUGHTS

DANGEROUS THOUGHTS
Memoirs of a Russian Life
Yuri Orlov

Translated from the Russian
by Thomas P. Whitney

WILLIAM MORROW AND COMPANY, INC.
NEW YORK

It is the policy of William Morrow and Company, Inc., and its imprints and affiliates, recognizing the importance of preserving what has been written, to print the books we publish on acid-free paper, and we exert our best efforts to that end.

Library of Congress Cataloging-in-Publication Data

Orlov, Yuri, 1924–
    Dangerous thoughts : memoirs of a Russian life / by Yuri Orlov ; translated by Thomas P. Whitney.
        p.   cm.
    ISBN 0-688-10471-1
    1. Orlov, Yuri, 1924–   2. Physicists—Soviet Union—Biography.
I. Title.
QC16.O64A3   1991
530'.092—dc20
[B]   90–48638
                                                                                         CIP

Printed in the United States of America.

First Edition

1 2 3 4 5 6 7 8 9 10

To the Memory of Anatoly Marchenko

Born, January 23, 1938, Barabinsk, Siberia
Died, December 8, 1986, Chistopol Prison

PREFACE

UNFORTUNATELY my life has not been boring. By nature I am an armchair man: I love to think alone, do calculations on a blackboard, look at what I have written from a distance. Instead, half my life has been lived in noisy and sometimes nasty places full of people. After a happy childhood spent among peasants, I worked as a laborer making T-34 tanks and then became an army officer, an active member of the Communist Party, a professor, a dissident, a prisoner, and an exile. I have traveled through nearly every layer of Soviet society.

It is problematic to write about such a life. Many people will declare that the author appears to be a decent man, but is certainly biased because his stories are absurd, impossible. And the rest will grumble that the author is certainly decent, but seems to be a trivial man because his stories are commonplace, nothing new. The fact is that the absurd is commonplace in the Soviet Union. This is simply the way things are, and my experience must reflect it. True, I was the only member of my family to get arrested, and I had the good fortune to be liberated from Siberia. But apart from that, my life has not really been extraordinary. I should like readers to see in this book a picture of millions and millions of other lives, as well as glimpse the

7

Russian tragedy of the twentieth century—indeed, the greatest tragedy of intellectual history.

Today, the brilliant and well-articulated idea of a just and rational society—the idea of socialism—has sustained a humiliating defeat. One of the main reasons it happened was that the intellectuals who created the idea did not take into account the nature of intellect itself. Intellect does not feel love. It does not feel physical pain. It is attracted to order and final solutions. Therefore, it is able to create any violent idea, including even the idea of self-destruction and the destruction of all living beings. "Just" and "rational" Soviet society buried itself in an ocean of blood, and then took three decades to swim to the surface again. Sixty-five million dead. *Sixty-five* million. Any future society based on an extremist conception of justice and rationality, on a final solution to social problems, will come to the same end.

As a Russian dissident, I took part in the movement to help Soviet society reach the surface. Today, as an exile, I watch with optimism as she begins to swim to the shore. I am certain that in the twenty-first century this adolescent of history will become a healthy, normal nation. Perhaps other nations will learn a lesson from her tragedy. But the greatest problem, that of the Violent Intellect, will remain insoluble.

ACKNOWLEDGMENTS

I should like to express my gratitude to Joseph Brodsky and Alexander Solzhenitsyn for their valuable stylistic comments on an early version of some chapters. I also owe thanks to Ludmilla Alexeeva, Alexander Ginzburg, and Valentin Turchin, for helping to confirm facts about our shared experiences. Gabriel Superfin of the Samizdat Archive in Munich sent me copies of my samizdat appeals and essays, some of which I had lost hope of ever seeing again. Slava Paperno of Cornell University guided me through the mysteries of word processing in Russian at home; Robert Cailliau of CERN provided critical assistance abroad. Edward Kline gave the support of steady and tactful friendship.

I am especially grateful to Thomas Whitney for being a wonderfully swift and sympathetic translator, and to Patrick Filley, my editor, for his patience, encouragement, and critical eye.

There is no way adequately to thank my wife for her help in organizing, editing, and polishing the material.

Nor can I adequately thank the thousands of people all over the world who fought for me. But for them, this book would have been written on cigarette papers and smuggled out of a camp—and would have been a very different book.

CONTENTS

	PREFACE	7
ONE	Pelageya	15
TWO	City Life	30
THREE	"If the Enemy Doesn't Surrender— Exterminate Him!"	43
FOUR	On the Eve of the War	58
FIVE	The War	69
SIX	The Officers' Group	80
SEVEN	Fog Beneath the Ceiling	90
EIGHT	"If Just One of You Becomes a Newton . . ."	98
NINE	Menshevik Songs	110
TEN	All Labor Is Glorious	123
ELEVEN	Armenia	137
TWELVE	Return	152
THIRTEEN	In the Opposition	163
FOURTEEN	Stompers	177
FIFTEEN	The Helsinki Watch	193
SIXTEEN	Arrest	210
SEVENTEEN	"Write a Book About Us!"	225
EIGHTEEN	Letters from Irina	241

11

12 CONTENTS

NINETEEN	Hard Days	245
TWENTY	In Transit	260
TWENTY-ONE	Exile	271
TWENTY-TWO	The Last Sunday in September	288
TWENTY-THREE	Falling from the Moon	299
TWENTY-FOUR	What Is to Be Done?	311
EPILOGUE		330
APPENDIX ONE		332
APPENDIX TWO		338
INDEX		341

DANGEROUS THOUGHTS

ONE

Pelageya

I REMEMBER everything after the wolves.

One day my grandmother hitched up our horse, piled sacks of potatoes onto the sledge, and tucked me among them all bundled up in an enormous fur coat. At this point she had to say, "Everybody knows there aren't any potatoes better than Pelageya's between Moscow and Smolensk," so she said it. Then she climbed in, jerked the reins, smacked her lips—"Let's go, Blacky, giddap, darling!"—and we were off to do business at Drovnino Station.

Grandmother sold potatoes straight from the sledge without unharnessing Blacky. He would bury his nose in his bag of oats, moving his ears whenever steam from the locomotives rolled over him. I sat in the sledge, wrapped in the sheepskin coat, and observed what went on.

"Pelageya! Grandma!" the passengers shouted. "Who is this Pelageya? Come on! Give us the best!" She dumped pailfuls into their shabby satchels and took their money as they hurried back to their seats. Sometimes they had no time to pay, sometimes none to get potatoes. And then rubles flew out of the retreating doors of the train, or Grandmother ran with a full pail after their outstretched hands, and cries of "Get up steam,

15

Grandma! Get up steam, you'll never catch up with Grandad!"
rang out from all sides.

"Never catch up!" she mimicked as she filled her pails for
the next train. "What do you mean 'never catch up'! We'll all
be there. God bless his soul. Are you freezing, Yegorushka?"

I had been baptized Yegor. "Yuri is from your mother's
side," Grandmother would explain. "But your real name is
Yegor."

Grandfather had died somewhere in Moscow even before I was born; I had never seen him. Now I was nearly four
years old.

After we had drunk hot tea in a noisy tearoom reeking of
tobacco and sheepskin, we drove on home. It was already dark.
There was no one but us on the forest road. Lying on my back,
I stared at the tops of the spruce trees and the fuzzy stars.
Blacky ran along at a jog trot. The bell on his shaft bow tinkled.
And then it turned into a station bell—I was a locomotive en-
gineer. A black-faced stoker smiled at me. . . .

I woke up. Something was wrong. Hooves were beating,
the sledge was bouncing. Grandmother was crying out, crying
out and praying:

"Holy Virgin, Mother of God! Have mercy and save us.
Have mercy! Save us!"

I lifted my head. Blacky was raising his hooves up high and
threateningly. Pelageya drove standing upright, an ax in her
left hand, the reins in her right. She was crouched as if preparing to leap. I turned around. One jump back from the
sledge, off to the left, raced a wolf. He was not looking at me,
but at the ax poised for a blow. The ax glistened. Grandmother's
face gleamed. I glanced up at the moon. It, too, was racing
along without falling behind us. Why was it that the moon never
fell behind?

"Hide yourself!" cried Grandmother. "Hide in the coat! In
the coat! Mother of God, save the child! The little one!"

Just as I buried myself in the coat I saw other wolves, racing
to cut Blacky off with powerful leaps across the snowy field.

"Save the child!" shouted Pelageya. "The child! Yegorushka . . ."

Hoofbeats rang out. Sheepskin got into my nose, tickled
my nostrils; I wanted to sneeze, but held back. Wham! I was

knocked over on my side: Blacky had banged the sledge against the village gate. He turned a sharp right, galloped downhill, his hooves drummed on the bridge. Now he went steeply uphill. Left. Right. Home! Blacky neighed. Grandmother scooped me up and ran onto the porch.

A bit later I sat at the table and ate millet porridge with milk, which had been keeping warm all day inside our huge Russian stove. Grandmother knelt in the corner before the icon of the Virgin and whispered her prayers. She crossed herself, bowed her head to the floor, and went on whispering. The icon lamp glimmered. Then, as usual at this hour, she brought out a wood tub full of warm herbal water, added a kind of salt to it, immersed my legs, and began to rub them and mutter something. I had lost the use of my legs almost two years earlier—why, I don't know.

Finally Grandmother climbed the short ladder to the top of the stove, smoothed out the sheepskin rugs, and carried me up. We lay on the soft fur. From the stove came the pleasant smell of the warm, dry clay that coated the bricks. I perched on the edge of the stove, stretched out my arms, pushed off with my legs, and extending my whole body in sweet delight, flew up to a window, turned over, pushed off from the wall, and flew back to the stove. Wolves began to rush, steam engines, train carriages . . . A horse beat with his hooves. . . .

The next day my uncles, Mitya and Petya, returned from the forest with firewood.

"What's all this, Mother, about wolves chasing you?" Mitya asked.

"That's the truth. The horse bolted, I turned to look, and good gracious! They were all over the field, just like your cavalry."

"Teeth unsheathed!" laughed Mitya. "What we have to do, Petya, is set out a guard."

"Go chase the wind in the field," Petya said.

"I went for the ax right away," continued Grandmother, "One of them caught up with us, the devil, bared his teeth, and kept looking at Yegorushka."

"At the ax," I said. "He was looking at the ax."

"They sometimes stick around," said Mitya. "We have to set out some bait "

"Ha, ha, caught some, didn't you!" Petya said.

"What do you mean?"

"I mean how you once caught some wolves with bait. Father ordered you to. Remember?"

"Oh, right. I remember everything I did when I was a boy. I remember, but as if it was in another world. Why's that, Mother?"

"You killed too many people," Grandmother answered, and went to the little kitchen behind the stove.

The brothers fell silent. The griddles rattled in the kitchen.

"Mitya, how did you catch wolves with bait?"

Mitya sat me on his knee.

"Do you remember Grandpa?" he asked. ("Just how do you think he could remember him?" rang out from behind the stove.) "Well then, all this was before the Imperialist War.[1] Your granddaddy Pavel, my daddy, ordered me to shoot a wolf. He'd been hanging around our farm, started a tunnel under the fence. He would've got the sheep. The cow and the horse, too."

"Blacky?"

"No, we had a different horse then, a gelding."

"A gelding?"

"A gelding. Blacky is a stallion."

"If there's any stallion around here, it's you," Grandmother remarked.

Mitya and Petya laughed.

"Well then, I tied a cow's head tightly to our oak tree. It had been lying around since Christmas. Come evening, I set myself in a bush near the pond and kept watch. The night passed. No wolf. It was March, not so cold but cold enough. I wrapped myself up snugly in my sheepskin coat, rifle underneath it, and then, dammit, dozed off. I was pretty young."

"Like me?"

"Like you, maybe just a bit older."

"Like in his teens," said Grandmother.

"Like you," Mitya repeated, and ruffled my hair. "I opened my eyes: wolves. Not just one. Two. They pulled and they pulled at the cow's head, but they couldn't pull it loose, and there was my rifle under my coat. I'm half-asleep, but somehow manage

---

[1]World War I.

to haul it out and fire. Bang! The smoke cleared. No wolves. I had missed. I went to Father, ashamed. He told me, 'Go climb up on the stove. You're still a mama's boy.' "

"On that stove? Where Grandma and I warm our old bones?"

"That very stove. Well, I slept it off, went outside, and our neighbor, Zyuzya, asked me, 'Was that your wolf bitch who's been waltzing around in the village?' 'What wolf bitch?' 'The one that's wounded,' he said. 'You wounded her, and she can't make it through the forest. She's out on the high road.' 'How long ago?' 'This morning.' I had overslept again! So it was on with my skis, rifle over my shoulder, and I raced off, following her trail by the blood."

"Blood?"

"Yes, she'd been wounded. I chased her a long way. Finally I caught sight of her. Sitting there on the road were two of them. The wolf-husband was taking her to the hospital. Now I would kill them both! When he saw me, he got up and pulled and pulled her by the scruff of the neck, telling her, 'Let's get going.' She got up, they ran off, and once again I lost them. And that's how it was every time. I'd catch up, he'd pull her, and it was off to the races again.

"Still and all, she was wounded. Here I was, completely fagged out, but what about her? I caught up with them again, and there he was pulling and pulling her by the neck, and she was lying there without moving. This was it! I'd tired her out. I quickly aimed at him. All right, I thought, so now I'd present Father with two wolves. Then what do you know? He didn't leave. He stood his ground and stared me in the eye: Go ahead, shoot. Do what you will, all the same I can't leave her. Okay, I thought, so you won't leave her. Then don't. That's your business, it's your life, not mine. So I kept aiming. And we stared at each other eye to eye. Why don't you run off? I said. This is no hunt, but an execution. Are you really going to give your life for her? She's already dead! And who are you anyway, just a wild animal! Suddenly she jumped up, and they were off again."

"Did you run them down?" I asked.

"No."

"Why not?"

"I stopped chasing them. I took mercy."

"On wild beasts!" Grandmother shouted. "But human beings? Have you taken mercy on them?"

"Some comparison, Mother. People and wild beasts. The beasts are better."

"Maybe they are better, but 'Thou shalt not kill'!"

"There is no God, Mother."

"You killed a deacon and put horses in the church. You shot down children."

"Military cadets are not children. And a revolution is not a wedding. Today he's a cadet but tomorrow an officer. If I pity him in the morning, he'll execute me in the afternoon. It's either me or him. And what's to pity about the blood of the nobility? I had my orders: Don't let the cadets out of their school. I had a machine gun. Even so, that morning they all ran out. I shot them down. Two hundred. True, Mother, for the first time that's an awful lot."

"Maybe you're bragging?" Petya inquired.

I was four when my grandmother got my legs to move again. Now I could run about with the other children and play Cossacks among the tremendous white willows, jump from haylofts, and catch lazy carp with a basket in the long village pond. But most of all I liked to spend my time alone, completely free, in the meadows and swamps. Every day at dawn I walked our cow, Mashka, to the herd in the common pasture. As the herdsman played on his pipe (there were still herdsmen and pipes in those days), the fog lifted from the swamps, and the swallows began to glide. A happiness would burst in me, and I leaped and jumped from tussock to tussock over the juniper bushes, and whirled until I fell. Then I strolled home along the cowpath, or ran off into the forest.

Our part of Russia, between Moscow and Smolensk, was all forest and swamp, wet places. The little villages had names like Mokroye ("Wet"), Kisselyovo ("Sour"), and Gniloye ("Rotted"). Gniloye was ours. We had so much moss that everyone used it instead of hemp to fill the cracks between the logs of their houses and barns. New houses made you want to stroke their yellow-green furry stripes. Most of the houses in the village were old and small, like ours, with a shed attached to the back for livestock and a vegetable garden and fields of potatoes, rye, and flax behind it. In our shed lived Mashka, Blacky, a pig, chickens, and a few sheep. Vaska, the cat, preferred a free life hunting a neighbor's chickens while a family of hedgehogs was on mouse-duty in our root cellar.

Inside the house lived birds. During cold winters, chicka-dees used to flutter about everywhere, and Grandmother never complained about cleaning up after them: birds were marked with the special favor of God. In summer we had nestlings brought by Mitya from his hunts, like the sandpiper who lived in a wooden washtub until he grew up and we put him out in the sedge. Once at night I was awakened by Grandmother, Mitya, and Petya trying to cure some baby owls of indigestion by feeding them milk from mouth to beak.

Our barn was across the dirt street, beside the village pond. Mitya and Petya used it for their workshop. Mitya had been a militiaman after the civil war that followed the Revolution, but it was a tense job and paid nothing, so he quit. Little by little, the two brothers had found work in the village, putting up houses and covering roofs with shingles they made themselves. Sometimes they also made elaborate frames for photographs with a fret saw, or glued together photograph albums—painting the Caucasus Mountains inside them, and handsome steeds and cavaliers in Circassian coats; for the faces they inlaid photographs of people in the village. After Mitya and Petya earned some money, they bought themselves an accordion, a mandolin, and a guitar to add to their harmonica and balalaika. They could play all of them, and Mitya even read music. Perhaps that was why the village girls adored my uncles, although Mitya was very pockmarked and Petya not exactly tall.

Mitya was an expert with the mother oaths, a master of multistory constructions with lace borders. And it was Mitya who cured me of profanity at the age of four. Our kitten, Vaska, scratched me, and I reproduced Mitya's language with great exactitude. The door of our second room swung open. Mitya came in and belted me very lightly with a strap. The peasants sitting there in the other room laughed, and I was ashamed.

Poor Vaska came to an awful end. Possibly he, too, imitated Mitya in some respects: he grew to love killing chicks, and didn't fear anyone on earth. Acting on their educational doctrine, the two brothers decided to hang him and chose our old willow as the gallows. But their performance was a failure. Vaska gripped the hanging rope with his claws and pulled himself up. He wanted to live. The brothers kept at it a long time. Finally, with a grin, Mitya untied the rope from the branch and began slamming Vaska against the gate. Even that was no help.

Petya got out his rifle and shot the cat.

"You Herods!" shouted Grandmother, gripping my hand. I broke away and fled to the forest.

During the last summer before collectivization, when I was almost five years old, the entire family gathered in our village home. My mother and father came, and my father's sister, Zina. At first I was a little shy of my parents; they lived and worked in Moscow, while I had nearly always been with Grandmother in the village. On doctor's orders my mother had brought me there when I was six months old and dying of the whooping cough. Later on, when I had nearly died of other illnesses, my grandmother carried me to Moscow, and my mother gave me her blood. But I had no early memories of her or my father. To be sure, there was always a great deal of talk about my father at home. He had begun studying at a worker's school. Mitya and Petya felt very proud of him for that, and so did I, even though I didn't understand what a worker's school was. Still, his brothers were a bit afraid of him. Mitya was then twenty-nine years old, Petya twenty-two, and Father twenty-six. When my father arrived he seemed gloomy; he had begun spitting blood. My beautiful mother was always merry.

For whole days at a time, that June, the women put up preserves, the men of course discussed politics, and I shuttled back and forth between them.

"Come on, Mother," my father said at one point. "We're bored. Let's get out the dragnet. You're a master at fishing."

"Right away, Fedenka," replied my grandmother, bustling about. "I'll be right with you."

She put on men's britches and boots, got the pails and the dragnet, and we set out for the stream. It was quite a small, slow forest stream with beautiful pools.

"It would be better for you not to go into the water at all, Fedya," ventured Grandmother.

"Mother!"

Father and Grandmother were covered with duckweed and slime as they hauled the dragnet along. Mitya noisily floundered about, driving the fish into the net. After five or ten paces they threw the net up onto the bank. In the muck flapped red-eyed perch and pike. We filled two pails in two hours, and Father cheered up.

After two weeks Father and Mother left. Their vacation had ended.

In July the rural idyll came to an end. It was 1929.

Mitya quickly understood where things were headed.

"Better wind things up, Petya. To hell with shingles and roofs, and the quicker the better. Time to get out of the village. Private traders are done for!"

"What kind of private traders are we?"

"It doesn't matter. We're going to get work in a factory. And if you want to know the truth, everyone here would be better off getting the hell out."

But they weren't able to get out that quickly. As a veteran of the Civil War, holder of a war medal, and mainly for having worked at one time in the militia, Mitya was ordered to carry out collectivization in our village. They promised to let him leave to work in a factory after he had achieved 100 percent collectivization of his fellow villagers. Petya acted as his helper. At home in our second room they drew propaganda flyers: *For Collectivization!*

"The faster we give those mothers their stinking hundred percent," said Mitya, "the faster we can get the fucking hell out of here."

And the rest of it I heard later from my grandmother when I had already grown up.

Mitya understood exactly what it meant to "liquidate the kulak as a class."[2] It was one more revolution, and he knew how revolutions were made. But here in the village were no cadets, only his own people. The concept of the collective farm, or *kolkhoz*, was almost universally repulsive; joining meant the loss

---

[2] The target of this well-known Party slogan was the class of prosperous peasants.

of personal liberty. Anyone who was a bit smarter and foresaw what was coming abandoned everything and fled. So when the warrants arrived with quotas for arrests of "kulaks and kulaks' henchmen" (their names not given, such details were up to Mitya), practically the only people left were the women. And not even all of them: In the two or three cleanest houses with painted floors, no one at all remained.

The higher-ups called Mitya on the carpet.

"Why didn't you give me instructions earlier!" he roared at them. "The kulaks and their kind have cleared out. After all, I thought and you thought that that was how it was supposed to be. Who needs them here? Let them go to industrialization —to the 'Five-Year Plan in four years.' You wanted me to organize a collective farm? I did. Are one hundred percent in it? They are. What else do you want?"

And this was true. Everyone was in the collective farm except for my smart old grandmother, crazy old Zyuzya, and a few outsiders who had jobs in the district center. Grandmother had escaped being collectivized because of her age and Mitya's influence.

Our not so rich, but not so poor village was ruined in the course of a single year. All the horses were handed over to the collective farm and became nobody's. Forced to work and fed any old how, they were quickly used up. Almost no cows remained: at the first rumor of collectivization the peasants had slaughtered them. No cows meant no milk, no manure. No manure, then not even potatoes. Machinery and fertilizers existed only as ideas.

Mitya and Petya left for Moscow, where my mother and father had a good room of 150 square feet. No sooner had Grandmother seen her sons off than she slaughtered Mashka and sold Blacky. She had nothing to feed them. The farmyard became empty. There was no point in having a farm under the new order, with prohibitions piled upon restrictions and taxes piled upon both.

"Don't worry," she said. "So long as our arms and legs are whole, we'll manage. There have been hard times before. We've got our little garden, and in two years I'll take you to school in Moscow."

* * *

Now large quilting frames took up all of our main room, and Grandmother made quilts on them. She sewed village coats by hand and simple dresses on the Singer sewing machine she had bought before the Revolution. In addition she treated the sick—illegally, of course. Many women had some wasting disease that consumed their hand muscles and bones. The doctors did not know what to do, but Grandmother discovered a remedy she kept secret from them. She would weigh out doses of mercuric chloride on her tiny pharmacy scales and dust it on the diseased areas. She also used to cast spells on toothaches and lance boils. And she would read fortunes from shadows, for the now solitary women.

"Tell me, Pelageya, about my husband. How are things there with him? Are we going to meet again or not?"

Grandmother would burn a newspaper on a big white plate, carry the plate to the wall, shine the kerosene lamp on it, turn the plate this way and that, and study the shadows cast by the burned newspaper. The shadows told much.

"What do you see there? Is Ivan coming?"

Grandmother would peer at the shadows:

"Aha, he's coming. Ah no . . . he is being led."

The woman would turn pale. Truly, truly, it even seemed as if his hands were bound.

Also disturbed, Grandmother would turn to her cards, laying them out and interpreting:

"I see a long journey. . . . A meeting . . ."

She laid out another card.

"Yes, a meeting. Darling, you are going to have a meeting soon. Just wait."

The woman would brighten up.

But Grandmother's most important work, the work that chiefly kept us fed, was to act as midwife. She refused to accept payment in money, lest she be charged with practicing a private trade. If the patient had a cow, she would accept milk, half a liter per day for a whole year for a successful delivery—and she never had failures.

I, too, earned money. I caught moles. Grandmother taught me how to dress the furs, and in Kisselyovo they would pay me one ruble per skin in the cooperative shop. Under her instruction I used to gather medicinal herbs—which she would dry and sell to the same shop—as well as berries, forest nuts, and mushrooms.

Between the edge of the forest and our village lay a swampy birch copse. I could always find brown boletus mushrooms there, even though, it's true, they were a bit on the scrawny side, with spindly legs. Once I came out onto the road after gathering some—the very road down which the wolves had once pursued us—and saw a man walking along thoughtfully, slowly putting one foot in front of the other. He did not look like a villager, in his dark blue riding britches, thin black boots, and black city-style jacket. I joined up with him and began taking big steps, not raising my bare feet, just pushing them along through the deep and pleasant dust. Flies, bumblebees, and gadflies buzzed in the heat. On the left, in the collective farm oats, someone's noncollective calf grazed lazily, trampling down more than he ate.

"That priest, we—we really fried his back good with that flatiron," the man blurted out.

I continued dragging my feet through the warm dust. If I lifted up my feet, my steps would no longer be big like his. The priest?

The year before, we had raided his apple orchard in Mokroye. It had been fun running back a whole two miles. Without apples. I was the smallest of all and had been behind all the rest. . . . What else would he say about the priest? But he didn't say anything else. I forgot about him and just shuffled along through the dust, enjoying the fountains leaping up from between my toes.

"As for his screaming 'There is no bread now!' " the man blurted out again, "there never had been any here. It used to last only till Christmas."

Once again he fell silent, and kept silent up to the village itself. There, we parted.

That evening when I went to bed, I wanted to ask Grandmother about him. But as I closed my eyes, I suddenly saw that steaming back beneath a hot flatiron, and did not ask. And I never did ask anything.

How many coats do women need? How often can they give birth? Now that Grandmother had more time for me, she took me on expeditions deep into the forest from early spring right through late autumn. We would bring a jug of milk, a chunk of bread, some boiled potatoes, a basket for mushrooms, pails for berries, or a big bag for nuts, and tramp barefoot through the tepid puddles, through the rusty swamps, through last year's pine needles. Grandmother was tireless in her marches, and so was I. We would sit down, eat some berries with milk, and go on further.

Grandmother was also tireless in conversation.

"We've come now, Yegor, to a secret place. No one knows of it except Zyuzya and me—and Zyuzya, you know, doesn't remember anything. But there was a time when he and I worked together in this garden here. Now everything has grown over with forest, but I can still make it out. Just look carefully, see how the lindens are arranged in rows. They were planted that way. This was a rich country estate, and the people were really educated. I used to work for them as a nanny. The books up in our attic—they gave them to me. When the mansion was burned down in 1906, the gentlefolk abandoned the place."

I had long since dragged those books down from our attic into my corner of the main room, and loved to look at the beautiful pictures with descriptions of amoebas, infusoria, the Pass of Thermopylae, and mysterious Leyden jars. My grandmother read Church Slavonic very well, much better than the modern writing in her many brochures on gardening. I had been reading them since the age of six, and she was proud of that.

"Everything was destroyed, burned 'to the ground,'" continued Grandmother, recalling the phrase from the "International" as she rapidly picked berries with her small hands. "They thought things would be better that way. We would build 'a new world.' Even I thought so, too. And now on the ruins tall weeds are growing. By the end of the Civil War I had been reduced to begging. . . . Come on there, Yegor, you're putting one berry in your mouth for every one in the jug. . . . So what does it matter that I went begging? Begging isn't a sin if there's no sin on your soul. I would take Fedenka and Petenka, leave Zinochka at home, and go from village to village. Someone would give us a piece of bread, or even a pie, or a shirt. So what? We're alive. We're fed."

She was smiling slyly with all the wrinkles of her lively little face, as if she had pulled the wool over everyone's eyes.

"And, you know, today it's like you and I are out begging. Right? Well, we're living."

A drizzle started and turned into a shower. We sat down beneath a spruce tree.

"It's possible to live, Yegorushka. Just work, work, work. God will provide."

I myself thought we were living wonderfully. And it was true that during those two years of long marches with milk-and-berry lunches in the forest, I became much much stronger.

Grandmother looked after Zyuzya.

"Do you know how Zyuzya used to be? At the age of fifty he could outrun a horse."

"A horse?"

"Yes. Zyuzya used to herd the horses. He was quick. But then the devil ensnared him, and no more Zyuzya. God punished him."

"In what way?"

"No way, no way. Let's go take him some milk."

We went into Zyuzya's stinking hut and put a jar of milk on the window ledge. Zyuzya was sitting on the stove, dangling his legs. A child's cradle hung near him.

"Zyuzya!" Grandmother rebuked him, "what have you gone and done in the cradle again?" The dreadful shaggy old man muttered something. Grandmother cleaned up the mess in silence.

"He doesn't let anyone at all remove the cradle. He's crazy, but very strong. And he keeps on going in it—right in the cradle."

Many years later, just before the war, I visited Grandmother and asked about Zyuzya. He was still alive, and she was still looking after him. Sitting with her beneath the bird-cherry tree alongside our house, I saw a new boy, tall and neatly dressed, make his way slowly along the dusty road. He was looking down at his feet.

"See there, that's his son and grandson. Zyuzya's," Grandmother said. I said nothing. I had ceased liking to ask questions.

"Just as soon as his daughter gave birth, she left to escape the disgrace. And she's never come back. She put a curse on her father. But now she's allowed her son to come and see him. Zyuzya is dying."

I understood then what the cradle was. It had been that unhappy boy's.

In 1931, when I reached the age of seven, my grandmother took me off to Moscow.

TWO

City Life

AT last we were all under one roof. My secretly adored father and my incomprehensible mother lived with me.

My mother loved roaring with laughter to the point of collapse. Grandmother would reproach her: "You're all tee-hee-hees and ha-ha-has."

"Horselaughs!" Petya would elaborate. Mama would be offended, set her lips in a pout, and leave.

"Priests' galoshes," declared Grandmother. "Those aren't lips that Klava has. They're priests' galoshes."

"Ha-ha-ha!" Mama chortled, reentering immediately. "Pretty Boy, ha-ha-ha, brought home a prostitute. And in the morning he threw her out the window, then shouted, 'Sweep up the rubbish, janitor!' But the janitor is Pretty Boy's own mother. She comes out with her broom: 'What's this? Look at the rubbish my sonny threw away!' Ha-ha-ha!"

"Phoo!" spat Grandmother.

Petya and Mitya laughed. Father, bent in thought over his drawing board, smiled absently. Looking at him, I also smiled, so as not to sob. That morning I had seen the woman lying there with broken arms, blood pouring from her mouth and

ears, while the crowd looked on. The gangster had hurled her
from the fifth floor.

The city shocked me.

My father decided that I was not ready for school: "Get
used to things first. Look, Carrot Top, run along and buy us
some bread." Clutching a ration card in one hand and money
in the other, I flew off to the store.

At the beginning of the thirties in Moscow and other cities,
bread began to be rationed as it was during the Civil War. The
villages had no bread at all. This was a price paid for collectivization. Fifteen years later, when I was in the army, a middle-
aged signaler from my platoon told me about another price
paid by millions of peasants for the same thing: "Our village
didn't want to be collectivized in '30. What's a collective farm?
It's forced labor—serfdom. We aren't going to join. The authorities go from house to house and take away all our grain
down to the very last kernel and lock it up in the church under
guard. Whoever made the biggest noise, they were labeled kulak
supporters, loaded in carts with their women and children, and
put out on the open steppe, on the snow: 'Go die out here
without collective farms. We won't force you to join' . . . Then
back to us: 'So, comrade peasants? Are we going to join the
collective farm now?' 'No.' 'No? Very well then. It's purely voluntary.' The most prosperous of the remaining peasants, meaning kulaks, were all rounded up in a single night with their
bundles of belongings in their hands, with their little children,
and taken under armed guard to the far north. I have to say,
Second Lieutenant, your tobacco is on the weak side. . . . Any-
how, the grain was rotting in the church, and we were still
resisting. It was a standoff. You won't believe it—"

He looked about. There was no one, just him and me.

"We even tried to storm the church. But we grew too weak."

"Did they fire on you?" I asked, also looking about.

"No, they drove us off with hoses."

"And then?"

"Then nothing. Those who didn't die of starvation were
saved by one of the authorities. He enrolled us in the collective
farm himself, the Dawn of Communism Kolkhoz. Those who
died are individual peasant farmers in heaven. And the girl

who boiled and ate her own baby—she was arrested and held in prison, then judged insane and put in an asylum. That's how it ended. Survival of the fittest."

Our family lived rather well in Moscow. "Better than in a sleeping car," Petya liked to say. We had a separate room for the six of us in a good pre-revolutionary building, a former shelter for elderly spinsters. The pre-revolutionary spinsters had lived two in a room. A common kitchen, common wash-basin, and common toilet with two toilet bowls had served fifty of them. The ladies did not even dream of a bath or shower. But apparently under the old regime there were no lines at public baths, nor for that matter any lines in general. Now we lived in a new era. That same single washbasin and those same two toilet bowls were used now by no fewer than two hundred people. On days off from work we stood back-to-belly in a line for the public bath that was five blocks long—all the way from the steam room to the district Communist Party head-quarters.

"What, in fact, would people do with their free time if there weren't lines?" Petya declared. "Smash each others' faces in? But their fists would get tired. I figure it's better with lines."

In our room Father's drawing board took up one quarter of the territory. My parents' bed took up another quarter. Mitya and Petya set up their cot at night and arranged themselves on it head-to-feet. The bed and cot legs all rested in tin cans of water, of course, so the bedbugs had to parachute from the ceiling. Grandmother and I slept on the lumpy sofa. "Crowded but friendly," she said.

Still, except for Grandmother we were all young, and we never stopped laughing. Our jokes were simple ones. "I was going through a gorge in my dream," recounted Petya. "I went in further and further, and the gorge got narrower and nar-rower. While only my shoulders touched the walls—no prob-lem. But when my sides started scraping, I began to lose my breath. But I kept on pushing ahead sideways. Finally I felt I'd gone as far as I could. My nose was caught, and I had nothing to breathe with. I was perishing. I woke up, and it was you, Mitya, with your foot up my nose. Your big toe."

Mama roared.

* * *

During the day I was on my own. Father worked in a design bureau. Mitya was a construction foreman somewhere. Petya operated a lathe. Mother sewed leather handbags in a factory, and Grandmother dispensed kerosene in a nearby shop. I would often go to the shop, listen to the gossip, and watch Grandmother work. Her mouth never stopped while her hands, wet with kerosene, swiftly ladled it like soup into the tin cans brought by the local women. The women came here to chat; it was like their club. Once Grandmother said to them, "Let's say I tell you that I am thinking about such and such. But in fact no one knows what I am thinking but not telling you about." This amazed me. She had in mind, probably, that there were some things it was better to keep quiet about. I didn't realize that, but instead discovered a puzzle:

Suppose I say to Mama, "I'm telling you, I want to go to school!" Can it be that I don't say what I'm thinking? I do say it, all right, but then again, I don't say that I know I am saying it. Since I know I am, then I'm thinking it. But I'm thinking it, not saying it. No—how on earth don't I say it? I just said it. . . . This riddle diverted me a whole day. The next day I forgot about it. (And then forty years later I remembered it when I studied logic.)

Having completed my call at the kerosene shop, I played by myself in the side street, or else watched what was going on in the world. A wagon thundered past; the enormous shaggy draft horse, the likes of which I had never seen in our village, beat out a tap dance with his horseshoes on the rounded surface of the cobblestones. A familiar woman with blue bumps on her face left the kerosene shop; without even stopping, she threw back her head, poured blue denatured alcohol down her throat from a pint bottle, polished it off within six paces, and continued steadily on her way. Schoolchildren ran by, taking no notice of me.

On days off, in the evening, Father rolled up his mechanical drawings, Grandmother set the table, and a celebration began. Father loved playing lotto. The pieces were like tiny barrels with numbers on them. Some numbers had their own names. "The Grandfather," Father announced after extracting the 99 from a little bag.

"How old is he?" cried Mitya and Petya merrily, waiting for the next number.

"Five years old. The Bolshevik," Father replied after drawing the 5. The 5 was called the Bolshevik because, fifteen years earlier, the Bolsheviks had been number 5 on the ballot for the Constituent Assembly that they themselves broke up.

We didn't drink much, but always sang a lot. In a quiet, threadlike voice Grandmother would begin: "Farewell happiness, farewell my life . . ." The gossamer web must surely break right then and there—but it never did. The song troubled me, because I thought it was a farewell to life, not love. When the song ended, Mama would begin another in her deep voice: "I'll die then, I'll die then. . . . They'll bury me there. . . . And no one will know. . . ." This was a song of the homeless children. "Probably a homeless child wrote it," I mused, "a boy without a father and mother. . . . Or a homeless girl, like Mama or her friend Rosa Gurfinkel. . . . *Why is she laughing again?*"

Mother had been a *besprizornik*—a homeless waif. There had been millions of them after the Civil War.

Before the Revolution Mother's father, my grandfather Pyotr Lebedev, worked as a mechanic on a big river steamboat that made trips from Perm on the Kama River in the Urals down to Astrakhan at the mouth of the Volga on the Caspian. The family lived well in a two-story house beside the river in the factory town of Motovilikha, and the children went to the local *Gymnasium*. Unfortunately revolutions are usually followed by civil wars. Our Civil War destroyed everything. The steamboat company disappeared first. Then the big steamboat itself. Then the big family—from typhus. Left all alone, the ten-year-old girl joined up with a band of orphan waifs like herself. They wandered all over the country and slept together inside abandoned barns and empty houses, keeping each other warm. They ate together, each getting whatever he could however he could. They stole and begged. But begging was difficult, because year by year people had become brutalized and persecuted the *besprizorniki* even worse than they did the Gypsies. With her friend Rosa, Mother lived this life for several years. And afterward she stopped respecting people, men in particular.

"Love?" she repeated in our last serious conversation, a month before her death at the age of forty-seven. She was very ill, and it was difficult for her to speak. "Love . . . I don't know what it is. There were . . . but I didn't feel anything except simple . . . I don't know what they mean by love."

"But Father?" I asked. "What about Father?"

"Your father!" she exclaimed. "What are you talking about? I respected your father like no one else on earth. Really, I didn't respect anyone else. A better or cleverer man I never met. He would carry you against his breast when you were a baby, tuck you into his shirt, and pace back and forth, back and forth . . . always thinking. . . . You would wet yourself, and he'd laugh." She also smiled. Then she began to weep.

My eighteen-year-old father saw my mother for the first time as a fourteen-year-old at the railroad station. She had a mass of red hair and a beautiful, impudent face.

"What are you staring at?" she demanded. "Are you fed up with living?"

Just a moment before she had torn herself out of the sweaty hands of the stationmaster. Smiling and panting, he had chased her around his desk. "I'll cut you up!" she hissed, and the stationmaster backed off.

"What's your name?" Father asked her.

"Scram!" she said irritably.

"Come on, let's—live together," he blurted out.

She narrowed her eyes: "Studs like you make me . . ."

But after looking carefully at his bright face, she said:

"Let's. My name is Klavdiya."

"Fedya and I lay there dying in each other's arms," my mother once reminisced to us when Grandmother was not home. "For the sixth day we hadn't had a crumb to eat. He had no work, and I had no work. He was ill, and I was ill. And pregnant. So we decided to end it all together. Suddenly Rosa ran in with sausages, butter, duchess pears—you probably don't even know duchess pears—they melt in your mouth. She spread all the goodies out on the floor.

" 'Eat!'

" 'Rosochka, darling, where did it all come from?'

" 'Well,' she said, 'I couldn't let you kick the bucket. I slept with an NEP man. Or a CEC[1] man—I couldn't make out which.'

" 'Rosa!'

---

[1] NEP man: The owner of a small factory or shop under the "New Economic Policy" (NEP), 1921–28, which aimed to revitalize the economy by allowing limited capitalism through private ownership of small factories, shops, and farms. CEC man: a member of the Central Executive Committee of the USSR (1922–38). The committee became the Presidium of the Supreme Soviet.

" 'What do you mean, 'Rosa!' One time isn't going to make it wither! It's the last time. I promise, Klava. Eat.'

"Ha-ha-ha! She couldn't make out which! Ha-ha-ha! It won't wither! Do you remember that, Fedya? Do you remember?"

Father kept silent; he was adjusting a template, drawing an arc. His eyes seemed to smile, but then his face became serious again. In general he was a touch severe with my mother, and she was even a bit ingratiating in his presence. For that matter so were the others in the family.

"Because all the rest of us are . . . impure," Mother once explained to me. "We're impure, but he's untouched. It's as if he is living with us, yet not with us."

A few months after Rosa Gurfinkel saved the three of us, including unborn me, Father at last found work—as a truck driver. In the mid-twenties it was not easy to get employment, and Father treasured his job. But he was unlucky. He was driving behind a tram when out of its doors shot a *besprizornik*, right beneath Father's wheel.

No one blamed Father. Nonetheless, the crushed child in rags tormented his soul, and he gave up truck driving. At that point he was called up for the army. After the army he began to work as a lathe operator in an aviation factory. Intelligent, industrious, and in love with technology, Father swiftly rose to the rank of engineer in the factory design bureau. There was a shortage of engineers at the time. Some of the older ones had fled from the Bolsheviks, others had been arrested, and still others had been killed during the Civil War or had starved to death afterward. It was difficult for the intelligentsia to get a professional education. New engineers were now drawn from among the workers. Most of them, like my father, were still studying at a night school.

There remained of his studies only a trifle. But there remained of his life also a trifle, one year.

Father had been spitting into a jar for a long time. Nurse Moiseyenko from the TB clinic visited regularly, collected the jar, and said to him, "You are getting along well, Fyodor Pavlovich. The analyses are not so bad. You'll be going again to the sanatorium in the summer, and you'll get completely well."

But in the corridor she whispered to Mother, "Ach, don't ask, Klava. Don't ask."

Once in the evening I was mindlessly watching him work, resting my chin on the drawing board. Suddenly—I shall never forget the despair that twisted his face for a second—he pushed himself back with a jerk and flung me away from the drawing board. I fell. He struck his head on the wall, I jumped up. Little streams of blood flowed over the drawings. The adults ran to get ice and laid him down. His ashen face was once again calm.

The illness went on the attack. Now, each day, he became worse and worse. The family went into a frenzy. "What he needs is the fat of a dog! It will make the lesions scar over." So Mitya stole a fat lapdog from some scrawny old lady and killed him with an ax.

"No, no. Not that! You've been told—not dog fat. Badger fat!" So the brothers went hunting and killed a badger. Father obediently gulped down the bits of rosy raw fat. The blood kept gushing. His face became emaciated. His eyes grew more and more sunken; they still shone, but already with an unearthly light. To be sure, they had always looked out from somewhere in another world.

"An amulet," demanded Mother. "I've been given a special prayer. I must put it in a walnut shell."

Everyone was silent. Why a walnut shell? Mother copied out the prayer, neatly folded up the slip of paper, and put it into a walnut shell. Petya glued the shell together, and they hung it on Father's neck by a silver chain. Grandmother added a cross to it. Father did not resist. He kept on bleeding.

Suddenly a close friend of my father, a handsome young military engineer, blew his brains out. He used to visit us almost every day; Father had been helping him design something or other. Then, wham! Why?

"Because of me," Mother gaily announced. "I wasn't what he took me for. He made a mistake in his design, the boy. So, I am a femme fatale! All he had to do was look at me and poof!—no more engineer. Fedya, I am a femme fatale! I am Carmen. Fedya . . . Fedyusha . . ."

But Fedyusha was already beyond human passions.

In March 1933, when I had nearly completed my first year of school, Father died. I remember that night. Father wheezed, stretched out on the bed. The adults took turns sitting with him and holding his hand. They had forgotten me. I was lying on the sofa across the room, looking at his blind face, listening to his endless and unbearable wheezes, gurglings, and whistles. I felt nothing except a slow, heavy weight, as in an illness when you keep having the same obsessive dream: the ceiling keeps getting lower and lower, and the closer it gets, the more depressed you feel. By morning Grandmother had begun to recite the prayer for the dying—in place of a priest. Where now could you find a priest? But Mother swooped down on her and whispered with rage:

"Stop it! He's not dying, he's not dying yet!"

Grandmother meekly stopped. The brothers kept silent, both sitting there on the bed, incessantly watching Father and holding his hands in theirs.

The factory organized a civil funeral: speeches and orchestra. They put me on top of the hearse, next to the coachmen. In the back lay my father. To the tune of funeral marches the white horses carried us unhurriedly. It was a warm spring day. Small boys ran around us in circles, eyeing me with envy. I felt embarrassed, and wanted to get there faster.

In the crematorium that had just been built alongside the fortress walls of the International Youth Day Leather Goods Factory, which before the Revolution had been the Donskoy Monastery, they burned my father. Curious people clustered around, waiting politely for the corpse, enveloped by flame, to raise itself a little, and for the muscles to jerk in spasms. But Father didn't raise himself.

"They cut the tendons in his arms and legs, here and here! That's why he didn't get up. You understand? You his son? Listen, he says he's the son. You got a mother? That your mother over there? Well, that's something. She's pretty young! She get along okay with your father? The mother's the main thing. Another father will come along, heh heh! Don't grieve."

In those years it was permitted to watch corpses being cremated, so that even the most ignorant citizens should know that there is no mystery in death.

The core of the family had been broken.

Mitya immediately became a drunk. One morning as I sleepily opened my eyes, Grandmother was flying toward the window. She banged against the windowsill and fell.

"Beast!" she said softly, got up with great effort, and slowly walked toward the door.

But she ran into Mitya's fist and again was sent flying.

"Beast!" she repeated sadly, and walked toward Mitya. Her face was all bloody. I cried out. She covered her face with her hands, pushed Mitya aside, and rushed out the door. Without looking at me, Mitya followed her. I shut my eyes. How awful it was without Father. How good it had been in the village. Playing in the hayloft, catching carp with my basket . . .

Well then, I would die. They would bury me to the accompaniment of an orchestra. There would be lots of people. Everyone would weep. All Moscow would follow the hearse. "He's a hero," they would say of me. "Our chief savior." And then . . . And then what? No, in actual fact, I would not die. Suddenly I would rise up and say, "I am alive!"

For a year after my father died, I was pursued by sweet daydreams about great feats, triumphal death, and miraculous resurrection. Perhaps his death had settled into my soul as the death of Christ. Not many children knew about Christ in those days. But back in the village Grandmother had haltingly read to me from the New Testament. It had been my first book.

Mitya perished. He lay drunk in the gutter one winter night in some other city, caught a chill, and died from galloping consumption among indifferent strangers. They turned Mitya's documents over to Petya but could not find the grave.

"People have started dying like flies," an old man from the morgue told him. "It's the famine. Can't keep an eye on everybody, who's got what name."

The doctors checked Petya: he, too, had tuberculosis.

They examined me and sent me off in a hurry to a children's group attached to the nearby clinic. Every day after school I was to have especially nutritious food, daytime rest outdoors in a fur cap, and a checkup by the doctors.

Mother turned out to be absolutely healthy.

She decided to make her way in the world. "Fedya's gone, he was my fortress," she said. "Now I'm on my own."

"What do you mean, you're on your own?" asked Petya. "You have a good job."

"You don't understand," Mother brushed him off. "What's a woman factory worker anyway? A minus zero."

She took a typing course, joined the Komsomol,[2] did volunteer social work teaching illiterates to read (there were many in the wake of all our wars and revolutions), and participated in amateur theatricals. Once she took me to a concert at her factory club, and there for the first time I heard classical music—the pastoral duets from Tchaikovsky's *The Queen of Spades*. It was Mother and another woman worker who sang them.

Mother's calculations paid off. She was noticed. Soon she was the secretary and typist for the chief engineer of the factory. She bragged that she could type with all ten fingers at once.

Almost two years after my father's death the chief engineer began coming to our apartment. It was near the end of 1934 and the beginning of a new phase of the Bolshevik terror. Newsboys shouted in the streets, "Kirov assassinated! Kirov assassinated!" Kirov, the first secretary of the Leningrad Regional Party Organization, had been murdered. Mass arrests began, not of peasants this time but of party functionaries themselves. They arrested each other by turns, and weren't squeamish about ordinary people either. Among the ordinary people was the brother of Mama's chief engineer. They held him in the Lubyanka[3] and then released him—for the moment.

During this period in which he was allowed to go on living, he came twice with his brother to our apartment. Heads bent down over our small table, they discussed in half-whispers what had happened to him. And what had happened was that they had arrested him and beaten him and asked him stupid questions. I had sometimes heard adults threatening each other with the NKVD[4] and the Lubyanka, and had wondered just what they were. Now I understood.

Yet the sufferings about which they whispered at the table did not move me. I disliked the chief engineer. I even hated him, although I could not yet have explained why. But then

---

[2]The Young Communist League.

[3]The Lubyanka was and is the headquarters of the Soviet secret police. Up until Stalin's death, it was also one of its prisons.

[4]The Soviet acronym for the name of the secret police at that time. The Soviet secret police has changed acronyms like a chameleon. It started out as the Cheka, and then became the GPU, the OGPU the NKVD, the NKGB, the MGB, and finally the KGB. Even today, however, people often simply refer to the secret police as "the Cheka."

once I awoke in the night. Mother's bed was just half a step from my sofa. Grandmother was no longer beside me; after Mitya's death she had returned to the village. Petya and his fiancée, Liza, slept in the dark half of the room, behind the partition that now divided our little territory in two. The window was in our half. A streetlight shone through it. On the bed were two people, and I saw what I should not have seen. For the first time I clearly understood why that man spent nights with us. The discovery was very unpleasant. I quickly fell back to sleep.

In the morning I had forgotten about it. Mother and I were sitting at breakfast, Petya and Liza had not yet gotten up. There was no sign of the engineer. None at all. But then I recollected everything I had seen and heard in the night. I vomited and went into hysterics.

"What is it? What is it?" Mother whispered. I cried so rarely. But she had already guessed what the matter was.

"Don't let him come, don't let him come!" I sobbed. Mother seized my hand and dashed outside with me.

Outside it was spring again—dry, warm, and sunny. I was crying. Mother was saying something to me, explaining as if I were an adult: "It's very necessary . . . and for you, too . . . you need a father. . . ." We walked along sunlit Yakimanka, down dark Shabolovka, and turned into Donskoy Lane. There in front of us was Mother's factory, the very same one near the crematorium where they had burned up Father. I kept on crying.

"All right, all right," Mother said. "You won't see him anymore. Stop crying, please, I don't have any time now, I'm late for work. Go, take a walk. I'll be home for dinner."

And she ran off to work.

I went into the courtyard at the back. It had once been the cemetery of the Donskoy Monastery. Usually I walked about there until Mother came for lunch. She would go with me to a workers' mess hall and then take me to the afternoon session of school. I sat down on the grass and began to decipher the inscriptions on the scattered gravestones. A gray crow stared at me, stretching out his head from behind a birch stump. A second crow arrived. I loved those ungainly birds; they were all around me when I was a child. Grandmother used to carry me to the kitchen garden, set me on a sheepskin coat, and begin digging up potatoes. "Frost tomorrow," she would say, and rapidly break up the beds with a pitchfork, collect the potatoes in pails, pour them from the pails into sacks, lug the sacks to the house, and empty them into the root cellar. Clouds flew past, and crows shrieked and glided in big circles on the wind. My legs did not move, but that was no matter. I was happy sitting beneath the circle of gray crows.

Now, waiting for my mother in the cemetery, I felt that I was no longer small anymore.

Mother kept her promise. I never did see "him" again. No, I did see him one more time. Two years later Mother married a very kind, very tactful man, and we moved to a different apartment. One night our door, which could not be locked, opened wide, and "he" came in. He was obviously very drunk. I leapt up, seized with my previous hate, just as if four long years had not gone by since I had seen him last. But my step-father, a lanky bean pole in long underwear, got out of bed, went up to him, and slapped his face. Loudly, but not hard. "He" gave a pitiful smile, murmured "Th-th-thank you," and went out, carefully closing the door behind him.

He may have been a quite decent person. Many years later my mother told me that at a Party meeting he had bluntly refused to condemn his brother, who had finally been arrested as "an enemy of the people." They then expelled him from the Party for "political immaturity" and, of course, fired him—first from his post as chief engineer, then as an ordinary engineer, and then even as a technician, because they could not permit such a person to be in a position of responsibility. He had turned to drink. After that night Mother lost track of him. No doubt he, too, had been arrested.

THREE

"If the Enemy Doesn't Surrender— Exterminate Him!"

AFTER the excruciating conflict with Mama over her engineer, I sensed that other lives existed, separate from mine, and that my own life could be lived in my own way. For the first time I experienced myself as having individuality. Of course, this was only a sensation. In my surroundings there was no concept of such a thing; the word *individuality* smacked of derision.

"You whore, look out, I'm going to bat you on your individuality!" a neighbor of ours would scream to his wife when he was in a good mood. And another neighbor, a militiaman,[1] used to advise the man who lived at the far end of the corridor:

"Wipe yourself, citizen! Shit and then wipe yourself dry with your certificate of individuality. Some in-di-vid-u-al!!!" But that was before I found the militiaman lying on the stair landing with a bullet hole in his stomach, . . .

And so that spring my independent life began.

"Don't go with me to school anymore," I declared.

We were standing near the gates of her factory. A stream of women workers flowed past. It was lunch break. Mother looked sadly at me, nodded, and handed me some coins: "Go

---

[1]A policeman.

43

along. This one is for the streetcar there. This other one is for the second streetcar. Be careful crossing the streets. Don't run. It's better to be late. Promise not to run?"

The intimacy, that sweet intimacy with a child when he is solely a part of your own being, had abruptly ended, scarcely having begun. She suffered. I felt it, but did not let her glimpse my sympathy for her. She kissed me good-bye on the walk. I rubbed at the place where she had kissed me. She tried to smile. I pretended that I was scratching my cheek. And day by day she kissed me less and less.

School was a two-story pre-revolutionary building with a broad stairway, high ceilings, and enormous windows. When the windows were opened, branches of linden and poplar trees came right inside our classrooms. Each class had thirty children. Now in the third grade, we were reading Tolstoi's story "Little Philip," taking down dictation for spelling, learning addition in arithmetic, and drawing leaves. We retold how the Winter Palace was taken by storm from the czar and the bourgeoisie. And in a separate room, seated in a circle, we sang revolutionary and peasant songs. Uniforms had not been introduced yet, and on me hung a somewhat large but lovely sweater—an award to the best pupil.

I adored school and thought of nothing else until one day, when I was going down the staircase during recess, someone's arms locked around my neck and a thin voice rang out: "Do you love me? Love me? Ha-ha-ha!" My neck was released, and a little girl dressed in yellow ran down past me.

I dreamed of her all night. The silvery voice asked, "Do you love me?" We sat on a bench beneath a linden tree and embraced and kissed—just like adults. The next day I waited for her when school let out, and from then on walked her home every day. She was ten years old, like me, and wore a threadbare gray coat. Her name was Lyusya.

Soon she became bored and thought up a new game. "Bring me some money!" she pouted, and forbade me to walk her home. The entire next morning I fooled around with the cat. Nowadays Mother left me at home alone when she went to work; I would heat up lunch myself and then go off to school. The cat was pink, with a red ribbon and a slit in its back. Ten-kopeck pieces flew out of it nicely. Twenty-kopeck pieces were more difficult. And as for five-kopeck pieces— they were perfect torture. But finally I accumulated a fair pile of small change.

"Here!" I said to Lyusya, trembling with excitement. And I opened my hand.

"Here what?" she asked, surprised, but nonetheless holding out her hands. I poured into them my love. We were standing outdoors. Suddenly her dear face twisted in revulsion. She clenched her fists, raised her arms, and with all her strength hurled the treasure into the dirt. Then she left. I was crushed. Why, why had she acted like that? I never even thought to pick the money off the ground.

That evening, when Mother dropped a new coin into the cat, the cat's belly answered her with an empty hollow thud. She turned to me. I sat there with sunken head.

"Why did you take it?"

I kept silent. And besides, did it make any difference now what might happen? Mother raised up my head, looked thoughtfully into my face, and went out. She returned with a switch and lightly hit me on my backside, as Liza and Petya watched in amusement from behind the partition. Mother never asked again what had really happened. Lyusya was my first and last schoolboy love. She soon took up with fifteen-year-old boys, and I sought out the Tolstoi Children's Library.

The girl who shared my desk at school had described it to me with delight. There were more books in the world than I had ever imagined, my eyes could not take them in fast enough. Scornfully I rejected the ones intended for younger school-children, and picked out a story about an orangutan who had lived with people and had nearly become a person himself. As I recollect, this was what did him in. I would be delighted to come across the book again, especially to look at the photograph of the orangutan dining at a table with his friends and conducting a decorous conversation.

The library workers were all Jewish women, and each one fussed over me like a mother hen over her chicks. "He's from a very poor family. And so pale!" I overheard them whisper. "We have to develop him."

They developed me.

"Developing the people" was a movement that began in Russia fifty years before the Revolution. Thousands of intellectuals, including even Lev Tolstoi, sacrificed their lives to it. The Russian intelligentsia had virtually ceased to exist by the time I was a child, but their old traditions had not yet been completely exterminated with them. There were still some good people alive who transmitted to children like me a love for general culture.

I began to spend all my free time in the library. The women offered me cookies and one thick volume after another: Pushkin, Gorky's *Childhood*, Turgenev, and of course books about Lenin, about glorious Bolsheviks, and about children who had courageously helped the Revolution. One day I read that the czar had already been overthrown before the October Revolution. It was the first blow to my child's faith in the truthfulness of books and teachers. I would have liked to ask Mother and Petya about what had really happened with the Revolution and the czar. Yet I did not. I could not have explained exactly why, but just knew with all my being: *it is better to keep silent,* better for all of us. Observing the way adults always shrank from an invisible border in their conversations, I had already begun to feel where the danger zone lay.

However, far removed from that zone it was possible—and even very interesting—to live. The library women organized a children's study group in which we learned about the great voyages and scientific discoveries with Natalya Nikolayevna, a quiet and inspiring young woman who soon after died of TB. I drew the routes of many explorers from Vasco da Gama to Perry, and prepared a report on Amundsen. Amundsen, among other feats, had eaten butter and cockroach sandwiches in his childhood in order to train his willpower. When I tried to repeat this exploit with a pair of cockroaches, I quickly found that I was no Amundsen. We also learned that Pasteur was not content being fourteenth in his class and took his science degree again—four more years. This second time he came in second, and became Pasteur. (Twenty years later, when I graduated from the university, I asked to be allowed to take my degree again. They replied, "You mean you want the state to spend twice as much on you as on the rest?")

* * *

By the time I reached eleven and my last year of primary school,[2] I had changed from a dreamy country boy to quite a lively city fellow searching out study groups to join. My school had also become more dynamic. Now that the second half of the thirties had begun, Spies and Enemies were everywhere; teachers would suddenly disappear; textbooks would suddenly be replaced. In readers for the lower classes there appeared border guards and child heroes who helped catch spies. One spy strolled about disguised as a mushroom gatherer. (There was a picture of him in the book.) Beneath the mushrooms in his basket lay hand grenades. (Also a picture.) Our class read and retold a story about a girl who discovered that a saboteur had damaged a railway track. (Picture.) In order to save the train, she cut her arm with a knife, soaked her handkerchief in the blood, and stood there on the track waving her red flag. The engineer saw her and succeeded in stopping the train. (Picture.) While my lips were retelling this nonsense, my mind was clean and empty. I knew that life in schoolbooks was a special universe created for examinations. Just once an idea did flash through my mind: where had this village girl, Masha, come by a handkerchief? I had never ever seen one in our village.

My mind was even cleaner and emptier when my hand wrote grammatically flawless compositions on such themes as "Thank you, Comrade Stalin, for our happy childhood!" or on Stalin's revelation: "Life has become better, comrades, life has become more jolly." Life was especially good and jolly in the collective-farm village. This was obvious right away from another story in the textbook, where a Young Pioneer[3] helped apprehend a "saboteur-clipper." This character went about with scissors and clipped ears of wheat from the fertile, rich collective-farm field into a little bag hung around his neck. I thought for a long, long time about that little bag—and about those scissors, too. This was an interesting saboteur. Some years later

---

[2] In my day the ten years of Soviet elementary and secondary education were divided into grades 1 to 4 (corresponding to American primary school), 5 to 7 (corresponding to middle school), and 8 to 10 (corresponding to high school). Children typically started school at age seven or eight. Now they begin at six or seven.

[3] A member of the Young Pioneers, a mass educational-political organization for schoolchildren.

I found out the truth. The "saboteurs" were starving people, and the weapon used against them was a stretch in the camps, or execution.

In the summer of '36, just after I completed primary school, my grandmother visited Moscow for the last time. She wanted to see Petya and me, and earn a bit of money. Life in the village had become more and more difficult. People were unable to pay for her work as a midwife and seamstress; she was too old to work in a factory, as she had during winters before the Revolution; her old job in the kerosene shop was not available. So she got herself a job in Gorky Park as an attendant in a public toilet, partly with me in mind. Every summer vacation my mother settled me with a peasant household in some village or other near Moscow. But she hadn't been able to find a suitable place that summer, and I was hanging about the city. Now, thanks to Grandmother, they let me into the park without a ticket and I no longer had to slither through holes in the fence. I would draw Red Squares in the graphic arts group, then visit Grandmother, and then look after rabbits and all kinds of peas in the tiny garden of the "House of the Young Naturalist." Experiments were being done with the peas there. Had Grandmother worked a little longer in her public toilet, I might have turned out to be a geneticist. (And been sent to camp for that.) However, she soon went back to the village. A few weeks later Mama finally got married.

The snag had been housing, and she solved that problem with two cells in a former monastery on Polyanka Street. True, it was on the grounds of a supersecret weapons factory, so we would have to pass by their guard whenever we went in or out. And, true, the communal toilet and other "conveniences" were awful. But at least our rooms would have separate entrances. Only three people were living in those two rooms, members of the very same family. They wanted to trade with us. My mother explained that there had been twice as many of them up until last year, and they wanted to give up the place because, maybe, in a new one, they would stop evaporating so fast.

"What about us?" I asked.

"We are not going to evaporate!" Mother replied. "Their problem is that someone doesn't like them."

"But what if someone doesn't like us?"

"We're ordinary people. Who would need to not like us?"

"And what if someone doesn't get to like them here either? What if someone here takes them for Japanese spies? Like Mustafa?"

"Go get your schoolbooks."

Mustafa was an engineer and a friend of my father. When I was not yet in school and Father was still alive, Mustafa and his wife, Talochka, often came to Moscow from Kiev on business and spent the night with us in order to save money. How we ever managed to sleep eight people is beyond me. Talochka was beautiful and perfumed. I kept staring at her; she would notice and laugh. Then, one day, Talochka came all by herself. She was not laughing.

"They arrested Mustafa," she declared, and began to sob.

"For what?" my mother asked very calmly.

"They say he . . . was not a Tatar, but a . . . Japanese . . . a Japanese spy."

"A spy?" asked Mother.

"Is he really a Japanese?" asked Petya.

"What kind of Japanese? I know his whole family."

"Well, they'll sort things out," said Mitya.

"Sort things out! What do you mean? They've already killed him!"

Everyone fell silent. She spent the night with us and during the day went off someplace; they ordered her to go home, and she left.

"I'll write Talochka not to come here again," said Mother firmly.

"What the hell for?" demanded Petya.

"Nothing. You know nothing about life."

"Meaning us?"

"Meaning you. Today it's Mustafa and tomorrow Fedya. Gone without a trace."

"What's with you? Have you been eating fish soup, or have you just gone fucking crazy?" Mitya asked.

Father was silent.

"Write her," Grandmother said.

The conversation broke off. Mother wrote the letter, and Talochka never showed up again.

* * *

We moved into the place on Polyanka. Our monks' cells were seventy square feet if measured by the floor and thirty-six if measured by the ceiling. Petya, Liza, and their little boy, Vovka, settled down in one cell, and my mother, my stepfather (also named Petya), and I settled in the other.

My stepfather, Pyotr Baragin, had studied in a school for applied arts. Then he had married my mother, exchanging the career of an artist for life with a beautiful and somewhat imperious woman who was five years older than himself and who came with a child. A student might live on bread and water, but not a family man. He dropped art school and worked as an apprentice in various factories, earning half the little my mother did. Once he got a job in a chemical factory for the higher pay. After taking one whiff of him, Mother decided to check up on what kind of work was so poisonous. She went to his plant. "Better to be without any money at all than breathe those fumes!" she shouted at the boss, and right there on the spot wrote out Stepfather's resignation.

No one could have been less suited to factory work than my thoughtful, dreamy stepfather. He really was an artist. At every free moment Stepfather took his easel, oils, and me off to paint landscapes. The walls of our room were covered with them. And we went dozens of times to the Tretyakov Gallery, where I learned from him about the artists' lives and techniques of painting. It could not have been easy for a widow with a child to find such a serious husband. He was a good comrade to me, just as my mother wanted, and he loved her. So she never, either by word or glance, reproached him for his low earnings.

However, all their energies were spent in getting us clothed and fed. After two years of this sort of life Mother summoned a family council. We needed, she announced, to have butter at least in the mornings. How could we get it? She already knew. We would copy by hand examples of telegrams and envelopes with addresses. Our copies would be hung on post-office walls throughout the Soviet Union. Agreed? Agreed. For long evenings all of us together—Mother and Stepfather after work, I after school—sweated over this miserably paid, exhausting job. But I did not notice these hardships. I had not seen any other kind of life in the city. And besides, I loved school and reading and study groups. If someone had said that we lived in poverty, I would have been astonished and replied, No worse than other people. We eat deliciously, you just have to know how to cook, and no one can touch Mama there. Potatoes fried in sunflower-seed oil with herring—how delectable! Our apartment? It's marvelous, just try to find one like it. Whenever you travel by railroad, for instance, you see barracks, barracks, barracks. Would they be better? You say we are working at night? So what, there's butter!

And not just butter. For thirty rubles[4] I bought a subscription to a lecture course for youngsters on the history of philosophy. . . . The enormous lecture hall at the university was overflowing. Professor Asmus began with the Pythagoreans. I took notes neatly and carefully, a little feverish. Here was a world of ideas whose very existence, only yesterday, I had not even suspected. Five lectures later, when Professor Asmus reached Zeno's logical paradoxes, my decision was made. I would become a philosopher. The age of fourteen surely could not be too late.

Everything was perfect except for a few details. Things were a bit like a loony bin, and in fact, if you could believe my aunt Zina, whose husband sometimes landed in a Moscow lunatic asylum, it even turned out that the genuine lunatics behaved more normally. One day some leader whose name we had learned by heart in lessons, whose portrait had been hanging on our squares, was convincing us that the Party never makes a mistake. And the next day the best writers, foremen, poets, and shock-workers[5] abused him in the papers and on the radio as a fascist spy, a despicable traitor, and a filthy murderer. And he himself confessed to this. And the next day he was shot. And then, with steel pen points, small schoolchildren would scratch out the eyes from his portraits in their literature, history, or geography textbooks, scrape off his ears with razor blades, cut out his nose, and to finish it off, neatly wipe his filthy mug with

---

[4] After World War II the ruble was devalued and ten rubles became equivalent to one. My references to rubles in Chapters 3 to 8 are to the prewar rubles.

[5] Workers who exceeded production norms.

spit. And the teachers wouldn't utter a peep. And when yesterday's leaders, except for Comrade Stalin himself, had all become spies, the textbooks were changed, and in the new ones were new portraits. And soon the schoolchildren began their new work: putting out eyes, cutting off ears, spitting on the filthy fascist mugs.

I was at my wit's end. If the Party never made mistakes and if these leaders were in actual fact traitors, then how were you to believe their words that the Party never makes mistakes? And in fact all these revolutionaries were *confessing* to their repulsive crimes. I heard this with my own ears during radio broadcasts directly from the courtroom; our whole family listened regularly to them. So that meant they actually were enemies of the people. Enemies of the people had made a revolution *for* the people? This was beyond all comprehension. I had been educated to think that people were neatly divided between those who believed in communism and those who did not. It would be a long time before I realized that people should be divided not between believers or nonbelievers in some faith but between those who are or are not prepared to kill for their faith or lack of it.

My generation was being taught to kill.

In school we all learned the declaration of the great humanist and leader of Soviet literature Maxim Gorky (written at the very beginning of the annihilation of the peasants):

If the enemy doesn't surrender—exterminate him!

And these verses of Chekist executioner and poet Bagritsky:

You look around—and see enemies all;
You reach out your hand—and there are no friends;
But if [the Age] tells you: "Lie!"—go lie.
And if it tells you: "Kill!"—go kill.

And this advice of the great Mayakovsky to follow the chief of the Cheka:

To make a life—with whom?
With Comrade Dzerzhinsky!

This was the atmosphere, the air, of the new, postrevolutionary culture. It was pushed by powerful pumps every day into our lungs.

What then did I *ex*hale? Practically nothing. I did believe that communism was "the bright future of all humanity." But the basic idea of the new culture, that the most awful violence is humane if its purpose is good, did not touch my soul although I still accepted it abstractly. The smoke rising from the back of a village priest prevented me from seeing the humanism of the Cheka. And still living on in books were the remnants of the old, totally different culture, which I had begun to love to the point of anguish. It alone would have been enough to preserve me from both the sacred cult of violence and the worship of leaders—including our Brilliant Leader and Teacher, J. V. Stalin. I had no attitude toward him at all. Even when my classmate Petrov told me that he'd like to get his hands around Comrade Stalin's neck, my reaction did not go beyond an academic interest in the idea. Thus, ideologically speaking, I was not a model Pioneer and Komsomol. I belonged because everybody did. (And I must say, the most interesting study groups were located in the Palaces of the Pioneers: you could look through a microscope there, or learn to write stories.)

In general, it was not our family's style to thrust ourselves forward. And more important, to thrust yourself forward now was dangerous. My bright and observant mother, hating police raids from her days as a *besprizornik*, evidently understood that all of life had become one solid police raid. But she never discussed with me anything that she knew and thought about what was taking place, perhaps because truth, like that priest's steaming back, could be beyond the capacity of a child's mind to bear. Or perhaps because a child might fail to keep a discussion secret, or might even joke about it. And then everyone would perish—the parents and also the child. This was something my mother knew exactly. And she was on perpetual guard like a beast of the forests. I felt it and automatically kept a thousand miles away from dangerous talk, always and everywhere. Except once.

One day in 1938, my mother, my stepfather, and I were riding in a streetcar, and they were carrying on their usual conversation about things at work.

"Levin is on the outs with the director," Mother said. "But

they're never going to find as good a purchasing agent as Levin."

"Is that the same Levin?" I asked playfully, referring to the doctor charged with poisoning Maxim Gorky.

Mother fell silent and grew pale. I looked at Stepfather— he couldn't possibly have been any paler. They began to make their way unobtrusively to the exit, Mother dragging me by the hand. As the streetcar rounded a corner, we jumped off and marched ahead in silence for half an hour without looking back. Then we did look. No one had followed us. At that point Mother let me have it. I had never seen her so furious.

"Fool! Idiot!" she cried in a whisper. "You found something to joke about! Don't you understand? Don't you?"

I was silent with guilt. I did understand. Only the day before we had listened on the radio to the trial of the rightist-leftist-Bukharinite-Trotskyite bloc. A man named Levin was in that bloc. He had confessed to everything, of course, and was, of course, condemned to be shot. The newspapers were publishing the enthusiastic reactions of foremen and writers. If a writer had been on the streetcar—I mean, a writer of denunciations—my silly joke would have been incontrovertible proof that both Mother and Stepfather, yes, and me, too, were participants in the leftist-rightist-Trotskyite-Bukharinite bloc, and also murderers, spies, and saboteurs. This was infallibly predictable. (Fifty years later the Party explained to us that there had never ever been any bloc at all. And there are grounds for suspicion that Gorky was poisoned by order of Stalin.)

We were lucky. No one in our family was arrested. Yet it was impossible to evade an age that demanded of each and every person, "Lie!" and "Kill!"

At the end of the sixth grade I had a school friend named Metalnikov. Perhaps he is still alive and will read these words. He lived with his mother on Zemsky Lane, not far from the Babiegorodsky Market. We often strolled about there after school together having intelligent conversations. But on this particular day he was stubbornly silent. I kept at him, noisily trying to prove something or other.

"Lay off," he finally said. "Yesterday they arrested my mother. I'm all alone."

Doom and alienation stared me in the face. We walked

along the Moscow River in silence. The ice was moving, children were making a racket, crows scouted for something of interest on the ice floes. We went on to the Crimean Bridge and then parted.

"Ma," I said that evening. "Metalnikov's mother was arrested. He's been left alone. Can he move in with us? You did say that two children are better than one."

Mother did not answer for a long, endlessly long time. She went out, came back in, and finally said:

"You don't know. It's difficult. It won't work out."

I lowered my eyes. For some reason I hadn't expected a refusal.

"Does he have relatives?" Mother asked.

"Don't know."

"Ask him tomorrow."

"Sure."

The next day, however, Metalnikov did not turn up at school. I went to Zemsky Lane. The door to their room was locked. I stood next to the door, seized with alarm. A little slip of a girl approached me.

"They took'm," she said. "They took'm. As an emily of the pleepull."

In the mid-thirties the age at which you could be legally arrested as an "enemy of the people" was lowered from sixteen to twelve.

In temperament I took after Uncle Petya, who loved being ironic. But for a while after the disappearance of Metalnikov, my taste for irony left me. I spent more and more of my time in libraries. There, in great European and Russian literature, real life lived. The life around me was unreal.

"Petya, why aren't you a Stakhanovite?"[6] I asked my uncle.

"Do you really know what Stakhanovites are?"

"Stakhanov produced one thousand, four hundred percent of the norm in a coal mine," I replied without hesitation. Everybody knew that from the newspapers.

"There's your one thousand, four hundred," Petya said

---

[6] A superproductive worker inspired by a coal miner called Alexei Stakhanov, who allegedly produced fourteen times the norm. An official campaign to increase workers' productivity was built around this fiction.

with a gesture. "One thousand, four hundred! In you it's still forgivable. But, you know, you'd have to be a cork to believe that. We have our very own Stakhanov at the lathe factory— Gudov. He's a fellow fresh from the country. The chief of our shop and the secretary of the Party Committee brought the blanks to his lathe for him. 'Get going, get going, we need a record.' Gudov kept puffing away. He had no skills. The girl working right next to him got her own blanks and produced more than he did on one shift. Just for fun. Well, Gudov is a husky chap, and he farted along for two shifts which got counted as one, and then they credited him with three times what he turned out. On paper it was five hundred percent. A record for the machine industry."

"What for?" I asked.

"What do you mean—what for? In the first place, the bosses could report back that we now had our very own Stakhanovite-Gudovite drive. In the second place, they were able to raise the workers' norms by fifty percent."

Eight years later I met that Gudov myself. After his record he had been "elected" to the Supreme Soviet, moved into an apartment in Government House, and become an important bureaucrat. He had a somewhat swollen and flabby face. It was obvious that his new life wasn't doing him any good. I never actually met Stakhanov, but one summer we shared a chauffeur. In 1956 I was tutoring Sasha Barabanov, the immensely talented son of the deputy minister of the coal industry. After each session a ministry car took me home. "Yesterday I drove Stakhanov," the chauffeur once complained. "The bastard vomited all over everything. He's eternally dead drunk."

"What does he do in the ministry?" I asked.

"He's an instructor of the Stakhanovite movement!"

In our apartment life flowed along rationally. No one arrested anyone. No one choked anyone. Except that when Mikolashka, the janitor, was drunk he would scream so the whole building could hear:

"I'll put you all in the clink! I'll write denunciations on all of you!"

True, he was drunk all the time. But our turn evidently had not come yet.

'It will come, all right," Petya remarked philosophically.

"Mikolashka will sweep us up with his broom. What we have to do is beat Mikolashka to the draw, and denounce him first. We've got to write."

"What are we going to write about, Petya?"

"It doesn't matter. It's only important that the grammar's not lousy."

FOUR

On the Eve
of the War

ALL my dreams had been shattered. My skull bones, thank God, were not—but they were badly strained at the seams.

I had decided to visit my friend Yevgeny Vassilev to hear him play on his concert piano. It was no distance at all to his home on foot, but in those days I was mad about Jack London, and perhaps because of that and perhaps because I was almost fifteen years old and spring was in full bloom, I had been practicing jumps onto streetcars and off streetcars while they ran at top speed. At that particular hour the streetcars were packed, clusters of bodies hung from the doors, and the tram drivers incessantly rang their bells. I took a running jump, caught hold of the handrails, got one foot on the footboard. But just then came a powerful surge from inside the streetcar. If both my feet hung in midair, I would slide down under the wheels. I immediately pushed off with my foot, tore my hands from the handrails, and flew headfirst into the asphalt.

The quiet Moscow summer wore on. My bed was by a window on the first floor. No one could visit. I had to be absolutely still. But every day someone was standing outside my window. Sometimes it was Mother and Stepfather, sometimes a silent and unsmiling Yevgeny. My whole class even came, together with its young supervisor. Flattening her freckled

nose on the windowpane and making silly faces, she showed
me my school record book. The grades were all A's. Middle
school was done. But I was depressed: the doctors had said to
put off school for a year or two. Would I ever return? My life
was finished.

By autumn, however, I felt completely healthy and Mother
decided to let me go. Adolescence, she warned me, was a dangerous period. If a boy interrupted his studies, he might get
out of hand, and then where would he end up? As a janitor?
My father, to be sure, had started from nothing. But that was
Fedya. . . .

With my excellent grades and a doctor's certificate, Mother
wangled me a place in a school rather close to home. School
#9 was special, although theoretically such schools did not exist.
The students were mostly children from privileged families,
who lived not in communal apartments but in individual apartments with their very own bathtub. Some lived in Government
House just beyond the Small Stone Bridge, some in Writers'
House near our communal baths on Ordynka, and some in
other such "Houses." Of course, there were also those whose
parents had got them in by pull. A handful of children like
myself and Yuri Kuzmichov, the best mathematician in the
school, came from very poor families. Yuri's mother worked
nearby as a janitor; his hydrocephalic brother walked the streets
all day, bouncing a stick along the pavement in front of him.
Half the children in our class came from Jewish families. In
1941, without completing school, nearly all the Jewish boys
enlisted as volunteers in the Moscow Home Guard and perished
along with the Guard.

Naturally a school for the elite had special teachers, some
of the most brilliant in Moscow. They had the best of us investigate a topic on our own and give class reports on it, which
everyone then discussed. This unusual approach introduced
me to a world of intellectual discipline. My research concentrated on what, as I saw it, was most important for my future
life as a philosopher: mathematics, literature, history. (But the
philosophy was a secret. And when my mother, lowering her
voice out of emotion, described how perhaps I might—who
could know, after all I was such an excellent student—attend
a military academy after graduation, I did not argue with her.)
I enrolled in the famous old reading rooms of the Historical

Museum, as well as the Rumyantsev Museum, which, along with
its large new reference library, had been renamed the Lenin
Library. I loved the ceremonial quiet, loved doing research in
the old books that could not be found anywhere else. There,
my numerous school reports on obscure writers were created.

All this inspired me to deliver a grand course of lectures
on Russian literature to my mother and stepfather. I prepared
myself very carefully. The enthusiastic audience lay down on
their iron bed and always fell asleep right away. The professor
sat on a rickety chair wedged between the sofa, the bookcase,
and the chest of drawers that my grandmother had long ago
dragged out of the fire and flames of the estate where she had
worked with the young Zyuzya. The lectern was a tiny table, a
specimen that today, perhaps even in the Soviet Union, no one
would bother to pick up from a dump. My lecture course lasted
for three months. I began in full detail with the ancient Russian
folk epics, but stopped on the eve of the nineteenth century,
feeling that this was a peak I could not yet scale.

In mid-September 1939, while I was moving deep into
medieval Russian poems, German and then Soviet troops
moved deep into Poland. People were thrilled that the Soviet
Union had quickly and easily acquired so much more land. As
usual, my own family was silent. The official story was that the
Soviet Union had not made war against Poland; had simply
liberated Polish Ukrainians and Byelorussians and reunified
them with their Soviet brothers. I was rather indifferent to this.
But our sudden friendship with Nazis startled me. It was only
a game, I told myself, in order to avoid being dragged into the
new big war already beginning in Europe. The blatant cynicism
of this game smashed what little faith I had left in official information, and I began practicing the great Russian art of reading between the lines.

That December my mother started to dry bread and rushed
out to buy salt, sugar, soap, and matches. Our "Winter War"
with tiny Finland had begun. I carefully read the newspapers
and listened to the radio. The reports claimed that the Soviet
Union badly wanted to push back its borders around Leningrad,
so it had offered the Finns an exchange: a well-developed Finnish district near Leningrad for an "equivalent" Soviet territory
in Karelia that I knew consisted of boulders and swamps. The
Finns impertinently refused, leaving the Soviet Union no exit

but—of course—to send in troops and a new government of émigré Communist Finns. The Finnish people put up stubborn resistance; Moscow hospitals were crowded with our wounded; rumors circulated about Finnish children and old women sitting up in pine trees with sniper rifles.

All the same, everybody remembered the August newspaper photographs of a smiling Molotov and Ribbentrop hugging each other in friendship. So no one expected a really big war, and life in our family went on more or less as usual.

Once a month we went to visit my stepfather's family. Not very much remained of it. His father had disappeared during the Civil War, and his mother had been unable to feed their six children. So she put my stepfather in an orphanage, and he survived, while all his brothers and sisters died except for his brother Vasya. Thanks to the shoe factory where they worked, Vasya and his wife now lived with their child and his mother in one semi-basement room carved out of a pre-revolutionary factory storage room. It was divided by a partition into two halves. We sat at the table and snacked, the adults drank and sang; Vasya's wife would immediately leave with the baby under her arm.

"Snake!" her mother-in-law would say. "She seemed like such a nice girl! But she turned out to be a snake. Of course Vasya drinks! When you live with a reptile, how can you not turn to drink? Just look what she's done to him!" Vasya's gaunt, pale face was swollen with red-blue-yellow-green fingernail slashes up and down and across, recalling the self-portrait of the earless Van Gogh. But once, decorated in blue and green on a ground permeated with machine oil, the victim was Vasya's unfortunate neck. His wife had twisted his long, soiled scarf into a sort of rope, looped one end around his neck while he was lying on the floor dead drunk, and strung him up from the bedpost. His mother came in by chance and cut him down. "May the wheel of fate run over you, snake!" cursed the old woman. And the wheel did.

Many workers, as opportunity arose, swiped things from the shoe factory—a piece of leather, even a whole pair of shoes. The best of the professional cutters could manage to use less leather than what the norm required, which meant there were extra pieces unaccounted for. A guard at the factory gate, who had to live on an even more miserable wage than a worker, might sometimes make a deal or pay no attention at all. But sometimes he was severe in enforcing the latest secret decree on struggle against petty theft. In that case everyone knew about it and behaved. Vasya's wife, however, had not earned her nickname of "the crosscut saw" for nothing. She would not listen to advice from others. They caught her with a small piece of raw material during the next such campaign, made a show of her trial and an example of her sentence, and sent her to camp. She never returned. Vasya became a hopeless drunk: he loved that woman. Soon afterward, the 1941 war with Germany began, and Vasya was immediately called up. He was killed within a month.

In that last year before the war the improbable combination of Lenin, genius of violent revolution, and Lev Tolstoi, champion of nonviolent resistance to evil, began to exert an enormous influence on me. I was bewitched by Lenin's passion, his rhetoric of sympathy for the workers, and his victory in the struggle for what seemed a just cause. At the age of sixteen I had yet to understand that means are more important than ends and that the Party slogan "Stalin is the Lenin of today" was a terrible truth. I read almost all of Lenin, devouring one volume after another in the library, and did the same with Tolstoi. Fifteen years later I was liberated from Lenin's charm, but Tolstoi remained the love of my life.

The teachings of Tolstoi about moral perfection and the possibility of moral resurrection at any moment of life were staggering and became part of my soul. I reread the novel *Resurrection* many times. Although I still did not really grasp his demand that we show our neighbor love and forgiveness, I felt very close to his compassion for people. Finally I had come to realize that the endless sufferings I saw everywhere were not an inevitable part of normal life.

Yet in school and the newspapers we were being taught compassion only for foreigners and our own pre-revolutionary workers and peasants, because in the era of Stalin our people lived so happily that the very idea of compassion for Soviet people sounded like a blasphemous slander. There was no one to be pitied. There were, however, plenty to be hated—the enemies of the people. The only people who could not hate them were even more inveterate enemies of the people. But I knew that there were many people to be pitied and that I was certainly not an enemy of the people.

The charwoman who worked in the weapons-factory offices on the floor above us earned 250 rubles a month. On these wages it was impossible to feed and clothe her two children until they completed regular school and after that a technical school. Yet the charwoman managed it. Then her children turned their back on her. She came to my mother in order to confide in at least one other soul what had happened. She was moonlighting as a prostitute. Her son and daughter lived with her in a single room and, no matter how hard she tried to conceal it, saw everything. Once they had completed their schooling, the children had given vent to their disgust.

"Bring them to me!" my mother commanded. "I'll introduce them to Rosa Gurfinkel. She's a kind woman. She'll explain everything to them. And do you know what she is? A secretary in a ministry. A ministry! And what was Rosa ten years ago? Bring them here!"

The charwoman shook her head. She hanged herself later that day. And I had just read in the newspapers that prostitution, being the result of bad social conditions, could never exist in the Soviet Union.

"But what's true is true," a neighbor declared, poking his finger at *Pravda*.[1] "Life *has* become jollier. There aren't ration cards. Just look at how the collective farms are getting rich." And he poked his finger at the newspaper again.

"So what were you telling us yesterday about your mother-in-law's village?" Petya cautiously reminded him.

"What mother-in-law? Oh, right, my mother-in-law's. That's only one place. But you've got to look at other places."

It amazed me how people could be hypnotized by the printed word. Nearly every summer vacation I had lived in some village, and they had all been the same. Meat, milk, and eggs were like relics of the past. Families ate somehow, but not off the collective farm, which gave them nothing except the opportunity to steal from it and the right to have a personal plot. A plot gave the family potatoes and a little money. Some-

[1]The word *pravda* means "truth" in Russian.

times, by hook or by crook, they still managed to raise their
very own pig or cow or chicken. On all this, even on fruit trees,
were imposed heavy taxes in cash and produce. When the hens
weren't laying or the cow wasn't giving milk, the owner would
buy eggs or butter from the state collection center, and then
she would hand them over to the same center! I saw this idiocy
with my own eyes. And I knew that the peasants could not go
away from the collective farm; unlike usual citizens, they did
not even have passports. They were slaves.

The workers were becoming enslaved, too—by new laws
so contradictory to the idea of a "workers' state" that I was
afraid of thinking the matter through. It was only after the war
that I found the courage to regard those laws as "anti-worker."
First came a law forbidding people to move from one job to
another in search of better pay, then a prohibition against ab-
senteeism. A tardiness of twenty minutes was considered ab-
senteeism, and the punishment for it was up to two years of
corrective labor camp. My stepfather almost got caught under
this law.

We had no alarm clock.

At six in the morning the wall speaker[2] sang out with the
anthem:

> I don't know any other country.
> Where a man can breathe so free. . . .

and we would jump out of bed. But one day the speaker was
out of order, and we overslept a bit. My sleepy stepfather was
scratching one hand with the other and one foot with the other,
dressed only in his long underwear, pulling on his shirt, when
my mother turned on the light and looked at the grandfather
clock: "You're late! Good God. What's to be done?" Barefoot
and in his underwear, Stepfather shot from the room. People
helped squeeze him into the streetcar, pushed him ahead, and
squeezed him out at his stop. He was only ten minutes late, and
got off with a reprimand.

That spring, in late May, our school principal called a Komsomol meeting, and without any explanation warned us that it

---

[2]People without radios plugged a speaker into a special wall outlet and received
state radio broadcasts.

would be better if we did not leave Moscow: "You may be needed here." Attaching no importance to his strange advice, I said nothing about it to my mother. And she, recalling the doctors' instructions, sent me off for the summer to my grandmother, whom I had not seen for five years.

This meant a hundred-mile trip westward by rail. Drovnino Station, halfway from Moscow to Smolensk, had hardly changed from the day when Grandmother had taken me off to school in Moscow: endless stacks of firewood, warehouses, an elderly guard with a rifle, long sheepskin coat, and tremendous felt boots. "Why not felt boots?" he protested at my smile. "No rain is forecast. See how good the weather is!" Rain, it was true, had not been forecast.

I had written Grandmother not to bother with a cart. It was only seven miles to Gniloye and I had brought hardly any luggage, so I walked along the cart track. The last third of the way I cut through the forest to our pasture, sat down on a hummock, and looked at the village. The log houses gray from rain, their dark roofs and tiny windows, the willows and crows . . . I realized that it was no longer my village. I was neither part of it nor part of Moscow. I was part of libraries.

Grandmother began to weep and bustle about, not knowing from which side to approach her educated, grown-up grandson. She was now very small and wrinkled. I wanted to hug and kiss her, but it was not our family's custom to demonstrate our love. I did not know how to begin. Yet in a day's time we had once again grown comfortable with each other. She was living in the second room and renting our main room, along with part of the vegetable garden, to a forester. Without this income she would have had nothing to live on.

There weren't enough farmers on the collective farm, so for lack of anything to do, I worked on the horse-drawn mower.

When Germany attacked the Soviet Union on June 22, 1941, I understood what our principal had been trying to warn us about. But how had he known what even Stalin himself had not known? It remained a mystery to me for fifteen years, until Khrushchev revealed that in 1941 the Soviet government had received many reports that Hitler was preparing an assault. But the Brilliant Leader of the Soviet People could not believe in the treachery of his friend, the Brilliant Leader of the German People. So that assault turned out to be as unexpected for Stalin as it was for all the Soviet people, who had been assured by him that the 1939 Molotov-Ribbentrop Pact would guarantee them peace.

Stalin pulled himself together after eleven days. On July 3 we assembled in front of a loudspeaker to hear his address to the people: "Comrades! Citizens! Brothers and sisters! My friends, I appeal to you." The farmers listened to the appeal in total silence and silently dispersed. About what were they thinking, those brothers and sisters of Comrade Stalin?

I was thinking only about entering military service. The first thing I did was head for Uvarovka to the military registration and enlistment office, three hours' hard walking away. When I got there, some fifteen young volunteers were already milling around. The military commissar looked sullen; he wasn't in the mood for us. After hanging around for five hours, we left. At that point I wrote a letter to the commissar of defense, Voroshilov: "I request that you send me to the front. I will soon be seventeen years old. Komsomol member since 1939." The reply came soon and said they would call me up when I was needed. I had no idea that in Moscow I could have volunteered for the Home Guard.

Meanwhile the Germans were advancing rapidly. Soviet deserters had already appeared in some forest villages, and our women openly gossiped about it. I had to get to Moscow soon in order to avoid the occupation. But it was hopeless: one after another, military trains rolled past Drovnino Station; passenger tickets were already not for sale. Along the Minsk Highway parallel to the railway, unbroken columns of ZIS trucks loaded with Red Army men tore westward, towing behind cannons and boxes covered with canvas. Trucks moving in the opposite direction were not to be seen.

One morning, from out of the forest mist, a Red Army infantry battalion crept into Gniloye. The soldiers immediately lay down to sleep in our houses and barns, and the collective-farm chairman assigned a cow to be slaughtered. The commander began to doubt whether the cow would be ready in time, and then and there my grandmother volunteered to prepare it. A kitchen was set up next to our house, and Grandmother was transformed. Once again I saw her as she had been before—swift, deft. Soon the cow was cooked and Grandmother took home her reward, the cow's head.

"Give us a horse, chairman, and a boy driver. I'll return them to you," said the battalion commander when they were done with the cow.

"Return?" laughed the chairman. "I'll give you a horse, naturally, but a driver—how? I'm not the boss. Now, if someone agreed on their own . . ."

I froze. Grandmother flashed her black eyes in my direction:

"*He'll* go!"

Half an hour later I was eagerly hitching up the horse.

The battalion once again faded into the forest, the horses dragging the cannons and the carts with artillery shells, ammunition, and men who had fallen ill. The rest, including the commander, went ahead on foot. They did not make any fires, and they fed on dry rations. Everyone came to a halt and waited beneath the trees whenever German bombers appeared—always at a high altitude—on their way to Moscow. None of our planes put in an appearance. In three days' time, without any misadventures, the battalion arrived in Vyazma.

I asked to stay with them.

"I don't know anything about that," replied the squadron commander, who had walked the whole way there alongside my cart. "The battalion commander said you were to return."

"I wrote to Voroshilov," I said. "I am a Komsomol."

"Listen to me, grab your rations and get moving! We're going to take the field, do you understand? Who's going to bother with you? Don't lose any time, lad."

The battalion departed.

After two days I got back to my village and returned the horse to the farm chairman.

"You got through to Vyazma, you say?" he asked. "To Vyazma? But the rumor is that the Germans are already in Vyazma."[3]

The Germans in Vyazma! There was not a moment to lose. Once again I went to Drovnino Station, and this time, on board a freight train carrying wrecked trucks, I successfully made my way to Moscow.

---

[3]The rumor was false. Vyazma fell to the Germans two months later.

* * *

Liza opened the door.

"Where's Mama?" I asked.

"In the hospital—an abortion."

"But why?"

"She saw your stepfather off to the front. They took him on the third day of the war. Then she did the abortion herself—they're illegal, you know—and did it badly. What a lot of blood! Sometimes it doesn't come off. They say she'll be in for a long time. Still, she's lucky to be alive."

I'd had no idea about the baby. In the spring my mother and stepfather had asked me whether I wanted a brother or sister. (I wanted one.) My stepfather, who could never quite manage to keep up with the norms on the lathes, had at last found work he liked—in an archive, with pay of 450 rubles a month and the prospect of promotion. Their life seemed to be working out. But when the war began and Stepfather was called up, Mother understood that there would be no more life, and gave herself the abortion. Evidently she was too tense when she did it.

FIVE

The War

AND so for the time being I lived alone. They gave me ration cards and Uncle Petya slipped me a little money. He had not been mobilized because of his tuberculosis. I started asking again to go to the front, but the enlistment office told me, Wait, your turn will come, don't worry. I had to earn money to live, so Petya took me to his factory.

The Sergo Ordzhonikidze Lathe Factory was perhaps the most modern Soviet machine-tool factory. They put me to work at a very comfortable lathe, the DIP,[1] which had been designed and developed right in this very factory.

The people's commissar for heavy industry, Sergo Ordzhonikidze, was no longer with us. Rumor said that he had either shot himself in 1937 or been shot after his brother's arrest. The brutalities committed by Sergo himself, during the Civil War, had probably not been forgotten in the Caucasus; yet they were not particularly remarkable, given the universal passion for violence in those days. Big deal, if he shot however many enemies of the Revolution he had to. Too bad for the people shot, but what can you do? You have to hit your enemies

---

[1] Short for *Dognat I Peregnat,* meaning "Catch Up With and Overtake" (America, of course).

"over their little heads," as Lenin says. However, Sergo's soul could not take it when, in accord with the natural logic of events, the Bolsheviks began to hurl each other into their very own meat grinder.

Sergo was popular with the workers in his day. Like all the outstanding Bolsheviks, he was a remarkable demagogue and an outstanding organizer of the military type. About ten years before the war, a still young Uncle Petya would recount with delight how the commissar, surrounded by workers, had cursed and even promised to shoot the factory director for neglecting his people. Now Petya wasn't so simple. He had cast off his belief in bayonet and bullet as cure-alls, and become ironic and skeptical about nearly everything. Even earlier, to be sure, he had not shouted out slogans and had not rushed off to join the Party. He enjoyed respect among the workers for just this reason, and also of course because he was a master at his trade.

Uncle Petya set me up as apprentice to his best friend and former apprentice, Mikhail Osipov. Mikhail, a lathe operator of the very highest category, was a serious young Russian with the thin, severe face of a Scandinavian. Once an illiterate, under Petya's influence he had completed seven years of night school by the start of the war. (Following the war he got a degree in engineering and became chief of a factory section.) After two months of keeping an eye on his apprentice, he came out with an astonishing idea:

"Listen, our ally now isn't fascist Germany but the democratic countries—without them we aren't going to defeat Germany. This must influence our postwar structure. I think the Soviet Union is going to become more democratic after the war. I'm sure of it."

"But we have democracy," I objected. "We don't have private property. That means there are no classes. If there are no classes, that means the whole people is in power. The power of the people—yes, that's democracy."

"Well, well," muttered Misha.

"Those who rule us own nothing and therefore exploit no one and defend only the interests of the people," I hammered away, beating off my doubts.

Misha kept silent. He never again returned to that conversation. But I always remembered it.

* * *

For the present, however, I could not manage serious political thinking. I was trying simultaneously to work at the factory at night and finish high school—my last year before university—during the day. It made me desperately tired. When the air-raid siren sounded on night shift, I did not run to the shelter but lay right down on the worktable or the joiner's bench. Anti-aircraft guns rang out as if in a pine forest, shell fragments and fire-bombs showered the roof, German planes whined and throbbed, bombs rumbled somewhere nearby, and I fell asleep at once.

When the Germans broke through Moscow's defenses at the start of October 1941, the factory was hurriedly evacuated. In two days we dismounted the lathes and loaded them onto flatcars, installed small iron stoves and two-story bunks in cattle cars, received a supply of flour from the nearby food warehouses, and headed for the east. My mother, just out of the hospital, traveled with me. Petya decided to be evacuated alone, and Liza stayed behind with my cousin Vovka, to hang on to their monk's cell for the sake of Vovka when he grew up.

"Who knows whether they'd let us have a room when we came back from the evacuation," Liza explained. "Then we'd eat our hearts out our whole lives, and move from barrack to barrack. But while I'm here, I sure won't give it up. I'll hang on to it with my teeth." (Teeth didn't help. Her room was soon taken away.)

Our trains barely moved, stopping for days at a time at junctions and halts and occasionally an open field when a station couldn't receive us or the tracks ahead of us had been bombed. We crawled thousands and thousands and thousands of miles, across the Urals, through West Siberia, through Central Asia —Tashkent, Frunze, and finally Tokmak, the end of the world, the end of the line. Before us towered the unbelievable heights of the Pamirs. The trip had lasted two months. We immediately unloaded the lathes.

The next day we immediately reloaded them. There was no electricity for a big factory here. And besides, the Germans had been beaten back from Moscow; there was no longer any need for us to be such a desperate distance away. The trains covered the thousands of miles back through Central Asia and

Siberia to the city of Nizhny Tagil in the Urals without a stop
in a matter of days. In a few more days, just as soon as we had
cleaned and set up the equipment by hand and the concrete
had hardened in the foundations beneath the lathes, under the
open skies at first the factory began to work. We were now a
small part of an enormous complex for producing the famous
T-34 tanks.

The lathes whirled, the fluffy December snow fell on our
heads. After working fourteen to sixteen hours, we slept on
portable cots in the office of the section chief without even
undressing. No one—neither workers nor engineers—left the
factory in those first months.

In Nizhny Tagil we were without Petya, who had been left
in Novosibirsk to repair milling machines for a new aviation
factory. My mother had got a typing job at the factory. She and
I were quartered in a just-excavated barrack together with a
pair of newlywed workers and an unmarried adjuster of au-
tomatic milling machines. The barrack had an earthen floor
three steps below the street, tiny windows, nails in the walls
instead of hangers, stools (there was no room for a table), and
four wooden trestle beds. All our belongings went into suitcases
under the beds. There was a small iron stove in the center and
firewood outside near the door. The walls got covered with
frost in winter, and with large drops of dew in spring and fall.
To make up for it, the barrack was not flooded in spring. Our
neighbors' did flood once, and their suitcases and stools were
left floating.

Outdoors things were rather nasty. To be sure, Nizhny
Tagil was charming in its way, although industrial, like all cities
of the Urals. There were well-built wooden houses with covered
courtyards not for livestock but people; high fences with sturdy
bolts for protection against strangers and drunks; clean old
streets; and all surrounded by mighty forests. But I saw almost
nothing of it, just the long path from barrack to factory—a clay mash you pulled your wood-and-cloth shoes out
of with a horrible sucking sound.

We spent twelve hours a day in the factory (with no days
off ever) except for the weekly changes of shift, when we
worked eighteen hours, rested another eighteen, and then
changed over to a different shift. The usual job assignment, to

mill 120 rods for holding the springs of tank suspensions, left me no time even to read a book; all my plans for high school and philosophy were forgotten. Yet I liked operating the lathe—the magical hypnotic rhythm when the cutting edge works without a hitch, the steel shavings curl beautifully, and you find pleasure in working even beyond the limits of your strength. Soon the responsibility of adjuster was added to my usual work on the lathe.

Everyone worked hard. It was impossible to do otherwise, of course: the factory was under military rule. Yet although we never had time or energy to discuss our feelings, I was sure that the other workers felt what I did—Tolstoi called it "the hidden warmth of patriotism"—even those who had no love for the Soviet regime, none at all, like the fellow adjuster who spent two years at timbering in a concentration camp just for being half an hour late to work. Or the one whose big peasant family had been pulverized by collectivization. Their terrible stories, recounted with a terrible calm, made a great impression on me. But they did not shake my decision to set aside all political doubts until the end of the war.

What I could not set aside anymore was a perpetual longing to sleep and eat, eat and sleep. After my shift I would throw myself right down to sleep on the shavings behind my lathe, or go over to the forge shop, where it was warmer, and sleep in a corner on the floor to the deafening accompaniment of the forge hammers. They worked the big forge hammers in pairs. A man turned the white-hot blanks, and a woman or a boy from the factory's vocational school worked the levers. A turn of the lever—boom! Another turn—boom! I would sleep well, wake up, and think about food.

It can't be said that they didn't try to feed the workers. We got 800 grams of black bread a day and three meals a day on ration cards. The meals consisted almost exclusively of *zatirukha,* a thin soup based on fried flour. Given our work, this was like feeding a mouse to an elephant. The children and other dependents of the workers got half that amount. The adolescents from the vocational school, who did a lot of work at the factory, were of course always starving, and one fifteen-year-old boy succeeded in forging ration coupons for bread. "Not for myself but for all," as he later explained. That's how the kids fed themselves until he was caught. They held a show trial in our section and gave the boy seven years in a strict-regime labor camp. He confessed to his forgeries but steadfastly "forgot" exactly to whom he had been giving his coupons.

By the summer of '42 everyone had begun to feel desperate hunger. There appeared "last leggers," as we called them, who collected the pitiful leftovers from other people's bowls. Some would trade their monthly ration card for any quantity of "living" bread, just so as to eat today, right now, this very minute. Then the foremen took away their cards and doled the coupons out to them one at a time, three times a day. I did not descend to such depths. I descended to worse.

There was a sort of hex on me: I kept losing my bread ration cards, or maybe someone was stealing them. Once I turned around and saw Vanya, an adjuster, pick up my ration cards, which had just fallen out of my pocket.

"Give!" I said.

"Give you what?"

"What you just picked up. Give them back."

"Have you gone fucking crazy?" asked Vanya. "You want to—go ahead and search me."

He looked at me with honest, condemning eyes. I decided that it had been an illusion.

The next month I lost my ration cards again. And the next month, yet again. Going three months in a row without bread—I had never done that. My monthly wages were already not small, eight hundred rubles, but part went to pay the factory mess hall and part went for clothing and for shoes that wore out while you watched. No money was left, while a loaf of bread cost one hundred rubles in the market. My mother did not know about my losses.

Now, too hungry to sleep every free minute, I roamed the market in hope of stealing something edible. If I could just snatch that loaf and run, would they catch up with me or not? Of course they would, there were so many people around. So what about grabbing something from the very edge of the market and then running off in that direction? But in the militia booth sat a German shepherd. From time to time the militia would carry out raids, and their dogs were always ready. And a German shepherd would certainly catch me.

I dragged myself into a store. On the counter lay a piece of bread that the saleswoman had somehow forgotten about.

It was small, but just what I needed. I grabbed the bread, leapt out of the store, and raced down the street, chewing and gulping it down as I ran. I had thought everything out beforehand: I would finish the bread while they pursued me, and then they could do what they liked. However, no one pursued me. I ran to where the firewood was kept and sat down on a log.

So, you are a thief. You've really gone off the rails. And not long ago you were dreaming of philosophy? The saleswoman will have to make good the loss out of her own ration. . . . Well, no, those saleswomen always give short weight, they have heaps of leftover bread. But maybe that woman doesn't give short weight? And maybe she has children? So, now you have become a thief. I was totally depressed by that word *thief*, which I had forgotten about when cooking up my plans.

A few hours later, standing half-asleep at my lathe on the night shift, I mournfully considered my life. A long scarf hung on my neck—the only time I ever forgot to take it off. My thoughts grew confused, and I fell asleep standing up. The scarf got caught by a whirling part of the lathe, jerked me downward, and began to strangle me. At that very moment Vanya jumped to my lathe and tore off the pulley belt with a crowbar. The motor began idling. I said nothing to Vanya, and he said nothing to me. We just looked at each other and went back to work.

I was unlucky that autumn. After one night shift it seemed to me that I had a fever. I ran to the polyclinic. Maybe they would give me two days' rest.

"One hundred five degrees," said the senior nurse. "Girls, take him away."

Two pretty nurses linked their arms through mine and led me to the hospital. I was in for a month. It was typhus.

When I left the hospital a month later, I decided to do everything to get to the front. For a start I enrolled in a school for tank drivers, and then on this basis asked the enlistment office for a mobilization order. But they asked to see my passport. I showed my factory pass; our passports had been collected from us and lay in the personnel office of the factory.

"You know we don't have the right to take tank plant workers."

"Give me a mobilization order anyway. It just might help."

They gave it to me.

"Here's my mobilization order," I told the chief of my factory section. "They're calling me up."

"Calling you up?" he laughed as he neatly tore up the mobilization order and threw it in the wastebasket. "By the way, you've been named a foreman. What more do you want, Orlov? You're in our good books."

"People are at the front!"

"People? And here aren't people? Forty tanks a day—that's not people? You're the only human being around?"

"They're people."

At last, in the autumn of 1943, I found a loophole. And besides, I had already driven the section chief up the wall with my requests. The factories of the Urals needed metallurgists, and, as the public notice stated, any factory whatsoever was obliged to release workers for study in the Mining and Metallurgy Technical College. Release would free me for military service. The factory let me and my passport go, and I enrolled in the college. Finally, in April 1944, the enlistment office called me up for the army at my own request.

"You are a gift for me," the military commissar said. "A volunteer. At present I have a quota to fill for the artillery school, but no recruits. Go there, please, you won't regret it. And if you won't go there on your own, I'll send you." That was not exactly what I wanted. They sent me to the Smolensk Artillery School. Smolensk had been bombed out and the school relocated a thousand miles away in the city of Irbit, not far from Nizhny Tagil. By comparison with factory life, life as a cadet was paradise no matter how hard the officers drove us. I was diligent and tried to be inventive, as I had at the factory. I proposed a shell with little wings that increased in size during flight; instead of the spiral threading of the gun barrel, there would have to be straight channels for the little wings and tail. My superiors liked it, but, they explained to me, its advantages were not yet clear and research on it would be impossible during wartime. And that was true.

Our intensive training allowed us no time even to go outside the college gates. I observed the city only from the windows. One window looked down upon an orphanage for small children—cripples of war. In its microscopic dirty courtyard, pale and terribly thin children, some without arms, some without legs, sat silent and alone, playing with the dust. Obviously the people in charge even stole their food. I pointed the unbearable courtyard out to our platoon commander.

"It's useless," he said. "They changed nannies, I heard, but it's still the same. It's the war."

A year later, in April 1945, with the rank of second lieutenant and a card certifying me as a candidate member of the Party, I arrived ready for action at the First Ukrainian Front. My regiment, however, turned out to be a reserve artillery unit of the chief command. As commander of the reconnaissance and communications platoon, I sat with my battery chief at our command post outside Prague and saw only the distant explosions of shells from our 122-millimeter howitzers. I do not know whether I killed a single enemy soldier. In two weeks the war came to an end. For the survivors, life could begin again.

I was almost twenty-one. During all four years of the war I had tried to get to the front, but instead spent almost three years in a tank factory and one more in artillery school. Four years of no real front, no education, not even a serious book in my hands. And now that I was an officer, I would have to slog pointlessly in military service for God knows how long.

Until mid-May 1945, our regiment was stationed next to a big farm outside Prague. (It was bitter to see how that flourishing farm differed from our pitiful collective farms.) Then we were moved to Hungary. Everywhere from Prague to the Hungarian frontier enormous crowds lined up on both sides of the roads, women and children showered our Studebakers with flowers, and cheers of *"Nazdar!"* accompanied us the entire way. We waved to them and shouted back: *"Nazda-ar!"* We caught their flowers. The Czechs loved us in those days.

In Hungary, which had waged war on the side of Germany, no one welcomed us, of course. But people were not hostile. The war was over. We encamped around the dainty city of Pécs, where I observed almost-free elections for the first and last time in my Soviet life. On walls hung posters for not one but two parties—peasant, which later won, and Communist. But none of us expressed amazement at this amazing spectacle, and I did not even feel any. Inside everybody sat a guard who kept him from crossing forbidden borders.

Officer life itself was monotonous: shooting practice, training the soldiers, officer training, political study (mostly of Stalin's speeches) from morning till night. The soldiers had to be kept busy without interruption—that was an army rule. If there were no training exercises and all buttons had been polished till they shone, then the men gathered pinecones in the forest. I tried to protest against the pinecones. At this time, however, many of the officers were intensely absorbed by the idea of reviving the traditions of the old Russian Imperial Army. The officer, according to the regimental theoreticians, was the decisive element in war; the soldier was merely the material of war. In a purely experimental plan one battery commander even struck one of his soldiers in the face for dragging his heels. That aroused intense discussion among the officers.

But here, abroad, I did not hear any serious political talk among them. Conversations revolved around military business and, of course, women. Women in fact were a real problem for the officers, who were far from their native surroundings. I was saved only by my immaturity. One afternoon a certain lieutenant and I got leave to go to town. We were sitting in a café, drinking beer, which I had not yet learned to like, when he suddenly whistled. I looked about for a dog. There was no dog. Approaching us was an attractive, buxom woman of around thirty; the lieutenant silently went off with her. They came back rather soon. My comrade then asked me whether I did not want to, too.

"Want to what?" I asked, not immediately understanding.

"Come on, stop pretending. Are you going to go?"

Ashamed to show my ignorance of this side of life, I got up from the table and let the woman lead me off. It is better not to describe what took place. I fled after seeing how businesslike she was in preparing herself for work. She got paid, but obviously felt upset.

"Everything all right?" my comrade asked.

I nodded. Somewhat later he discovered that he had contracted gonorrhea. Several of the other officers got it, too. Things were much better for the soldiers. Not having official leave to go to the city, they went AWOL at night and ran off to healthy and lovable peasant women. Sometimes one of them was caught out, put into a detention cell, and it was a real holiday for him and his buddies. His Hungarian girlfriend would bring him huge baskets of lard, white bread, and grapes.

But my own life was boring—no girlfriend, no interesting conversation, and only Soviet newspapers to read. Once, however, a couple of issues of *Britansky Soyuznik*[2] miraculously appeared in the mess hall. They contained two shocking articles by American scientists. The first was "Why Did I Leave the Soviet Union?" by George Gamow, whose name I did not know. (Actually it was forbidden even to mention it.) He turned out to have been a famous Soviet physicist. At the beginning of the thirties he gave a lecture in Leningrad on the future of atomic energy and proposed building a particle accelerator. After the lecture he was approached by Nikolai Bukharin, who was then responsible for scientific development in the Soviet Union. Bukharin offered him all the surplus electric power of Leningrad at night for his scientific research. They became friends. However, as Bukharin's political status grew unstable, Gamow felt the earth getting hot under his own feet: it was imperative to flee, and the sooner the better. In 1933 he got permission for an official trip abroad with his wife, and did not return.[3]

In the other article the geneticist Hermann Muller described a similar story. After the famous anti-Darwinist "monkey trial" during the twenties in the United States, Muller came to regard Russia as the country most free of religious fanaticism. In 1933 he left America to live in Russia, where he worked with Nikolai Vavilov, the leader of Soviet biology. But in 1936, genetics in the Soviet Union began to be destroyed under the banner of a fanatic anti-religiosity. Muller left the Soviet Union that year and later decided not to go back. (Ten years later he would receive a Nobel Prize for his discovery of "the dance of the chromosomes.") Nikolai Vavilov was arrested in 1940 and died in prison.

What the hell sort of place was my country?

---

[2] A newspaper published in Russian by the British government for Soviet readers during and after the war.

[3] Bukharin was arrested in 1937 and shot the following year.

SIX

The Officers' Group

"You betrayed us!" screamed an elderly Polish woman. "You didn't attack at Warsaw until the Germans suppressed our revolt! You shot our officers at Katyn!"[1]

Our regiment was being shifted in railway trains from Hungary to the Northern Caucasus. Right now we were at a station in Poland, waiting for a green light. Standing alongside us, headed in the other direction, was a trainload of Poles from Lvov. They were being removed to Poland from the territory Stalin had captured in 1939.

"You killed them in '40!" she screamed again.

Although our newspapers had said that more than four thousand prisoners of war at Katyn had been shot in '41 by the Germans and that Soviet medical experts, academicians, and Alexei Tolstoi, the country's best writer, had confirmed the fact, I immediately believed the old Polish woman. It sounded like us. After what the signaler in my platoon had told me about

---

[1] In 1939 the Soviets invaded Poland, imprisoning over 15,000 Polish officers. In 1943 the Nazis announced the discovery of 4,443 corpses of murdered Polish officers in the forest of Katyn near Smolensk, and claimed that the atrocity had occurred in 1940—before the Nazi occupation. After decades of denial, in 1989 the Soviets admitted that it had been the work of the NKVD.

collectivization, after all my own experience, there were no criminal charges against our regime that I could not find credible. By now, nothing shocked me.

When we reached the Soviet Union, Banderists—Ukrainian nationalists led by Stepan Bandera—sprayed us with machine-gun fire in the Western Ukraine; I had heard even before the war that Western Ukrainians hated the Soviets because of collectivization. No one was injured. At the next large station the commander of the regiment asked his superiors whether we should turn our cannons against the "bandits." No, they said, just keep going. So our trains, with cannons and trucks on flatcars, rushed farther to the east. Sitting atop my train as duty officer, I looked with sadness at the neglected fields, the smashed cities, the makeshift stations with angry crowds around the boiling water taps.

But I was happy to come home.

It was the start of 1946. We were stationed on the outskirts of Mozdok, a small city on the banks of the broad, rushing Terek River. I remembered the Terek from Pushkin: "Beating against the gloomy cliffs, the billows roar and foam." The billows, to be sure, did roar and foam. But there were no cliffs. We were on the Mozdok steppe. As soon as my routine service duties began, I snatched time from them to glue together the five-year break in my education. I found the city library and enrolled in the Moscow Industrial Institute (a correspondence school), studying higher mathematics and physics as part of its program. And I returned to the question I had put off for so long: "What kind of society do we have?"

Now that our officers and sergeants were back in their native land, they became more thoughtful than they had appeared to be abroad. For the first time in my twenty-two years I encountered serious political talk. It amazed me to hear a tow-headed sergeant, surrounded by about twenty men, argue that Stalin should not be given the credit for all victories.

"The people won the war," he said. "We did, not Stalin." Of course, it was a trivial point—but not for that time! And absolutely not trivial was the fact that no one informed against the sergeant. Otherwise we would have seen no more of that victor. In those Stalinist conditions it was almost impossible to hope that no one would denounce you, on whatever grounds, and that state security[2] would not inflate some monstrous case against you.

On one occasion in the officers' mess there was talk about the Stalinist constitution. "Constitution?—Prostitution!" rhymed the chief of staff. The next day all the officers were summoned one by one for interrogation. As the youngest in the regiment, I was the first to be called in. On two chairs in the middle of an empty room sat the deputy political commissar and a security officer. By a happy coincidence they both had faces like pigs. Had I heard, asked one of them, what the chief of staff had said in the mess hall?

"I heard."

"You heard?" the pig faces cried in chorus. "What did you hear? And how do you evaluate it?"

"Well, they were talking about the French constitution. And about French prostitution."

"How do you know?" asked the deputy political commissar.

"What do you mean, how? In the Soviet Union there is no prostitution. You know that, don't you?"

Silence fell. It was now their turn to make an evaluation. They were old hands. And who knows this fellow Orlov anyway? He pretends to be a fool. But maybe he'll write to the proper authorities and say that the deputy political commissar has got it into his head that prostitution exists in the USSR. And he'll say that none other than the deputy political commissar himself has begun to link Stalin's constitution with something unspeakable. We could get into such a mess with this we'd never get out.

"Go, Orlov."

All the other officers, one after another, repeated my baloney. And that's where the denunciation ended.

After that the other officers trusted me. Three or four of us began regular walks out to the steppe, away from unfriendly ears. All of us were Party members, I was a candidate member, but everybody had his own independent opinions. They were rather radical.

"Two things fuck us up in Russia," said the captain, sweep-

---

[2]The Cheka (in those days, the MGB).

ing his bold, bright eyes across the steppe. Around us the feather grass tinkled and invisible quail whistled their "Time-to-sleep! Time-to-sleep!"

"Two things," he repeated. "The first is the central plan. The second is the 'indissoluble bloc of Communists and non-Party people.' Which non-Party people signed any agreement on such a bloc?"

"And who ever saw the text of the agreement?" I asked. We all laughed. It was ridiculous to discuss an unknown. It was merely described as "an indissoluble bloc," and everyone had to guess for himself at the essence of it. "The essence is the dictatorship of the Party," said the captain.

Two political imperatives were clear to us already in the summer of 1946: renunciation of central planning, and renunciation of the one-party system. Nevertheless, socialism was the postulate of our discussions, at least for me. Socialism—but not communism, which Marx said would necessarily follow socialism. I unexpectedly realized that I did not understand what communism would be like, and that it was impossible to understand it.

"They just give us a slogan," I said. " 'Communism is from each according to his abilities and to each according to his needs.' Nothing more. It's absurd to build a new world without knowing anything at all about it except for a one-line slogan. It's ludicrous.

"And who is going to sign the decree on needs, anyway?" I continued. "The decree that says, for example, now it's time for you to have meat, while your next-door neighbor has to go on a diet because there isn't enough meat to go around. Or that your neighbor needs a separate room, whereas you don't feel such a need; go sit there in your barracks for now. Who will decide? The police? The trade union? A freeze on needs and a prohibition on the invention of new needs—that's what is required for communism!" I paused for breath.

"Yes. Time-to-sleep," said the senior lieutenant. We turned back toward camp in order to get there by taps.

Those talks of 1946 seem astonishing to me now. I'd never taken part in such bold discussions before, and never did afterward until 1956. *Why were we not afraid of one another?* Perhaps we felt unfettered because it was an uncertain period of military reorganizations and demobilization. The eyes of state security in the army had become crossed for the moment. Now it is known that the Chekists were occupied elsewhere, with the so-called prophylaxis: the transfer from Nazi to Soviet camps of hundreds and hundreds of thousands of Soviet soldiers taken prisoner during the war. In general, state security worked silently; people and families dissolved into the air, and it was sometimes difficult to feel the genuine scale of the danger. In any event, we trusted one another.

Our walks on the steppe continued throughout the summer; during our discussions my opinions and life experience fell into a kind of system. "Our society is not a dictatorship of the proletariat—but a dictatorship of the bureaucracy," I declared to my friends. "The workers, in fact, have no rights. There's no grub, no housing. A worker has the right only to work and to wait until the bosses solve their endless 'objective difficulties.' Engels wrote that if the workers come to power, they will have to defend themselves from their own officials."

I was still seeking confirmation of my own ideas in the "classics of Marxism," whereas my friends respected the classics but set more store by experience and common sense. I wanted to reorganize society on the basis of Engels's idea that there must be industrial-agricultural units. Factory workers would help agricultural workers with technology and in the fields, and agricultural workers would help out in the factories during winter. And because the only way to achieve radical social change was by force, according to Marx and Engels, my plans included the creation of a new revolutionary party.

All my projects assumed the complete absence of bureaucrats. Workers decided problems by voting.

"That's a lot of shit," said the captain.

In my free time I continued studying in the city library, but now looked more often at the librarian than at *The Phenomenology of Spirit*. Finally I invited her on an outdoor date. We sat side by side in an open airplane, a light two-seater, pilot in front, mountains and valleys below, clouds above, and wind in our ears. The plane started to shake, our arms dangled over the side, there wasn't so much as a seat belt; it seemed that one good jolt, and we'd be tossed out. But Sonya—that was her name—was unruffled. Her beautiful Ossetian face, slightly pockmarked and hawklike, was as tranquil as if she were sitting in her library and not in some rattletrap without seat belts. After that, she and I spent long summer evenings together on the steps of her house.

Her older sister lived there, too, with her child. "Her husband was killed?" I asked one day, thinking of the war.

"Her husband is a Chechen."

"So what?"

"Even though he was a Party official."

"What are you talking about?"

"You really don't know?" I didn't know.

"Two years ago all the Chechens were rounded up in one night and carted off somewhere. The Chechen children were also deported, but my sister is an Ossetian, so she was permitted to keep her daughter with her. And now the daughter has no father."

"Why?"

"They said the Chechens collaborated with the Germans. Her husband was not a collaborator!"

"The *children* were collaborators?"

"Her husband was not a collaborator!" she repeated. And then she was silent for the rest of the evening.

The sky almost fell in September.

"Second Lieutenant, be at the special section of the division at eight P.M. tonight."

The special section! What did state security want? Had they learned of our conversations? How?

I immediately got excused from my service duties and began burning up all my notes, all my projects, everything, including my citations from the classical authors of Marxism. The citations supported my own views, but certainly not the official Soviet ones. Nor, by the way, did they support other views held by the classical authors themselves. Their writings were full of self-contradictions. But then, they had lived a long time ago and had written freely and voluminously, unafraid of the interrogators and prisons of that future system they were battling for. I had never had an appointment with the Chekists, yet felt in my bones that neither Marx nor Lenin would save me. I burned everything in sight, transforming the authors of Marxism into smoke and ash. My thick notebooks burned slowly.

Children were underfoot, offering advice in four different languages at the same time. (I was renting a room from an Armenian family who had been under German occupation in Ossetia, which was a part of the Russian republic.) Finally everything had burned. So far so good, I thought to myself. The classics have been consumed.

In the special section of our artillery division, three look-alike officers conducted the conversation.

"Are you a candidate member of the Party?"

"Yes."

"As a patriot and as a young Communist, it is your duty to help us."

"Yes. Understood. But help—how?"

"No, no, strictly speaking it's just your ordinary duty. You yourself know the imperialist intelligence services are acting more and more boldly. It's no secret they are sending spies into our army. And recruiting spies. From among morally degenerate, politically unreliable people."

They gave me a searching look to see whether I myself had not suffered moral-political degeneration.

"Morally degenerate and politically unreliable people may turn out to be in your very own regiment. The officers, even right at your table in the mess hall, talk very freely about service affairs. They can accidentally touch on secret matters. In the army everything is secret. We have to stop them in time. If necessary—stop them decisively. Do you understand?"

"I understand."

"And?"

"Yes, I understand. 'And' what?"

I was calculating feverishly. Do they know or don't they? Why are they talking about our table? That's in fact our group. Or do they only suspect? I have to keep the conversation going. Maybe I'll understand something more. I have to find out.

"Yes, 'and'—what?" I asked again.

"What? Simply write down everything you hear and the next day hand it over to the chief of your regiment's special section. Just don't sit down to write there at the regiment! Do it at home so no one sees you."

"Yes . . . But what . . . what do I write down?"

"Everything! Everything. We will sort it out ourselves."

"But . . . sometimes . . . they talk about broads."

"Don't write about broads. Well, it depends on what broad. Ha-ha. Remember the names."

"Names? Uh-huh. And?"

"Write them down and turn them over to the special section."

"Got it. But . . . they . . . about the weather . . ."

"Second Lieutenant, what are you talking about? You're an educated officer! Figure it out for yourself. Yes—and pick a name."

"A name?"

"A name. Don't use your own."

"A name. What name?"

"It's unimportant. Just so it's not your own."

"All right. Notov." (This was the name of an agent of the czarist secret police in a detective story.)

"Very good. Notov. Sign here."

"Sign? Sign what?"

"For the time being, nothing. We will meet with you again. Right now you are pledging not to reveal the content and the very fact of our talk with you."

I looked it over. Yes, it was only about nondisclosure. I signed.

All night long I pondered the "conversation." Did they know or not? I concluded that they knew nothing except that we were friends and loved to chatter. Otherwise that "conversation" would have had a different tone. They would not have said to me, "Figure it out for yourself." They would have tried to scare me by saying they knew something—in order to push my back up against the wall. To make me immediately sign a pledge to collaborate. No, they would have tried not to give me any room to maneuver. Everything was clear. There was nothing more to discuss with them.

The next morning I told the chief of the regiment's special section, "Listen, I won't be able to inform on my comrades. It's not in my character."

"How's that? You do understand this will cost you?"

I shrugged. Everyone kept asking whether I understood. I understood. An hour later he led me to the state security officer of the special section of the military district.

He was an elderly-looking, fairly young man. Our conversation was tête-à-tête.

"I can't keep a watch on my comrades," I said. I wanted to say "spy on," but just in time recalled that we do not have spies in our country. It's the imperialists who do. What we have are intelligence agents and patriots.

"It's impossible," I continued. "It's not right, and it's unpleasant."

"I understand that," he replied. "It is unpleasant for me, too. But don't you understand that it is impossible not to have monitoring? Foreign espionage. Secrets."

"I understand. But after all, that's not the only thing you watch for. You can arrest people simply for—"

He shot a glance at me, and I broke off. Idiot, what was I saying?

"What else are we on the watch for? For what else do we make arrests?"

"Not just for secrets. You have various tasks."

"What tasks?"

I fell silent. Why had I changed the direction of the conversation? I was like a beginning cyclist running into a telephone pole.

"Don't be afraid," he said soothingly. "Don't be afraid. We're alone here. Tell me frankly, what do you think of us? " I was still silent. "What do you think of us? Why do you think we're like the Gestapo?"

I shuddered. He had compared them to the Gestapo! I had never yet thought of such a comparison.

"Gestapo?"

Now he was the one to fall silent. He stared straight at me with attentive gray eyes. There was no malice in his look. We had gone very far. Too far.

"Well—"he finally said, "be off with you."

Our chat had no immediate repercussions. The regiment was being reorganized and I never saw those Chekists again, but I still awaited the promised misfortunes. My plan had been to leave the army, take my high school exams, and enter the university. Now I considered alternatives. If they don't accept me in the university, I reasoned, if they don't let me study science, then I'll find the underground groups that the sergeant had been talking about.

This was not the sergeant who had spoken of Stalin, but another one, a man of around thirty-five. Something about me

had aroused his curiosity; he had come up to me one day and
we'd talked.

"So you want to go into science?" he said. "Before the war
I was a research fellow in science. And what do you plan to
study?"

"Just a month ago I wanted to be a philosopher." (The
sergeant pulled a face.) "I read Hegel and Bacon. But then I
realized that philosophy won't explain how nature is ordered.
So I decided to study physics—just now I'm doing some physics
problems. Philosophers merely propose various ideas. But that's
not science."

"And Marxism?"

"Marxism—is also not a science."

"Good for you," he said. We were walking through our
camp.

"I'm going back to the same institute I worked in before
the war," he went on. "And I do know that in the institutes,
there are underground discussion groups."

Groups! I did not have to ask him to explain what kind of
groups. Political. I, too, would join such a group. We will develop a program to restructure society! We—I had started
shouting. The sergeant looked at me bleakly. I stopped. Looked
around. At that very moment we were walking past the open
windows of the special section.

He never came near me again.

I asked to be released from army service in order to continue my education. In November 1946 I was demobilized and
headed for home.

SEVEN

Fog Beneath the Ceiling

WE had lost our monk's cell.

The factory had taken over the communal apartment, and on Mother's return from evacuation they had quartered her in an annex, a former storeroom. When I entered it, I saw on my right a bed that took up the entire length of the room from the door to the tiny window. A bedside table stood by the window, in the fifteen-inch space between the bed and the left wall. That was all there was. Well, I thought, I guess I'll have to sleep with Mother on the same bed, head-to-feet. It was warm, but the walls and the ceiling, six feet or so high, were covered with drops of moisture. You could have written novels on them with your finger. In the fog beneath the ceiling burned an electric light bulb.

We had shared our news in letters to each other, but wanted to talk it all over again. Confirmation had come that my stepfather was killed at the front in 1942. Just as soon as Uncle Petya returned from evacuation in Siberia, he had been put to bed ill and in two months was dead from tuberculosis. Even before that, Liza and Vovka had been evicted from their cell. But she got herself fixed up pretty nicely; she worked in a dormitory now and lived in a room there. Nothing had been heard about Grandmother. As for Mother herself, she had heart trouble. And all her teeth had fallen out, every last one, in the final year of the war. "You bite into a piece of bread and your tooth sticks in it," she recounted. "I even swallowed two teeth." She smiled with her toothless mouth. "Soon they'll make me dentures." Mother was thirty-seven.

"I now believe in God," she said when we were lying down, arranged head-to-feet. "I go to church. Only I've forgotten all the prayers. As a girl I used to know them, but when was that, and did it ever exist? Maybe that little girl died and her soul migrated into me? What do you think? Is it possible? . . . I remember my father taking me fishing on the Chusovaya River. The riverbanks were thick with raspberries. We caught gray-lings. What a tasty fish! . . . And my mother—didn't I ever tell you?—used to go to Persia for Persian fabrics. She would go with my father downriver to the Caspian Sea, he was a steam-boat mechanic, you know, and then go on farther by herself, on a small boat, at night. So, you had one grandma who was a witch doctor and another who was a smuggler."

She burst out laughing like a young girl.

"She would wrap herself in Persian fabrics and bring the merchandise all the way home that way, under her dress.

"Are you asleep? You know, you could get housing. I've been talking to Vassily. Your cousin, Aunt Zina's son, remember him? After he was demobilized, he got a job with the militia. He's already put out a feeler on your behalf, and they'll take you. It's difficult to get in without pull, they favor out-of-towners. They'll give you a room right off and you'll have only a four-year wait for better housing."

"Mama, I can't go into the militia. I have to go to the university."

"Idiot, from there it will be easier to go wherever you want! Once they give you an apartment, you can up and leave. And they promised you'd have time for correspondence school."

"I need much more time than that. Correspondence school isn't education. I've lost more than five years. Anyway, to work in the militia would be disgusting."

"It wouldn't really be like the militia, you'd be behind a desk, not on the street."

"I won't do it."

She didn't insist.

I truly killed her with my refusal. She had neither healthy

housing nor healthy food for the rest of her short life. That was the price of my education.

The university entrance examinations would be in July, and before that I needed to take my secondary school equivalency exams. So I had just seven months. I began to work as a stoker for the factory in the Donskoy Monastery, where my mother was working again as a typist. I would have earned more working on a lathe, but had less time and energy to study. As a stoker, I worked one twenty-four-hour day and then had two days off. Work did not take up much time: once an hour you threw in the coal, raked out the cinders from the stove, hauled them in pails up from the cellar and out into the factory courtyard, threw in more coal again—and went back to your textbooks. No one disturbed you as you read physics and solved equations twenty-four hours at a stretch, sitting on a pile of coal in the semidarkness. To burn my bridges behind me, I declared to everyone that I would hang myself if I didn't pass the exams for the university. It was no joke.

After taking the secondary school exams in the spring, I immediately began to prepare for the entrance exams to the Physico-Technical Department of Moscow University. Just then the furnaces at the factory were shut down and I was reclassified as an unskilled laborer, which meant working at the factory every day and among people. I was on the point of quitting when I got the chance to see Grandmother again, assuming she was still alive. The factory had equipped a truck to buy potatoes in the villages for some of the women workers but mainly for the bureaucrats to eat and, if they had a garden plot, to plant. The driver insisted that to get good, cheap potatoes you had to go 150 miles westward on the Minsk Highway. So he would be driving not very far from my village. I volunteered to help him.

We were on our way back, loaded up with bags of potatoes, when the driver said:

"Listen, my girlfriend is nearby. Want to drop in? What a girl, too! She'll tank us up, feed us, and hop into bed with us. She loves me. Men are a hot item nowadays, I'm more precious than gold." I nodded. He turned right, and we drove up to a prosperous-looking house at a railway station. The girlfriend turned out to be a stout woman named Kapa. "Hello there, Kapychka!" he said in a buttery voice.

"Hello yourself. What are you here for?"

"Here for? We've driven by."

"I see you didn't fly. And who's that?"

"What do you mean who?"

"That curly redhead in the truck."

"Oh, him. We went for potatoes."

"I can see you didn't go for oranges. If you had oranges, I just might invite that redhead in to listen to the radio. But I have my own potatoes."

"He's a redhead but quiet. He won't bother us, Kapychka."

"What's this 'us' business? This is the first time, darling, I've laid eyes on you. Well, not the first, but the last."

"Kapychka!"

"Kapychka yourself! You missed the boat. I told you that, remember? Bye-bye, sweetie!" And Kapychka waved her white hand.

"You fucked-over whore! If I'd known—"

"Quiet down, darling. I have a husband now. He'll show you who's a whore!"

"What kind of a husband can you have, you bitch? I'm the one with a decent wife. There isn't an unfucked spot on you!"

"Pussycat!" hollered Kapa. The driver quickly leaped into the cab.

"Oh fuck, it won't start!"

"Pussycat!" Out onto the porch crawled tremendous, shaggy Pussycat.

"Get out there and crank, for God's sake!" the driver bleated at me. I took the crank and jumped out of the cab. He slammed the door.

"Hooligans!" said Kapa. Just then the motor caught, I jumped aside, the driver stepped on the gas, and this time the truck literally flew.

"Fooligans?" Pussycat growled and started after me. I looked reproachfully at Kapa.

"No, not this one. That one," said Kapa.

"Fooligans?" Pussycat growled again and continued his advance.

"I said it wasn't him!" shouted Kapa. I turned my back to

Pussycat and fled the battlefield for the station, where I boarded
a train headed for Moscow.

The forests of Smolensk flew past, heavily cut on both sides
of the railway during the war. Now came the sign announcing
Uvarovka, our district center. Not one single house was intact,
not one wall, not one brick. Everything had been smashed to
smithereens and leveled, apparently by tanks.

And here was Drovnino. I got off.

Drovnino was whole. Those same endless stacks of firewood and an elderly guard almost the same as the one before,
coat down to his heels and felt boots, except now he had galoshes
and a handgun instead of a rifle. I made straight for Gniloye
through the forest. It was a quiet and beautiful summer day.
The walk took three hours. Finally, light appeared through the
trees. That must be our pasture. I emerged at the edge of the
forest.

The village was gone.

There wasn't even forest beyond it, just a vast flat emptiness
to the horizon. No mill pond, no bridges, not even the stream
itself. Not a splinter, not a bump. Not a trace of our house.
Had there ever been a village here? I went farther, crossing
familiar gullies, and discovered a solitary barrack in place of
Kisselyovo village. Inside was a small iron stove, potatoes cooking on it in an open pot. A narrow-shouldered soldier and a
broad-shouldered woman sat on opposite sides of the stove and
watched the pot.

"Greetings," I said. They looked at me in silence. I went
up to the stove and also stared at the pot. They remained silent.
I went out.

She ran after me. "Don't take offense. They're not my
potatoes."

"Of course I'm not offended."

"Listen, tell Petya—I mean Pyotr Pavlovich—that Marusya
sends her regards."

Now I recalled her.

> Petya, Petya, Little Rooster
> Golden comb
> Gleaming head
> Silky beard . . .

Standing beneath our window, she used to sing that nursery rhyme about a fox calling to a rooster. And Petya, to Mitya's amusement, would leave the house as if he had all the time in the world. "You forgot the beard!" Mitya would shout.

"Grandmother," I said. "What about my grandmother, Pelageya?"

"She died in the first year of the war. There were Germans put up in her house. She went out walking, and just fell down and died. You won't forget to give Petya my regards?"

"Petya died."

"Died!"

"What about you? Are you working here?"

"I'm working. On my back!" Glancing at me, she corrected herself: "I'm hired help. The soldiers are timbering. I keep house for them."

"And where are the villagers?"

"The ones still alive have scattered. At the start they lived in dugouts, then they moved away to wherever they could. I stayed on. All the graves are here."

I did not want to intrude on her weeping, and left. I, too, felt like weeping. The graves were unmarked.

Back in Moscow they broadened and deepened our housing. In place of the storeroom, where we could only sleep head-to-feet on the same bed, they gave us a somewhat bigger little room, in a very deep cellar. Only rats had lived in the cellar before the war (and they were not squeamish about the place now). After the war the municipal authorities had set up rooms there for people, using partitions of wooden planks: four rooms of fifty square feet, each with a window; one closet of a room of twenty-five square feet, without a window; and one kitchen for everyone, also without a window. We lived in a room with a window. Of course, when I say "window" I am speaking Soviet. It would be useful to have a Soviet-Russian dictionary in which, say, Soviet "freedom" would be translated into Russian as "necessity." But come to think of it, given what we had in that cellar, Soviet "window" would be impossible to translate into any human language.

If you looked from the street, you saw only gratings laid flat on the sidewalk bordering our house. Each grating covered a shaft one foot across, two feet long, and three feet deep. The "windows" of our cellar gave onto these shafts. The windows provided neither air nor light; it was impossible to open them. I don't even want to describe the filth in the bottom of the shafts. Passersby thundered with their heels on our gratings and spat.

To build a toilet in such a grotto would have been ludicrous and costly for the state. Why bother? On the first floor there was a beautiful hundred-year-old toilet. Build an inside staircase to it and—*voilà!* If a citizen feels the urge, then he or she can hike up the slippery wooden stairs to the wet wooden cubicle and, thanks to the beloved Party, clamber up onto the bowl like a hen onto a perch.

At least Mother and I lived passably, with our window. Now she slept on a homemade couch; I had a mattress on the floor. In the closet without a window lived a janitor with her schoolboy son, who had something wrong with his legs and went about on crutches. The mother moonlighted as a prostitute on the bed. At such times, the son slept on the floor on a narrow mattress wedged into the space between the bed and the plank wall.

And all this was in the heart of the capital of a nation that wished to teach the rest of the world how to live!

Having left my job at the factory, I had lost the right to ration cards. Experienced by now, I soon arranged to sweep and hose down the big courtyard of a worker's dormitory in return for dinner. Dinner came without meat and bread but with plenty of potatoes, and the job took only one hour a day. It was pleasant to work alone and out-of-doors, thinking about something or nothing, and leaving behind a clean, wet, shining space. Had I not become a scientist, I would probably have worked as a janitor. (There do exist planets on which janitors are not obliged to collaborate with the police.) I cut short my janitorial career when the university examinations began. For the moment there would be no potatoes.

The admissions office of the Physico-Technical Department had warned that the examinations were extremely difficult. But as soon as they started, I realized that I had overprepared. On August 15, 1947, my name appeared on the pass list posted on a wall of the university. Now it was not necessary to hang myself.

It turned out, however, that this still did not mean I was accepted. I had to fill out a questionnaire for the department's state security unit, stating:

> That neither I nor my closest relatives had served in the White armies;
> That we had not participated in the opposition;
> That we had not been abroad;
> That we had not been subject to punitive measures;
> That we had not been expelled from the Bolshevik Party;
> That we had not vacillated in carrying out the Party line.

All of that was the pure truth about my relatives, except maybe Petya (who had vacillated). But as for myself, I was already intensely vacillating. Yet you would have had to be a real idiot or intent on suicide to answer all the questions in questionnaires honestly. Answer a question and get a questioning. I did not vacillate one second in hiding my vacillations from the authorities. There was no other way to get a good education, indeed, any higher education at all; questionnaires like these were required in every Soviet institute and university.

Waiting for the verdict, I wondered about the threat of the regiment state security officer: "This will cost you!" Maybe it would not take effect. There were probably hundreds of thousands of people like me about whom the Chekists had sent routine reports upward. Just try sorting out a huge pile of information like that. I resolved that if the university accepted me, I would temporarily push aside thoughts about underground groups and programs for reorganizing society. Science would come first. Then philosophy and politics.

Before we got security clearance, the department asked us to begin our studies. We attended lectures and worked in laboratories for three months, then suddenly some of us were transferred to other institutions. I was allowed to stay.

University!

EIGHT

"If Just One of You Becomes a Newton . . ."

PEOPLE said that Stalin himself signed the order establishing the Physico-Technical Department after the war. It was really a pact between scientists and the devil. The department prepared specialists mainly for fundamental nuclear and rocket research. Scientists badly wanted that for the sake of advancing science itself, and Stalin for the sake of producing bombs and rockets. The students were party to the pact, too. Most were untroubled by the idea of doing military work someday; others, like myself, believed we could manage to avoid paying that price for our education.

Our teachers included the best Soviet scientists, such as Kapitsa, Landau, and Landsberg. Leading nuclear experts and rocket scientists had shaped the department to fit their idea of scientific training, and the result was an unheard-of autonomy and a wildly un-Soviet regime. We, the department's very first students, took great pride in that. Only laboratory work, examinations, and problem-sets were obligatory. We did not have to attend seminars and lectures—not even the lectures on Marxism, although official doctrine still declared that without thorough study of Marxism it was impossible to understand science! We were exempt from military training. And instead of the usual school spirit of collectivism and support for the untalented and backward, we met respect for individual uniqueness and a spirit of competition.

I liked the competition, but had yet to understand that there are exceptional individuals whose achievements cannot be approached by any group, however large. Still partially hypnotized by Marxism, I did not believe very much in the uniqueness and the irreplaceability even of geniuses. So when Pyotr Leonidovich Kapitsa declared at a general assembly of the students, "If just one of you becomes a Newton, we will be happy," I was amazed. He doesn't believe there are *many* future Newtons among us? I protested to myself. Why can't *I* become a new Newton?

Notwithstanding my high opinion of myself, I was infected by society's contemptuous attitude toward individuals. "There are no irreplaceable people!" declared the official ideology. "Those who are needed will appear just as soon as circumstances call for them." And who creates the circumstances? The masses. They do it unconsciously. Only the "wise Bolshevik Party, armed with the triumphant teaching of Marx-Engels-Lenin-Stalin," comprehends the laws of development and is that "conscious force which accelerates the course of history." And why accelerate that history? Because ahead lies Communism, "the bright future of all humanity." Someone would always arise to carry out the assignment—if it wasn't Ivanov, then it would be Petrov, or Sidorov. The women could always give birth to more. It turned out that individual human beings were not very precious. For Stalin-Lenin-Engels-Marx there were exceptions made, of course, because they were gods, not men.

Where in particular lay the value of each, even the most ordinary, individual personality? I had not begun to ask myself that question. But step by step, entering the circle of science and scientists, I escaped from my primitive understanding of the role of exceptional individuals. Now before me every day stood individuals who were indisputably exceptional.

Kapitsa, who had not yet won his Nobel Prize, gave us a lecture course in experimental physics. Professors also attended it. He was about fifty years old, and his sparse gray hair did not make him seem any younger, but his face had preserved the features of an inspired boy and his sky-blue eyes were the eyes of a child. They teared a little, as happens sometimes with very young babies. In his first lecture he remarked that he had wasted rather a lot of time in his own life. It was a tactful bit of advice to us—don't waste time. Listening to Kapitsa was rather difficult because he organized his course as a history of measurements and discoveries, and understanding it required from the very start a good knowledge of all of physics. Besides that, he would erase with his left hand what he had just written with his right. But these difficulties could be surmounted, and the lectures were fascinating. Kapitsa would tell us about people—their discoveries, their mistakes, their bright ideas, and sometimes their "accidental" successes—so that we felt we were together with them in their laboratories. Kapitsa's personality fascinated us, too. Stories circulated about his unheard-of independence, about how, for example, when he inexplicably returned from England to his homeland, he stipulated that there should be no special personnel office in his institute, and the Politburo went along with it just because he was Kapitsa, the great physicist.[1]

Lev Davidovich Landau, who had not won his prize yet either, gave a lecture course in general physics from a theoretical standpoint and was even more difficult to follow than Kapitsa. His elegant concluding formulas derived almost "from nothing," from general physics ideas, astounded us. Tall and lean, with a naturally elegant manner and a face bright with intelligence, Landau was the supreme model for me. My fellow students even claimed I consciously imitated his hairstyle, but that was untrue. I was the first student in the department to take special theoretical "Landau examinations" at his home, which was next to Kapitsa's off the courtyard of Kapitsa's Institute of Physical Problems in Moscow. After the examination we would usually chat. On one occasion I asked him not quite tactfully how many hours a day he spent in bed. It seemed to me that if I knew how this great scientist lived and worked, it would help me achieve a success like his. "Nine," he willingly replied. "Sometimes more. One must work only with a fresh mind."

---

[1]We had no idea that Kapitsa was virtually a prisoner. He had been working for years in England at the Cavendish Laboratory, and had refused several official invitations to return home for a visit. Finally he accepted. Once he got to the Soviet Union, he was never again permitted to visit the West until he was an old man. Niels Bohr and Ernest Rutherford, director of the Cavendish, tried in vain to get him released. Rutherford then shipped Kapitsa's laboratory equipment to him. There was nothing else he could do to help.

Abram Isakovich Alikhanov, director of the Institute of Theoretical and Experimental Physics (ITEP), where my study group did its practical work, was not such a genius as Landau or Kapitsa. But he was a distinguished scientist and honest man who gathered in his institute the same kind of men, and transmitted to us students his awesomely high standards. Once, after learning that only one student in our group (myself) had passed a theoretical physics exam with flying colors, an enraged Alikhanov summoned us to his office.

"You are shit," he began without any preface. "Either you intend to be researchers or not. If you do, then please be so good as to study theoretical physics thoroughly—whether you intend to become theoreticians or experimentalists. If you do not, then we'll bid you good-bye." The students did very well on the next examination.

I lived in a dormitory next to the department, which was located outside Moscow. It would have been quite impossible to study while living in our Moscow "apartment" and commuting three or four hours a day. Once a week or more I went to see my mother—to chat, buy her something, carry out the slops and the chamber pot, and also wash down the floor, which unfortunately never acquired a clean look. The boards had long since rotted. When it was her turn, I washed down the common corridor for her, the kitchen, and the toilet, but couldn't manage to wash away the smell.

My mother was hopelessly ill. Worn out by high blood pressure and her first heart attack, she could no longer work, and lived on a monthly pension of 150 rubles. I gave her 200 rubles every month from my 400-ruble stipend, and one third of my bread ration cards; but this was only a small part of what she needed. I did not drop my studies—the one thing that could have made her life easier.

The first year in the dormitory I roomed with Victor Trostnikov, a mathematician and future religious philosopher. He came from a cultured family and had a very sharp mind and tongue, along with haughty good looks that brought him great success among women. We spent many evening hours heatedly discussing physics, and trusted each other enough to debate philosophy and politics, too. Victor was the first person I ever met who believed that individual rights were the most important ones. I had not even heard of them before, and in fact Victor did not use the term itself. It was my discovery. "That's right," he said in confirmation. "I *am* talking about individual rights. Clever boy."

Our lectures, laboratory work, and nocturnal debates left us hardly any free time, but the little we had was never boring. Although our fourth-floor room was just next to the toilet, we would crawl out our window, make our way along a narrow cornice, face to the wall, fingers clutching the bricks, and go in through the window of the toilet. We also mastered the art of jumping into the water from taller and taller bridges. Victor once bet another student one hundred rubles that he would jump from the Crimean Bridge into the Moscow River fifty feet or more below. The student, however, got scared or began to regret the one hundred rubles, and decided to warn the militia. When Victor arrived at the bridge, a militiaman was already patrolling the parapets.

"Has something happened?" Victor asked in his best intellectual and authoritative tone.

"You bet, I expect a suicide."

"Ooh! Then I'll help you. You take that side, I'll take this one." The militiaman moved off, and Victor immediately jumped. Our committee of referees, floating down below in a boat, awarded him the victory.

The year after my expeditions with Victor to the lavatory via the cornice, I was assigned a room with three other demobilized officers—Borisov, Voitsekhovsky (a future academician) and Maslyansky. We spent every free hour studying in that room and discussing physics problems. I do not recollect our ever going out, except to the movies once or twice. I had not yet worked my way up to women, and besides, in all of our enormous department there were only three or four of them.

Like the other roommates in the dormitory, we lived as a voluntary commune. Every morning the duty person in our commune cooked porridge for everyone. We often did not have time to eat breakfast before our train left for Moscow and our research institutes. In that case the duty person would shove a pan with porridge and spoons into his rucksack, and we ate it on the train. Naturally, we bought a railway ticket for only one of us. If the conductors showed up, Voitsekhovsky, the ticket concealed in his pocket, would rush past them into another car.

"Your ticket!" they would shout.

"I have a ticket," he would toss back at them en route, but without showing them a thing. The conductors, sensing a fine, would trot after him, and he would lead them a long way off to the other end of the train. Only then would he show them his ticket.

"You, you . . . why didn't you show it right away?"

"I told you I had a ticket."

Maslyansky was arrested. One morning he said, "Panov has asked me to go to the military records office in Moscow. Damn, I'll have to skip classes. I'll be back by evening." He shoved a book by Einstein into his map case and left. It was altogether strange that Professor Panov, the administrative head of the department, should have personally informed a student of such a trivial matter as a summons to the military records office. Maslyansky did not return either that evening or during the following days.

When I came back from one of my regular visits to my mother, Maslyansky still had not returned, and Voitsekhovsky reported that there had been a search of the dormitory. Three weeks later, I was summoned to the Lubyanka. Strictly speaking, I was summoned to Petrovka 38, which is also a famous Chekist address, and taken from there to the Lubyanka, in the sad, notorious main building of the MGB on Dzerzhinsky Square. The time set for my appointment was 10:00 P.M. My interrogation started at 11:00 P.M. and ended at 1:00 A.M.

I was interrogated by two captains.

"Your name? . . . Your place of employment? . . . You don't work? . . . Well . . . What do you do? A student? . . . Well, of what institute? . . ." This comedy went on for a long time. Finally:

"Is Maslyansky, former student of the Physico-Technical Department of Moscow State University, known to you?" Former? Things are bad, I thought to myself.

"What sort of relations did you have with the former student Maslyansky? What can you say about his moral cast of mind?" What, indeed, could I say about his moral cast of mind, except that he was a brilliant mathematician and studied very intensely. Did he cook good porridge? I decided to describe our student life in detail. How we lived as a commune. How we would sometimes have belt battles in the style of the Caucasus, or catch one of the students, tie him up, and throw him on top of the wardrobe. They wrote it all down.

You shouldn't give even neutral testimony! But it was my first experience of real interrogation. I was still rather naive and did not know that they were capable of manufacturing a "case" from *any* details whatsoever, just so long as there were details, and the more of them the better. Only out of nothing at all, from absolute zero, was it psychologically rather difficult for them to concoct something.

Finally they got tired of my anecdotes.

"What things of a suspicious nature did you notice in the conduct of Maslyansky during your joint residence in the dormitory?" asked the officer on the left.

What did that mean—"suspicious"? One was not supposed to ask this question. Every Soviet citizen knew what sort of conduct was suspicious, and what was not. All the same, I should have asked for a clarification. But it was midnight. To hell with them, I thought. Anyway, if there had been something "suspicious," I wouldn't tell them.

"I did not notice anything of the sort," I replied.

"What things of a suspicious nature did you hear about Maslyansky from the other students, and who are those students?" asked the officer on the right.

"I heard nothing. Not from anybody."

"Inform the investigation about the anti-government statements of Maslyansky," said the officer on the left.

"There were none." What did "anti-government statements" mean?

"We possess all the necessary information. Keep that in mind. Inform the investigation of everything you know about Maslyansky!" said the officer on the right.

Their tone became more and more threatening. After two hours of interrogation I felt tremendous psychological pressure. Finally an idea occurred to me. The Soviet press had begun a frenzied persecution of "cosmopolitans," which in translation from Soviet to plain Russian meant "Jews."

"I've remembered," I said.

"Well now, there you are, see. . . ." said the officer on the left.

"And you said you heard nothing from anybody," amicably scolded the officer on the right.

"I had forgotten. I only just remembered. Maslyansky is an anti-Semite. He cursed the Jews a lot, and often." This, alas, was true.

Disappointed, they fell silent and puffed away on their cigarettes.

"But you do understand that that isn't a crime against the state," the officer on the right said at last, looking suspiciously at my red hair.

"I understand." There was nothing to understand.

In the end they released me. I signed the interrogation protocol just on the last page, at the very bottom. (You shouldn't do that either! Many years later, Ivan Yemelyanovich Bryksin told me that he did the same thing when he was interrogated on his own case. And then at his trial he saw springing up from the protocol such pages against himself that even the devil himself would not have signed.)

They did not call me back for interrogation, and we never saw Maslyansky again. Afterward there was talk in our dormitory that he had listened to the BBC. There existed only one radio in our dormitory, in a room occupied by only one student, who was still in it, safe and sound. Dark rumors began circulating about him, and he was soon transferred to another institution.

The fact was that the students worked very hard, arranged seminars, went on summertime hikes together, argued with inspiration—and informed on each other. Denunciations were being written by no less than one quarter of our own study group. I found out about this only in 1956. Apparently I was much more naive than I could have imagined.

During our last years in the Physico-Technical Department, seven of us from the group had been temporarily given a two-room apartment near ITEP. This meant good conditions for studying. We lived as a friendly commune and took turns cooking soup and kasha, discussed physics, and even organized a choir for Russian songs in which everybody sang. I was its conductor. We were genuine friends. At least three of the seven were writing denunciations at the time. True enough, no one denounced any of his friends, no one exploited anyone's slip of the tongue. But, for that matter, did we make any slips of the tongue? Did we ever discuss politics? We did. Yet no one ever said anything dangerous to himself. We had inner gyroscopes that kept our torrents of speech within safe channels. *In our hearts, deep down inside ourselves, no one trusted anyone.* In such circumstances there were not, and could not be, simple and pure relations among us.

Apart from myself, Zhenya Kuznetsov was the only one in our group, who came from a family of workers. Gersh Itskovich Budker, the brilliant physicist who led our seminars and went by the Russian name Andrei Mikhailovich, thought him the most quick-witted of us all. Zhenya Kuznetsov once roomed in the dormitory with Zhenya Bogomolov, the offspring of a family of provincial teachers. The two Zhenyas lived as a commune, cooking porridge in turns and eating it together right out of the pan, scornful of such prejudices as individual bowls. They ate together, but wrote reports on each other separately. It is not difficult to see the internal contradiction here—which, in accordance with Marxist philosophy, ought to lead to a qualitative change. And it certainly did. The chief of the department's special section demanded that Zhenya Bogomolov steal Zhenya Kuznetsov's address book from his pocket and hand it over to the section. Zhenya Bogomolov's soul rebelled. He confessed to Zhenya Kuznetsov.

As Kuznetsov told it to me in 1956, their conversation ran something like this:

"What whores," said Zhenya (Kuznetsov). "What real whores. You know, they asked exactly the same of me. But, you know, you don't have any address book."

"No, I don't," muttered Zhenya (Bogomolov). "But do you have one?"

"I do, but there's nothing in it. It's blank," said Zhenya (Kuznetsov), playing the fox just in case. "Give it to them, let them wipe their asses with it."

"And what do we do next?" wearily asked Zhenya (Bogomolov), who always tended to be a little depressed.

"From now on we'll only write together," said the never-depressed Zhenya (Kuznetsov). "Together about me and together about you. We'll minutely describe each move of our spoons from the pot to our mouths and back again.

They had been dragged into this sewer gradually: "You only have to do this once. You're Komsomol. Just describe your life and your conversations. You only talk about physics? Well then, write about physics. . . The reason we have sent for you again is this: we have been warned that some students are manufacturing gunpowder. Have you heard anything about that?"

Each wrote down all sorts of nonsense, lest they think he was hiding something, and finally signed a pledge to observe and report. Why not simply refuse to write reports on each other? They both desperately wanted an education and did not know what a refusal would mean for them. I knew the force of that powerful blackmail myself.

In artillery school, as a future officer, I had automatically been put up as a candidate member of the Party during the war, and that seemed natural at the time. But after the war my views changed considerably, and I tried not to move up to full membership. As a stoker in the factory, I simply concealed the fact that I had a Party card in my pocket; in the university that was impossible. To refuse to move to full membership meant giving up the university, and that was impossible, too. After being a candidate three years instead of one, I was seriously asked by the secretary of the Party bureau in the university why I was dragging the thing out. So I decided to become a full member. But that was not the end of it. Because I was an older student member of the Party and doing well in my studies, they asked me to join the Komsomol bureau. And I agreed.

The more deeply I studied science, the more confused I became about the Soviet Marxist teaching that all the basic sciences—quantum mechanics, relativity theory, genetics, and cybernetics—rested on a false foundation. Either Marxism was wrong, indeed, anti-scientific, or the science that I had come to know and passionately love was not science at all. The scientific status of genetics became crucial for me because of its direct bearing on the Soviet doctrine of Communist reeducation.

Back in 1948 the renowned Trofim Denisovich Lysenko, with the inspired face of a hungry wolf, had liquidated genetics once and for all and switched the agricultural sciences onto the rails of the one and only true scientific teaching. I vacillated in relation to his theory, according to which no such things as genes existed, and acquired traits could be transmitted by inheritance. If, I reasoned, genes do exist and have transmitted all the important traits of human beings from generation to generation for thousands of years already almost without change, then the Soviet slogan "We will rear a new Soviet man!" was a nightmarish delirium. But if, on the other hand, such traits as, for example, selfishness and possessiveness were not constant but depended on milieu and indoctrination, then the only thing to be done was to change the social system—and press ahead with indoctrination—in order to rear "the new human being." There was much to be said for such a view.

This became for me the question of questions.

Finally, two years after Lysenko's scientific decision that genes were something dreamed up by the priest Mendel and the American pseudo-scientist Morgan, I decided to look with my own eyes upon the astonishing successes of Lysenko in reeducating plants. The Soviet press had written about that: "Egyptian wheat, reeducated by Academician Lysenko, will soon ripen on the fields of the Soviet Union. Each stalk of the miracle grass has ten times more grains than ordinary varieties." I got on an electric train at Paveletsky Station in Moscow and rode to Lysenko's famous station at the state farm named "The Lenin Knolls."

Wandering among the pitiful experimental plots, I asked myself whether I was not in an insane asylum. Yes, indeed, on the full stalk of this wheat there *were* about one hundred grains. But the heart of the matter was that out of every one hundred stalks of it, ninety were completely empty! This wheat did not want to be reeducated.

So it was a fraud, moreover, a grandiose fraud. The theory of environmental reeducation was blown to hell. This was something I saw, to be sure, only for wheat. But what if the human species also would not surrender to reeducation? What if, out of every one hundred people, ninety would, all the same, love themselves and their own children more than they loved society as a whole? What could be done? Should their heads be cut off? Then we would get a headless society in which the headless people probably would love themselves even more.

Deciding that it was time to consider the matter without joking, I traveled farther on the railway for a walk in the forest. But there was nowhere to walk. There was barbed wire—a camp. Still more barbed wire—another camp. And still more barbed wire. I turned back.

NINE

Menshevik Songs

ONE year before completing the university, I married a very serious young woman with big, beautiful, dark brown eyes. Her name was Galina Papkevich and she was half Polish. That is how, in the summer of 1951, I came to move with my suitcase out of the student dormitory and into a room in the very center of Moscow, where Galya and her aunt were living. To honor this event, my student friends presented me with a suit—the first I ever had. At the end of 1952 a lovely son was born. We named him Dmitry. Galya worked as a technician at the very same aircraft factory where my father had once worked. I was carrying out research under the supervision of Vladimir Borisovich Berestetsky. Since we were helping my mother, money was tight, and to get diapers we had to sell all of Galya's library. But we were happy. At night I would rock the baby carriage with my left hand and calculate with my right the transitions of the orthopositronium into the parapositronium. Once when I was figuring something, Dima kept crying to be picked up, the number 2 got lost in my calculations and wouldn't be found, and Dima still kept crying. Finally I raised him over my head, and started to shake him: "Come on, come on, go to sleep, kid!" He began laughing his angel's laugh. I was ashamed and covered his face with kisses. What more was needed for happiness?

The absence of guilt.

The summer we were married, the Physico-Technical Department had been reorganized into an independent institution, and like many in our group I was transferred to the Physics Department of the university. However, under the pretext of the reorganization the Jewish students were not sent there but to provincial and minor institutes, depriving them of access to "secret" work. This meant exclusion from future jobs in serious scientific laboratories. They were my friends, and I felt guilty when we met, but we did not trust one another enough even to discuss the situation. I wanted to graduate, to do science, to be with my wife. And so I kept silent like everyone else.

The following winter, shortly after my graduation and the birth of our son, the Chekists revealed the plot of the "poisoner doctors" and threw them in KGB prison; even if the doctors had not drunk the blood of our babies, they had poisoned the blood of our leaders. Ordinary and not so ordinary Soviet people were discovering new poisoners here and there—poisoners of our children and our minds. Soviet ladies writhed in hysterics in the waiting rooms of Jewish doctors. Jews were being openly abused. Because of my curly red hair, people jostled me on the street, spat, and cursed: "Jew!" I refused to say that I was not. But I said nothing; to do otherwise seemed pointless. People had turned out to be so unutterably stupid and cruel that even my old dreams of a new revolution now seemed pointless, too. I felt guilty, ashamed to look into the eyes of the stoically cheerful Jewish wife of Galya's uncle Tadeusz.

"The whole deal stinks of kerosene," said Mother's plumber-neighbor in the cellar. "If I was Jewish, I'd make a dash for the North Pole. Better yet, the South Pole."

The student Eskin, one of the best in our old department, made a dash out of a seventh-floor window onto the road. At an emergency meeting his Komsomol group, one third of it Jews themselves, condemned his conduct as *unworthy*.

After a two-month wait for security clearance following graduation, my scientific career began. I had been offered three good choices of where to work: ITEP with Berestetsky, Kurchatov's institute, or the Institute of Nuclear Research in Dubna. I had already collaborated with Berestetsky; he had entrusted me with checking the calculations in the chapter of his book where electrons scatter on electrons. He was an outstanding theoretician and a sympathetic, cultivated man. Apart from that, I simply liked ITEP. So I began to work with Berestetsky in ITEP's theoretical division. Headed by Isaac Pomeranchuk, the division was the patrimony of Landau and consisted entirely of his disciples. Landau himself worked there half-time and ran his own division in Kapitsa's institute. My research went well from the start. I worked so hard that calculations whirled about in my head even in dreams. At first I investigated the passage of particles through matter, and Berestetsky advised me to publish the results. However, they struck me as too small-scale; my first publication had to be something unusual. I dreamed of solving the problem of superconductivity, and began studying mountains of books and articles about it night and day. My new colleagues were similarly fanatic. "Science," lectured Pomeranchuk, his spectacles and eyes sparkling, "is the most jealous of mistresses!" He did not just work evenings, as we all did, but at lunchtime snacked on sandwiches in his office rather than going to the institute's canteen.

Goading me on in my work was the opinion of Landau, which Volodya Sudakov had told me about when we were students. Orlov, he had said to Volodya, is talented but lazy. It would have wounded me less at the time had he said that Orlov was diligent but dull, for I had grown up in a family where lack of diligence was something immoral, and I was certainly not lazy. Yet Landau had correctly seen that I was not burying all of myself in theoretical physics, which demands very great abstraction from life around you. The fact was that more than just physics interested me. Indeed, I had come to physics from something else. It was impossible not to think about philosophy, social problems, and Soviet politics. Especially, now, about Soviet politics in science.

Not long before Stalin's death a general attack on physics was being prepared—an assault on quantum mechanics and the theory of relativity. At a special session of the Academy of Sciences, scientists were going to be forced to condemn publicly and without reservation the obscurantist and subjective, in a word, pseudo-scientific, concepts of Albert Einstein and Niels Bohr. The philosophers and the most progressive Communist physicists had already begun the assault. The Ministry of State Security was rolling up its sleeves.

It was not so difficult to imagine the indignant thoughts of some righteous, hardworking colonel from the Lubyanka: "It is time to begin sorting out the actual professional, political, and moral qualities of these so-called scientists. They talk about 'unpredictable atomic transitions,' just as if we're fools and can't understand what's going on. We will arrange for them a quite predictable transition to here, the Lubyanka. They hint that the universe could have originated in one moment from one point, forgetting that it is also possible to die in one moment at a given point. Who needs these people? Outrageously little work has been done with the physicists, and it is time to find out who has sabotaged that whole business. Gamow escaped. Landau spent only a year in prison before the war; we had to release that kike—because of the interference of the untouchable Kapitsa. Again because of that Kapitsa, it was impossible to keep that Fock locked up. Kapitsa himself—and who is this son of a bitch anyway?—is sitting things out at his country house. And Rumer, that insect, didn't kick the bucket as he was supposed to in labor camp. Before the war the shit got himself a place with Tupolev and Korolyov in a posh *sharaga*. He had figured out what kind of prison was better, and even if it was in Siberia, it wasn't a labor camp. It was a resort! The geneticist Vavilov left prison feet first, in the normal human way, yet his physicist brother is not only alive, the bastard, but even president of the Academy of Sciences.[1] No, we can't go on like this."

Budker, with whom I became friends during the last years of his life and of my freedom, told me how the catastrophe had been prevented. Igor Vasilyevich Kurchatov, the head of the

---

[1] Except for Yuli Borisovich Rumer, a theoretical physicist and collaborator of Landau, who spent too many years in camps to become famous outside the Soviet Union, these scientists were world-renowned: Vladimir Alexandrovich Fock, theoretical physicist; Nikolai Ivanovich Vavilov, geneticist and botanist; his brother, Sergei, experimental physicist; Andrei Nikolayevich Tupolev, airplane designer; Sergei Pavlovich Korolyov, chief designer of the Soviet sputniks and space rockets. A *sharaga* was a labor camp for scientist-prisoners; their labor consisted in doing science for the military. Fock was once temporarily arrested simply because one of the *sharagas* needed his expertise to solve a particular scientific problem!

nuclear program, warned Stalin that even the slightest distraction of physicists by a "philosophical discussion" would wreck the production schedule for nuclear weapons. The entire nuclear program was based on quantum mechanics and the theory of relativity. Everything will plunge off the rails, Iosif Vissarionovich. Stalin grasped this. Leadership in nuclear and rocket weapons was the primary goal of the state. These were weapons for future world domination. To achieve this goal with the aid of Leninist "beatings over their little heads" was a pleasant idea, but unfortunately premature. Stalin had learned Lenin's dialectic: to get to heaven it is necessary to pass through hell; to get to absolute supremacy it is necessary to pass through relative relaxations. So he ordered that the physicists, with their pseudo-scientific but, for mysterious reasons, powerful science, were not to be touched for now. Given the scale of things at the time, this was a small but remarkable retreat.

And so physics was saved with the help of the atomic bomb.

Alas, it was the bomb, too, that had given us our freedoms in the Physico-Technical Department and had saved our professors. Budker described to me how, at the entry checkpoint of Kurchatov's institute, where he was permanently based, the security guard had blocked his way and said, "Budker? You don't have a pass!" Budker needed no explanation of what this meant and what the sequel could be. He immediately phoned Kurchatov, who immediately explained to the proper quarters that Budker was a participant in the atomic program. Budker's pass was quickly given back to him. In the Physico-Technical Department the only one of our professors to disappear was our super-independent Kapitsa; but the general retreat of the regime from physics saved him, too. He was merely dismissed from his Institute of Physical Problems and from all his other jobs for refusing to work on nuclear weapons, and set down in his dacha instead of the Lubyanka. After Stalin's death they apologized to him.

No, we in the Physico-Technical Department hadn't really smelled gunpowder. We hadn't even had an arrestometer. I learned about this Leningrad University apparatus from Berestetsky. In the thirties they had a gallery of professors' portraits that the students, among themselves, called "the arrestometer." Portraits began to vanish from the walls. A portrait disappeared—the professor disappeared. Another portrait disappeared—and that professor disappeared. Finally the apparatus indicator went off the scale: all the portraits had been taken down.

Physics was lucky. Biology was not. Cybernetics was not, because no one dreamed that the bourgeois science of control would be useful for the control of rockets. Agronomy and the whole of agriculture lay in shit. Comrade Stalin himself translated this into Soviet language: "We are all delighted at the successes of our agriculture," he wrote in the article "Economic Problems of Socialism," which was studied and cited by all thinking and progressive humanity. The delightful successes of our scientific agriculture were right in front of us. In the very center of Moscow, where I now lived, peasant women with hemp sandals and children feeding at their breast were begging alms from Muscovites. Up above them against the night sky glowed an enormous neon advertisement:

BUY MOSCOW CUTLETS!

There was no translation for this from Soviet into Russian. It was useless even to ask what the advertisement might possibly mean. I had still never succeeded in seeing such cutlets, even though I sometimes did see enormous lines waiting for them, almost as long as the lines at Lenin's mausoleum.

Marx wrote that the criterion of truth in science was practice, and this claim was true even though it was taught in the network of special Party seminars. They also taught that "the Party is building society on the only true scientific foundation." The practice of this Party was clear to me; that Marxism was its foundation was also obvious (I knew Marxism well). From which I could draw only one conclusion.

Thus, by the end of the Stalinist era of Soviet history, which coincided with the beginning of my own scientific career, I had already found ridiculous the claims that Marxism was "scientific." In my view Marxism as a serious theory no longer existed. Considering also the inefficiency of the Soviet system, I reached the conclusion that it sometimes could be very efficient, but only in narrowly focused fields of activity such as the rocket and nuclear race, where the stimuli at the top were extremely strong. On the whole it was inefficient. However, when I asked myself whether I wished to see a return to capitalism, at that

time I firmly answered, "No." My rejection was purely emo-
tional. The idea of working not for an impersonal "state" but
for some specific person seemed unpleasant and humiliating.
This attitude was, and to an extent remains, typical of many
people in Soviet Russia. Therefore, I had no positive economic
philosophy at the time, apart from a vague idea about self-
government by workers.

That was how my views were being formulated when, in
the spring of 1953, Comrade Stalin finally died. His death on
March 5 made no impression on me whatsoever. I sat out those
days of national mourning, glued as usual to my desk in Berestetsky's office. He asked me what did I think would change?
In which direction? I replied that in my opinion nothing could
change. And suddenly I added, surprising myself, that so many
people were already in prison, there was already nothing else
you could scare ordinary people with. Of course, I was over-
estimating the possibilities of "ordinary people" and underes-
timating the probabilities of change from above. My remark
simply reflected an instinctive desire for a people's rebellion—
a desire that I consciously and firmly suppressed after several
years and then rejected entirely. Berestetsky looked thoughtfully at me. I do not know what he was thinking, but from that
time on he became much franker with me than before.

Not everyone was so indifferent to the death of the Father
and Teacher. The people wept for their Leader. Officers shot
themselves (most probably while drunk). Some of our old student group decided to force their way to the body, which had
been exhibited for farewell in the House of the Unions, but it
was hopeless. People had flooded the entire center of the capital.
Zhenya Bogomolov made it. He pushed his way to the rear of
the House of the Unions, climbed to the roof by the fire escape,
then descended by the drainpipe on the front side of the building, landed on the shoulders of the people who, like himself,
had thirsted to see the corpse, and pushed into the Hall of
Columns, accompanied by piercing yells from the children,
women, and men being trampled on. "Stalin is dead, but his
cause lives on," Berestetsky commented about the idiotic death
of multitudes at Comrade Stalin's funeral.

The event reminded me of the celebration on Khodynka
Field at the start of the reign of Nicholas II, when the corpses

were also laid out in piles. My grandmother had told me how people trampled each other because of spice cakes even before the living czar appeared at the fair. Now they were being trampled on without any spice cakes, because of a corpse.

Soon afterward a conflict sprang up between myself and Director Alikhanov. After reviewing old experiments, his laboratory discovered an anomalous scattering of muons. This being a serious matter, Pomeranchuk asked me to check the calculations. I discovered a mistake: because of the antiquity of the measurements, they had confused definitions of what had been measured. Alikhanov had to be told.

"We've worked for so many years!" Abram Isakovich shouted. "But you—!"

"How many years is irrelevant," I said ruthlessly. "You made mistakes in the calculations." He walked out, slamming the door with a crash; I was left alone in the office. In a few minutes he came back, listened, and understood. After that he became extremely friendly and warm to me, and I began to love him with all my heart.

A few years later ITEP decided to build a proton accelerator with an alternating gradient. When Budker pointed out an important physical effect that might cause it not to work, Pomeranchuk, remembering my muons, included me on the accelerator team. His plan was that I would check this effect and then go right back to my usual subjects. I interrupted my study of superconductivity and in two years constructed the necessary theory of nonlinear oscillations (the effect turned out to be harmless for us), became a coauthor of the accelerator proposal, sent articles off for publication, and on orders from Pomeranchuk wrote a dissertation. "Writing a dissertation has no relationship to science," he explained, "but it does to having bread. You urgently need an increase in pay." Salaries depended on scientific degrees. And by now a second child, Alexander, had made his appearance. We definitely needed more money.

However, our life had already improved a great deal: ITEP hired Galya as a technician and at the end of 1955 gave us a self-contained apartment of two rooms in a new building near the institute. It was like living in a palace, after the single room for the five of us. That room had been inherited by Galya from her mother, who received it from the Soviet government for contributions made to the Revolution by her parents, Polish revolutionaries. The very same Soviet government had confiscated the two-story wooden house from an NEP man, a factory owner imprudent enough to believe in the stability of the New Economic Policy. The only things left of the NEP man by the time I lived there were the recollections of his former cook, to whom, for some kind of services past and future, the authorities had allotted twenty-seven square feet separated from the communal toilet by a thin board partition. On that account the old woman hated all her neighbors, especially "Poles-and-Jews," raised Cain in the communal kitchen from morning till night, and frightened little Dima whenever he happened to be alone in the corridor. That genius of architecture Le Corbusier, who was such a tremendous enthusiast for building communal boxes on the site of old Moscow, should have been sentenced to live for one month and a day with that woman, who in fact was a typical denizen of Soviet communal apartments. The ITEP apartment was our salvation from the old witch.

With my dissertation finished, I could finally go back to my previous investigations. But in February 1956, Nikita Khrushchev delivered his dramatic report at the Twentieth Party Congress and left me an accelerator specialist for the rest of my life.

Khrushchev's report on the atrocities of the Stalinist epoch was read at closed Party meetings and shattered even those who, like me, were already anti-Stalinists. For the first time I realized the fearful scale of the crimes. Gangsters had been in power, and could get there again because in principle the structure had not changed. What should I do? There came that moment for which I had, in effect, been preparing my whole life—a life of tensely scrutinizing this strange, murderous, self-devouring society. I must state openly everything I thought about it.

By order of the Central Committee, all Party organizations had to carry out closed discussions of Khrushchev's report. The discussion at ITEP would be led by our Party bureau, which I had now been a member of for two years. Although Director Alikhanov, his deputies, and his division heads were nearly all non-Party, they tried to influence the composition of the bureau, as well as the trade-union committee, in order to have good or at least harmless people there. It was like organizing an all-round defense. So I had not declined to be elected to the bureau, believing that I could be of additional benefit to science in this way. Given all the twists of Soviet politics, even unexpectedly favorable ones like the death of Stalin, scientists always had grounds for fear. In the event of a general or local assault against physics or particular physicists, the position of the Party bureau could, I thought, prove decisive in their defense.

The bureau met twice to plan our March meeting. We decided to set its tone by speaking first. Klava, a typist, would record the speeches in shorthand. The opening speaker was Robert Avalov, a Georgian and orthodox Leninist who had graduated with me from the Physico-Technical Department. "What must be done to prevent a new 'Stalin cult'?" he asked."We need what Lenin proposed: to arm the workers. The working masses must have some organized, armed power to suppress the bureaucracy!"

My speech followed Avalov's. Despite my excitement I spoke loudly and distinctly. "The terror carried out by the government," I began, "has affected not only the economy of the nation but also every aspect of Soviet life. It has changed us ourselves." We all, I said, from an ordinary worker to a writer, had been taught to sense where the wind was blowing and to adapt our souls to the current policy of the government. Everyone had got used to raising his hand obediently "in favor"— the members of the Supreme Soviet, and the members of the Central Committee, and all of us.

In the conference room sat members of the Party who, like myself, were neither careerists nor fanatics. Now many of them, some timidly, some boldly, were opening their eyes and thinking about how to avoid a recurrence of Stalinism (although that term still did not exist). They seemed to like what I was saying.

Under capitalism, on one and the same industrial base, I continued, various political superstructures can exist, from fascism to democracy. There is no determinate link between industrial strength and political structure. It is exactly the same under socialism. Murderers like Stalin and Beria can be in power, as in the Soviet Union, and there can be a more democratic regime, as in Yugoslavia.

"In order for what has happened not to happen again, we must switch to democracy on a foundation of socialism!" That's how I ended. My words about terror and murderers had not shocked the meeting; the anti-Marxist idea (which I was so proud of) about indeterminate development was a theoretical subtlety no one seemed interested in. What was noisily being applauded was the idea of "democracy on a foundation of socialism."

Volodya Sudakov, a talented theoretician and the secretary of the Party bureau, did not come forward himself but quietly offered the platform to everybody who asked for time to speak. He gave it next to Vadim Nesterov, an experimentalist (whose father later hid a copy of my speech at home, for safekeeping). The last to speak was Shchedrin, a worker and member of our bureau.

People excitedly applauded our speeches and wanted to make their own. Since it was already late in the evening, we voted to continue the following day. I planned to lay out my economic proposals then—essentially the same ones I had formulated in 1946 on the Mozdok steppe. But we were not permitted to conduct the next meeting. It was conducted instead by the chief of the Political Directorate of the Ministry of Middle Machine Building, Mezentsev himself,[2] an experienced Chekist. People said that in 1944 he had been in charge of deporting the Tatars from the Crimea.

"No one is permitted to criticize the Central Committee!" Mezentsev shouted, pounding his fist on the table. The audience was nervous. I came forward to speak against his thesis, people shouted things from their seats, and no one publicly backed up Mezentsev.

"We must pass a resolution condemning the anti-Party speeches of Orlov and the others!" he demanded. His proposal got voted down. Klava accurately recorded it all.

The meetings over, the institute was frozen in expectation of what would happen next. The affair was being examined at a high level, we still did not know which one. All the speakers were ordered to write explanations to the Central Committee.

---

[2]ITEP was formally, but secretly, a military unit. Therefore, ITEP was just like the army with respect to Party control at that time: not subordinate to the nearest district Party committee, but to a special political administration—in our case, Mezentsev's. The political section of ITEP was appointed by Mezentsev and existed parallel to our elected Party bureau.

Transcripts of the speeches were going there, including the statements of Mezentsev. Mezentsev would dispatch to the Central Committee a separate report of his own. Klava was typing everything up, checking it against her shorthand record.

"You know," she said to me, "Mezentsev had touched up his statements and misrepresented your speech in his report. The son of a bitch is steamrollering you. Write about it to the Central Committee."

"Won't you catch it?" I asked. She shrugged. Klava had spent the entire war as a machine gunner at the front. I wrote the protest. Mezentsev called Klava a "traitor," but nothing else happened to her. Luckily for her, the Political Directorate was dissolved, and Mezentsev was made deputy minister for personnel.

A week later an order came from somewhere in the sky, firing the four bureau members who had made speeches, "owing to the impossibility of any further utilization." Alikhanov called us in. We stood before him as he paced back and forth.

"Listen, if you knew what you were doing and what could come of it, then you are heroes. If you didn't—fools!"

We kept silent. Were we fools—or heroes?

"I telephoned Khrushchev on your behalf, but he said that he was not the only member of the Politburo. Other members demanded your arrest. He told me, 'They should be glad they got off with dismissals.' Good-bye." He firmly shook our hands.

We went out into the street.

"Well, so be it! We simply won't work for as long as the Party orders," I joked. It was strange, but I felt only liberation—from a moral burden and from the incessant racing about at work. Buried in my science, I had forgotten the color of the sky and not noticed the change of the seasons. Now I discovered that out-of-doors it was spring.

On April 5, 1956, *Pravda* ran a big editorial on problems of ideological purity. It mentioned the four of us and said we had "sung with voices of the Mensheviks and of Socialist Revolutionaries." I had not read anything by Mensheviks or Socialist Revolutionaries, who had existed before my birth and whose writings had been prohibited even earlier. If, as *Pravda* said, they had "sung" like me, then this was in their favor, and what I had to do was try and get hold of their works.

Several days later the four of us were driven from ITEP to Mezentsev's ministry, where we were formally expelled from the Party. They also took away the Party cards from the other members in ITEP, but returned them to whoever declared in writing that they condemned our anti-Party speeches and profoundly regretted that they had not opposed them at the meeting. Nearly everyone did exactly that.

Yevgeny Tretyakov, a war veteran who had been in our student group at the university, refused and was expelled from the Party. Fortunately he was not fired. On a betaspectrometer of his own design he went on to carry out a great many first-class experiments. Yet he would never do a dissertation, regarding the dissertation business as degrading and outside of science. They should have conferred a doctorate on him anyway, because of his work. But how could that be? After all—expelled from the Party, an unstable citizen!

They warned me that I would not be permitted to defend my own dissertation, which had already been published. The articles I had sent to Soviet journals were blocked. Fortunately the European journal *Nuovo Cimento* managed to publish the first part of one article; it was impossible, now, to transmit the second part. My name on the title page of the accelerator proposal was painted over with black Indian ink and omitted from the lists of coauthors of several reports sent to an international conference at CERN.[3] But they misfired with one report. When they proposed to Yevgeny Kuprianovich Tarasov, my sole coauthor, that he drop my name from it, he preferred to drop the whole report. Although he was a well-known specialist on accelerators, he thereby lost any chance of travel abroad.

During our visit to the ministry I had inquired why my name was being removed from all scientific publications.

"It is very simple," they replied. *"Your name is a discredit to Soviet science."*

---

[3]The European Organization for Nuclear Research.

TEN

All Labor Is Glorious

I LOUNGED against a wall inside the tiny entrance checkpoint of the institute. The workday had started. Staff members rushed past, nodding to me on the run and unfolding their security passes in front of the elderly security guard dressed in military blouse and khaki skirt—with a pistol at her side.

Why the pistol? I wondered. Oh yes, "the pile." But it's not a bomb. It's a research reactor, they show it to foreigners. Still, we Soviets have to be put through a Chekist sieve to get clearance for "secret installations," even when they aren't secret. It's a madhouse.

I went on standing there. It was obvious that they were trying to torment me. Deprived of security clearance, I was now forbidden to go inside even for my own documents. As for that pile of scientific notes left in my desk—I could just forget about it. Yet I hadn't even been working on military problems (and had firmly resolved not to).

No, it's not a madhouse, I corrected myself. It's a continuation of the Revolution, the psychology of people in the underground. The whole country is a goddamn underground. We're all entangled in a net of "secrets."

I was waiting for the head of the personnel division to bring me my workbook, military ID card, and assorted papers. Instead of him, Sergei appeared, a skinny redheaded physicist who had been in my study group at the university. He took out a notebook and a pen and stared.

"How do you evaluate your dismissal?" he asked in a businesslike tone. His sharp, freckled nose became even sharper. It was astonishing: he was posing questions officially and making a show of it.

"The dismissal was unlawful," I responded.

"Un-law-ful," he wrote down. "In that case how do you evaluate your anti-Party speech?" he asked sarcastically and put a check mark in his notebook, evidently opposite his first question.

"That's precisely what's unlawful. What connection is there between my speech at the meeting and my work ability?"

"What? You're kidding!" he said, jotting down one more check mark and writing something in his notebook.

I recalled a conversation with him back in our student days. "Only Communists are of value as citizens," he had said. "The rest can't be trusted. It's simply stupid to." At the time I had felt it better not to argue. He lived in the center of Moscow in a densely populated communal apartment in an ancient one-family house opposite the Ministry of Defense. His family was herded together in a tiny little room. Of course, every room contained a family—except that one small room, nice but windowless, had been given to him all for himself and was crammed with radio equipment, which he'd had a passion for since childhood.

What nice parents and what nice neighbors! I had thought to myself when visiting him there once. Because even a windowless room was a room for which his neighbors could write some pretty denunciation indeed. But now as I listened to his questions, I belatedly grasped the fact that the people being nice to him had obviously not been his neighbors but the Chekists, who had permitted the boy to play around with ham-radio communications in the very center of Stalin's Moscow.

Some thirty minutes later, as if on secret cue, the head of the personnel division appeared. Sergei neatly closed his notebook and departed.

"Here are your documents," said the personnel man.

"But the papers that show I've passed the qualifying exams for my degree are still lying in your office."

"That's right. But you won't need them anymore."

"Why? Sometime, in the future . . ."

"Don't you understand, Orlov? You'll *never*—get it?— never *ever* need them!"

"But all the same they aren't yours. Give them back, please."

"Wait, I'll get them," said his deputy, who had probably turned up just to have a look at me. And she brought the documents.

Three years earlier, at the end of 1952, when the Jewish doctors were still being tortured at the Lubyanka, when journalists and writers and some scientists as well had spontaneously combusted with rage at the degenerates who had wanted to poison Comrade Stalin himself, I, a Russian, had been accepted for work here. This woman had brought a brand-new security pass out to me in the entrance checkpoint. Looking me over, she had smiled and poked her finger at the photo: "Russian? Russian, yes?" I had looked at my photo and looked at her: an attractive, dark-complexioned brunette. You silly, they won't take you for a Slav either, I had thought to myself. However, there are times when a word is silver but silence is golden. She actually turned out to be a decent woman; she just wasn't very bright.

When people took me for a Jew, I wanted to reply, "No, I'm not Jewish, I'm Russian,"[1] but to say such a thing would have been indecent during a period of awful persecutions of Jews.

Finally I went outside. There was a ringing in my head. One way or another things really weren't very jolly. The best physics institute had been closed to me. And, no doubt, other institutes as well . . .

"Orlov, get in!"

I turned around. A black Volga limousine had floated up silently, its door already open. "Where to?" I asked.

"To hell and gone," cheerfully replied an official from Mezentsev's ministry, peering from the depths. "Sit down here."

ITEP was located on the southwest edge of Moscow. The car rolled along toward the center of the city. We passed the Danilov Cemetery, old and overgrown, where our whole family—

---

[1] In the Soviet Union, Jews and Russians are officially considered—and consider themselves—distinct nationalities, like the Armenians, Georgians, and so on. The term "Russian Jew" exists only in the West.

Father, Mother, Petya, Mitya, and Grandmother—used to visit my grandfather's grave, straighten the wooden cross, and pick up the branches and leaves fallen during the winter. We would sit down and have a picnic, then I would wander around. (How could I have not sought out his grave?) We drove out on to Polyanka, the street of my childhood, down Crooked Knee past Mother's building (I didn't say good-bye to her!), and then came to a stop in front of GLAVATOM—the State Committee for Atomic Energy. Well, for that matter, Maslyansky had not gone first to the Lubyanka . . .

I was piloted right through all the security guards and into some room on the second floor. The ministry man sat down heavily on a chair, looking grim, whipped—an old man. I studied the cabinets with their files, the green cloth on the table, the bureaucratic curtains on the windows.

Three men in civilian clothes entered. The ministry man pulled himself together, and now looked like a bold young fellow.

"Ivanov," one introduced himself.

"Petrov," said another.

". . ."

"Sidorov?" I asked.

"Yes, how did you know? No, in fact, I'm Nikolayev."

They all laughed, sat down, and lit up.

"You don't smoke, Yuri Fyodorovich?"

"No."

"Very good. Smoking is bad for the health. Maybe you'll teach us something about abstention?"

They laughed again. Then they frowned.

"You were invited here, Orlov, for a serious conversation," said Nikolayev. "Perhaps our last conversation with you."

"No, no, God forbid, not the last one," said Petrov. "Eh, Yuri Fyodorovich, not the last one, right?"

"We are very disturbed, Orlov, by what I would call your frivolous behavior after your expulsion from the Party. It is not clear to us that you realize, Orlov, the full seriousness of your crime—to call things by their right names." Nikolayev's face became stern and important.

I kept silent.

"He hasn't realized a thing," said the ministry man. "That whole business was a provocation they planned ahead of time."

"I don't understand," I said.

"Don't understand? We'll explain things to you."

"He understands everything," interjected the ministry man.

"No, why not, we will explain," said Nikolayev. "We are in essence what I would call an educational organization. You, Orlov, set up that meeting. You delivered a slanderous, anti-Party speech, which incited people—"

"What did I incite them to?"

"Shut up. You aggravated your slander against the Party and the Soviet people in your alleged clarification to the Central Committee. It was not for that that they demanded a clarification from you."

"But I had to explain to the Central Committee why I thought I was correct."

"Just who are you to instruct the Central Committee? You were supposed to explain: (a) how you arrived at, (b) what got you started in, and (c) who led you to your anti-Party actions." The faces of Ivanov and Petrov lit up as they raptly listened to Nikolayev.

"You ought to have explained to us that you have now realized your mistakes and also just how you have come to realize them. In the contrary case, these are no longer mistakes, Yuri Fyodorovich, but something worse. Is that clear?"

"It's all clear to him," said the ministry man.

"It wasn't you I wrote to."

"He's still being stubborn—even now!" said Ivanov.

I fell silent. They also fell silent. Finished their smokes. Looked at the clock and at one another.

"Here's what, Orlov. For the present we are warning you. For the present. The party teaches us humanism."

"Humaneism he's not going to understand. He doesn't know what humaneism is," remarked the ministry man smugly.

"You are a young man, Orlov. You have everything ahead of you. But if you do not admit—Then you have only yourself to blame. Another time our conversation will be—different. And in a different place."

So, it wasn't off to the Lubyanka! They weren't taking me away!

"But what about work?" I asked merrily. "I have children."

"He's remembered his children!" exclaimed the ministry man.

"We do not have any unemployed. In Soviet society everyone is obliged to labor. But we regard scientific work as leadership work, and you have demonstrated that you are unable to do such work. You should have set a moral example to lower-ranking employees. But you yourself still need educating. You are not mature enough for scientific work, Orlov. That is not a mortal sin, of course, all labor is glorious. We will help you get work in a factory. Our working class will educate you."

"But I *am* working class," I said.

"You—!" Ivanov jumped up.

"Calm down," said Nikolayev. "Calm down. Politely, please. We must be patient with those who have stumbled."

I understood only when I was outdoors again that however much they wanted to, they could not do anything terrible to me. It was stupid to have feared them. Because, just as Khrushchev had told Alikhanov and Alikhanov had told the four of us, the Politburo had decided not to arrest us. And you couldn't jump any higher than the Politburo. But they had certainly blocked my scientific work. I would not be able to jump over that.

GLAVATOM was only two steps away from my mother's stinking cellar. An electric light bulb burned in her room, but everything seemed to be in a thick fog after the April sun outside. Mother was lying facedown on the couch.

"What's wrong?" I asked.

"Pain," she groaned. I ran to the polyclinic on Ordynka Street. It was quicker than trying to find a telephone somewhere.

A young nurse ran back with me to Mother and started to prepare her hypodermics. Shots were given free. "Me first," said the nurse. She pulled her skirt way up, stuck the needle into her haunch, and emptied out the morphine. "You've got lovely eyes," she commented, pensively scrutinizing my face after she lowered her skirt and prepared Mother's shot. Mother smiled, but she was in no mood to laugh. She had already suffered two heart attacks, and walked with difficulty. She was tormented by pain.

"The doctors tell me everything is a wreck," she lamented. "Only, in the female department everything is fine, as if I were quite young."

I listened to her with anguish. The most awful thing was

that she did not want to move into my ITEP apartment. For the first time in our life we had a place fit for human beings—and she refused it!

"Where would I fit?" she asked when I raised the subject again after the nurse left. "There are five of you, including the children; I'd make six. It's on the third floor. At least here I can go into the courtyard and sit for a while. Quietly . . . I'm tired of people. . . ."

"There things are clean, we have air. We can look after you."

"There! They can take away your apartment. Where will you go then? You know, it's still uncertain what will happen to you. But here is emergency space. You can all live with me."

The thought was staggering. They did hold in their hands not only my employment but my housing. The apartment belonged to the institute. If they fired Galya, who was still working there, then they would in fact take the apartment away. There were plenty in line for it. Families often spent a lifetime waiting for a separate apartment, and in vain . . . But how had Mama found out I'd been fired? Evidently someone had shown her *Pravda* with my name in it—and she, who knew all about our Soviet life, had drawn her own conclusions.

"They won't take it away," I said. "And in general everything is all right with me. Don't worry."

"Really? I hope so. Listen, Yurochka. I have a feeling I'm going to die soon. When I do, have a burial service in church. But don't put my body in the earth. The worms . . . Brrr . . . Burn me in the crematorium. I'll be alongside Fedya. Bury the urn in the ground there at the crematorium. I've found out how and what to do. I even have the photographs to go on my grave."

She grew animated and took out from under her pillow some recent photographs, retouched to make her look quite young.

"Pick whichever you want, the best one. Make me beautiful on my grave."

I promised.

"Don't forget to return the books from the library after I die."

"I will."

Mother had always read a great deal. She especially adored

Charles Dickens, perhaps because his books reminded her of
her homeless childhood. The only schooling she'd had was two
grades of pre-revolutionary *Gymnasium,* but the neighbors in
her courtyard knew nothing of that.

"Klavdiya Petrovna is an intelligent woman," they would
say. "Well-educated."

Alikhanov was pressured to fire Galya, a highly respected
technician, but he swept aside the attempt. Everything was all
right, then, with our apartment. While Galya was working, we
had for the five of us her twelve hundred rubles a month, minus
something to help my mother, plus the small pension of Galya's
aunt. This was not enough for meat. But bread cost only one
ruble a kilo, so the situation was not catastrophic, and thanks
to the solidarity of scientists we soon had almost the equivalent
of my salary.

Because of the *Pravda* article and a letter that the Central
Committee had sent to all Party organizations, the names of the
four rebels from ITEP became known everywhere. Scientists
came to our aid, distributing to each of us one thousand rubles
every month. At the Lenin Library metro station, future Academician Boris Chirikov twice secretly passed me funds gathered in the Siberian Institute of Nuclear Physics. One month
someone presented me with funds gathered in Moscow at ITEP
and the Lebedev Physics Institute, and the next month, funds
from the Leningrad Physico-Technical Institute. This was perhaps the first time that scientists in the Soviet Union had taken
collective action to help their repressed colleagues. Under Stalin
it would have been absolutely impossible.

I decided to work on theoretical physics at home as if nothing had happened. Although it was dispiriting to live off the
support of my friends, the formal end of my scientific career,
which had begun so well, did not concern me overmuch—I
believed in my ability to get good scientific results under any
conditions. Galya, however, felt deeply disturbed. "You have to
choose," she said. "Either science, or politics." The uncertainty
about my future worried her, not my political opinions. Had I
decisively chosen the dangerous path of politics, with its almost
inevitable prospect of arrest, I am sure that she would have
supported me. After all, she was a Papkevich.

The Papkeviches were descended from Polish rebels who

had been exiled to the Siberian gold mines back in the nineteenth century. Galya's grandfather, a Polish social democrat, had joined the Bolsheviks after the Revolution, and during the Civil War had been a railway commissar. Galya's mother had been the friend of a young female relative of Trotsky. On one occasion when Trotsky's premises were being searched, his relative asked her to stand guard outside to warn away his visitors. She agreed, although she was pregnant. The first person she warned turned out to be a Chekist, and he arrested her immediately. But she was soon rescued from prison through the intervention of Dzerzhinsky, the creator and leader of the Leninist Cheka, who evidently sympathized with his fellow Poles and perhaps even with Trotsky himself. So Galya was born in freedom.

Our case became a notorious example of the contradictions in the Khrushchev "thaw," when the most bloodstained Chekists were purged and the press was given some freedom, while at the same time the heroic Hungarians were brutally suppressed abroad and critics of the regime were punished at home. My colleagues often visited me to show support, cheer me up, and talk over the whole political situation. During these conversations I grew very close to Tarasov and discovered another lifelong friend in Valentin Turchin, a physicist and mathematician, who discussed with me that eternal Russian question: "What is to be done?" I proposed that someone (but not I) should create a workers' party; Turchin argued for a non-party system. After thinking a great deal about our discussions, I concluded that the existence of different political parties and unions was necessary to prevent the moral and intellectual decay of society. The danger lay not in political struggle itself, but in how it was carried out.

My old friend Zhenya Bogomolov came to visit, too. Now he was a scientist at ITEP. "Yur," he confided, his always guilty eyes wide with embarrassment behind his thick spectacles, "they didn't bother me for three years after the death of the Great Leader and Teacher. I was convinced they would leave me alone. But see, now they've called me in again and ordered me to learn what you think about the Party policy, about politics generally, and about yourself—you know, what your plans are. I've told you this so you would know why I came. Spout everything you think you should, and I'll write it down." No longer astonished by anything in my country of wonders, I spouted at him three bushels of nonsense.

A day later my old friend Zhenya Kuznetsov turned up. He was also now a scientist at ITEP.

"Yur! For three years they haven't called me in. . . ."

"So now they've called you in and ordered you to learn what I think of the Party policy and what I think in general and what my plans are?"

"Ha-ha-ha. You mean you're also on their hook?"

"No. Zhenya Bogomolov came to visit."

"Ah, Zhenka!"

And Kuznetsov told me the whole story of their tragicomic relationship and who else, to his knowledge, was writing denunciations. Then, in my presence, he wrote a report on me, composing it in such a way that its utter emptiness contained a crystalline plausibility.

Both Zhenyas perished a few years later. Zhenya Bogomolov drowned in the bathtub in his own apartment, which he got when he married a woman with a child shortly after graduating from the university. The woman had not loved him and was openly unfaithful. Zhenya Kuznetsov's hacked-up body was found in his home village in a little shed where he had spent the night with a girl. His father ran to the militia with a bloody ax and a declaration that he had killed his own son, but the militia did not believe him because he had been badly shell-shocked at the front and suffered from seizures. They reasonably supposed that the man's mind was confused by grief and that the son had been murdered by local village boys on account of the girl. The investigation showed, however, that it was the father who had killed Zhenya—in some sort of fit. Everyone took pity on him and his unfortunate wife, for Zhenya had been their only son. The old man was put into a psychiatric hospital.

One day in June when I was lounging on the bed and feeling a little sorry for myself, Lev Okun, the theoretical physicist, dropped in and asked why I was lying there belly-up.

"What can I do?"

"Earn some money!"

"But how?"

"Give lessons to students preparing for entrance examinations. It pays well. I'll give you one telephone number, and you can take it from there yourself."

Among the Moscow intelligentsia this was a well-known way to make a living in hard times. But I still wasn't very close to the intelligentsia, and by myself would probably never have guessed that well-to-do bureaucrats paid well—fantastically well, on my monetary scale—for preparing their children to enter institutes. Okun's advice changed the whole situation. Soon I had a multitude of private lessons. I worked all summer from 6:00 A.M. to midnight, seven days a week, and could stop accepting money from my friends. For the first time in my life I purchased a refrigerator, a radio, and a good suit. I sent my mother and Galya to stay in vacation homes, and even began saving money so that I could devote the coming winter entirely to theoretical physics.

Despite running around all over Moscow to my pupils, I rarely missed seminars and conferences that did not require special permission to attend. Most of the scientists I encountered there tried to keep my spirits up. "Why are you hanging your head?" asked Budker, although I wasn't letting my head hang. "Remember that you are a hero." But Lev Davidovich Landau was, as usual, dissatisfied with me: "One can help a person who knows what he wants. But if he doesn't know what he wants, it's impossible to help him."

"Lev Davidovich," I objected, very much stung by his remark, "you used to tell how in prison in Kharkov where they stuck you in '38 everyone thought, I'm not guilty of anything but the others must be guilty; it's impossible that they've been imprisoned for nothing. And now you consider that I was dismissed for cause?"

"You've missed the point," Landau calmly replied to my unjust charge. "In those years it was impossible to calculate anything. People would find themselves being punished as a matter of chance. Now things are different. You could have calculated the consequences but did not want to. You consciously took a risk, then did not want to set things straight, and you gave up a good institute—for what? Do you really need physics?"

The reaction of Bruno Pontecorvo was purely ideological. While traveling from one private lesson to another, I encountered the mysterious "professor" in the center of Moscow. The Italian physicist and Communist, who for some reason had moved from the West to the USSR, was gradually being "revealed"; a mere two years before, it had not been permissible even to utter his name. I had last seen him in Dubna, strolling along the shore of the Volga, his bodyguard twenty paces behind. Dubna, with its nonsecret synchrophasotron, had been at the time reliably protected against spies and saboteurs by barbed wire and a zone of plowed earth around its perimeter, just like a good concentration camp. Surrounded by swamps, Dubna was in fact built with concentration-camp labor. It rested on their bones. The physicists were well aware of this, but absolutely none of them ever seemed disturbed.

Pontecorvo greeted me and asked in his pleasant Italo-Russian accent:

"What was the essence of your demands at the meeting?"

"We called for the merging of socialism and democracy."

"Under socialism, bourgeois freedoms are impossible," he objected.

At the time I did not understand the deep truth of this remark. It struck me as absurd. But I did not yet know the "professor" well enough to say so.

"It's nonsense!" I fumed soon after to Alexander Gerasimovich, my old chemistry teacher, the very same school principal who, in May 1941, had asked Komsomol members not to leave Moscow. Now, in 1956, as principal of another school, he was helping me pick up students for private tutoring. I had stopped by his office on the way to visit my mother. We sat there drinking tea and speaking with complete candor about my conversation with Pontecorvo.

"Nonsense! Why label these freedoms 'bourgeois'? The right to free trade unions, to strikes, to labor parties—aren't these freedoms for the workers? With these 'bourgeois' freedoms the workers of the West have achieved a life much better than ours. These are freedoms of the whole people. I know that stupid argument: 'Since we have no classes, then, first, we don't need freedoms, and, second, they can lead to the restoration of capitalism.' It's wrong."

"No. It's true about restoration," objected my teacher. "But I sometimes think that when there are no capitalists, they somehow have to be invented. Otherwise we're going to die of starvation under a leaky roof."

Right up to that moment I had been thrusting away the idea of socialism becoming transformed into capitalism. Now I found myself ready to confront it. Gathering up the parcels of bread, butter, and ham I had bought for Mother, I strolled deep in thought down the streets leading from the school. It was already dark when I turned onto Crooked Knee, went down the cellar stairs, and opened the door.

My mother's body, arrayed in her very best dress, lay there on two chairs drawn together, her hands crossed on her bosom. Her face, with closed eyes and a white kerchief tied under the chin, was sad, severe, and calm.

"We've bathed her," said a neighbor. "Her suffering is over."

"When? How?"

"Today at dawn. She cried out. As if my heart felt it, I ran in—she had already stopped breathing."

"And the doctor?"

"Of course we called, everything was done properly. Even the doctor said, 'Her suffering is over.' You taking her to church?"

"Yes, of course."

"She was really counting on it."

"She asked—first church, then the crematorium."

"How on earth, church and crematorium? Is that possible?"

"That's what she asked for. I promised. Thank you."

I buried my mother's ashes in the tiny crematorium cemetery near the Donskoy Monastery, which housed the International Youth Day Leather Goods Factory where she had worked the best part of her life. One hundred yards from the crematorium began the compound of the Ordzhonikidze Lathe Factory, where Petya and I had worked, and with which Mother had been evacuated east to the Urals tank factory, leaving behind there her health. If you went on further and crossed the bridge over the Circle Line railway, then it was easy to find the world-famous Institute for Physical Problems where Kapitsa had again become director, and where I continued to attend seminars. But if you did not cross the bridge, then you saw on the right two semicircular apartment houses built for the sci-

entific elite and the upper ranks of the KGB, with beautiful
parquet floors that had been laid after the war by a political
prisoner as yet unknown to the world—Alexander Solzhenitsyn.

The next month, in late August, Alikhanov's brother summoned me to his home in Moscow. He was director of the
Yerevan Physics Institute of the Armenian Academy of Sciences.

"My brother has advised me to hire you for work in Yerevan," said Artemii Isakovich Alikhanyan. "We're going to build
a large electron accelerator. Will you come?"

I discussed it with Galya. I did not want to go far from
Moscow because Galya and the children were here, and my
friends, and the best physics centers. My work as a tutor was
paying well. I could privately discuss any scientific problem at
all: none of the leading scientists denied me that; these were
not Stalinist times. Nevertheless, the future hung by a thread.
Today the authorities would put up with this, tomorrow—who
knew? I had children. Anyway, they were not going to let me
do scientific work in Moscow. But to leave our Moscow apartment for a distant province, with two small children and Galya's
elderly aunt, and no key in my pocket for at least one single
room—only a lunatic would do that. And then there were our
residence permits for Moscow. We could not have kept them,
which meant losing forever the right to live in Moscow and the
opportunity of a Moscow education for the children.

We decided that I should accept the job, but would live in
Yerevan alone. It was the biggest mistake of my life.

ELEVEN

Armenia

Twelve hundred miles from Moscow to the capital of Armenia, three days of looking through windows. For the last day the train ran past watchtowers, guardhouses, border guards, and multiple rows of barbed-wire fences. Beyond the fences lay empty fields, and beyond them more fences, and more again, and beyond that we could see Turkey.

"There aren't any barriers over there," I said aloud.

"What do you mean, there aren't any!" shouted a citizen, hastily dropping from the top bunk. Another just as hastily climbed up there to occupy his sleeping place.

"They have underground barriers, don't you understand? Under the ground! What—you don't like our border, is that it?"

In Yerevan I moved into a dormitory for five people off a lovely green courtyard on the bank of a gorge. From the chasm rose the thunder of the Razdan River, and beyond the Turkish border, high up in the bright blue sky, the bald spot of Ararat gleamed in a wreath of curly clouds. I liked my new home in this pleasant, uncommon-looking city. But without my family it was lonely. All of us should have been living together in Yerevan. Should have, should have . . .

The Armenians welcomed me. Smiling strangers came up to me on the street and said:

"We know you. Do you like Armenia? Here no one is going to do anything bad to you. Here everything is going to be fine!"

They regarded any public criticism of the government and even of the dead Stalin as a dangerous gamble. Who knows, maybe Stalinism has just temporarily fallen out of favor? The Armenians loathed Stalin. After World War II he had planned the final solution of the Armenian question—not in the barbarian style of the Turkish Janissaries, but in the spirit of socialist humanism. It was decided not to massacre the Armenians as the Turks had done in 1915, not rip open their bellies, but to transplant them to Siberia. The technique of mass deportations had long since been worked out. One night, selectively, according to a list, they took away part of the population of Echmiadzin District, the religious center of this Gregorian Christian nation. For some reason the deportations were then suspended, perhaps because that sort of business has to be carried out quickly, has to be a good clean job. However, quick and clean did not work out. There was only one railway in Transcaucasia, and too many Armenians were spread around the region. In any event, when a certain technician whose name I have unfortunately forgotten returned from a business journey, pleased that he had obtained spare parts for the collective-farm tractors, neither his wife nor his children were waiting at home. There were also no neighbors. The militia had nothing to say. They hinted that he should drop in at the KGB. He dropped in. We don't know a thing, they said, but we'll find out. Come again. He came again. Your family was moved out, they said, on suspicion of espionage.

"My wife? My mother? My little girls? Spies? Impossible!"

The security organs know best whether it is or not, they told him. You don't mean you're going to argue with the security organs?

"No, no," he said, "good God, no. Only what should I do?"

"This is a difficult situation," they said. "We sympathize but can do nothing to help. The train is gone."

And that was the truth. The technician had been listed as a spy before the deportation, but since he happened not to be on the scene that particular night, they had crossed him off the list and replaced him with some bachelor who also understood technology. But they certainly had carted off his family.

The technician and the local Chekist racked their brains over the situation and found a way out. The technician (an Armenian) wrote a confession of espionage (for Turkey), and it traveled with him under guard in pursuit of his family. The Chekists, as the Party had taught them, treated the man with understanding. He caught up with his family at one of the Construction Projects of Communism. He did not find his daughters—they had perished on the way. Soon his wife died. The technician survived.

His story was just a run-of-the-mill incident in those days; only the technician seemed not to be run-of-the-mill. But when I got to know the Armenians and their attachment to their families a little better, I understood that even he was not extraordinary.

In 1956, when I was told about all this, the times were of course radically different. You could now live without hysteria and need not fear arrest merely because they needed slave labor for the great construction projects; or because your apartment, your furniture, and your wife appealed to your neighbor; or because you had not said, "Long live Comrade X!" at the right time, or had said it at the wrong time (when X had just been arrested); or because you had poorly chosen yourself a father and grandmother, and failed to renounce them publicly. Anyone who has not skated on that surrealist rink will never comprehend how enormously liberated people were by Khrushchev's turn to elementary legality. Society remained totalitarian, but at least had ceased to wallow in blood and vomit.

To be sure, not all Russians felt as liberated as the Armenians. If you do not count the Soviet intellectuals, who had almost all become anti-Stalinists after Khrushchev's famous speech at the Twentieth Party Congress—including even those intellectuals who just the day before had written verses praising the Great Leader, or thundered against the Jewish doctors as poisoners—if you do not count them, then 50 percent of Russians were in favor of Stalin because of the Soviet victory in the war. Also, for many Russians socialism was still a magic word, an *idée fixe*, no longer intoxicating but still a dream that justified everything that Stalin did. In Armenia, however, almost no one cared much about any social idea whatsoever; all attention was riveted on the national idea. Whether there was capitalism or socialism, it was all the same to them for the time being: "You Russians made yourselves a revolution—in 1917, was it?—so you can go eat that porridge yourselves."

This rather engaging attitude confirmed the view I had begun to form about social ideas. As I saw it, people are not born all alike and cannot be made all alike. Since many of their values and interests are bound to be different and even mutually contradictory, there can be no single social idea that everybody will accept. To try and impose one is a crime against human nature and therefore will fail sooner or later. So the health of society requires a multitude of ideas, however mutually contradictory. Each of us should pick and choose whatever suits him best. Perhaps from someone else's point of view our idea will seem awful—that is not important. *What is important is that we do not use violence against people whose ideas we do not like.* And we must always be on guard, because the more holy or scientific our idea seems to us, the more we will want to use violence against heretics, and the easier that violence can grow into gas chambers and endless thousands of graves with corpses piled one on top of the other, all with bullet holes in the back of their heads.

"What motivated Khrushchev? Why did he feel compelled to expose Stalin in such a way?" Alikhanyan asked in one of our first conversations. We were sitting in his Yerevan house. On the wall in front of me hung a photograph of the physicist Nina Shostakovich, wife of the composer. She had suddenly died not so long ago in the institute's cosmic-ray station. Alikhanyan often repeated that it was not he who had stolen Nina from his friend Dmitry Shostakovich, but that it was just the opposite. During their student days Shostakovich had taken her away from Alikhanyan. After many years she had finally come back to her first love.

"The Communists got tired of devouring themselves," I answered. "When they gobbled up others—the peasants, the old intelligentsia—I'm sure they didn't gag."

"The peasants? Ah yes, collectivization. No one remembers

about them, really. It's true. More coffee?" He fussed about the table a bit.

"I'm interested in knowing, Yura. Could you in principle become a spy?"

"A spy? I don't know. If I were terribly convinced of something . . . and it was something like a war . . . and it was vital to find something out . . . No. Why do you ask?"

"It's just interesting."

He had thought at first that only a KGB agent would talk so freely.

A. I. Alikhanyan had been a *besprizornik* during the Civil War until a rabbi picked him off the streets of Tiflis. The Armenian boy received a strict Jewish upbringing. But unlike his austere older brother, A. I. Alikhanov,[1] Alikhanyan was a true Medici. The best painters, writers, and musicians—many of whom had been in trouble with the authorities—adored him as a courageous patron and distinguished scientist. His scientific colleagues valued him most for his intimacy with "unofficial" painters and the dazzling banquets he put on for people who might be useful to him and his institute. Alikhanyan was, in fact, an active scientist and an excellent director, and helped several physicists in trouble. But he expected absolute loyalty in return, and could be a dangerous man when he thought he had not received it. According to rumor, he had his own stable of spies in Stalin's day, to protect himself and his colleagues from the spies of the KGB. It would have been quite in character for him to have kept some of them around in my day.

"You're lucky to be in Armenia, Yura," he said. "Don't rush back to Moscow. There they'll write a hundred denunciations against you straightaway."

Maybe so, but in Armenia letters were opened. While I lived in the dormitory, mine came to me at the institute, and the secretary, Amaliya, delivered them to me unsealed. I would not have died of astonishment to learn that the insatiably curious Alikhanyan was reading them as well. "Don't take any notice, Yura," he said. "Amaliya is as much at home with a keyhole as you are with an integral. I hope that no one is writing

---

[1]Because the brothers were both physicists and had the same initials, Alikhanov had changed his last name slightly so that people could tell them apart in print.

you anything—'pornographic.' " No one was writing me anything "pornographic," and I myself did not write anything dangerous. We had all learned a lot in Stalin's time. Still, it was very unpleasant.

Amaliya was a master of all trades. She even ran the special section for a time, until they sent a professional security officer. All my numerical calculations for the accelerator had to be surrendered to her after work, whereupon they immediately became "secret" and I no longer had the right to take them back, even one hour later, since I had no security clearance. I therefore always kept copies of my "secret" papers in my open desk; otherwise it would have been impossible to do any calculations. The accelerator design had to be finished before the autumn of 1958, in order for the Council of Ministers in Moscow to have time to approve the project and incorporate it into the state's next Five-Year Plan. I was in charge of the theoretical side of the design; Semyon Kheifets in Yerevan and Yevgeny Tarasov in Moscow were helping me. At the start of the last, hectic stage of our work, eighteen months after my arrival, Alikhanyan presented me with his own office so that I could write up my part of the project proposal and even sleep on the couch without interruptions.

We got it in on time. The reviewers praised the proposal, noting my key role in it, and the Council of Ministers approved the project. I decided the time had come to try and defend my dissertation, which had been lying around for two years without movement in Yerevan University. They would be glad to let me defend it, they said, but couldn't do it without permission from the top. I wrote an aggressive ultimatum to Alikhanyan: "Consider me discharged in two weeks' time. I am going to look for employment elsewhere because here I will not be permitted to defend my dissertation, which I used in the accelerator calculations." Alikhanyan, not a Party member himself, promptly ran to the Central Committee of the Communist Party of Armenia.

Everyone involved understood the not-so-profound meaning of this game. They realized perfectly well that I knew I would not be permitted to defend my dissertation anywhere else. But it was also clear that I was determined to leave Armenia at a time when the accelerator project had been accepted at the very highest level and I was needed more than ever. In October the Armenian Central Committee quickly reached an understanding with Moscow, and a directive came down from the top: let Orlov defend his dissertation. Vladimir Borisovich Berestetsky flew at once from Moscow to serve as one of my referees, and the defense went without a hitch. I had painted myself into a corner. Now, instead of going home to my family and to the physics problems I had once hoped to solve, I was morally obligated to stay in Yerevan. I felt that I had betrayed my family and myself.

After the defense I was given a raise in salary and a pleasant apartment where my family could stay. Galya and I were still afraid to move everyone to Yerevan, so we continued to live apart, I flying to Moscow on official trips, and Dima and Sasha sometimes visiting me with Galya or a baby-sitter. I took our clever and inquisitive children to the mountains for long rambles around the cosmic-ray station on Mount Aragats, thirty miles from Yerevan. We would roam the alpine meadows and picnic on bread, cheese, and tasty wild herbs plucked right there, washed down by the naturally carbonated water from a small stream.

Life in general had certainly become easier after the approval of the accelerator project. Although I now had my own group of physicists to lead, and a lectureship in Yerevan University, I could often find time in the evening to walk down into the gorge of the Razdan River, through the thickets of wild fruit trees alongside the rushing waters, and then up to the garden of my former dormitory. The old dormitory guard would put his copper coffeepot into a pan of hot sand on his stove and begin our usual conversation: I listening, he speaking. Years before, he had been a partisan struggling against Turkey and then against the Red Army invasion of Armenia. The Red Army had "liberated" the republic, which had been governed until then by the Dashnaks—social-democratic Armenian nationalists.

The fortieth anniversary of that event arrived in 1960, and Khrushchev himself came to the official festivities. Alikhanov also attended. Once more he rose to my defense, and the KGB counter that kept registering his sins gave yet another click. At a reception honoring the general secretary given by the president of the Armenian Academy of Sciences, Alikhanov asked

Khrushchev, "Nikita Sergeyevich! What about returning Orlov to me for the institute? Do you remember the business back in '56? He is working now in Armenia, and doing good work."

"Listen," replied Khrushchev, "it's high time that business was forgotten."

This was heard by "those who needed to hear." The next morning I was summoned to the special section and immediately given a security pass for "secret" work. At first I supposed I had been awarded clearance in honor of the festivities so that I could study my own calculations in the special section. Nobody explained anything to me at the time. Alikhanov went straight back to Moscow while Khrushchev continued his visit. Alikhanyan later described it to me.

The Further Adventures of Nikita Sergeyevich in Armenia

After a successful excursion to the famous cognac distillery, the Armenian leadership took Khrushchev to famous Lake Sevan.

"Look, you've been going on and on to me about this Lake . . . er . . . Sevan. You say that your . . . this . . . national pride and joy of yours is perishing, the hydroelectric stations will come to a halt, the trout will die out," Khrushchev complained in an absolutely steady voice. "Where are they, these trout of yours? I haven't seen any."

"Nikita Sergeyevich, you ate some yesterday!"

"Yesterday, how do I know where they came from? Maybe you flew in some trout from America for me, ha-ha-ha-ha, just so I would sign off on this project of yours. From America? Eh?"

"Nikita Sergeyevich!"

"What do you know about fish? Now I—when I was a boy this big, I used to catch pike this big—no, this big—with a fishing pole. A fishing pole! So get me one. I want to find out whether this pride and joy of yours is worth a damn or not." Out of thin air materialized fishing poles with bobbers, and Nikita Sergeyevich began fishing for trout like a veteran.

(The beautiful mountain lake was truly perishing. They had channeled the water to hydroelectric stations through tunnels punched in the rock, and by now had lowered the lake

by some thirty to forty-five feet. They should have cut back on using lake water and compensated by closing down energy-intensive operations such as the synthetic-rubber factory with the awful orange smoke above it. Instead, they came up with a project for a tremendously long mountain tunnel to bring the waters of the Arpa River into Lake Sevan. This insane project required insane millions from the federal budget, in other words, a signature from on high. And if there hadn't been that fortunate date of the "liberation of Armenia," it would have been soon forgotten.)

. . . Meanwhile, Nikita Sergeyevich was not catching any fish. In that lake it was next to impossible to catch trout from the shore. The patience of the general secretary was running out. Bright hopes were fading. The issue was no longer to save the lake: decorations and careers might be lost. That decisive moment had come when the future course of history depends on a single step. And the step was taken. The secretary of the local Party committee arranged to send down a diver with live trout in a net bag. The diver fastened two trout onto the fishhooks. He could have put even more on, but the secretary had not ordered more than two. So Nikita Sergeyevich caught two big trout. The catch was a glorious success. The whole exalted company went up to the Akhtamar Restaurant. The table was loaded with trout; for Nikita Sergeyevich they cooked the ones he had caught himself. Then and there at the table, he scrawled his signature on a decree to construct the tunnel, and that very night the Armenian newspaper Kommunist *prepared an article on the remarkable new construction project symbolizing the inviolable friendship of the peoples of the USSR.*

Several years after these events, when Khrushchev no longer worked in the Kremlin, but I was still working in Armenia, that same local Party secretary invited me to visit his Lake Sevan district on the May Day holidays. I was interested and accepted. He took me around to see the hydroelectric stations, the plant-selection station, the trout hatchery, and so on. The next morning I stood with him on a little wooden platform in the center of the small town of Sevan and reviewed the Demonstration of Workers' Representatives. I was a nobody, a physicist long since expelled from the Party, but the demonstrators knew nothing of that and shouted "Hurrah!" to us both in equal measure. Several poorly dressed female workers from a haberdashery factory, I believe, marched past bearing a slogan about Communism. A group of Pioneers from nearby villages rode past silently in a truck, blue with cold and looking like wolf cubs in their white shirts and red neckerchiefs. After waiting for hours, standing in the rear of the truck to the right of the platform, they drove past us in one minute. That was the kids' demonstration. Then other representatives marched past, some in twos, some in threes, and at the end a solitary person bearing a slogan about the Party.

"Who is that?" I asked.

"The diver."

"*That* diver?"

"The very same. We have only one."

"Maybe we can talk with him?"

"Of course, it's not a secret anymore."

But the diver wisely evaded reminiscing about Khrushchev.

There were many sides to Khrushchev, of course, but on the whole I have a liking for him. He was the first Soviet dictator who was not utterly insensible to people. He dethroned Stalin. He freed the surviving innocents from the camps. He made the decision to buy the Soviet people grain from the bourgeois West. He began large-scale construction of housing, the first in all the years of Soviet power. He raised pensions for urban pensioners who had been living on the edge of death from starvation. He punched a little window in the Iron Curtain. We aren't even going to start to count what he did *not* do. Khrushchev reorganized the country from a regime of total self-destruction to a moderately totalitarian one, in which the average citizen could at least die peacefully in his own bed.

My position at the institute continued to improve. By 1961 I had become chief of a laboratory and produced over fifty scientific publications. Nevertheless, I was tired of accelerator physics and tired of living apart from my family. But when I told Alikhanyan that I wanted to return to Moscow, the old Medici angrily threatened to block all possible avenues. True enough, his institute desperately needed my help in building the accelerator I had designed. I was trapped. It was already five years since I had come to Yerevan, five years of family life at a distance.

The next year I destroyed it.

She worked as an electronics engineer in Alikhanyan's institute. Lively and talented, she played the piano, played table tennis, and drove a motorcycle. Her maternal great-grandfather was Pypin, a well-known literary scholar of the nineteenth century, and she was related indirectly to the nineteenth-century democrat Chernyshevsky—which interested me but explains nothing at all. My Yerevan friends tried to bring me to my senses. They meant well, but handled it badly. The physicist who headed the trade-union committee called a meeting of the union in order to discuss the unworthy conduct of trade-union member Ira, my girlfriend, who had broken up the family of a married man. He believed that this would save me. They of course "discussed" with joy and rage and then condemned her. I was not present, having resigned from the trade union at ITEP in 1956 for its refusal to defend its fired members. The meeting only strengthened my determination to stay with my ostracized girlfriend.

The following year, still outraged by Alikhanyan's crude threats, I got a half-time job on the side at Budker's Institute of Nuclear Physics in Novosibirsk, where I began a collaboration with Vladimir Baier on quantum depolarization of electrons, and defended my second doctoral dissertation. While I commuted between Siberia and Yerevan, Ira, now pregnant, went to live with her parents in Novosibirsk. Budker had created a remarkable ensemble: everyone, technicians and workers included, was a first-rate specialist Budker had chosen himself. He was wise as an old rabbi, and even looked like one now that he had started growing a beard. After first meeting Ira, he told me with light regret, "Yura, you're living in a regime of hysteria." But he gave us a huge institute apartment to help begin a new life.

Our marriage could not be a happy one, even after the birth of Lev—named in honor of Lev Tolstoi, perhaps to ingratiate myself with the memory of the great moralist. My sense of guilt toward my two other children, for whom all of this was a catastrophe, poisoned my happiness. My egotistic hopes that the children would live "in two families" turned out, of course, to be unreal. Still thunderstruck, Galya forbade the children to visit me. It soon turned out that Ira and I had very different concepts of life. She was disappointed, and two years after Lev's birth she fell in love with someone else. We continued to live together, but I was in despair. Deciding to leave the matter to chance and a moonless October night, I set out to climb the eastern peak of Mount Aragats.

Millions of years ago Aragats had been a volcano. Now there remained of it three peaks roughly three miles high around a five-hundred-yard-deep crater like a saucepan, in which clouds swirled and spun. October often brought snow and fog, and it was difficult to climb. I arrived at the cosmic-ray station in the morning, wandered about the laboratories all day, left while it was still just light, and, before darkness fell, got to the base of the peak. Suddenly night descended. Stones, hands, feet, everything disappeared along with my desire to climb. I scrambled upward, groping my way around the steep walls, crawling on my stomach over boulders. Finally I came to a grass-covered gully among the rocks and collapsed. The night was majestic. I woke up to a beautiful mountain morning. An enormous, bright raspberry-colored cloud hung over the horizon. Feeling like a fool, I made my way back.

Soon I tested fate again, by walking along the very edge of the bridge slung over the deep canyon of the Razdan River. When I finally calmed down several weeks later, I got hit by a truck. I had been working all night long, and that morning had to make an urgent appearance at an academic council. Running for the bus, still half-asleep, I glanced up and saw a truck rushing straight at me. The last thing in my recollection was a feeling of regret.

I came to on the seat beside the driver, mind fuzzy, blood pouring over my eyes. Where were we going? Vineyards . . . I came to once more. Stones . . . Don't lose consciousness again! Where were we going?

"Turn around," I told the driver. He didn't answer or even look at me. "Turn around!" Again, no response. The truck was rushing God knows where.

"Turn, you motherfucker!"

Still without looking at me, the driver swung the truck around and tore back to the city. He braked at the nearest polyclinic, I tumbled out of the cab, he drove off, orderlies ran up to me. . . .

After six years of not very successful life together, Ira and I finally parted. But a year before that I was able to help her move to Moscow as she had always wanted. On the recommendation of Alikhanov and Pomeranchuk, the academic council of ITEP unanimously elected me as a senior scientist in Pomeranchuk's division. It was understood that I would continue working part time for Alikhanyan in Yerevan. The council's decision gave me the right to exchange my Yerevan apartment for an apartment in Moscow and to acquire a Moscow residence permit again. But just as I got the permit, giving Alikhanov the official right to hire me, I was summoned for a chat by an official of the Military-Industrial Committee—an organization of whose very existence the ordinary Soviet citizen was not supposed to know. His name was Burlakov.

"We will help you transfer to any institute at all, even to Serpukhov, okay? But we're putting ITEP off limits. For you ITEP is, as you physicists like to put it, a singular point."

"Why?"

"Why? I will tell you frankly. Right up to the present moment an unhealthy moral-political environment has prevailed there."

I went to Pomeranchuk. "Won't this be harmful to you?" I asked him. "I've been elected to the academy. Nothing is going to harm me now," he replied. Alikhanov had already issued the order to hire me at ITEP, and if I went to work he would stand by it. But now, after the conversation with the Military-Industrial Committee man, I understood that it would be monumentally selfish to accept the job: everyone could hear the KGB sharpening its knives over Alikhanov's refusal to fire Alexander Kronrod. Kronrod, the brilliant organizer of the mathematics division and its computer center, had worked alongside Alikhanov for decades. He had signed a letter to the Ministry of Health, defending the heroic dissident mathematician Alexander Esenin-Volpin, a completely sane person who had been incarcerated in an insane asylum. Alikhanov was then ordered to fire Kronrod. When he refused, a big meeting was convened at the institute to "discuss" the professional qualities of the head of the mathematics division, one of Alikhanov's deputies (a Party member) was forced to sign an order for Kronrod's dismissal, and almost all of the mathematicians submitted their resignations in protest.

I thought everything over and dragged myself back to Armenia to help start up the accelerator. Ira and Lev moved to Moscow, and the Yerevan Institute managed to find me a temporary small apartment. Not long afterward Alikhanov suffered a stroke, and then was demoted from director to chief of a laboratory—"for reasons of health." In his place they sent a Party member, I. V. Chuvilo, a physicist from Dubna.

In its ten years of slow construction the Yerevan electron accelerator had become obsolete. After all, an accelerator is not a candy factory. We were nevertheless supposed to start it up in November 1967 for the fiftieth anniversary of the October Revolution. On this special anniversary, decorations, promotions, big prizes were expected, and for that it was very useful to present big achievements. In view of my anti-Party attitude, no awards awaited me (although the academic council of the institute had proposed me for the Order of Lenin). But, keyed-up over the launch of the machine, I did not care. Once the accelerator was assembled, we swiftly got it going. I was satisfied and finally free of my moral obligations to Alikhanyan.

Then the goodies were handed out. The Order of Lenin —the highest award—went to the deputy director, Sergei Yesin, a very intelligent engineer and an orthodox Leninist to the point of stupidity. "The Order of Lenin is a sacred honor for me!" he declared. "I could not go on living if it were proven to me that Leninism was incorrect." The secretary of the Central Committee of the Communist Party of Armenia approached me. "If you submit an application to the Party right now," he said, "we will arrange with Moscow not only to readmit you but even to restore your Party seniority for the entire twelve-year period since 1956. Don't lose a minute!" That was my prize.

Curious as to what people thought of this ludicrous honor, I surveyed public opinion on the question: "Should I accept the offer to join the Party again?" Everyone answered, "Yes."

In Moscow I put the same question to Alikhanov, who was by now no longer director of ITEP.

"What do you need that for?" he asked.

"I certainly don't need it. Of course, people say I could have permission to go on scientific trips abroad."

"I wouldn't crawl into that bucket of shit even for the sake of trips abroad!" Alikhanov snapped. This was what I expected to hear from Abram Isakovich.

I did not crawl into the bucket.

TWELVE

Return

In August 1968 the Soviet Army, heading the armies of the Warsaw Pact, occupied Czechoslovakia. "Prague Spring" was crushed.

In those dramatic days I did not encounter a single intellectual among my enormous number of acquaintances who was not excited by the Czechs' idea of transforming their Soviet type of socialism into "socialism with a human face." There were hot private conversations in kitchens in Moscow, Novosibirsk, Leningrad, and Yerevan. Nobody was on the Soviet side, nobody liked the government, and— And nothing. Debate went no farther than the kitchens. No one with high status protested publicly against the Soviet military action. Interfere in foreign policy? Never! It is too dangerous, you can be prosecuted for high treason. This was the post-Stalin "inertia of fear," as my friend Valentin Turchin later called it.

The problem also was *how* to protest. Write? You would not be published. March on the street with placards? Nobody would follow you except the KGB—not in Yerevan, where the Armenians did not care much about politics outside Armenia; and especially not in Russia, where ordinary people cursed the ungrateful Czechs for forgetting that the Soviet Army had saved them from the Nazis. During spontaneous street discussions in

Yerevan, some Russians and Armenians expressed this view as well. "That is completely just," I agreed. "The Red Army freed the Czechs from the Nazis. And once you have saved a woman from rapists, of course you have the right to rape her yourself every day." But they pointed to the newspapers, which clearly proved that had it not been for the invasion by our brilliant armed forces, Czechoslovakia would have been seized by the armies of West Germany and the United States. Their stupidity incensed me.

By this time I had already come to prefer the Scandinavians' reliable and tested model of "capitalism with a human face," and doubted whether the Czechs' plans were realistic. Nevertheless, my sympathies were wholeheartedly on their side because they rejected the methods of dictatorship.

On hearing my statements on this subject, most Armenians kept silent and merely smiled carefully now and then. There was one Armenian, however, who was silent then but found his voice when the KGB needed help in prosecuting me. "Orlov conducted anti-Soviet agitation and propaganda against the introduction of Soviet armies into Czechoslovakia," I read ten years later in his written testimony. This Akop Aleksanyan had once been just an ordinary physicist in our institute. But then everything changed when his attractive daughter married the son of the first secretary of the Central Committee of the Armenian Communist Party. Akop suddenly discovered in himself a severe party zeal. His star rose. He was elected secretary of the Party Committee of the institute. He bought himself a big briefcase.

Several weeks after the Soviet invasion of Czechoslovakia, a samizdat[1] report from Moscow typed by some brave anonymous typist on the thinnest of transparent copy paper appeared in Yerevan. It announced that in August, seven people had demonstrated in Red Square against the invasion. Among the names, I recognized that of Larisa Bogoraz, dissident and wife of the imprisoned dissident-writer Yuli Daniel. The group just

---

[1] "Samizdat" means "self-publication" and refers to the system of copying and circulating materials privately and secretly, in order to bypass the authorities. Such materials typically included political essays critical of the government and documents containing information that the authorities wanted to suppress. During the sixties Samizdat exploded as a homegrown source of independent information and opinion in the USSR, and played an enormous role in revitalizing the intelligentsia.

had time to unfurl a poster reading FOR YOUR FREEDOM AND OURS! before they were seized, beaten up, and dragged into a black raven[2] that had rolled right up. In reading the report, I felt shame. Since 1956 I had done nothing to change this terrible and idiotic regime.

By now I had become a professor and a corresponding member of the Armenian Academy of Sciences. But it was not these titles, or the high salary connected with them, or fear, that had held me back from public action against the regime. The main point was that to open my mouth meant to be expelled from the science I loved. This had happened once already, and would not be easy to accept again. In any event, it would be best to pay that high price for creating something really important. To me that meant presenting a clear program for the kind of democracy our totalitarian system should be changed to, and how. So far I understood only the "what," not the "how." Although I did not believe in planned socialism, I understood that any proposal to move back toward capitalism would be rejected in the Soviet context and would therefore be practically useless. Something intermediate was needed, yet what it was eluded me.

But time was passing, and I had still done nothing at all. This was not the first time that I felt so uncomfortable. At the beginning of the sixties, savage suppressions of workers' unrest had occurred in several cities. I had known about them, yet not lifted a finger to inform the public. I had even investigated one such case—the strike and shooting down of workers in Novocherkassk in 1962. Most people were not aware of it; official information had been tightly sealed off. In 1965, when I visited Novocherkassk with Ira to give a lecture at the polytechnic institute, friends told us a lot about it and the city's history. On a visit in 1967, I learned more.

Novocherkassk had been the capital of the Cossacks of the Kuban and Lower Don. At the end of the nineteenth century they erected an enormous Orthodox cathedral there, an even more enormous majestic polytechnic institute, and monuments to the great Cossacks—heroes of Russian history. The Cossacks and their monuments were liquidated by the Bolsheviks, and an anti-religion museum organized in the cathedral. But the

---

[2]The colloquial term for a paddy wagon.

polytechnic institute continued functioning just as under the czar; the city was still full of students when I lectured there.

In the summer of 1962, at the big electric-locomotive factory seven miles from Novocherkassk, wages were cut by about 30 percent, and, simultaneously, state prices for meat, milk, and eggs increased by 30 percent. The price changes were like the famous price cuts under Stalin: prices did exist, but there was no food in the stores. Housing for the workers was terrible—barracks and overcrowded communal apartments—but for that matter it was the same all over the country.

The workers struck.

The authorities responded by sending troops and tanks into the factory, into the workers' settlement, and into the city of Novocherkassk. Troops sealed off all roads leading to the area. People were arrested and received the usual beatings. The Kalashnikovs were silent for now, but the factory steam whistles continued to hoot, calling for a general strike. People stopped work at other Novocherkassk factories.

It is popular in the West to talk about the allegedly natural submissiveness of Russians, their fatal love for the cult of authority. But just try to stand right in front of tanks: in which direction would you walk or run? Under the tanks or away from them? The workers of Novocherkassk walked *through* the tank barriers. Columns of workers from the various factories began flowing to the center of the city. They marched singing the "International," with portraits of Lenin and red flags. All the people of the city came out onto the streets; children climbed onto roofs and up trees. When the demonstrators broke through the cordon of troops and occupied the building of the municipal Party Committee and the militia, the order was given to fire.

The soldiers fired their submachine guns at the roofs and the trees full of curious children, at the dense crowd, at the tanks plastered over with workers who had plugged the vision slits with clothing. The tank crews did not fire.[3]

All night long the fire brigades washed blood off the street. The bodies of the dead and severely wounded were hauled away in trucks and buried outside the city in some gullies, hid-

---

[3] Today we know that their commander, Lieutenant General Matvei Kuzmich Shaposhnikov, ordered them not to shoot. For that, he was fired from the army.

den away from their relatives. There was talk about the escape of a wounded teenager from the rear of a truck crammed full of corpses. Hospitals were overflowing with the wounded, but many of them hid or disappeared. One soldier was killed.

The unrest lasted another month. Two or three members of the Politburo, including Mikoyan, came from Moscow. They threatened that the people of Novocherkassk, everyone down to the last person, would be deported from the city. More than a hundred workers were tried and sentenced; seven were condemned to be shot. Wage rates for labor stayed reduced, but the food supply improved and prices were not raised. I had known all about it . . . Now, after the Czech tragedy, I reconsidered my life again and decided that I could not leave science voluntarily: that would be the equivalent of death. I would continue my scientific work until stopped by force. But it was unpleasant, disgusting, this totalitarian civilization crawling all over the world like a cancer, and not to oppose it meant living with a constant feeling of shame. I had to do something. At least I could make contact with the Moscow dissidents. Afterward, I would see.

That same autumn, after making the painful decision to separate from Ira, I met Irina Valitova, a Muscovite living with her mother and youngest brother in a communal apartment where every one of the six rooms contained or had contained somebody who had been in prison—half of them on political charges. Irina worked in the Pushkin Museum as a guard and studied art history at night in the university. We met in the museum, I asked her out for a movie, and a few months later we rented a room together in Moscow. Irina traveled back and forth to Yerevan with me, and ended up living there two years later when the Ministry of Middle Machine Building in Moscow began to limit my official trips. The Yerevan Institute was controlled by this ministry now, just as ITEP was.

Apparently the ministry had not imagined that I, a Russian, would be elected to the Armenian Academy of Sciences the previous spring. It was Alikhanyan who had promoted my candidacy. I had long ago decided to pardon him for his attempt to make me a slave, and except for that insulting episode, he had always acted as a good friend. When I was elected to the academy, the deputy minister for personnel at the Ministry of

Middle Machine Building—Mezentsev, my old Chekist friend from ITEP—summoned the director of the Yerevan Physics Institute to his office. Mezentsev was enraged. His genealogical tree probably went back to the czarist secret police. It is known that a Mezentsev was a high police official in the last century; he was stabbed to death by a revolutionary in St. Petersburg.

"How could Orlov have been elected to the academy?" Mezentsev bellowed at Alikhanyan. "How could you, the director, permit such a thing? The decision of your academic council was in your power. The academy's vote depended on your stand. But you—you did not even let us know where the thing was heading!"

Alikhanyan did not report to me how he had gone about defending himself. But knowing him very well, I could picture how he had bent low at the waist, inclined his bald pate—this good and famous physicist—and portrayed repentance for the political foolishness he had committed. I felt uncomfortable. "Still, the thing is an accomplished fact!" Alikhanyan said to me, smiling. "They elected you. They can't vote over again." (He was mistaken. In 1979, when I was in labor camp and he was in his grave, the academy expelled me.)

In 1970 the ministry produced a formal written order announcing that "to economize on funds," scientists could travel to Moscow on official business no more than twice a year, for six days at a time. There was an additional clause: "In exceptional cases it is permitted . . ." My case was never exceptional. The ministry's restriction of my travel could not have come at a worse moment. I had conceived the idea of building a huge (100 GeV) electron-positron collider, my Yerevan laboratory had begun to design it, and discussions with scientists in Moscow were essential. I wanted to develop contacts with dissidents. And my relations with Galya had improved; now I could meet Dima and Sasha in Moscow at any time.

During my now-rare scientific trips outside Yerevan, a rat-faced ministry bureaucrat named Makarov-Zemlyansky often crossed my path. And he actually blocked it during a small meeting in Tbilisi on the Soviet program for elementary particle accelerators. Alikhanyan had unofficially invited me to it; my new collider project was going to be discussed. Makarov-Zemlyansky ordered me not to enter the conference room. I missed all the reports, including Victor Weisskopf's review of the Soviet program, which he had specially come from the United States to deliver. As Weisskopf left the hall, he looked reproachfully at me, but I decided not to make a fuss and explain.

I worked two more years at Yerevan under these conditions, developing the collider project. In 1972 my patience finally ran out. A telegram had summoned me to a meeting in Moscow of the Academy of Sciences council on accelerators as a member of the council presidium. Having already exhausted the two official trips to Moscow permitted me that year, I made an agreement with Alikhanyan and traveled to the meeting at my own expense. Makarov-Zemlyansky saw me there. When I returned to Armenia, the ministry response was already waiting: a reprimand and a deduction from my wages for the days I had been "absent from work" in Yerevan. Enough was enough. They had evidently forgotten that I still possessed my Moscow residence permit. I was not absolutely dependent on them. I resigned.

Just then, Artemii Isakovich Alikhanyan was removed as director. He could easily have ended up in prison. When the accelerator started up in 1967, it had been necessary for the workers and technicians to go all out, ignoring the clock, which meant paying them extra for work above the legal limit. Alikhanyan did that by putting on the payroll wives who had never seen an accelerator. This sort of thing went on all over the Soviet Union, and because it worked, the authorities usually shut their eyes unless a conflict with higher authorities arose. In that case it was no trouble at all to send the sharp manager to prison or at least fire him from his job. They decided to fire Alikhanyan. Fortunately he had a lab in the Lebedev Physics Institute; he left Armenia for Moscow shortly after I did.

To my surprise, after sixteen years of a kind of exile in Armenia, I found myself rather sad to leave. I had fallen in love with the mountains covered with sunburned grass, the lichen-painted stones, the terraces with children running up and down them, the old courtyards and narrow side streets, the benevolent, peaceful, hardworking people. However, in our country there is not much room for melancholy—and even less for boredom. To get the official discharge and back pay due me, I had to hand my temporary apartment over to the institute.

It was all emptied and ready, when the wife of my colleague Garik entered it in my absence, locked the door from the inside, and sat on the floor. She was expecting their second child at any moment and had decided to occupy the territory by force. Somehow or other their family always got passed over for good institute housing. For many years they and their child had been living in one room at the institute's hotel. Garik's study was their tiny lavatory, where he worked sitting on the toilet and writing on a table he had specially built.

Meanwhile, my sons Dima and Sasha were at the Black Sea, waiting for Irina and me to arrive. But I preferred to leave with an official discharge. Besides, the Party secretary, Akop Aleksanyan, had begun announcing all over the place that Garik (who rarely had twenty kopecks in his pocket) had bought the key to the institute apartment from me for twenty thousand rubles.

"Garik," I pleaded with my colleague, "for God's sake explain to her!"

"You know her." Garik shrugged. "When she digs in her heels, it's impossible to dislodge her."

"Liberate the apartment!" I demanded, putting our long-standing friendship at risk. After half a day of negotiating through the door, Garik prevailed on his wife to leave.

Finally settling things with the apartment, I went to get the signature of the special section. The head of the section, a pleasant and efficient man, signed my checkout document and held out his hand. I shook it without thinking and only then remembered—just the day before I had been told that some old woman had suddenly grabbed him by the hair in a trolleybus and begun to scream, "You tortured my husband! You tortured my husband!" He could barely get away from her. The case, apparently, went back some twenty years. Soviet Armenian soldiers who had escaped from German prisoner-of-war camps and then fought in the Italian Resistance had of course been arrested on returning to the USSR, because they had mixed with foreigners. Then they had passed through the hands of this security man, who, people said, had brutally beaten them during interrogations and sent them on to Siberian camps. Who knows, I thought as I left, maybe those camps will become familiar to me, too. And I decided to spend my last hours in Yerevan with Kostya.

Kostya was lying on his couch dead drunk. Among Armenians drunkenness is rare, but Kostya was an Armenian only in his passport. The young Kostya had fought the Nazis and then the English as a Communist partisan in the mountains of his native Greece. "For us there was no difference between German and British imperialism," he explained. In one clash they captured a hundred English soldiers, and Kostya was ordered simply to shoot the prisoners down. So he shot them all down with a machine gun. For this feat a Greek court condemned him to death in absentia. After that he and his parents, also Communists, were evacuated to the Soviet Union on a Soviet ship, carrying documents as repatriated Armenians.

In Yerevan he began to study in the university. Very soon three repatriated Armenian students proposed that he flee with them back to the West across the Turkish border. They told him that when they came to the Soviet Union, they knew about socialism only from books, and it had sounded good, but in their worst nightmares they had never dreamed of what they actually saw here. Kostya, of course, declined to go. One of the three was wounded but managed to swim across the turbulent Araxes River to the other side; a second was killed by the border guards; and the third, too scared to try to swim across, was captured. Under interrogation he testified that Kostya had known about their plans. Kostya was arrested. Refusing to give any testimony, even during face-to-face confrontations with this idiot, because he did not know what had happened to the other two, he got pasted with twenty-five years for treason against the Motherland that he wasn't yet a citizen of. When Stalin died he was released, having served only seven years—in all the famous camps. He had a job at our institute in the warehouse, wrote stories that were read in broadcasts from Budapest to Greece, and also worked in a film studio. Unfortunately he was rarely sober. I looked at his pale face and went away.

And so in the summer of 1972 I finally went home to Moscow. Now I could join up with the dissidents, especially the great Sakharov, who had openly broken with the state ideology and nuclear-arms program. Most scientists, neither brave nor independent even in their own kitchens, had erected an invisible wall between themselves and him. We had met before at scientific meetings; he knew the old ITEP story of 1956, and saw my desire to support his struggle for human rights. At first shyness kept me from visiting him until 1973, to discuss our respective points of view. Then I learned that he and his wife, Yelena Bonner, always kept their door open for like-minded people. Their home was an oasis of free thought and perpetual readiness to help people suffering from the authorities for their ideas, criticism, or nationality. In logical, quiet, sometimes seemingly asleep Andrei Dmitriyevich and his quick, explosive Yelena I found kindred spirits.

That autumn Irina and I got married and moved to the very center of Moscow. Our small room was in a communal apartment on the fifth floor of a fine old building with no elevator. The caretaker, Nina Sergeyevna, the loud and jolly fifty-year-old widow of a pilot-general, lived next to us. In another room a little shrimp of an old lady somehow survived on her pension. Nina's ancient loyal fox terrier also lived in the house; she always kept forgetting to take him out.

One morning loud, jolly Nina Sergeyevna lay down on a railroad track and put her plump white neck on a rail. But first she phoned the old lady and asked her to take the dog for a walk. All this took place shortly after her son, a soldier home on Sunday leave, had thrown himself out of her window headfirst right in front of her eyes. That he was drunk was beside the point. The point was that Nina Sergeyevna, with her old connections, could have got her son exempted from the draft. Instead, she had pushed him into the army. Everyone said to her, and she said to everyone, that the service would make a real man of her son. However, her picture of military service was based on what it had been like in the forties, the days of her husband's youth and my youth. The service then was different, something better. No beating of junior soldiers by their seniors—and on a scale undreamt of even in czarist times. The boy could not endure his military service. We never found out what became of Nina's poor dog, because we had to move to another place.

It was in the old house on the Arbat where Pushkin had lived with his young wife Natalya just after their wedding. A friend of mine passed it on to us after his father died. We were not permitted to be registered as residents, and nobody else had a right to occupy our room, since the house was scheduled to be restored and turned over to the Pushkin Museum. So we were going to live there until the police showed up. The room was large, with two windows and a Dutch stove. It pleased me to think that this stove remembered Pushkin himself warming his back at it 150 years before.

Once again I was in Moscow without a job, earning money by giving private lessons. At least I also collected 150 rubles a month as a corresponding member of the Armenian Academy of Sciences—enough altogether for us to live on and help out my sons. Being without a job at the age of forty-eight was more unpleasant than at thirty-two. It had been entirely unexpected. Just before leaving Yerevan, I had made a firm agreement to work as a professor in the new physics sub-faculty being organized at Moscow University by the theoretician Alexei Abrikosov. They had even accepted my documents. But now they informed Alexei that he would not be appointed because he had made an unauthorized marriage to a Frenchwoman, and that Orlov would not be appointed because he had been expelled from the Party sixteen years ago and had never been reinstated. The Leningrad Physico-Technical Institute was likewise unsuccessful in hiring me.

I remained unemployed for several more months, until academicians L. A. Artsimovich and R. Z. Sagdeyev helped me get a position as senior scientist in the Institute of Terrestrial Magnetism and Dissemination of Radio Waves. My having work gave us the right to buy an apartment in a housing cooperative. An old friend lent us money to make the initial deposit, and for the first time in Moscow Irina and I lived in tolerable conditions. By a happy coincidence our new place was in the heart of the "dissidents' quarter." Living close by was my old friend Valentin Turchin, who together with Sakharov and Roy Medvedev had already written a famous samizdat appeal to the authorities; Alexander Ginzburg, a journalist and one of the founders of samizdat; Ludmilla Alexeeva, a historian and editor; Yelena Armand, the granddaughter of Lenin's mistress; and several families of refuseniks.

"You know very well that was no coincidence," Irina said mournfully seven years later. "You got just what you wanted."

THIRTEEN

In the Opposition

In September 1973 the rabid persecution of Sakharov began. *Pravda* published a statement by several famous academicians condemning his "unpatriotic activity." There followed vicious letters by factory foremen who, if they really existed, had probably never read a word Sakharov had written. But those famous academicians certainly did exist. I knew that most of them were genuine scientists, and also knew the value of a public pronouncement like theirs. I remembered the statements published in the thirties, in which academicians demanded the death penalty for people who had been arrested; then some of those academicians were arrested themselves, and other academicians publicly demanded the death penalty for them. A number of denunciations written by academicians about each other even found their way into the KGB archives, as I learned from samizdat. That was the 1930s. As for the 1970s, a bureaucrat in the Academy of Sciences had informed me—without naming names—that some academicians were secret agents of the KGB and that the KGB had backed or at least not impeded their scientific careers in exchange for this nice service. The moral value of the academicians' statement about Sakharov was, as my mother would have put it, minus zero. No honest academicians signed it. Some, like Budker, deliberately avoided it; a

163

heroic few, including Kapitsa and Sagdeyev, even refused point-blank.

Sakharov, whom I knew well by now, had to be immediately supported. By the end of the next week I finished writing "Thirteen Questions to Brezhnev," and the state security people put in their safe the first exhibit of my future criminal case.

"Thirteen Questions to Brezhnev"[1] was a letter not so much in defense of Sakharov as in his honor. Since my views somewhat differed from his, I could best defend him and offer him moral support by voicing my own criticism of the Soviet regime. The basic thesis of the letter was that fanatic adherence to an ideology that denied the existence of freedom of choice and expression as an innate human need had resulted in a feudal relation between citizen and state as well as scientific, economic, and cultural decline. I proposed abolishing press censorship and instituting the free exchange of ideas and *glasnost.* My economic proposal was to keep the framework of state ownership while imitating the West through such stimuli to large-scale economic development as establishing domains where managers had free initiative and salaries dependent on their profits.

Thus I tried to give a preliminary answer to the tormenting question of how we could begin the peaceful transformation of the system from thick-headed Soviet "socialism" to a modern democracy. Given the practical focus of the letter and the large amount of ground it aimed to cover, it seemed best not to elaborate on the subject of human nature, so I omitted my view that contradictory social beliefs unavoidably coexist in the same social system and even in the same believer since human nature pulls in several directions at once. But this coexistence now deeply interested me from a scientific standpoint, and I had already begun to seek a mathematical apparatus for describing it. (A year later I called the apparatus "wave logic.") As for my economic remarks, I proposed the interim path of freedom of private initiative within a framework of state ownership because a direct leap into the modern, Western form of capitalism seemed a psychological impossibility in Russia. The masses had too great a mistrust of private entrepreneurial activity. Fifteen

---

[1] It has now been officially published for the first time in the USSR, in the weekly magazine *Ogonyok*, No. 35 (September 1989). See Appendix I for the full text.

years later some of what I proposed was reinvented by Gorbachev—although not, as he himself has often said, to create a Western democracy. Yet what was moderate and timely when I proposed it is far too conservative and too late today.

Of course, I did not believe for a second that constructive conversation with the regime was possible, but decided that my first public appeal should not proceed from such a postulate. The authorities had to show in practice that they rejected a pluralist approach to ideas and would not conduct serious dialogue with me. I sent the letter—typed, signed, and with my home address on it—to Brezhnev and the editorial offices of the official newspapers, and circulated it among intellectuals in Moscow, Novosibirsk, and Yerevan. Brezhnev's reply consisted of one anonymous telephone call ("Was it you who sent the letter?") and ten look-alike characters who began to stroll outside the entry to our building, slipping and sliding and stumbling beneath my nose in order to get a good look at my face. When they sorted that out, they got themselves an apartment nearby. For the next three and a half years, one shift of KGB would enter the apartment to sleep (they slept quite a lot) while another left it to stroll about the neighborhood and keep watch on me. The Chekists sometimes followed by car or on foot until I formed the Helsinki Watch Group; after that, they followed me everywhere.

Since much of the writing by official economists, philosophers, and social scientists in the USSR was obviously primitive and corrupt, intellectuals welcomed any new, honest, and reasonable idea from nonspecialists. My letter to Brezhnev was therefore read with interest and duplicated in various cities by many nondissidents, some of whom even came to Moscow to discuss it with me. And that had been my purpose. The dissidents read it but were not so excited, because each had long since worked out his or her own ideas.

Solzhenitsyn read "Thirteen Questions," which is how our acquaintance began. Late one autumn evening I was taken to see Alexander Isayevich by Anya Bryksina, the daughter of a common friend. We disembarked at a railway station outside Moscow whose name I deliberately forgot, and after half an hour of walking entered a dark lane in a village of dachas. Before us loomed a tall, solid fence; behind the fence stood a

large unlit house. Anya disappeared into the darkness, where
she was already expected, returned for me, and we followed a
compactly built man of medium height. We silently passed
through the gate, which he immediately locked behind him—
now I recognized him by his enormous forehead—and went
on into the house. He carefully closed the door and leaned
something against it.

"A pitchfork," Anya whispered.

"Just in case they try to raid," Solzhenitsyn quietly explained. The narrow beam of a night lamp illuminated a man-
uscript on the table. In the small room stood an electric heater,
a chair, and a bench. The windows were heavily draped over.

"Hello!" he said.

He asked me about myself. I gave him the letter to
Brezhnev.

"Yes," he said, after reading it through. "It is possible to
approach the problem from different angles, but whichever
you choose, the result is the same: the system has no future."

"What would be your minimal demand for a truce with the
regime?" I asked.

"Freedom of the press."

Anya and I left an hour later.

In Stalinist times Anya's father had been imprisoned with
Solzhenitsyn in the *sharaga* described in *The First Circle*. It was
Ivan Yemelyanovich Bryksin who managed to sneak out of that
camp the well-known portrait drawing of the prisoner Solzhenitsyn. Anya's mother, Yekaterina Mikhailovna, had also been
imprisoned, taken away from her two small children after remarking in her communal kitchen that the Germans had not
behaved badly in her hometown during the Occupation. The
Bryksins met each other as prisoners, got married on their
release, and were "rehabilitated" after Stalin died.

By the time I met him, Bryksin was the head of a large
electrochemical laboratory, the elder children lived with their
own families, and the youngest, Anya, was studying in an institute. She and her parents lived now in a three-room Moscow apartment. On Sundays it overflowed with their relatives
and innumerable friends—eating, drinking, discussing politics,
and dancing fox-trots. Sometimes we sang Russian folk songs
and romances. Anya, her mother, and her sister Nona all had
remarkable voices. Being with them I felt that no, not every-

thing had been killed off in the Russian people. Only, in the eyes of Ivan Yemelyanovich you could still see the shadows of camps, body searches, and prison transports.

Anya gave her student friends Solzhenitsyn to read. Naturally, right in the middle of final examinations she got a telephone call at home from the Komsomol secretary asking her to come at once to the Komsomol Committee. Something struck her as suspicious in his voice and untimely request, but there was no way out of going. Just in case, Yekaterina Mikhailovna swiftly removed from their apartment all of the samizdat and tamizdat.[2] At the doors of her institute Anya was met by a pair of husky strangers who took the lovely girl by the arms and courteously piloted her not, of course, to the Komsomol Committee, but to another room entirely. There they began the interrogation.

Anya took after her mother and father. From beginning to end she stuck to denial-of-everything, the very best way not to put anyone else on the spot.

"Come on now, Anna Ivanovna," said one of the young men. "After all, we have evidence."

He rummaged about in his briefcase for a file and extracted a piece of paper. A student had reported that at a rehearsal of their choral group, the student Bryksina had given him a copy of Solzhenitsyn's *The First Circle.*

"That's no kind of evidence—there's no signature," said Anya.

"Why do you need a signature? Well, if you do insist . . ."

He got another piece of paper out of the file. This was the last page of the report and had a signature.

"I don't know a thing about it," Anya said. "He made that all up for some reason. Maybe he was jealous?"

"An-na Ivanovna! We have other evidence as well."

He rummaged about and produced one more document. This was not just a report but the nervous confession of a student, in which he kept repeating, Yes, such-and-such did take place, but he himself had asked Bryksina for a book.

Anya knew who had written it, but there was no signature. "It's not genuine," she said. "There's no signature on it."

"But, Anna Ivanovna! Isn't it all true?"

---

[2] Literature from abroad.

"No, it's all lies!"

She astounded them, and they released her. She was expelled from the Komsomol, which was no big loss in itself. Then they tried to fail her in her examination on scientific atheism, but she knew all the proofs for it by heart. Finally she was given her diploma. It is certain that the authorities feared the scandal that Solzhenitsyn, a friend of the family, would have created: her father and mother had been imprisoned for nothing; now even the daughter was going to serve time? So they left her alone, and she began working as an engineer at the ZIL automobile factory.

Anya, like my Irina, became a founding member of the Soviet Amnesty International Group, organized in October 1973 by Valentin Turchin as part of our general plan to help create more and more unofficial human rights groups in order to involve people in peaceful activity independent of the government. Andrei Tverdokhlebov, a physicist and cofounder of Sakharov's Moscow Committee for Human Rights, handled most of the practical side—getting people together, establishing contact with Amnesty International in London, and drawing up something like a set of statutes. There were twenty-five or thirty of us, mostly scientists and writers from Moscow, Leningrad, Kiev, and Tbilisi, passionately concerned with showing the Russian public an example of commitment to pluralism and to tolerance of any ideas that were promoted without violence. Accordingly, we defended a South Vietnamese trade-union leader, a Yugoslav rightist, an Indonesian Communist, and worker-strikers from Poland.

It would have been natural for the Soviet authorities to arrest us immediately. After all, they hated peaceful pluralism even more than they hated any hostile ideology, and had long since proclaimed to everyone in the USSR that Amnesty International was an agency of the American CIA. But arresting us just then would not have been opportune. That month, Soviet politicians had set up a show in Moscow, a Congress of Peace-Loving Forces. Sean MacBride, now in his next-to-last year as chairman of Amnesty's International Executive Committee, had been vice-chairman of the Preparatory Committee of the congress. So there were no immediate reprisals against us.

* * *

In slushy November the trade-union committee of my institute unexpectedly offered me a cheap holiday at a vacation home outside Moscow. I walked alone all day there in the wet woods, going indoors only to eat and sleep, no one watching at my heels. The other vacationers were file clerks, technicians, workers, typists, with whom things were easy and uncomplicated. During downpours, I spent my time in pleasant conversation with an elderly former bookkeeper who had an infinite number of stories.

"That's our people for you. They need a fist and then another fist," he pronounced one afternoon, sipping a good strong cognac. "They're not people—they're anarchy. I remember the Revolution. They sent us sailors into the villages to organize Committees of the Poor. We came to a village, assembled the peasant men, and explained to them: peace, freedom, and land to the peasants, be off with you. There was an estate there—the manor house was completely preserved, two floors, luxurious, all boarded up. The estate owner, they told me, had already been killed at the German front, and where his family was no one knew. I hung up a sign on it: 'Do not touch! The People's Property.' The peasants read it. One, two days passed, and an orderly raced in: 'They're looting!' We rushed there on a machine-gun cart. What a picture! The peasant men, women, children were hauling off everything they could get their hands on. Whatever wouldn't get through the door they didn't dismantle but sawed or chopped and threw the parts out the window. They dragged off halves of chests of drawers, divans—it was a mob scene, just like at a fire. We shot over their heads with the machine guns. Screams. Then they poured out of the doors and windows, scattering like peas in all directions. But what was the point? Nearly everything was all smashed up or hauled off, and whatever wasn't would be later on. I gave the orders myself: all right, take what's left, but don't break things up, you scum! So what did they think up then? They very carefully carted away a grand piano and a huge cheval glass—you see, they could be careful when they wanted to, the sons of bitches—and set them down at the village well. But the mirror wouldn't fit in any of the peasant huts. Then let all the village women enjoy the mirror while they're going for water, they said, and let the piano stay here on the street for amusement until we find some use for it.

"But the cattle also used the street. The bull looked at himself in the mirror and didn't like what he saw. Bang! One mirror in little pieces. That was all right, too. Every house could have a fragment of the mirror. And they found a use for the piano. The strings went for wire. They also carried off the house, brick by brick. That's how it was. And you talk of 'democracy!' Those people need the kind of 'democracy' which wasn't even dreamed of at hard labor under the czar. Don't tell me."

"Did I say anything?"

"I don't know. Here folks are chattering that maybe you stole something—otherwise why are people keeping an eye on you? What I think is that you blurted out something you shouldn't have. Well?"

And I'd thought I had freedom here.

"Why is the intelligentsia stirred up?" he asked. "It's a new intelligentsia, from workers, but all the same they're dissatisfied with something. You tell me. You're a scientist—tell me, what is it you don't have that you want?"

"Origin isn't important." I said. "Once a person has become an intellectual, he needs freedom to express his thoughts. That's a condition of his existence. Without it he's not an intellectual."

"So that's how it is!"

Returning to the institute a week later, I learned that Moscow University and the Lebedev Physics Institute had nominated me along with Sokolov, Ternov, Kolomensky, and Lebedev for a state prize, and that I was fired as of January 1. The director of the institute looked straight into my eyes and claimed it was on grounds of redundancy. Sakharov and the mathematician Igor Shafarevich jointly wrote a protest to the Academy of Sciences and passed a copy of it to foreign correspondents. Without pressure from abroad any internal protest was virtually useless.

For the third time in my life I found myself without a job. There was no hope of finding one in Moscow. My being a corresponding member of the Armenian Academy of Sciences did legally require the academy to provide me with work in

Armenia. And Armenia was beautiful, and had been kind to me. But I had no wish to live outside my native land again. Still, there was nothing for it. In Moscow I reached an agreement with the president of the Armenian Academy, Victor Ambartsumyan, to work in his Byurokan observatory, and a little while later flew to Armenia on my last funds. The first day, Ambartsumyan greeted me cordially and showed me the telescopes. The second day, he vanished. Understanding that he was not going to give me the Byurokan job after all, I descended from the mountains to Yerevan and spoke with Dzhrbashyan, the director of the academy's Mathematics Institute. He agreed to hire me—but, he said, in a case such as mine the president of the academy would have to agree, too. So I went to Ambartsumyan. Our conversation was extremely brief.

"We helped you eighteen years ago, back in 1956," he said. "But we cannot do it a second time."

Evidently Victor Ambartsumyan, distinguished in science, omnipotent in Armenia, member of the Central Committee of the Communist Party of Armenia, had asked for—and received—instructions directly from Moscow. A year later, in 1975, along with seventy-one other scientists, Ambartsumyan signed a protest against the award of the Nobel Peace Prize to Sakharov. Four years after that his academy secretly expelled me, and he lied about me in *Le Monde*.

It was futile to point out their legal obligation to give me work. I returned to Moscow with nothing, and never again worked as a scientist in my country.

Soon afterward, Kolomensky and Lebedev asked to meet with me at a private apartment.

"Listen, Yura," said Andrei Lebedev, "we were warned that if we didn't exclude you from the list of nominees for the prize, there would be nasty articles about our work in important newspapers and we wouldn't get the prize. I don't like this, but I'd feel sorry to have our work go by the board; after all, it was good work. What can we do?"

"There's just one way out," said Andrei Kolomensky. "Yuri, you have to remove your name from the list. We were told that you had signed some sort of 'collective' document. You know yourself what that means."

"No, I don't know what it means," I remarked. This "collective" document was obviously the first declaration made by our Amnesty group.

"You signed some sort of document against the state, and the state naturally has the right to refuse to give you its own prize."

"I don't like that logic," said Lebedev.

"It's just a paranoid state," I said.

"But nonetheless you live in it," said Kolomensky.

"I won't play," I said. There were no nasty articles in the newspapers, and I did not keep track of the matter any further, so I never learned the fate of our prize.

At the end of January 1974 Solzhenitsyn paid his last visit to the Bryksins. Usually he was economical with his time and did not drink at all, but on this occasion he sat with us for more than two hours and drank a little glass of vodka. The previous August, state security had discovered the hiding place of a copy of *The Gulag Archipelago*. He told us the tragic story of the typist.

This elderly Leningrad woman, having secretly typed *Archipelago* for Solzhenitsyn, had held on to the last poor-quality copy. Solzhenitsyn insistently demanded that she destroy it. He wished to publish this explosive document much later on, and until that day he was keeping it in his own archive, which the KGB could not get at. She lied to him—and kept her copy as a souvenir. A certain amount of time passed, and, not understanding what she was doing, she gave it to a close friend to read. More time passed, and this old man blabbed about it to his close friends. The chain ended, finally, with the KGB. Tracing the chain back, they silently arrived at the typist and detained her. After five days of interrogation she revealed her hiding place. *Archipelago,* together with the names of witnesses whose testimony Solzhenitsyn had used, fell into the hands of the KGB. The old woman was released. When she got home, she hanged herself.

Her friends had known about the interrogation. Lev Kopelev, who once, like Bryskin and Solzhenitsyn, had been imprisoned in that *sharaga* in Marfino, immediately phoned Solzhenitsyn from Leningrad and reported what had happened. Solzhenitsyn at once ordered his lawyer in Geneva to publish *Archipelago*—and made a public announcement to that effect.

Now he awaited arrest. He was living, these days, in Moscow.

"I don't see any shadows," said Solzhenitsyn. "That means they will arrest—if not today, then tomorrow."

He spoke of this calmly. Intellect and firmness were written on his face with extreme, fantastic sharpness.

Less than two weeks later Solzhenitsyn was arrested and accused of "treason to the Motherland." But after the personal plea of Heinrich Böll and the agreement of the West German government, and without, of course, asking Solzhenitsyn himself, they deported him from Soviet prison directly to West Germany. He left stripped of his citizenship.

Right after his exile I added my name to a protest-appeal by Moscow intellectuals, which proposed establishing an international tribunal (like that of Nuremberg) for investigating the crimes described in *The Gulag Archipelago*. I thought then, and still do, that given the passage of so many years after the crimes of the "Red Terror"—no matter how nightmarish its methods and scale—there should not be executions or imprisonment of those criminals who are still alive. The former leaders, the members of "troikas," the prosecutors, the interrogators, the guards, the writers of false denunciations, the numerous theoreticians and propagandists of that terror—let them live. But they must be publicly tried. And all the atrocities must be publicly investigated, regardless of whether the criminals are living or dead.

As always when I needed it, financial help soon came from my friend Yevgeny Tarasov, who now headed a laboratory in ITEP. Within a few months funds came from colleagues in Yerevan, from Budker in Novosibirsk, and from Solzhenitsyn in Zurich. Later on, when Sakharov received the Nobel Prize, Yelena Bonner transferred money to me for my sons from her "children's fund." My journalist friend Igor Virko asked other journalists to help organize free-lance work for me in Moscow: I edited scientific filmstrips, wrote and produced my own on the history of nuclear physics under the pseudonym of Y. Fyoidorov and published a small book for nonspecialists entitled *The Sources of Fast Neutrons*. (Before Gorbachev such free-lance jobs were not officially considered work, and had I not been a corresponding member of the Armenian Academy, a charge of "parasitism" would have been slapped on me; that happened to the poet and future Nobel Prize winner Joseph Brodsky.) However, my main source of income, just as eighteen years earlier, was private tutoring. Irina and I typed one hundred announcements—"Doctor of Sciences gives private lessons"— and stuck them up in entries to apartment buildings.

Despite unemployment, my morale was high. By now I had become intensely involved with the democratic human rights movement, managed to translate into mathematical language my ideas about belief and doubt, and joined an independent physics seminar led by the physicists Alexander Voronel and Mark Azbel. The seminar met every week and was attended by unemployed physicists, nearly all refuseniks.

That spring Voronel and Azbel organized an unofficial scientific conference scheduled to coincide with President Nixon's summer visit to Moscow. No support for our conference had come from Soviet scientists, including most of the Jewish ones who were not refuseniks. But many foreign scientists, among them Nobel Prize winners, were seeking visas to come. The Nobel laureates did not get their visas, and at the end of June, Voronel, Azbel, and other seminar participants got deposited in a lockup outside Moscow. Veniamin Levich, a corresponding member of the Academy of Sciences of the USSR, was placed under house arrest, and so was I.

The arrest was not formally announced. Living as we did on the first floor, we simply saw from the window on June 27 that a militiaman in uniform was standing at our entry and stopping visitors; three sturdy Chekists sat on the bench beneath our windows; on another bench further off sat three more; and on the paths between the nearby apartment buildings there milled about not ten characters as usual, but twenty, with concealed, squawking walkie-talkies.

"Can my husband leave the house?" Irina asked the militiaman from the balcony.

"All right with me," he smiled. "But those guys might haul him in."

Now, whenever she went to the store, she was closely escorted by two thugs who pressed her tiny body between theirs. "Do you get paid well?" she asked. "Enough for vodka," they answered. When she tried to telephone her sick mother from a pay phone on the street (our own telephone had temporarily been disconnected) they pushed down the hook from behind her. When she tried to break away from them to catch a bus, they caught her and threatened her with arrest. "Aren't you parasites ashamed of yourselves?" she sometimes asked. They were silent. She gave them her heavy groceries to carry.

But everything living wants to go on living, as Nikita Khrushchev liked to say. At night they dozed off, at night we had guests. The first to arrive, clambering through our side window, was Anya Bryksina with a bouquet of flowers. We talked till early morning, and she climbed back out at five o'clock, when their slumber was deepest. Then she stopped a militia car with four officials in it and pushed into their hands a copy of a protest I had written to the Moscow Soviet. Some unidentified men, I wrote, were molesting my wife on the street. Irina must be protected against a potential violation. The protest helped: the KGB men began to walk ten paces behind her.

Our second guest was redheaded Venya, one of my pupils, who lived in the building next to ours. His father, Mikhail Agursky—an unemployed Ph.D. in engineering, Russian Orthodox-Jewish refusenik, and participant in our seminar—had been put in a lockup. A militiaman stood guard at the door of their apartment. Venichka's Russian mama, Vera, a district physician, went on her rounds escorted by her very own pair of gorillas, who served in shifts. Venichka himself was convoyed to and from school and about our neighborhood by just one gorilla, because he was only a small boy of ten. He enjoyed walking about with the state security men. "Jump!" he would say, and fly over a fence like a bird. While the old fellow behind him was still grimly climbing over it, Venichka had already disappeared around the corner. That's how he got to us—he simply flew in.

Unrecognized by the KGB, Valentin Turchin burst through our apartment door to discuss my situation and his own. Valya was in the process of being fired from the computer center of the industrial institute where he had gone to work after being forced out of the Institute of Applied Mathematics for political reasons. He decided that if his period of unemployment dragged on, he would leave the USSR to accept a long-standing invitation from Columbia University in America.

The house arrest lasted ten days. We knew it was over when the telephone started working and the militiaman and extra Chekists disappeared.

Later that month three representatives of Amnesty International came to Moscow. They met first with officials and handed them a list of Soviet religious prisoners of conscience. Then they came to Turchin's apartment for talks on the still-unrecognized status of our organization, which had been formed nearly one year before. On our side were Turchin as chairman, Tverdokhlebov as secretary, myself, and Tatiana Litvinova, daughter of the famous Commissar of Foreign Affairs Maxim Litvinov. Litvinova acted as translator. Our guests delivered arguments against a Soviet "section" of Amnesty. It was difficult, they said, to deal with a totalitarian country; one might run up against provocations by the KGB; sending our delegates to Amnesty congresses would be problematic; Tverdokhlebov would be well advised to devote himself to some activity more effective than Amnesty, "if you wish to overthrow this system." "We are not setting ourselves any such goal," I remarked to the walls, just in case.

After many hours of negotiation they finally agreed on a compromise: in two months' time they would register us in Amnesty as a "group"—the lowest status, carrying no right to send delegates to Amnesty congresses. It seemed to me that they found us troublesome. Perhaps, bewitched by the Soviet political game, the Amnesty leadership had decided not to complicate its relations with the Soviets by establishing close ties with dissidents. By 1977, when Sean MacBride received the Lenin Prize, many of us were prisoners of conscience.

FOURTEEN

Stompers

THERE was no free press. Few families had a telephone at home Yet in the mid-seventies desperate people came to Moscow from all over the enormous country, found us, and asked for help. The dissidents were their last hope. At least we could report violations of human rights to the world. We defended rightists and leftists, monarchists and Trotskyites, believers and atheists, regardless of their ideas, provided that they did not advocate or use violence. Our small community numbering several dozen people, no more, led a hectic life attending political trials all over the country and writing protests, appeals, news releases, and reports. In the summer of 1974 I began to receive letters asking for help even from criminal camps. I passed them to a friend, a professional lawyer. Twice Pentecostals asked me to attend their trials in the autumn of 1974.

Fundamentalist Christians and pacifists, the Pentacostals faced persecution wherever they lived, even in the Soviet Far East. The authorities invaded their prayer meetings, confiscated their religious materials, and sent their young men to labor camps for refusing to serve in the army. My first Pentecostal trial was a civil one in an industrial city outside Moscow. The second, in the city of Kaluga, was the criminal trial of a worker and Pentecostal bishop, Ivan Fedotov, charged with organizing an illegal congress disguised as his own wedding. Not only his fellow believers, but also his worker friends and neighbors, had been invited to the wedding. The investigator in the half-empty courtroom nevertheless took the line that all this was a "smoke screen." And although all the witnesses other than the militiamen denied the accusation of a "congress," the prosecutor, who gradually worked himself up into a state of ecstasy, as often happens with prosecutors, demanded five years of strict-regime camp.[1] He called this a humane sentence, and that was true. Under Khrushchev, when Soviet journalists and "leaders of the arts" portrayed Baptists and Pentecostals as fanatic bigots, Reverend Ivan Fedotov had served ten years.

Interrupting the prosecutor's closing speech, I declared in a loud voice that no proof of the defendant's guilt had been produced at the trial. The astounded judge opened his mouth like a fish, then mumbled, "You cannot decide for the court"; the prosecutor continued his speech, but without the ecstasy. When the verdict was read a few hours later, the accusation about the "congress" had been dropped. Fedotov received two years of intensified-regime camp for two anti-Soviet utterances: exclaiming "Fascists!" when a detachment of militiamen once invaded his home at night in hope of discovering a prayer meeting, and "Your policy goes against Lenin's decree!" when a commission of the district executive committee was carrying out an indoctrination-prevention session with him. As people say, "Once you're charged, you're convicted."

That same autumn I flew to Yerevan with Tatiana Sergeyevna Khodorovich for the trial of Paruir Airikyan, founder of the underground Armenian National Party. Tanya Khodorovich, a linguist and a decisive, severe person, was one of the courageous editors of the famous samizdat periodical *The Chronicle of Current Events*, which gathered and published detailed, accurate information on human rights abuses—and managed to do so for years despite frantic KGB efforts to stop them. Tanya coedited the *Chronicle* with the biologist Sergei

---

[1] Labor camps are classified by the harshness of their "regimes" with respect to housing, quantity of food, and the number of letters, family meetings, and food packages a prisoner can receive. Going from least to most harsh, the regimes are: "ordinary," "intensified," "strict," and "special."

Kovalyov and the mathematician Tatiana Velikhanova. They had a dozen or two selfless helpers, Anya Bryksina among them.

In Yerevan I pulled rank as a corresponding member of the Armenian Academy of Sciences to get Tanya and myself admitted to the courtroom. (When Airikyan's fiancée tried to enter, she was put into a preliminary detention cell.) Airikyan's steadfastness was astonishing. Since his student days he had gone from prison to camp, from camp to prison, and now was being tried for "agitation and propaganda" on account of some letters from camp that a camp censor had confiscated. So he had been "propagandizing" the censor. But that in no way bothered the prosecutor, who demanded a sentence of ten years of special regime and four years of exile.

Before the verdict was announced, I went into the room where the judge was deciding Airikyan's fate. Alongside the judge sat the prosecutor. "You are violating the law," I said. They looked at me in silence. "And on what basis are you demanding such a sentence? His letters never got to the addressees, and for that matter there's nothing in the letters anyway. Ten years of special regime! Have you decided to kill him?" I left without waiting for an answer.

Shortly afterward the judge read out the verdict:
". . . sentenced to . . ."

Paruir's mother collapsed. The well-trained audience did not stir, the judge fell silent, the guards seized Airikyan, the state security people and the prosecutor rushed to the mother, began to pry open her mouth with a table knife, and after breaking off five of her teeth, well and truly succeeded.

". . . is sentenced to seven years of corrective labor colony under strict regime . . . three years of exile."

That evening we went to the Airikyans. The mother lay on her bed with a happy, tearstained face. Her son would survive.

While we were in Yerevan, the KGB put on a fascinating performance. The fact that black Volgas jam-packed with Armenian Chekists followed not behind but abreast of us—we on the sidewalk and they on the road—that was trivial. The fact that they sat there in the auditorium when I gave a scientific report in the Physics Institute, and patrolled outside the door of the office where my old friend Garik and I were discussing a joint physics project was trivial, too. What was not trivial, however, was the fact that they shut down the *entire* telephone link between Yerevan and Moscow when they discovered the unpleasant information Tanya Khodorovich had begun transmitting to Moscow. "The lines to Moscow are out of order," telephone operators replied to citizens the whole day long. I would not have believed that the KGB could make such simple, costly, and effective decisions, had there not been an analogous case when Tanya Plyushch once tried to carry from Kiev to Moscow particularly shocking information about the torments being visited on her dissident husband, Leonid, in a special psychiatric hospital. At the railway station there were no tickets to Moscow. Finding this suspicious, Tanya went to every ticket window and questioned every cashier. One of them finally confided, "There are tickets—but we were just ordered not to sell them for the time being." Tanya rushed over to the bus station. There were tickets. But at the first stop the Ukrainian KGB made her get off and returned her to Kiev.

Still, what was the sense of cutting off information temporarily, knowing that all the same it would get through later on?

Just in case. Late information is not nearly so dangerous. And then, maybe tomorrow they'll arrest the bearer of the information—so it won't get through.

But why not arrest immediately?

Because they haven't arrested him or her before. Sound ridiculous? It's not. Their case has only just been started, the case file is still not very thick. And it promises to be thick. What they need are big cases. Big cases mean big promotions in the service. So they'll wait.

Although we dissidents were absolutely united in our struggle with the Soviet regime, we were far from agreement on the question "What is to be done?" None of my friends seemed to share my view that political reform in the Soviet Union could come from the very top as a result of our pressure. No doubt Gorbachev didn't share it either in those days. On December 10, 1974, International Human Rights Day, I distributed an open appeal to the regime in which I said that possessing an unlimited apparatus of repression, the government could without the least fear carry out *from above* certain minimum reforms urgently needed by the state. Among them were a general political amnesty; free movement of citizens out of, into, and within the country; independent publishing houses; and creation of legislation on strikes. This last point was unacceptable to some of my friends. Valentin Turchin and Andrei Sakharov, for example, argued that strikes could destroy the economy. I agreed, but saw them as the only weapon workers had for improving their lives. And so, in principle, strikes had to be considered a normal part of a healthy society.

At the end of December, Sergei Kovalyov, one of the most respected of the dissidents, was arrested.

Later on, in camp, I would recall 1975 as the last happy and peaceful year. The children were healthy and often came to visit. I finished three physics articles, two of which my coauthors managed to publish in Soviet journals (the third was held up by Makarov-Zemlyansky and his comrades). The Institute of Philosophy, without consulting the KGB, sent my first article on wave logic to an international conference in Canada on methodology, logic, and the philosophy of science, which published it in the conference proceedings. I had a stable pattern of work, dividing my time equally among science, private tutoring, and human rights activities. No one searched, interrogated, or arrested me. And there were only ten plainclothesmen around. The black Volga limousines carrying four Chekists each plus one driver were not yet keeping watch in shifts beneath our windows. (All of that would begin next year—unmuffled motors, squealing brakes, squawking walkie-talkies round the clock, seven days a week.)

The plainclothesmen stomped up, down, and across the diagonals of our microdistrict.[2] Irina would go up, poke them in the stomach, and say:

"Tell your boss to replace you!"

The stomper silently went off and did not reappear. He was indeed replaced by another, but they all had the same imprint on their faces. Irina would go up to the next one and declare, "We've recognized you!"

---

[2] A planned group of twenty or so big apartment houses that share a school, heating system, and some shops.

This one also disappeared. It is quite possible that the entire student body of the university law department was sent to us for practical training.

However, they still did not accompany us into the woods on our usual Sunday trips to the country—not even during the summer, when we often visited the Bryksins in their rented country house. Inexhaustibly creative Ivan Yemelyanovich was constantly improving something around the place, and I helped him a little. A year and a half later we would part forever: the KGB arrested me, and the summer after that he was murdered out in a field, on the path from his country house to the station, by still undiscovered gangsters. But in that year of 1975 all was peaceful for us both. And the KGB was leaving Anya alone.

The previous autumn they had summoned her to Kuznetsky #24, one of their buildings. The topic of conversation was a summertime trip she had made with Ivan Yemelyanovich and Solzhenitsyn to visit Ivan Yemelyanovich's brother, who lived in a village in the province of Tambov. Solzhenitsyn wanted to record folk language. The brother's family had been extraordinarily delighted, not in the least afraid of being with Solzhenitsyn. Samogon (moonshine vodka) was put on the table not just every day but every hour. Anya and her father drank enough for three; Solzhenitsyn did not drink. Yet Anya, for some reason, could not seem to recollect anything about this visit. Nothing at all. She had even forgotten people's names.

"We know everything about your relationship with Solzhenitsyn," the Chekist told her. "Shall I show you the photos?"

He dug about in his desk, watching her all the while with his cold eyes. He slowly opened the drawer and began to take something out of it: a blank sheet of paper. He turned it over—also blank.

"Listen here! Would you like to go abroad?"

Several days later they again telephoned her and again invited her to Kuznetsky #24.

"What garbage! Just ignore them," we told her in a family council. "Let them send an official notice. You are obliged to put in an appearance only after receiving an official notice."

She ignored their invitation, and they dropped her. It had just been a fishing expedition.

* * *

Despite continual KGB efforts to stop her, Tanya Plyushch kept getting through to Moscow to bring us information about her husband. Leonid Plyushch, a Kiev mathematician and member of one of the earliest dissident organizations, the Initiative Group for the Defense of Human Rights in the USSR, had been put into a special psychiatric hospital in part for having signed a petition criticizing the political abuse of psychiatry. The KGB used incarcerations in special psychiatric hospitals as a punishment for active dissidents and a deterrent against potential ones. Even more than labor camps, people feared these hospitals where political patients were forcibly given agonizingly painful neuroleptic drugs, freely beaten by orderlies, and put together with the violently insane. The only way to struggle against this monstrous perversion of medicine was to send information about it abroad. That struggle had been begun several years earlier by Vladimir Bukovsky and the Kiev psychiatrist Semyon Gluzman.[3] By the mid-seventies other Soviet dissidents had seized it with their teeth.

A central figure for us was a major general and much-decorated veteran of World War II, Pyotr Grigorenko. He had become a critic of the Party in the early sixties and later a leading human rights activist committed to pluralism and opposed to all violent and underground methods. His punishment was to be stripped of his rank and pension, and twice confined in a special psychiatric hospital. Under pressure of international public opinion sustained by information from his courageous wife Zinaida Mikhailovna, Sakharov, Igor Shafarevich, and other dissidents, General Grigorenko was released from his second psychiatric incarceration in June 1974. He came out as he had gone in: a passionate, kindly, noble man of complete inner freedom.

I concentrated my efforts on the Plyushch case, joining Tanya Khodorovich in giving interviews to foreign correspondents and writing appeals to international organizations of mathematicians, psychiatrists, and lawyers. Our information came mainly from Plyushch's wife, Tanya. In the spring of 1975 I went with her to confront the chief Soviet psychiatrist, Pro-

---

[3] Bukovsky and Gluzman landed in the same labor camp, where they continued their collaboration.

fessor Snezhnevsky, in his huge Moscow apartment. He was a criminal rather against his will in the sphere of psychiatric abuse; the real criminal was the director of the famous Serbsky Institute, Professor Georgy Morozov, a KGB collaborator since his student days. Going to him would have been useless.

Snezhnevsky realized why we were there as soon as he saw Tanya, but it was too late to retreat. I immediately began with the case.

"We are asking you to intervene in the actions of Professor Blokhina against Plyushch in the Dnepropetrovsk special hospital-prison. After every single reexamination of the case she writes more and more horrible protocols. He was admitted with your diagnosis of 'sluggish schizophrenia,' and is now being diagnosed as having 'schizophrenia of a paranoid type.'" The illness of "sluggish schizophrenia," something intermediate between normality and a true illness, was a creation of Professor Snezhnevsky.

"Your husband is ill," he said politely but firmly, replying to Tanya instead of to me. "Before we reached this diagnosis, we held him under observation."

"Yes, but the people observing him were common criminals," I interjected.

I meant criminals in a literal sense. Plyushch's behavior had first been directly observed in ordinary prison, and who could have done that other than the common criminals imprisoned with him? However, Snezhnevsky took my remark as referring to himself and blushed slightly.

"I have no reason to doubt the qualifications of the Dnepropetrovsk doctors," he said. "They are in constant consultation with me."

"That is very interesting," I said. "I do not know whether *you* have read your textbook on psychiatry . . . but I, at any rate, have read it. It is written there in black and white that your sluggish schizophrenia *never develops* into paranoid schizophrenia!"

He fell silent. Tanya looked at this gray-haired "chief psychiatrist" with anguish and anger.

"Just tell me," he asked finally, "would things be better if Plyushch were imprisoned in camp?"

"Better!" we cried simultaneously.

"You have trampled his human dignity," Tanya spoke out

with hate. "You have condemned him to endless torments instead of seven years of camp. And what torments! He's all
swollen up from injections. They're giving him shots of triftazin;
you can go mad from the pain. They keep him locked up with
the violently insane. You . . ."

Snezhnevsky stood up. So did we.

"When you report to whomever you have to report," I said,
"then kindly explain to them that psychiatric repressions subvert the prestige of the state."

Snezhnevsky grew pale. "You are insulting me again!"

We left. "He nearly bit your ear off," said Tanya.

At my trial I requested that Snezhnevsky be summoned as
a witness, so that he could repeat this conversation. After all,
my five appeals defending Plyushch were in the charges against
me as slander against the Soviet system. Snezhnevsky refused
to testify, claiming that he was being sent on an official trip at
the very beginning of my trial.

The turning point in the defense of Plyushch was a huge
meeting in Paris organized by the non-Communist "leftists without illusions" in the autumn of 1975. I dictated a speech for it
over the telephone. The French Communists refused to participate, then realized their tactical error. Georges Marchais,
general secretary of the French Communist Party, spoke with
Brezhnev about Plyushch, and right after that, in the middle
of a deeper and deeper descent into schizophrenia, Plyushch
instantaneously recovered. In January 1976 he was deported
abroad with his family and went to live in Paris. After his deportation we joked that only an insane man would flirt with
Trotskyism in Russia. Plyushch had been probably the only
Trotskyite left in the Soviet Union. In Paris he gradually moved
away from it.

Just after my visit to Snezhnevsky with Tanya Plyushch,
the KGB actively started in on our Amnesty group. It had been
only a matter of time. They searched Turchin's place and made
search after search of the one-room apartment of Tverdokhlebov, our secretary, removing documents and archives the
group needed for its work. Sakharov, Turchin, and I were
present during the last Tverdokhlebov search. Just as the dissidents went to the trials of their friends, they attended searches,
exploiting the KGB rule that an ordinary citizen who came in

during a search could not leave until it was over. The KGB never managed to conduct one without some of us being present as supporters and independent witnesses. This search at Tverdokhlebov's began in the afternoon and lasted until late at night; Irina and Anya Bryksina tossed us sandwiches through the transom. On April 18 Tverdokhlebov was arrested. That same day, the authorities detained Mikola Rudenko and pressured him to quit the group. (He refused.) We wrote a protest against all this to Podgorny, chairman of the Presidium of the Supreme Soviet, and continued our work. When Vladimir Albrecht undertook the duties of secretary, the black Volgas began following him, but Volodya was not yet to be arrested. The KGB went on summer vacation.

That summer I wrote "Is a Nontotalitarian Socialism Possible?" essentially an elaboration of ideas in "Thirteen Questions to Brezhnev," and even the 1956 speech at ITEP. The essay warned Western leftists about the potential danger of a centralized economy: if, in some critical circumstances, centralization of political power were temporarily needed, the combination of both economic and political centralization could create an irreversibly supertotalitarian system—a trap from which escape would be almost impossible. For those who liked the idea of socialism, I proposed an intermediate system that was formally socialist but in fact capitalist. As a necessary stimulus to activity, large-scale means of production would be in the hands of the state, while professionals would manage them freely as if they were private owners; their salaries would depend on the profits of their enterprises. The workers would have to be provided with all democratic rights, including free trade unions, uncensored newspapers, and the right to strike. This would automatically create pressures toward the full democratization of this society of "private initiative without private ownership."

I circulated a draft of my samizdat essay among my friends for comments and criticism. The first reader was Andrei Amalrik. He liked it, but for that matter he liked everything I did, perhaps because I liked everything he did. In his most renowned and elegant essay, "Will the Soviet Union Survive Until 1984?," he predicted the rapid breakdown of the Soviet system, and he was not far off either. The KGB hated him for his independence, quickness of mind, and implacable hatred of the regime—all wrapped up in lightness and mockery. He had just returned from exile, and before that had been in camp, and in exile before that. Forbidden to live in Moscow, he could legally live at his wife's place for only three consecutive days. The militia usually woke him up in the middle of the third night and incarcerated him in a stinking vomit-covered temporary detention cell full of criminals and homeless tramps. Eventually Andrei and Gyuzel found an illegal apartment not far from us and disappeared, going out for walks only after midnight. Irina and I used to visit them, zigzagging between apartment buildings and trees. They finally came out of hiding in 1976, when the Dutch government received permission for them to go to Holland. Amalrik then began to prepare for his departure and take English lessons. Anatoly Shcharansky gave them in my apartment: we needed English, and Tolya needed an officially registered source of income.

In December of 1975 dozens of dissidents from Moscow, Leningrad, and the Baltic traveled to the Lithuanian city of Vilnius for the trial of Sergei Kovalyov, arrested a year earlier for editing *The Chronicle of Current Events* and now being tried for "anti-Soviet agitation and propaganda." While Sakharov was there, Yelena Bonner read his Nobel Prize speech in Oslo. Only Sergei's wife and son were allowed into the courtroom—and even that was amazing. The trial was "open" to the public, but, as usual in trials of well-known dissidents, a special "public" was hauled in on buses, and then it was announced that no seats were available. As usual, too, we gathered in the evening at the apartments of local dissidents and worked up a transcript of the trial proceedings from reports of the defendant's relatives. The official transcripts were always secret, but they were false anyway. During the day we assembled outside the court, surrounded by plainclothesmen and KGB officers, and argued with the militiamen near the doors, signed appeals and petitions, collected funds, discussed the events, worried, tried to catch sight of the accused and wave to him, and shouted "Seryozha! Seryozha!" whenever a metal-covered paddy wagon passed by in which, perhaps (we did not know for sure), they were carrying off Sergei Kovalyov. And we ran after the paddy wagon, calling out "Seryozha!" until it disappeared, in order to give moral support to our comrade.

None of the intellectuals with a stable position inside the Soviet structure openly came forward to defend Sergei. It was not only fear. "There's no question but that the people on the top are a mafia," the physicist Igor Kobzarev told me. "But I'm for them because I fear those others out there"—he pointed to the street—"even more." This was a popular theory. Intellectuals simultaneously sympathized with the dissidents and feared that their propaganda against the authorities would awaken the dark instincts of the masses. However, the intellectuals were being suicidal by not pressing the authorities, *from inside the system,* toward speedy democratic reform. Without it, an explosion of those very dark instincts could indeed be expected. I wrote urgent private letters in this vein to several academicians of the older generation—V. L. Ginzburg, N. N. Bogolyubov, among others—asking that they use their influence to liberate the persecuted scientists Plyushch and Kovalyov, and trying to persuade them to help push the government toward democratic humanization of the system before it was too late.

One Thursday in March of 1976, while I was talking with Amalrik's genius of a cat, and Irina boiled potatoes for my biweekly scientific seminar at home, Tolya Shcharansky arrived with a proposal. Let us appeal to the foreign public, he said, to form committees for monitoring human rights on the basis of the Final Act of the Helsinki Conference on Security and Cooperation in Europe, which the USSR has signed. If they do that and it becomes the norm in the West, then after a while we can create the same sort of committee at home with less risk of persecution.

Ever since the Helsinki Accords had been signed on August 1, 1975, many of us among the dissidents, including some religious activists and even a group of political prisoners in the Mordovia camps, had invoked them in appeals to the West about Soviet violations of human rights. And when the American congresswoman Millicent Fenwick met with Turchin, Levich, and myself in Turchin's apartment that August, we had argued that the West should use the Helsinki Accords to pres-

sure the Soviet government to honor its human rights obligations, and monitor how well it honored them. So Amalrik and
I found Shcharansky's idea timely.

The three of us quickly edited the draft appeal that he had
brought with him, and agreed to collect signatures of Moscow
intellectuals. In the end we did not gather the signatures, having
lost interest in our appeal because it was unlikely to stir up the
West. I understood very well, however, that the Helsinki Accords were very important for the USSR because they actually
took the place of a peace agreement and *fixed the postwar boundaries in Europe*—which were advantageous to the Soviet bloc—
in exchange for human rights and other obligations. (Later on
I developed this idea in our Helsinki Watch Group *Document
No. 10.*) The Accords moved human rights from the sphere of
"internal affairs" and kindhearted international desire to the
sphere of concrete international politics, although this was a
fact that the Soviet government did not admit, and Western
governments did not exploit at the time. But appeals to the
public would not help. We had to create our own committee
and send expert documents to governments about the USSR's
violations of the political agreement it had signed.

So I decided to begin where Shcharansky's proposal left
off. In the course of the next two months I discussed the idea
of the group with Alexeeva, Ginzburg, Larisa Bogoraz, Vitaly
Rubin, and Shcharansky, and wrote up a concise declaration.
It stated that the documents of the group would be handed
over to the heads of the governments that had signed the Accords, and called on the Western public to create analogous
groups for monitoring observance of human rights in their own
countries. I named the group "The Public Group to Support
Compliance with the Helsinki Accords in the USSR."

All that was left was to make the final choice of members.
I invited Tanya Khodorovich, but she categorically refused:

"This whole game with the Helsinki Act is pure Soviet and
only useful to the Soviet regime! Your committee's name, for
that matter, is outrageous. Whom are you intending to support?
Supporting these Accords means supporting the Soviet regime.
No, I won't participate."

"I don't agree with you," I replied. "These are political
Accords; that's their defect but also their value. Political levers
can be used to defend human rights."

"That's exactly what is bad, that you're playing at politics. You're not going to outplay them. They'll outplay you." Like Andrei Dmitriyevich Sakharov at that time, Tanya Khodorovich thought nothing could be changed in Russia; this was probably one more reason why she rejected using any political tactics.

In much the same words as Tanya's I was turned down by Malva Landa, a geologist and flaming defender of human rights.

"A group for support!" she boiled over. "Support of the authorities?" She looked at me with pity.

"Dear Malva," I said to her, "it's not the name that's important. What's important is *who* leads it."

She looked me over appraisingly and left.

Finally the group was almost formed, the members nearly all veterans of the human rights movement: Ludmilla Alexeeva, Mikhail Bernshtam, Alexander Ginzburg, Alexander Korchak, Anatoly Marchenko, Vitaly Rubin, and Anatoly Shcharansky. Marchenko, in his Siberian exile, had learned about the group from his wife, Larisa Bogoraz. I had never met him, but had written appeals in his defense and read *My Testimony*, his memoir of camp life. He did not have much formal education and had spent many years of his life in camp. Yet this, his first book, was a masterpiece. In its purity, courage, and intelligence I felt that I knew Marchenko himself. To have him in our group was an honor.

I was in no hurry to announce the existence of the group, since the final draft of our declaration had not yet been discussed by everyone. But on May 12, 1976, I discovered in my mailbox an official notice to appear at the district KGB at 11:00 A.M. Published laws regulating the mutual relations between citizens and the KGB do not exist, so I violated nothing in ignoring their notice.

At one o'clock a jeep rolled up and two young men approached my balcony, where I stood watching them.

"Yuri Fyodorovich—"

"Sorry, I'm busy."

"Very well, then. Here is an official notice for you to appear at four P.M. today. Don't be late. The address is on it." I took the card so that they wouldn't take me. They drove off.

The KGB clearly knew of my plans and wanted to block

them. I had to announce the creation of the group at once, before they got their machinery in gear. Luckily the energetic young dissident Mikhail Bernshtam was in my apartment. It was necessary for us to canvass all those with whom I had an understanding. Were they agreeable to an immediate disclosure of their names as members of the group? We arranged to meet at Sakharov's apartment at ten-thirty that evening.

By ten-thirty only Shcharansky could not be reached. Everyone else confirmed their acceptance, and General Grigorenko had joined the group. I gave Sakharov the text of our declaration, asking whether he did not wish to be our head.

"Yura, my experience with groups is rather negative. I am not going to join. But your document is a very serious one, and I support it." I did not insist. To tell the truth, I thought I might be better as an organizer.

"I'll join," said Yelena Bonner, and she immediately sat down to retype the text of the declaration with the names of the participants, their addresses, and the telephone numbers of those who had phones.

Andrei Dmitriyevich had invited a correspondent from an English newspaper. As soon as he arrived, I read the declaration aloud:

" 'The Public Group to Support Compliance with the Helsinki Accords in the USSR has been founded, May 12, 1976, in Moscow. The Group's aim is to support observance of the humanitarian articles of the Final Act of the Conference on Security and Cooperation in Europe. . . .

" 'The Group considers its immediate aim to be that of informing all Heads of States signatory to the Final Act of August 1, 1975, and the public as well, of direct violations of the articles mentioned above. Given this aim, the Group:

" '1) will accept directly from Soviet citizens *written* complaints that concern them personally and relate to violation of the articles mentioned above, and will forward such complaints in condensed form to all Heads of States signatory to the Final Act, as well as to the public. The Group will retain the original complaint signed by the author;

" '2) will gather, with the assistance of the public, other information about violations of the articles mentioned above, organize it, and forward it along with our appraisal of its reliability to the appropriate Heads of States and to the public.

" 'In some cases, when the Group encounters specific information about extreme acts of inhumanity such as:

- removing children from the custody of religious parents who wish to raise their children in their own faith;
- compulsory psychiatric treatment aimed at altering a person's ideas, conscience, religion, beliefs;
- the most dramatic cases of division of families;
- extreme inhumanity in treating prisoners of conscience,

the Group intends to ask Heads of States and the public to form International Commissions for verifying such information on the spot . . ."[4]

After reading the names of the members, I gave our declaration to the correspondent. It was midnight.

I returned home at 1:00 A.M. In the morning the KGB was going to come and perhaps arrest me. Correspondents would pay more attention to my arrest than to the important news about the creation of the group. They had to be given two or three uneventful days to report *only* about that.

I dressed as warmly as possible. Irina turned off the light. The apartment was bugged, so we pretended to go to bed. Irina opened the window. I climbed out first. The thick bushes and trees concealed us as we went along the wall. She kissed me, and I disappeared. I was on the lam for the next two days.

---

[4]See Appendix II for the full text.

FIFTEEN

The Helsinki Watch

I lived buttoned up in the apartment of my friends, the Korchaks, in a small town outside Moscow. Dr. Korchak, an astrophysicist, a war veteran descended from Orenburg Cossacks, and a newcomer among the dissidents, worked in the same institute I had been expelled from two and a half years earlier. He regularly monitored the Voice of America and other foreign radio "voices." At last, on May 14, he heard them comment on foreign newspaper reports about the creation of our group. This was all I needed, and just before dawn on May 15 I returned home. The stompers were slumbering away.

That morning Malva Landa and a few other people dropped by to see me. At ten o'clock we all left. When we were crossing the avenue, I was seized from behind, pushed into a car that had silently crept up on us, and driven off at high speed. They took me to KGB district headquarters and left me in an empty room.

It was evidently someone's office. On shelves lay bulletins stamped "For Official Use Only." If you put me here, it's your problem, I thought, and began to read them. Leafing through some on China, I found nothing at all like the customary ravings of the Soviet press about China's alliance with world imperialism. They contained real information.

Finally I was escorted to the chief of the district KGB, a run-of-the-mill colonel in civilian clothes. In a bored voice he recited some decree of the Presidium of the Supreme Soviet and then issued a formal warning: if the group I had organized should begin to operate, the matter would be turned over to the Prosecutor's Office. (This meant that I had won the first inning—the whole matter had gone a step higher. Three days earlier they would have warned me not against beginning to operate the group but against forming it.) I refused to sign a document to the effect that I had been warned. The decree of the Presidium that the colonel read had not been published, and therefore, according to another decree, was not a decree. "This decree is all samizdat," I said, "just like your warning. I'm not against your samizdat, but *you* haven't signed *my* declarations."

Our political gains were in fact much greater than I had expected. At the very hour the KGB discovered I was not going to retreat, Tass had issued a declaration, solely for the West, on the formation of the group. It said that the Soviet government was not against monitoring the Helsinki Accords. (This was a lie.) But what was important was who was involved. (That was true.) The person involved was Orlov, a professional "anti-Sovietchik" who had long since left science. (This was a lie.) The group was unconstitutional. (That was absolutely true. Under the Soviet constitution every organization had to be under the leadership of the Communist Party.) The group had been formed, it said, in order to subvert détente and sow doubts as to the faithfulness of the Soviet Union to its international obligations.

As for our sowing doubts in signing the Helsinki Accords, the heads of the Western governments *had not doubted* that the Soviet Union would *fail* to discharge its obligations in the area of human rights, but they went along with this as an unavoidable evil. The purpose of our group was, first and foremost, to change this "Munich" approach of the West.

So far as détente was concerned, that was precisely what the West was prepared to sacrifice human rights in the USSR for. Yet in actual fact, under Brezhnev the West did not even get détente. While the talks on détente proceeded, there was a rapid growth of Soviet medium-range rockets in Europe, and the Soviet military presence in Latin America, Africa, and Asia sharply increased. Meanwhile, the dissidents had not only no opportunity to protest against the Soviet government's reckless subversion of détente, but even no chance to get the information necessary for protest. All the democratic dissidents understood that only democratization of the USSR—including freedom of information and protest, as well as open borders—could ensure mutual security. However, few people in the West understood this; even fewer believed that democratization in the USSR was possible. The Moscow Helsinki Watch Group acted as if it were, in principle, possible—and ten years after us, it became clear that we were not mistaken.

One way or another the May 15 declaration of Tass gave us the publicity that helped clear a path to Western governments for our documents. At the same time, thanks to the foreign radio "voices," more and more people inside our country began to seek an international defense of their rights with the help of our group. Appeals for assistance to international organizations, so commonplace in the contemporary civilized world, had up until then been uncommon in the isolated USSR.

Not knowing how the KGB's seizure of me would end, all of our group with the exception of exiled Anatoly Marchenko assembled at the Sakharovs', determined to announce the start of our operations. They invited foreign correspondents. Malva declared that in this situation she considered it her moral duty to join the group. I went straight home when the KGB finally released me, learned of the meeting in Sakharov's apartment, and raced over there to issue a formal statement: as of that day, May 15, 1976, the Helsinki Watch Group would get down to work. What astonished me at the time was the astonishment of the correspondents. They kept asking if we would really begin our work despite the KGB warning and the Tass declaration. One of them had even filed a report that we had dissolved the group.

The Seventh-Day Adventists had an underground printing plant with very good typefaces where they published books about their interpretation of Christianity and about the rule of terror by Soviet state atheism, which, they wrote, contradicted Lenin's decrees. Their leader, Vladimir Shelkov, a very old man, would be arrested for this and perish several years later in a Siberian camp below Yakutsk. The Adventists established a tie with Ginzburg and me, and using our designs printed letterhead stationery for our documents. They were prepared to print the documents themselves, but that would have broken the extremely fast tempo we had adopted for "publication."

For almost nine months the KGB held off from arresting any of the group, busy preparing big cases against us. None of us said aloud that we needed to make haste while we were still at liberty, and perhaps it was only Alexander Ginzburg and I who foresaw the arrests. The rather dramatic beginning of the project, the fear of losing momentum, and the strong personalities of the participants gave us a swift pace. Every two weeks we put out a large, numbered informational document, plus announcements. Each was scrupulously accurate, deliberately academic, even pedantic in tone, and focused precisely on specific violations of the Helsinki Accords. All the documents were edited and typed by Ludmilla Alexeeva. I established the elastic rule that each member signed only what he or she wished to sign, because a requirement of consensus would have held up fast production of useful documents.

We presented our very first document on May 18 at a press conference in Sakharov's apartment. Written by Grigorenko and Bernshtam, and signed by all members of the group, *Document No. 1* described the dramatic trial of Mustafa Dzhemilyev in the Siberian city of Omsk. Sakharov traveled there, but was refused entry into the courtroom; his wife was rudely pushed around by the militia—for which Sakharov slapped a militiaman across the face. The principal witness against Dzhemilyev, himself a prisoner, proclaimed in court that he was renouncing his pretrial testimony because it had been forced from him under physical and moral pressure by the KGB. The judge, nonetheless, sentenced Dzhemilyev for propaganda on the basis of this prior testimony.

Dzhemilyev was the leader of the peaceful movement to return the Crimean Tatars to the Crimea. In 1944, every last one of them, including newborn infants and centenarians, had been deported from the Crimea to the East, and people said that half had perished in the course of the deportation. In 1967, fourteen years after Stalin's death, they had been officially cleared of the charges that they had collaborated with the Nazis during the war, but had not been permitted to return to their homeland. This restriction on freedom of movement and choice of a place of residence, as well as on equality under the law regardless of nationality, violated rights established in the Helsinki Accords.

Document No. 2, on Soviet disruption of postal and telephonic links between the USSR and the West for political reasons, was written by Shcharansky, Vitaly Rubin, and myself. We covered cutting off of telephone communications, failure to deliver telegrams, letters, and the like, demonstrating that both the practice and even the official rules of the Soviet communications services failed to meet the obligations undertaken in the Helsinki agreements. The participation of refuseniks such as Shcharansky and Rubin in our group was essential; dissidents who, like me, did not intend to emigrate were not nearly so familiar as they with Soviet practices concerning freedom to leave a country or return to it, particularly for reasons of family or employment. Of course Shcharansky, Rubin, and Vladimir Slepak, who later on replaced Rubin, did not restrict themselves to this issue. They were true dissidents, fighting for the human rights of all people.

Dr. Vitaly Rubin, a sinologist specializing in Confucius, and an old acquaintance of my wife Irina, was an intelligent, brave, compassionate man like Shcharansky, but closer to being an armchair scientist than a born leader. One day shortly after Rubin got permission to emigrate, I stood looking out of my kitchen window and saw him headed for my apartment with somebody else. Having inherited caution from my mother, I opened the door but blocked their entry. This was terribly rude to Rubin, whom I liked very much; however, I simply could not let in this other person. I did not like his face.

"Yura," said Rubin, "this is Sanya Lipavsky, an excellent person, and he is going to replace me as head of the seminar on Jewish culture. But he is also prepared to help you, too. He's a physician and has a car—two virtues right off."

"Very well," I said. "Do you have a telephone?"

Lipavsky gave me his telephone number, address, and compliments, but all the same I did not move from the door. Finally they went away.

Lipavsky, a secret agent of both the KGB and CIA, had wormed his way into Shcharansky's confidence and rented a Moscow apartment with him. One year later he gave the false testimony that the KGB needed to charge Shcharansky with treason. I myself never saw the man again and never asked him for anything, just simply crossed him off my mind. Vitaly Rubin whom I named an overseas representative of our group, perished in an automobile crash in Israel.

Amalrik had not joined the group because he and Gyuzel were going abroad. The farewell party for them took place in our apartment. They passed out to their friends everything they possessed—we came into a concert grand and enormous bookshelves—and left for the Netherlands, taking with them only a change of linen and their genius cat. Several years later Andrei Amalrik was en route to Madrid for the third Conference on Security and Cooperation in Europe. He was driving the car. Alongside him sat Gyuzel; dissident friends were in the back. Down the road in the opposite direction came a truck loaded with thin pipes, one of them sticking out to the side. The windshield shattered, the car came to a stop. Gyuzel laughed, then screamed. Everyone was still sitting in his seat. Andrei's throat had been pierced by the steel pipe.

The KGB followed hard on my heels—by foot, by car, by train; in cities, in towns, in villages; through the forest and on the waves of the sea. It was a fascinating game for the children of our friends. One day we went to the forest with the family of the psychiatrist Marat Veksler. His daughter, Katya, kept screaming with delight, "I see him! I see him!" as she spotted the dark jackets of the Chekists now behind one birch tree, now behind another. They were a bit too numerous, with their boundings back and forth, all of them dressed for city work. Evidently they had pursued us all the way from Moscow. Nonetheless there were fewer than a thousand of them, and when it started to bore us, I swiftly led our group away. How could I not lose them in a forest?

But to escape them elsewhere was a real art. Irina and I were once going in a bus to hunt mushrooms, when I noticed a car two hundred yards behind us; it moved and stopped synchronously with the bus. Even a tree stump could understand what it was all about. The shift was relieved and the car changed color but repeated exactly the same maneuvers. We weren't about to go looking for mushrooms with them. "Jump out!" I whispered to Irina at one of the bus stops, just before the door shut. We jumped, the bus promptly drove off, and we sat down behind the bus shelter. Four of them leapt out of their car and ran past us toward the houses on the right, eyes fixed on the ground. It was hard for those boars to raise their heads, so they didn't notice us. When they disappeared, we stood up, waved to their driver—who had seen us but whose walkie-talkie certainly did not work—and crossed the road to the forest. We had won back a free Sunday.

Sometimes the Chekists landed among my now-numerous visitors. One of them naively tried to leave with me a fat briefcase containing, he said, correspondence with the Ministry of Defense on the illegal shutdown of a nursery school. Another left behind his camera loaded with film; Irina noticed it, grabbed the camera, and caught up with the benefactor. The film, he had said, contained shots of the militia beating people up. People are beaten by the militia, of course, who didn't know that? But he had added that the main snapshots were buried in a place we happened to know was just across from the district KGB. He actually believed we would rush over there with a little shovel. The KGB was indeed full of fools.

Insane people burst in on us.

Most of my visitors, however, were not Chekists or lunatics but normal people who came to tell me about real misfortunes. From distant provinces they brought hair-raising stories of illegalities and sufferings. Typically there would be an attempt to expose local corruption; then dismissal from a decent job; a visit to Moscow bureaucrats, in search of justice; expulsion from the Party; imprisonment in a psychiatric hospital; disintegration of family, disintegration of everything; then an attempt to break through to the American Embassy to ask for refuge; and finally a psychiatric hospital again.

Among the workers who visited was a crane operator named Dubov from the Urals, who had distributed pages from the *Program of the Communist Party of the Soviet Union* on which promises were made of a better life just around the corner. Dubov had rubber-stamped the pages "Unfulfilled." For that he had received a year in a special psychiatric hospital. And there was the remarkable Vladimir Klebanov, a former miner who had been sent to a psychiatric hospital for his independence as an official trade-union leader. Now he wanted to organize an unofficial trade union. After my arrest, he was sent to a psychiatric hospital for the second time.

The most regular visitors were activists of religious minorities, whose problems directly related to the human rights articles of the Helsinki Accords. Our group collected an enormous amount of information about the persecution of religious families—fines, demolition of their houses, and removal of their children on the basis of the Code on Family and Marriage, with its cryptic demand that parents educate their children "in the spirit of the moral code of the builder of Communism." The phenomenon of removing children from their families for ideological reasons appeared in Russia before the Bolsheviks; Lev Tolstoi struggled against it in the last century. Irina and I already knew a great deal about the situation of such children from our worker friend Anatoly Vlasov, a Pentecostal.

The right of spiritual ties between parents and children was, from my point of view, the most vital of all rights; it was necessary to fight for it with all possible intensity. I composed a detailed exposé (*Document No. 5*). Later, after interrogating many dozens of religious witnesses, the KGB could not obtain a single refutation of this document. One of the typical episodes they obviously did not want to go on the record was described in an appeal by peasants of a Ukrainian village. Seventh-Day Adventists brought it to me. The militia had gone to this village to remove someone's young daughter to an orphanage, but the little girl ran away to the forest. The militia left with nothing, and the mother was compelled to keep her child hidden, because without official documents the growing girl would be an outlaw in the state.

Unfortunately, few atheists in the USSR ever protested against this abominable policy of confiscating children. But the protests and information sent to the West by dissidents and members of Christian groups certainly did have an effect, and the situation of children in religious families improved even before Gorbachev.

Eighteen documents were produced by the group in the nine months before my arrest, including an analysis I made (*No. 10*) of how the Helsinki Accords could be used in the struggle for human rights. The others covered a broad range

—from the situation of prisoners and psychiatric abuse, to persecution of religious and national minorities, and lack of freedom to emigrate. The group's documents on the situation of prisoners were prepared by Malva Landa, Ludmilla Alexeeva, and Alexander Ginzburg—who by now had become administrator of Solzhenitsyn's Russian Social Fund to Aid Political Prisoners and Their Families. Possessing broad contacts with prisoners and dissidents in Russia, the Baltic states, and the Ukraine, they were able to obtain information secretly from camps and from extracts of regulations stamped "For Official Use Only." (The authorities' classifying of such information as secret was itself a violation of human rights.) *Document No. 3* described with great precision the food, work, and criminal medical service in the camps and prisons, as well as punishment by hunger and cold in isolation cells. Other documents described the persecution of prisoners' families as well as administrative persecutions of prisoners after their release, and listed new arrests.

One document (*No. 9*) was entirely devoted to the case of an ethnic Russian village, part of which wanted to leave for Israel. An elder from the village of Ilinka in Voronezh Province had appeared at the Moscow synagogue, seeking activist refuseniks. He had a certificate from his village Soviet, in place of a passport, which permitted him to be absent for just five days. He told the story of how there were people in his village who had long been practicing Judaism; this had always been difficult, and now they wanted to leave Russia for Israel. But the invitations sent to them had been confiscated by the chairman of the village Soviet. Could they possibly obtain new ones? Shcharansky and Slepak arranged invitations, then drove with Lipavsky to Ilinka to deliver them—and at the same time verify all the information about the village. Eight months later the KGB charged Shcharansky with making this journey for purposes of espionage, and charged me with complicity.

Journeys of this sort, simultaneously aimed at verifying information and helping people, were constantly being undertaken by members of our group. Ludmilla Alexeeva traveled to Lithuania on the cases of two persecuted Roman Catholic priests and several school pupils who had been expelled from school for participation in a religious circle. Lidiya Voronina traveled all the way to the Far East to verify on the spot the status of a large congregation of Pentecostals, numbering about two thousand, who had decided together with the Pentecostals of the North Caucasus to emigrate from a country where they had suffered decades of repression. Alexander Ginzburg and Valentin Turchin traveled to Lvov, Shcharansky and Slepak to Leningrad.

With Irina and my son Sasha, I went to the Western Ukraine in order to understand its spirit and problems; meet the Horyns—intellectuals and former (and future) prisoners now working as stokers; and encourage the family of the prisoner Hell. Needless to say, Ukrainian state security kept us under massive observation, which initially amused Sasha and in the end bored even him. After visiting the families and looking round Lvov, Irina and I traveled by bus to see Ivan Kandyba in the settlement of Pustomyty, leaving Sasha back in Lvov for safety's sake. Kandyba, a lawyer, had just completed fifteen years of special-regime camp with his colleague Lukyanenko merely for restating the legal right of the Ukraine to independence; now he lived under administrative supervision, a sort of parole. We already knew him—right after camp he had come to visit us in Moscow. He was a smallish man, with a worn but lively face. We gave him gifts, had a little to drink with him, and went for a walk. Like Ginzburg and Turchin before us, we tried to dissuade him from joining a Helsinki Watch Group (he joined the Ukrainian group along with the Horyns, following my arrest). At 8:00 P.M. we left, because after eight he did not have the right to poke his nose out on the street. But just as he stepped a bit beyond his gate to hug us one more time, the Pustomyty militia seized him and hauled him off. They drew up charges, adding half a year to his administrative supervision. One more violation would mean trial, and camp or exile, like Anatoly Marchenko. They detained Irina and myself half the night in their headquarters.

Then, with heavy hearts, we went on vacation. From Lvov a Ukrainian woman took the three of us off to a distant Carpathian village where her recommendation—"They're Russians, but nice"—made it possible for us to rent a house. Our ostentatiously visible tail was not there, so we freely walked in the beech forests, gathered mushrooms, and observed delicate black salamanders with bright yellow spots. I studied a clever earthworm who got down from a stone six inches high by curling himself into two and a half spirals, half an inch in diameter, and rolling off to the ground. After a month of rest we returned to Moscow.

In the late autumn and winter of 1976–77 the Helsinki Watch movement began.[1] It grew quickly. In November the Ukrainian and Lithuanian groups were created with the help of our group. In December Gleb Yakunin created the Christian Committee for the Defense of Believers' Rights in Moscow with our support. In January the Georgian group was created, and in February an English group, and a group composed of parliamentarians from nine European countries. The Armenian group was created in April, after my arrest.

The provincial Helsinki Watch groups could not work without our help, because they were addressing their documents to the heads of the thirty-five countries that had signed the Helsinki Accords, and all the embassies were concentrated in Moscow. We undertook to transmit their documents for them. Right at the very beginning I had tried sending our documents to Brezhnev and the embassies by mail. From Brezhnev's office came a notice of delivery; from the others, nothing. I had not expected anything else, but the attempt had to be made. After this we announced at one of our biweekly press conferences that we had been forced to abandon postal communications and would transmit our documents to embassies via foreign correspondents. In practice this was not so easy. Although several Western correspondents generously took documents at our press conferences, not all of the Western embassies were prepared to accept them, and the journalists of the socialist bloc pretended not to be interested in us at all.

"Your group has been declared illegal," explained the political secretary of the West German Embassy, a Social Democrat. "We cannot have anything to do with you." Our documents were invariably accepted by the Americans (who transmitted them to the British and the Canadians), the Italians, and the Belgians; sometimes by the French and the Scandinavians. In the Belgrade Conference volume of my criminal case file I saw

---

[1]That autumn and winter also saw the creation of important human rights groups in Eastern Europe: the Workers' Defense Committee in Poland (September), and Charter 77 in Czechoslovakia (January).

only English and Italian translations of all the documents of the Moscow group.

The KGB began its general offensive after December 18, 1976, the day the brave imprisoned Vladimir Bukovsky was traded for the imprisoned Chilean Communist leader Luis Corvalán. Under cover of the noise created by the exchange, the KGB began intensive searches of the homes of Helsinki Watch members.

On December 24 they searched the apartment of Mikola Rudenko, leader of the Ukrainian group, and planted some dollars on him so as to charge him with violating foreign-exchange laws. (He beat off this attack, and the charges were not left in his sentence.) The very same day they searched the homes of two other members of his group, planting pornography on the writer Oles Berdnyk, and a German rifle of wartime vintage in the garden shed of the country schoolteacher Oleksy Tikhy. On January 4 they searched the apartments of members of the Moscow group—Lyuda Alexeeva, Lidiya Voronina, and Alexander Ginzburg—and planted foreign money in Ginzburg's toilet. (They were forced to retreat on this one, too, and drop the charges.)

Later that day they searched our place. At about ten o'clock we heard a commanding knock on the door. "Don't open it, Irina," I said. "Burn these papers and those, and I'll flush the rest down the toilet." The knocking ceased; then someone came with tools, and they started breaking down the door. We only managed to destroy papers that might get other people in trouble. When they did break in, the kitchen was full of smoke, and we were sitting calmly and sadly, side by side, in our chairs. "On what grounds have you burst in here?" I demanded. There were four of them: a public prosecutor named Tikhonov, two interrogators, and a witness. They showed me the prosecutor's search warrant and their identifications. At that moment, calculating that there might be a search going on at our apartment, Alexander Podrabinek entered. They emptied his pockets as well, and refused to let him leave—but that was how he had planned it.

Three of them rummaged around, setting aside doubtful papers and books. Poems of Akhmatova and Tsvetayeva, in Western editions, were unhesitatingly seized. Tikhonov put on

his pile Andrei Bely's novel *Petersburg*, in the Soviet edition of
the thirties, which I treasured; then he put it back on the shelf,
then on his pile, then on the shelf, then on his pile. The process
ended with the book back on the shelf. I sympathized with him.
It was difficult to make judgments in the absence of definitions;
class intuition might betray you. The witness, a somewhat embarrassed young man, stood in the middle of the room. "Don't
go near the things," I told him. The three of us supervised the
three of them—not stepping back even one step, for even a
second. "You aren't going to manage to plant anything in this
apartment!" I warned them. They said nothing, their movements were nervous. We discovered why when Irina turned on
the radio and we heard on the BBC that according to Tass, a
search *had* been carried out at Orlov's and documents *had been*
discovered linking him to the NTS. (The NTS is a genuine
émigré organization in the West, but at the time I believed it
was simply a KGB fiction.) The interrogators, who had not yet
looked through half of what was there, interrupted their search
and attentively listened alongside us. "One can expect anything
from you, you have no conscience!" Irina shouted at them. "But
you aren't going to plant a thing on us!" And they didn't, because it would have raised a storm. Those poisonous Orlovs
would have told correspondents about the unprofessional work
of the KGB, and asked that more competent people be sent
next time.

The search lasted about eight hours.

The next day, when members of the group were leaving
Turchin's home for a press conference, two men ran up to us
and tried to seize me. The women—Malva, Lyuda, and Lidiya
—remembered Solzhenitsyn's instructions in *Archipelago* and
encircled me, shouting, "Help! Help!" to get the attention of
passersby. I quickly told them what I had planned to say at the
press conference. Other KGB men came running from all sides,
pulled me away, shoved me into a car, and drove off.

They delivered me to the Moscow Prosecutor's Office, to
that very same Tikhonov; I was formally there for interrogation
as a witness in the case against *The Chronicle of Current Events*.
It was always done this way with a person whose fate they had
long since decided: first interrogate him as a witness in some
case, then subsequently as a suspect in his own case, and only

afterward as a defendant. In the role of a "witness" maybe the
person would talk about himself. By law a defendant has the
right to refuse to testify; a witness does not. The penalty for
refusal is comparatively slight, but interrogators deceive the
witness and threaten a heavy one. Tikhonov asked about the
papers confiscated during the search, among which there was
not even one copy of the *Chronicle*. I replied that in persecuting
people for their beliefs and for having information on violations
of human rights, they were violating the Helsinki Accords,
which had been signed by the Soviet government.

Prosecutor Tikhonov was simply a pawn. He conducted
the interrogation unenthusiastically, then phoned somewhere:
"What are we supposed to do with Orlov?" Evidently instructed
to release me for now, he led me out to the street himself. On
the way he began a discussion about the division of legislative,
executive, and judicial powers. Uniting these functions, he said,
permits swifter achievement of a given goal. "Means are more
important than ends," I objected.

"Are you trying to tell me that the means can destroy the
end?" he asked, astonishing me with some comprehension of
the problem.

That very same day, January 5, 1977, Alexander Podra-
binek's commission announced the start of its operations. The
Working Commission to Investigate the Use of Psychiatry for
Political Purposes was formally affiliated with our Helsinki
Watch Group and worked to a high medical and legal standard.
Its members included two psychiatrists and one lawyer. To cre-
ate such a group at such a time!

On January 8 an explosion occurred in a car of the Moscow
metro. Tass reported that many people had been killed, and
the Soviet journalist Victor Louis, who was openly connected
to the KGB, at once informed the West that the explosive had
been planted by dissidents and nationalists. Rumors circulated
about some explosions in stores. In interviews with correspondents I suggested that the explosions had been KGB provocations, comparing them with the Reichstag fire of 1933 in
Germany, which the Nazis used against the Communists. The
KGB, I said, wished to use the explosions to crush the dissident
movement.

A few days later at a press conference in my apartment,
all of the Helsinki Watch groups and other human rights or-

ganizations issued a joint declaration condemning the terrorism. After a few more days, the secretary of our Amnesty International group, Vladimir Albrecht, was interrogated about the explosion. But when I was questioned "as a witness" twice more, there was no mention of it. Automobiles without license plates continually accompanied me on the streets now. In between these interrogations my old teacher, Professor Berestetsky, died. I was already so cut off from the scientific community that I had not even known about it. His wife, Olesya, asked me through Zhenya Tarasov to attend the funeral service at ITEP, and Lev Okun got me in. When I told Olesya that the moral example of Vladimir Borisovich had played a crucial role in my life, she wept.

On the day of the funeral some friends who worked in publishing warned me that an article attacking me was being prepared at *The Literary Gazette*. It had been taken to the Central Committee of the Communist Party of the Soviet Union for checking, had been corrected, again taken to the Central Committee, and so on several times more. The article appeared, on February 2—a very primitive slander saying that I had abandoned my children without any financial support, and Alexander Ginzburg had purchased anti-Soviet information from Pentecostal priests. That afternoon, Valya Turchin told me some man had come to inform him that I would be arrested the next day. I did not ask Valya to elaborate. For a long time I had felt they were preparing my arrest.

"In Stalin's time," Valya said, "people used to go off for a while and then sometimes the arrest was canceled. Maybe you ought to try it? You could wait things out at my brother's, he's not under suspicion." I reflected that if I went into hiding as Amalrik once had, I could in principle still work with the group and meet regularly with foreign correspondents in unexpected locations. Emigration was out of the question. As I had declared several times to correspondents, I would leave the country only by force.[2]

That evening we held a press conference at Ginzburg's apartment about the article in *The Literary Gazette*. Witnesses,

---

[2] Although the KGB had blocked my mail and telephone calls ever since the creation of our Helsinki Watch Group, they had recently let through an invitation to address the Norwegian Parliament. Clearly, they hoped I would leave the country. Just as clearly, they would have prevented my return—which was why I declined the invitation.

including Anatoly Vlasov and his wife, who had come from the other end of Moscow with their three small children, talked about the "author" of the article—not, that is, the Central Committee, but the man behind whose back they were hiding. He was a notorious swindler who at one time had managed to rob a trustful congregation of Pentecostals by representing himself as a persecuted Pentecostal. (Ten years later I encountered his name again: he was serving one more term for some swindling, in a camp up north. The slanderous article obviously had not helped him.) After the Vlasovs spoke, Ginzburg delivered a report on "the Russian Social Fund." I wondered why he was giving it at such a press conference, and then realized that he expected arrest, too. He had been harassed by searches and detentions all these years. As a former prisoner, he was not allowed to spend more than three consecutive days in Moscow with his wife and two children. The only thing restraining the KGB was his close connection with Solzhenitsyn and Sakharov. And Ginzburg knew it.

When we got home, I told Irina that I had to disappear for a while. I did not have the heart to tell her directly about the arrest, but she understood. At ten o'clock, just as I was preparing to leave, the doorbell rang. We now had a peephole in the new door that a worker from the repair shop had installed free. ("They told me to help Orlov," he explained.) Irina looked through the peephole. A militiaman. Alone. So it was not an arrest. I went into the back room and put out the light. The very courteous captain had brought a notice calling me for interrogation in the morning. That meant they had to be arresting me there. That's how it was with Sergei Kovalyov. Irina refused to take the notice. It was not addressed to her. "Your husband?" "Away." "Where?" "Don't know. He's away." The captain left. It was all the same to him.

Now I had to leave immediately; they would be looking for me soon. Marat Veksler was visiting us. I traded coats and caps with him, embraced Irina, and climbed out the window. I would not be seeing my home again.

First I kept a long lookout at the entry of the apartment house next door. When there was no one in sight, I emerged and walked in a direction away from the center of Moscow, disguising my normal stride. At the very first crossing I saw a KGB Volga full of people keeping watch. At every big avenue—another black Volga. They couldn't really have managed to raise the alarm while I was getting ready at home, I thought. Still, there's some big KGB operation in progress, and it doesn't matter against whom: I can get caught in the net. After walking for an hour, I jumped on an empty bus headed for the city center and got off somewhere beyond the Circle Line railway. Parked on a side street in the small courtyard of some industrial institute was a truck labeled BREAD. There were no bakers nearby. Two people and four eyes looked straight at me from the cab. It was 2:00 A.M. Once out of their field of view I started to run as fast as I could. Glancing back, I saw that the truck had come out of its hiding place but was not moving in my direction. Across the avenue a black Volga was rounding a corner. Now I had reached some sort of microdistrict. Halfway down a passageway between buildings I was suddenly blinded by the headlights of a car standing there at the end, nose pointed toward me. I jumped sideways into the shadows. At the end of the next passageway the headlights of another car shone straight in my eyes. I went back into the depths.

A large, well-lit avenue ran along the side of the micro-district. There were no black Volgas near the bus stop. When a bus approached, I left the shadows and jumped into it. This was the bus I needed—what a piece of luck! I got off near the apartment building where Tarasov and my sons Dima and Sasha lived, slipped through the fence, entered the building, and rang Tarasov's doorbell. Zhenya opened the door. Everyone was asleep. In whispers I quickly explained the situation. He gave me his padded jacket, a cap, and an address. I went back through the fence and took a bus to the Kursk Station. It was three in the morning.

The long-distance train that went through Tula left at 5:00 A.M. The third-class car was full, people sitting and lying on the benches and shelves. One side shelf was unoccupied. It was very dirty, but now that didn't matter. I lay down to sleep without wiping it off.

SIXTEEN

Arrest

As KGB captain Victor Orekhov told the dissident Mark Morozov while sitting with him in Morozov's apartment, and as Morozov recounted to me five years later while sitting with me in our camp, KGB generals were shouting into telephones day and night, directing the search for Orlov. But I had never actually given anyone a pledge to sit tight in my apartment, and certainly no one had asked me to.

At 5:00 A.M. on the morning of February 3, I got off the train at Tula, passed through the outskirts of the city, and stopped on Lock Street in front of an old wooden house surrounded by a solid wooden fence with a door built into it. I knocked. Zhenya's mother, a little woman with a friendly, lined face, opened the door.

"Zinaida Afanasyevna, can you take me in for a few days?" She instantly grasped that I'd had to leave Moscow.

"Come in, come in, Yura, don't even ask. Just stay here as long as you like. We have plenty of room." She bolted the door behind me.

I had never been there before. It was a typical village house in the middle of a modern city, with three small rooms, a Russian stove, a kitchen, and a lavatory outside in the garden. The

Tarasovs had built it before the Revolution. Zhenya's father, a worker, was dead, and his mother lived alone now. I had known her just as long as I had known Zhenya, and Zhenya and I had been friends since the beginning of the fifties.

The street was called Lock Street because at one time, Zinaida Afanasyevna told me, all the households along it used to make locks in addition to working at the factories that were the center of all life in this ancient industrial city. Later on, Lock Street switched to the production of concertinas. Each household made one particular component, and they all divided up the profits. Unfortunately the merchandising was a problem: Soviet law persecuted cottage industries aimed at profit. Once when Zhenya was still a boy, Zinaida Afanasyevna sent him to the bazaar to sell a concertina, and a militiaman seized him. He put Zhenya in a booth until he could send the boy to a preliminary detention cell, but turned his back and Zhenya escaped. The concertina was inherited by the militia. From that time on, Zinaida Afanasyevna swore not to send him there—she had almost got him put in prison! However, all that was in the past. It was years since the workers had made anything serious in their time off; their desire to do so had been destroyed. They just worked at the factory and drank.

As if I were an ordinary guest and nothing had happened, Zhenya's mother sat down at the table with me over tea, and began conversation about Tula in the old days. It was a pleasure listening to her soft, quiet voice, her beautiful Russian speech. I, too, tried pretending that I was a simple guest. But what was happening in Moscow? How long would I wait here in Tula? And wait for what to happen? We had no radio in the house, no news.

Then it turned out that Zhenya's sister sometimes listened to foreign radio broadcasts; she lived with her husband and two children in an individual apartment a five-minute walk away. On February 8 she heard on her radio that the U.S. State Department had expressed concern about the arrest of Ginzburg. He had been arrested on February 3. This changed the situation. It would be immoral for the chairman of a group to stay in hiding when a member had been arrested. And not only that. A suspicious black Volga full of people had appeared at the end of Lock Street, hanging about at the same spot. Twice on the street I noticed looks that were too insistent. To let myself get arrested here would be unfair to the Tarasovs. I had to return at once to Moscow.

On the night of February 8, when I was just about to leave, Zhenya's wife, Mila, came with a note from Turchin and Alexeeva. They thought I should go back to Moscow. I began to say my farewells. "You've thought it over?" asked Zinaida Afanasyevna. "Of course," I replied. "Thought it over well?" "Well." Her wise old eyes examined me. We kissed. I was again fitted out in a new set of clothes, as well as her spectacles—which made me completely unrecognizable. To be sure, I recognized nothing in them myself.

When the train delivered me to the southwest outskirts of Moscow, buses to the center of the city were already running. In the center I transferred to a trolleybus and doubled back to the southwest and Lyuda Alexeeva's apartment house. I had wanted to go home, but Mila warned that security men were posted right at the door to our apartment. My son Sasha had come there, she said, and they had hurled themselves on him in a mob; then they looked him over and backed off.

It was eight in the morning, and stores were already open. I bought bread, a frozen chicken, cheese, and, holding them piled up in front of my face, entered Lyuda's apartment house—a resident back from shopping. The elevator could be observed from the street, but the staircase could not. I climbed up the fifteen stories. Lyuda's mother opened the door. Everyone was home except Lyuda; she was being questioned by the police.

Time was running out. I had to wait for Lyuda to call the press conference, because my voice would be recognized on the telephone. Meanwhile, I would draft personal appeals to give to the foreign correspondents. My paramount duty was to try to get immediate support for Ginzburg. I wrote an appeal to the Soviet authorities, protesting against his arrest and suggesting that they would do better to think about feeding the people than to hunt dissidents. Next I wrote a proposal to the Belgrade Conference on Security and Cooperation in Europe, describing my old idea to hold a series of international conferences, within the framework of the Helsinki Accords, on declassifying secret information in the humanitarian sphere:

illnesses, crime, nutrition, the state of prisoners, and so on. All of this was classified information in the USSR. No matter, I thought, whether these appeals have any effect or not. I must make them.

Lyuda returned from the interrogation ten hours later. I asked her to call our friends and then the correspondents. To be on the safe side, she used a phone on the street. Valya Turchin and Tolya Shcharansky soon arrived to discuss the situation. But first I went with Valya and Lyuda's son, Misha, to explore the attic; if there were a way to get to the other side of the house, I could leave by a different staircase. There was a way. When we returned to Lyuda's apartment, I proposed that I go into hiding again, leading the group and meeting with correspondents from there. Lyuda, Valya, and Tolya firmly vetoed the proposal. The leader of the Helsinki Watch Group, Valya said, must not hide. This would discredit the very concept of the group, which functioned openly as a matter of principle.

It was true. Openness was our principle—although one we had never discussed carefully. Now I had only two choices: to hide myself from the KGB, or permit the KGB to hide me in a camp. The only unclandestine action left now was to be arrested.

"It seems somehow ridiculous to go get myself arrested," I said.

"Of course. But why such a panic?" asked Tolya.

"It's not panic. It's common sense," I replied.

"They aren't going to arrest you," Lyuda said. "They'll summon you to interrogations, yes, but nothing more."

Tolya and Lyuda were totally unconvinced that I was about to be arrested. And Tolya did not believe that he would ever be arrested. It was astonishing. Ginzburg, Rudenko, and Tikhy had already been seized, and it was absolutely obvious that the KGB had decided to finish us off. But that, I reflected, wasn't the problem. The problem was that if we hid, official disinformation would make people believe that we were criminals. So probably I was wrong. In any event, I had no moral right to go against the will of members of the group. I would leave nevertheless Lyuda's place via the attic and spend this night at an apartment the authorities did not know about. I announced my plan.

The newspaper correspondents arrived, two Americans

and one Englishman. They explained that interest in our group had now shot up because of the arrests (which was not so pleasant to hear), asked their questions, got their answers, took my appeals, and left. Lyuda's telephone was immediately shut off, and three black Volgas rolled up to the entry. Her son opened the door and saw one man standing right there, another on the staircase, and another at the entrance to the attic.

"It's too late," I muttered to Lyuda reproachfully. She looked at me reproachfully, too. The very idea of going underground was distasteful to her.

But the KGB held off entering the apartment, and Tolya and Valya were not detained when they left. I wrote down the order in which the members of our group should pass on the leadership, as each was arrested in turn, and gave the list to Lyuda. This is my last free night, I thought, as I lay down to sleep on a folding cot. I am surrounded.... It really would have been better to have gone on home, at least I could have said good-bye to Irina.... No, I would not have been able to break through to her....

At ten in the morning they knocked. When Lyuda opened the door, eight men hurtled into the apartment. One of them rushed to the wardrobe and looked for me inside. Idiot. I was sitting right in front of him on a chair.

They all led me out, and two of them accompanied me in the narrow elevator. One asked the other, "What about Alexeeva?"

"Let her go rot in the West!" the other replied. I smiled.

"And what is so funny?" I did not answer. They really believed that in the West people usually rot.

Down below in the entry hall, twenty street agents of the lowest rank crowded together, some dressed like students, others like hippies. There were also seven or eight old women pensioners with worn shopping bags, "mushrooms" Irina called them, who earned an extra twenty or thirty rubles a month working for the KGB.

I was taken first to the district militia, where Prosecutor Tikhonov formally greeted me and asked me to sign the protocol of the detention. I took the protocol only to write that Tikhonov had planted foreign currency on Ginzburg during his search the previous month. Perhaps after fifty or a hundred years Soviet historians would want to have a record of the truth. Then nothing happened; they were waiting for something. I asked to go to the toilet, and an indifferent militiaman pointed to where it was. I stood there alone, brooding in front of an unbarred window. It was still possible to—

No. Lyuda was right.

They came in a black Volga. I was put in the rear between two Chekists. There was a third up front, plus the driver. Another full Volga drove behind us. They took me to Lefortovo Prison, the interrogation prison of the KGB. It was February 10, 1977. I saw everything as if it were happening to someone else, as if I weren't there at all.

The landscape that unfolded along Red Barracks Street, my last street before prison, looked much more interesting than the one in Lyuda's entry hall. Every half mile, standing by the right-hand curb like a dreadnought, was a black Volga full of men. Every half mile. Im-pres-sive.

Inexhaustible is our Mother Russia. KGB generals catch in a thousand obedient hands intellectuals speaking their own minds. General secretaries train a thousand obedient minds to hunt citizens selling concertinas made with their own hands. General engineers rattle out "Prisoner Korolyov!" and "Prisoner Tupolev!" a thousand times, and the thousand and first time are suddenly freed and—Look! There they go! Korolyov's rockets fly into space and Tupolev's airplanes plow the skies. . . . But this is an illusion. Nothing is eternal. Russia is almost used up.

After numerous questions and a search of every crease and tooth in my body, I was finally given back my clothes and taken to a cell containing two made-up iron beds, one empty bed, and one man. The iron door thundered shut behind me. The peephole opened. The peephole closed.

I lay down on a bed and stretched out. Scientific work, the race to produce documents, the games of the KGB . . . all over. Finally I could rest, even if it was in prison.

Lefortovo is a prison of quality. It has absolutely no bedbugs. The cells house two, three, or four persons, not fifty-two, fifty-three, or fifty-four. Wake-up is 6:00 A.M., which gave me time to do my exercises together with my stoolie cell mate, whom the KGB periodically changed. Sometimes an officer came in with a doctor whose main concern was whether we had been drying our socks out on the radiator. The radiator, solidly boxed in by plywood, had a small grated opening in the top, and, as everyone in Moscow knew, a microphone beneath the grating. My cell mates would conduct political conversations for it, trying to get me to reveal something. I used the same method to transmit remarks about my interrogators. Once I said loudly, "Jerk Face Yakovlev is copying the psychopath Dzerzhinsky. He sits nose to nose with me and tries to hypnotize me with a fiery stare." After that, Yakovlev kept his distance at interrogations.

Breakfast was at seven and nasty—claylike bread and peculiar noodles or kasha poked through a small food hatch in the door that the prisoners called a *kormushka* or "feeding trough." Prison veterans swore the food was royal compared with other Moscow prisons and the camps. After breakfast you had a one-hour walking period that could be called at any time. It was ten echoing paces from the exit of the prison block to a walking yard via the prison courtyard surrounded by four-story walls with barred and shuttered windows. But with the broad sky above, those felt like ten paces of near-freedom. The walking yards were really just cells without roofs, three by five yards, the walls three yards high. You got locked in, and a guard kept watch on you from above. As I jogged from wall to wall, I kept my gaze fixed on the sky or watched sparrows. Families were created and destroyed before my eyes. An old husband carelessly absented himself from his wife, and a new lover occupied his nest beneath the roof of the prison block. The old fellow flew in and began a fight, while the lady sat nearby and watched with admiration. The young lover won, of course.

At nine o'clock a guard usually came in, frisked me, and led me out. We walked from floor to floor and passageway to passageway in the graveyard silence of this very quiet, dark prison block, I ahead, hands behind my back, and he in the rear, clicking his tongue or snapping his fingers so that people proceeding from the opposite direction would know we were coming and not cross paths with us. It took fifteen minutes before we reached the well-lit block where the interrogators had their offices.

Throughout the long months of interrogation, striding past the large, unbarred windows of this block, I excitedly investigated what was outside them. What if I broke through the glass and jumped? Just look, down there is a two-story annex, you wouldn't smash yourself up, and beyond it there's no fence. Well? But I wasn't brave enough or crazy enough.

During the first ten months they interrogated me on my case and on the cases of the other Helsinki Watch groups seven or eight hours a day, from nine or ten in the morning to five, six, or seven in the evening, with an intermission for lunch, six days a week. Sundays were "days off." Evenings and Sundays I often played chess with my cell mates or read books from the prison library. It was a good library, full of classic Russian literature confiscated from intellectuals in the thirties. We were given a copy of *Pravda* every day, and I read that, too.

During the next two months there were supplementary evening interrogations, especially on the Shcharansky case, from six or seven o'clock to ten or eleven and sometimes taking up Sundays as well. Thus, by the end of the investigation I was being interrogated from six in the morning to ten in the evening, with intermissions for lunch and dinner. It was a battle every day, week by week, month by month. But fury and disdain, the conviction of my innocence and their guilt, gave me a kind of equilibrium.

The interrogators worked alone or in pairs, and all the interrogations followed the same pattern. An interrogator dictated a formal question to me, then wrote down my formal answer as I dictated it to him. Whenever there were distortions in what he had written down, I refused to sign that page. For the first six months my answers were mostly "I do not remember," or "That is a leading question," or "I do not reply to questions about other people." In my responses I never named names and, except for special cases (when, for example, the person was no longer in the USSR), did not confirm episodes relating to other persons. The interrogators attacked this approach over and over, without success.

"You maintain that your activities and those of your group have been open, but at the same time you conceal facts from the investigation, you do not reply to the questions directly put to you. Explain your actions."

"Because," I dictated, "the KGB will use any answer I give in defense of other people as a charge against them and myself.

If I explained and defended the legality of someone's actions, you would write in his or her verdict that I *admitted* and *confirmed* the very existence of those 'illegal' actions. You're not conducting an investigation but an execution."

Sometimes I gave long, convoluted answers bristling with subordinate clauses, and then counted my interrogator's grammatical mistakes—ten to fifteen per page on the part of Yuri Sergeyevich Yakovlev.

"Socialism rests on the shoulders of the KGB, on our shoulders!" shouted the insulted interrogator. He had hit the nail exactly, exactly on the head. "That's all very clear, Yuri Sergeich." I said. "The closer we get to Communism, the bigger the KGB staff becomes. What else is socialism going to rest on?" But usually I avoided informal conversations.

I pointed out when the interrogators and the KGB in general violated the laws and the interests of the state. And I smoked. One of my interrogators had informed me that he didn't smoke. I didn't either. I started.

"Why?" he asked, coughing.

"To poison you."

After six months of all this I decided that there was nothing more to talk about, and merely wrote down each question, replying, "Refer to the answer to the preceding question." In response to the very first question I had said, "I refuse to respond to your question." Many pages in the fifty-eight volumes of my case consisted of this algorithm. Fifty-eight volumes arose very simply: Yakovlev filled entire volumes with spoiled sheets. A stack of blank letterhead of the group could constitute several volumes.

Four months later the interrogations began on the Shcharansky case. I changed my algorithm for those sessions· so that my interrogator would say more, giving me more information. I needed to know how the KGB wanted to use the crudely falsified Shcharansky case against our group, in order to try and deflect the blow both from the group and from Tolya himself. One of the charges against him and us was that he used the group and human rights activities generally as a front for espionage. Not, of course, that they believed this for one moment.

"Didn't Shcharansky transmit espionage information to foreigners at your press conferences along with documents of the group, just like this?" asked the interrogator. And he demonstrated how this was supposedly done. I responded that no one specifically passed documents from hand to hand—they simply lay there on tables.

"Who laid them out there and how? Who took your documents and how?"

"I laid them out myself. Whoever wished to, took them."

And so on and so forth. But once you commit yourself to giving some replies, a trained interrogator will ask the sort of questions that can make selective silence dangerous. You feel as if you are walking on a razor blade. Physically I was at the end of my strength when I finished up these sticky nighttime interrogations.

The interrogations on my own case at this time were being conducted as if the KGB had proved no less than "treason to the Motherland." Namely, that I had used the Helsinki Watch Group as a front to help "foreign states carry out hostile activity against the USSR."

"Do you acknowledge the full gravity of the crimes which you committed?"

"See the reply to the preceding question."

"Are you prepared to expiate your guilt before the Soviet state and the Soviet people?"

"Refer to the preceding answer."

"You just keep on laughing," warned Yakovlev. "But we have a case for treason right here in this folder."

The so-called "proofs" consisted of a letter to me from U.S. Representative Dante B. Fascell, chairman of the Commission on Security and Cooperation in Europe, which had been proposed by Millicent Fenwick and established by the U.S. Congress in May 1976. The letter said that their delegation had been refused visas to visit the USSR, where they had wanted to meet with me, and that he wished me the greatest of success. The KGB was interpreting these wishes for success as a "letter of instruction." I interpreted their interpretation as intimidation, but could not rule out something worse. With the KGB, anything is possible.

During all those months in Lefortovo I got no news about my family, and they got none about me. I knew only that Irina had not been arrested: she wrote and signed inventories of the food she brought once a month, and I had the right to check them against the food I was given. Had I been cleverer, I would have arranged some food code in advance, to learn from her what was going on outside the walls of Lefortovo. At the start Irina had been informed that I had simply been "detained"— that is, not arrested—in order to avoid a fuss. Then she was told that I had been charged with Article 190-1, the lightest of all the *political* articles of the Criminal Code. Meanwhile, inside Lefortovo, they had started out by saying to me, "You are going to have many criminal charges against you, all the way from currency speculation to treason." I couldn't fathom at the start what they could be referring to. Eight months later, all the talk was of treason.

My main problem, however, was not a charge of treason but the toilet. Prison food and an almost sedentary life swelled my belly, and I found it unbearably shameful to sit down on the bowl of my cell in the presence of other people. Sometimes I went to interrogations as to salvation, for there the guard could take me to the private lavatory of the interrogators.

Although I was locked up in a prison, no one could have accused me of parasitism. In Lefortovo I provided the salaries for a whole troop of interrogators working full time on my case. I fed their children, dressed their wives, and sent them all to the Black Sea for a rest. The interrogators themselves revealed a great deal about their heroic labors, and I learned even more when I read my case file at the end of the investigation. Conscientious workers, they dedicated all of 1977 to finding ways of charging Irina and me with criminal "foreign currency operations" and "speculation." They interrogated dozens of our acquaintances and combed the state commission stores, which resold used goods on commission, for something left there on consignment. Hurrah! Orlov had consigned some wool! There were three receipts—"speculation!" Three consignments were as legal as one, of course, but the laws weren't written for the KGB. Fortunately I recollected that there had been in fact just *one* single consignment. After I wrote protests naming the interrogators Yakovlev and his boss, Trofimov, as outstanding inventors of new methods of charging citizens with speculation, they were forced to interrogate the clerk who had accepted the consignment. "It was I who divided up the wool into three parts and who wrote out three receipts for Orlov," she testified. "It's much easier to sell it that way. It was *one* consignment only. I repeat again, *one single* consignment." They urgently interrogated another forty receiving clerks from state commission stores, and utterly failed to squeeze "speculation" out of them.

They interrogated academicians, too: Roald Sagdeyev, Lev Okun, Alikhanyan, Vadim Belotserkovsky, Mikhail Leontovich, Vladimir Migulin. No, Orlov had not conducted anti-Soviet conversations with them. Academician Leontovich, one of the creators of the thermodiffusion separation of isotopes, asked them to write down in his protocols that I was a productive physicist and had published numerous articles. But in a separate report sent to the KGB, corresponding member of the Soviet Academy V. V. Migulin contradicted Leontovich, saying that I had not worked in physics for a long time and had not published since 1963. I had actually published more in journals than Migulin himself. However, he had been one of my teachers, and I did not want to disgrace his name when defending myself against the KGB accusation that I had long ago stopped being a scientist. "The academy will never elect him a full member after that," I explained to Yakovlev when I asked him to withdraw Migulin's report from my case file. But Yakovlev did not withdraw it, so I was not silent about it at the trial, and Migulin was never elected. Academician Budker, the inventor of colliding beams and electron cooling, was not interrogated. After my arrest he had sent a telegram to Irina, asking her to come to him in Novosibirsk to talk about me. Alas, the telegram had been intercepted by the KGB and bound into my case file. Budker died soon afterward.

My family was interrogated, of course, as well as Galya and Ira. Galya decisively refuted the moral accusation that I did not provide financial support for our children, saying that I had helped them more than the law demanded. Ira refuted the same accusation. Lev was not interrogated because he was not of age. Sasha spoke only of my positive qualities. Declaring, "I love my father," Dima refused to be interrogated. Irina demanded that she herself write her answers in the protocol. Her testimony consisted of "Carrot Top, I love you." The last letter of her message turned into a line running down the whole page. The interrogator had pulled her hand away.

In the evenings I often wrote protests to the Prosecutor's Office. After they interrogated me about the "forbidden" books seized during the search at my apartment, I complained that the KGB had not yet even attained the standard of the Holy Inquisition, which, unlike the KGB, at least had lists of forbidden books so people knew what was forbidden. . . . I wrote that either the state was schizophrenic or Plyushch was not, since Shcharansky was condemned for allegedly exporting state secrets of Soviet parapsychology while Plyushch had been judged schizophrenic for his interest in the same parapsychology. . . . I demanded that the intellectual capabilities of the interrogators be tested. . . . A whole volume of these protests piled up. Although the prosecutor responded to all of them with the cliché, "No violation of the law has been found," as an embarrassing record of KGB contradictions and arbitrariness they helped wreck the KGB's dream that "You are going to have many criminal charges against you, all the way from speculation to treason."

The "investigation" came to an end in February 1978, a year after my arrest. In a breaking, trembling voice rising to a shriek, Yakovlev announced the revision of charges from Article 190-I (a mild version of Article 70) to Article 70 itself: *"Anti-Soviet agitation and propaganda, with the purpose of subverting or weakening Soviet power. Slanderous fabrications defaming the Soviet social and state system."* I hardly recognized him. He had held out all year long, and suddenly had broken down. Had this been a difficult interrogation? Had he lost his nerve? I recalled his once remarking with genuine hurt, "You are the one who considers himself a humanist, but you write such terrible protests against me!" At the time I had been frightened that my jaw would become dislocated from laughing, as my stepfather's often did. (But I knew how to solve the problem. You just slammed the jaw back in place with the heel of your hand.) Yakovlev was evidently angry, because instead of the expected range "all the way from speculation to treason," the only thing left was just the one clean and honorable Article 70. Had I spoiled his career?

A few days later they brought to my cell his literary essay

entitled "Indictment." Then, for several weeks, the interrogators retyped all fifty-eight volumes of my case file with their
very own hands. "Why aren't you using a typist?" I asked the
interrogator Katalikov.

"But that would be distribution!"

"Distribution—of what?"

"Anti-Soviet propaganda—your documents and declarations."

"Distribution of my propaganda among your own typists???"

This was the same Katalikov who had once asked me, agitated
and nearly blushing: "Yuri Fyodorovich . . . Tell me . . . is it true?
You do not have to answer. . . . Do the dissidents actually condemn
the conduct of Pavlik Morozov?" Pavlik Morozov, the hero of
Komsomol members, betrayed his father, who, according to the
newspapers, had hidden the kulaks' grain (it was really the
kolkhoz grain). With Pavlik's help the authorities found it, seized
it, and arrested his father. The furious kulaks (really the *kolk-
hozniks*) then killed Pavlik. In my childhood we were taught to
be honest and brave Leninists just like Pavlik Morozov.

They granted me two months to acquaint myself with the
finally completed volumes of my case, taking me out of my cell
for this work every day. Under surveillance by the interrogator
Kapayev in a special room, I filled four notebooks with extracts
from the volumes of my case file and from the Code of Criminal
Procedure. Usually they refused to let prisoners see the code,
but for some reason made me an exception. The law forbade
me to see my lawyer until this stage of the case. Now, every
day, he joined me in this room. It was impossible to find a
defense lawyer who was both honest and experienced in political cases, yet not forbidden to practice. Yevgeny Shalman was
honest—but up to this point he had handled only ordinary
criminal cases.

On one occasion when Kapayev left the room, Shalman
wrote "NOBEL" on a scrap of paper, adding out loud, "They
aren't going to give it, of course, but . . ." So our Helsinki Watch
groups had been nominated for a Nobel Peace Prize. I was glad,
but felt no shock. We certainly deserved the prize, and certainly
would not get it.

After studying the case, Shalman wrote out his formal judg-
ment: he considered me not guilty. My interrogators were outraged, evidently not expecting this quiet, sensible lawyer who

wrote works of literary criticism about Pushkin to act as a real lawyer for his client. The KGB summoned him for high-level talks. Then again, and yet again.

"Yuri Fyodorovich," he told me afterward, "I will undertake to defend your honor, but you are going to have to handle the political part of this trial entirely by yourself."

SEVENTEEN

"Write a Book About Us!"

IN the good old Stalinist days they knew how to handle a case. Show trials sparkled like diamonds. But now with these new dissidents, it was really a mess. The defendants didn't follow the script, the stage managers were sloppy, the witnesses forgot their lines, even the judges didn't know their part—and by the time they ran back from the prompter's box to their chairs had forgotten everything.

My trial opened May 15, 1978, almost exactly the second anniversary of the Moscow Helsinki Watch Group, a careless reminder of what was really on trial. In front of the courthouse crowded Sakharov, a hundred dissidents and sympathizers, foreign correspondents, and an observer from the American Embassy. I had been held incommunicado for fifteen months, and we were not supposed to see each other now. However, that did not work out. At six in the morning the guards would put me in a paddy wagon, drive a whole hour to the other end of Moscow, and back the paddy wagon right up to the door of the courthouse. But in the short stretch between the wagon and the door I managed to glimpse my friends two hundred yards away behind a cordon of militiamen and raise my arm in greeting. Immediately a militiaman shoved me in the neck and back, and I flew through the door. Then they would lock me in a preliminary detention cell stinking of vomit, and keep me there in the cold semidarkness for the two or three hours before the session started. After that I was led into the courtroom, where at least I could see Irina, Dima, and Sasha at a distance.

Because of the international attention it had attracted, the trial was declared open to the public. The role of the public was played by people delivered by bus and provided with special passes. The real public was outside—the house was full, they were told. So inside, except for myself, my family, and my lawyer, were only actors playing for themselves and the authors. One author sat through the very first performance until lunch-time: deputy KGB chairman and brother-in-law of General Secretary Brezhnev, General Semyon Kuzmich Tsvigun, modestly dressed in civilian clothes. The other actors did not know it yet, but Tsvigun was one of the greatest actors in the nation. Together with the minister of internal affairs, Shcholokov, and General Secretary Brezhnev's son-in-law, Churbanov, and hundreds of other high-ranking officials of the Party and the KGB and the militia and the Prosecutor's Office, he was guzzling at the state trough. It was the largest-scale corruption of the century in the USSR, perhaps of modern times. Several years later Tsvigun disappeared in mysterious circumstances; people said he shot himself. But now he was still at the peak of his power and needed political cases like air in order to divert attention from his swindles. Naturally he had the best seat in the house, front row, directly opposite the judge's table.

The table was beautifully arranged with the black volumes of my case file, which by now numbered fifty-nine and with the protocol of the trial would increase to sixty—this no doubt being the magic number. All the volumes had miraculously sprouted white labels saying "Secret." At the table sat the judge from the Moscow City Court, V. G. Lubentsova. She was flanked by two "people's assessors," familiarly known as "nodders" because their role is very simple: to agree with the judge. Once upon a time there really were juries in Russia, even under the czar. . . . I sat behind a waist-high barrier, guarded by two soldiers. Opposite was Yemelyanov, the prosecutor, and between me and Tsvigun sat my lawyer, Shalman. It was only here, and only at a distance, that I saw Shalman now. The KGB had thoroughly frightened him. I did in fact have a lawyer who would have been unafraid to conduct a real defense, but he was in London—John Macdonald, Q.C., a well-known Liberal barrister. The Soviet authorities denied him permission even to enter the country.[1]

My guards adjusted their pistols and the play began. Lubentsova started to speak, looking nervously for approval at Tsvigun's honest face; her nodders started nodding. First she refused to call the dozens of witnesses I had requested—not to mention the dozens more I did not know about, who had written to the authorities from camps and abroad, offering to give testimony. That was her prerogative, and a smart move. Then she forbade the "public" to go to the windows lest they become confused by the sight of the protestors on the street. Another smart move. But then she declared that the Helsinki Watch Group had nothing to do with Orlov's case,[2] and forbade both prosecution and defense to quote from any of the documents in the fifty-nine volumes on the table, and even to refer to their titles. Her ukase covered not only my appeals and the Helsinki Group documents, but the KGB evidence against me as well— evidently the KGB was afraid of it all. Even Vishinsky, Stalin's attorney general, would have turned in his grave at this lack of finesse. After all, under the law a trial *means* investigation of the documents on which the indictment is based. Really competent people, he would have said, don't slap "SECRET" labels on documents in open court. If they make you nervous, create your own documents or close the court.

I had to decide whether to participate in such a trial. I wanted to demonstrate to my children, foreign journalists, and the real public the absolute truth of the Helsinki Group documents and the absolute stupidity of the KGB. So I stayed.

---

[1] While I was in Lefortovo, Lyuda Alexeeva emigrated to the United States. En route, she was invited to London by the leader of the British Liberal Party, David Steel, who put her in contact with Macdonald. Lyuda then arranged for Irina to invite him to represent me. Donating his services, Macdonald worked tirelessly on my case and took all the steps that a Soviet defense lawyer should have taken—and more. During my trial he mounted a parallel defense in London, with testimony from émigrés in Europe and the United States about each of the Helsinki Group documents alleged to be "slanderous." In London, after my trial, he sent a formal appeal of the verdict to Moscow. The authorities did not reply.

[2] Three days later, according to *The Times* of London (19 May 1978), Tass accused the British Foreign Office of violating the Helsinki Accords by expressing concern over the trial!

* * *

Before the prosecutor examined me, that first day of the trial, I was permitted to make a statement to the judge: "So as not to waste time, kindly explain to the prosecutor that I bear full responsibility for the content of the documents of the Moscow Public Group to Support Compliance with the Helsinki Accords in the USSR—but that I refuse to answer questions about where, when, and to whom they were transmitted." Nobody else wanted to waste time either. To be sure, the judge ran to the phone every five minutes for guidance, and she and the prosecutor kept interrupting me when I spoke. They still managed the whole trial in three days. The questioning of witnesses took six hours. Six hours for witnesses, after fifteen months of investigation and fifty-nine volumes of documents, was probably rather a lot for the KGB.

And it's not as though they weren't busy with other things. During the trial they searched my sons and Irina four times a day and even punched them when confiscating the tape recorders that Dima and Sasha had hidden under their shirts. (After that, Irina, Dima, and Sasha reconstructed the trial from memory every day. The judge had forbidden any note-taking.) On the third day, during a search, a policewoman stripped Irina down to her brassiere in front of several men. If she had resisted, she would have been arrested and sentenced under criminal Article 190-3. She did not resist, yet neither did she help them. The fools dressed her carelessly, thinking she would just cry and run home, but she marched outside in this state of disarray to show everyone what was going on at the trial. When President Carter publicly condemned the entire course of the trial, he mentioned this episode with Irina.

I was also very busy behind my barrier, the top of which I used as a desk for my four thick notebooks of extracts from the case file and the Code of Criminal Procedure. As Shalman had made clear in Lefortovo, my defense largely depended on myself. So it was I who cross-examined the witnesses on the second day of the trial. According to Soviet law, there are no witnesses "for the prosecution" and "for the defense," because a case has only one side—the side of Truth. Prosecution and defense nominate witnesses; the judge decides which ones will serve the cause of Truth. Lubentsova had decided that only witnesses put forward by the KGB were qualified to do that.

They were almost unbelievably underrehearsed, especially the ones who appeared before lunch. Granted, it must have been difficult to try to prove that my various public appeals and the Helsinki Group documents were slanderous without mentioning them. They did their best. That morning I asked one of the psychiatric witnesses, Professor Blokhina, why Leonid Plyushch had been released from a special psychiatric hospital, and she replied with terrific self-assurance that it was because his mental health had steadily improved. But my case file contained an affidavit from Blokhina testifying that Plyushch's mental health had steadily deteriorated. The KGB had put it in the file to refute my old charge that Plyushch had been kept in the hospital solely for political reasons. Over the shrill objections of the judge—"It is forbidden to cite documents! Forbidden!"—I cited this document from my notebooks. Red-faced and angry, Blokhina kept silent. Another witness that morning was a man called Varna, whose task was to show that, contrary to one of our Helsinki documents, there never had been a strike in the port of Riga. His evidence? He had never heard of the strike. I cross-examined him, and it turned out that he neither worked in the port nor lived in that area. "What are you here for, then?" I asked. Like Blokhina, he was suddenly struck dumb.

The afternoon witnesses all prefaced their testimony with exactly the same statement: "First of all, I confirm all the testimony I gave during the preliminary investigation." Their "second of all" was nonexistent. This was all they had managed to memorize at a lunchtime rehearsal with the KGB. The testimony of all the witnesses was so idiotic that half their names did not appear in the judge's explanation of the final verdict, and the rest were barely mentioned.

On the third day Prosecutor Yemelyanov and I had to present the documents supporting our case. But how could we, when the documents for both sides were in those fifty-nine volumes on the table and we were forbidden even to cite their titles? Yemelyanov simply cited volume numbers and pages. I cited virtually the same ones—but with titles. After that, he gave his speech for the prosecution: "Comrades! Sixty years ago the greatest revolution in the world was carried out. The workers and peasants, under the leadership of the Communist Party, took power into their own hands. . . . At the present time the Soviet people have begun to build communism. . . . In order to slander our society, fabrications about 'various versions of socialism' are invented, for example about 'democratic social-ism.' . . . The imperialists are better informed than anyone about how well Soviet people are actually living, and this arouses their hatred . . ."[3]

Just after Yemelyanov drew out the last note of his rather hysterical aria, I fired my lawyer: I wanted the right to make the speech for the defense myself. Until this moment the "pub-lic" had been more or less quiet. But now the script called for cacophony. From the beginning to the end of my speech— nearly two hours—they shouted, "Better you should tell us about your crimes!" and "You're carrying on propaganda even here!" and various other things I could not make out. The "public" paused for breath when the judge and prosecutor made their usual interruptions. Then I began the final state-ment that every defendant is permitted to make: "You can sentence me to seven years in prison, to five years of exile, you can shoot me, but I am sure that similar trials will not help to eradicate those misfortunes and problems of society about which the documents of the Helsinki groups testify and about which I have tried to speak here. And if—" At this point the judge and her nodders walked out of the court-room, and the guards removed me. As I left, Dima cupped his hands like a megaphone and shouted, "Father, you've won the case!"

The verdict and sentence were read on the fourth day. Out of disrespect for the trial Irina and Dima refused to stand up for the reading. Lubentsova asked Irina three times to stand. "I do not respect your Soviet court," Irina answered, then sud-denly pounced on the bench and locked her arms around it. Three men tried to pull her off the bench, Dima tried to pull the men off Irina, and I had to restrain myself from jumping over the barrier and hurling myself at them. Then a couple of hulking men grabbed Dima's arms and hauled him out of the

---

[3]This speech against democratic socialism did not prevent Yemelyanov from be-coming chief Moscow prosecutor under Gorbachev.

courtroom. Sasha had been at his institute preparing to defend his degree. By the time he arrived, Irina was standing upright between two huge men.[4]

At the end of the reading the "public" broke into enthusiastic applause and yelled, "You should have given him more!" The sentence was seven years of strict-regime labor camp and five years of exile.

KGB captain Orekhov had known before the trial that the KGB had decided on "7 + 5," and through Mark Morozov had alerted the dissidents in the Moscow Helsinki Watch Group and in Sakharov's circle. They should, he said, publicly declare that the trial would be a fraud. But no one believed him.

Hardly anyone ever had.

Through Morozov, he warned Turchin of my arrest. Only I believed the warning. I was arrested. After my first arrest he warned that Podrabinek would be searched. No one believed him. Podrabinek was searched, and then arrested the day before my trial.

The dissidents did not simply find it hard to believe Orekhov. They refused as a matter of principle to engage in any secret collaboration, especially with someone from the KGB. Even when Orekhov gave them passes for the trial, the dissidents did not use them. Part of the tragedy was that Orekhov did not realize how fundamentally his idea of resistance differed from theirs. For him, the path of underground resistance would have seemed the most natural. The KGB and the top level of the party bureaucracy are an "underground" organization, closed off from the people, and the history of resistance exalted by the Soviet government has been the history of the pre-revolutionary Russian underground. The peaceful and open work of the liberals in pre-revolutionary times, the tradition followed by the democratic dissidents now, was either buried in total silence or ridiculed after the Revolution.

---

[4] I learned only in 1989 that while Dima was being thrown out of the court, the Sakharovs were trying to force their way in. "The tall, balding Mr. Sakharov shouted: 'Let me in! Under Soviet law all citizens are allowed in when the sentence is read.' The police appeared to be trying to calm the situation. But, according to witnesses, there was a scuffle. Mrs. Sakharov slapped a policeman in the face, and her husband hit a policeman who was trying to restrain him. The police then seized Mr. Sakharov by his arms, bundled him and his wife into a bus and drove away with them. 'Nobel Prize for Orlov!' Mr. Sakharov shouted as the bus drove away. [They] were released after five hours." *International Herald Tribune*, 19 May 1978.

The tragedy lay also in the fact that many dissidents, convinced that Orekhov was a provocateur, discussed the mysterious KGB captain more or less openly before the microphones planted in every dissident's apartment. No doubt the person most to blame was the half-deaf Morozov himself, who was so careless about controlling the volume of his voice that the dissidents thought *he* was a provocateur. Unfortunately he was the only person through whom Orekhov could pass on his information without arousing suspicion; his official assignment had been to "cultivate" the dissident Morozov.

In the autumn of 1978 Morozov and then Orekhov were arrested. Morozov was first given exile and after that eight years in camp. Orekhov got ten years of camp and was due to be freed in 1988. Alas, no one seems to know whether my unknown friend is, in fact, free.

I remained in Lefortovo until the end of July. It took a couple of weeks to receive an answer to my formal appeal of the verdict, which I'd had to write and file myself because Shalman sent word he was busy. He would have done a much better job. I was fed up with the case. Then it took the KGB two months to produce transportation. Meanwhile I did physics calculations and drafted a paper in wave logic. When Shalman finally came to see me, he was too frightened to deliver them to Irina for safekeeping, and I did not have them on me when Irina was unexpectedly granted a short visit just before I was moved to camp. Two officers confiscated them the day I left.

"Where will I be going from here?" I asked the chief of Lefortovo Prison. It was a silly question, but I hoped to gauge the impact of the Nobel Prize nomination and the protests in the West that Irina had told me about during our brief meeting.

"From here the only place people go is to Siberia!" he replied. "And I imagine you and I are going to meet again. . . ."

The prisoner transport from Lefortovo to Perm Camp 35 in the Urals lasted only a week. During the journey I had a cell to myself, but it was impossible to isolate me entirely from the other prisoners. They already knew who I was. "Orlov! Write a book about us!" "Yes, write about us, Orlov!" they shouted from the neighboring cells of the Stolypin car,[5] where people were so packed in that for twenty-four hours they stood pressed against one another.

When I arrived, I was first kept outside the camp in a hospital that served several political camps, a piece of luck because I had a bad cold and fever. Usually a newcomer, healthy or ill, is put straight into an isolator—a special punishment cell—in the camp's internal prison, by way of introduction to his new life. But the Chekists treated me with caution, waiting for the decision of the Nobel committee. It also helped that I was a corresponding member of the Armenian Academy of Sciences. The chief of the hospital turned out to be a man called Sheliya, who had been a witness at my trial; he testified against our documents on medical treatment in the camps. Sheliya now confided that he had asked to be sent here after medical school because it would be convenient to practice surgery on prisoners. After leaving his hospital, I learned that six prisoners had died in it the previous year.

I felt happy there during the two-hour walks in the hospital courtyard—it was full of greenery, and beyond the fence you could see forests all the way to the horizon. The local KGB man, from Camp 35, strolled in the courtyard with me one day and asked what I would do with the Nobel Prize. "Certainly not give it to you! I'll divide it up among the prisoners of your camp," I said.

In the middle of August I was removed from the hospital to that camp and put to work on the lathe forty-eight hours a week, turning screw taps. Like other camps, Perm Camp 35 consisted of a living zone, with barracks; a working zone, with a factory; and a prison zone, with prison cells, special punishment cells, and cells for work. Zones were separated from each other by barbed wire and fences. Prisoners often called the whole camp, or sometimes the camp minus the prison, "the zone." I was surprised by how well-organized the political prisoners were. Many had long been known to me through samizdat, and amazingly, despite their isolation, many knew me. We met as if we were old friends. Ukrainian nationalists predominated, led by Valery Marchenko, who perished six or

---

[5]Named after the czarist prime minister Pyotr Stolypin (1862–1911), a Stolypin car is a railroad car specially designed to transport prisoners. It is usually attached to the end of an ordinary passenger train. See page 263 for a description.

seven years later in prison. Almost all of them had written renunciations of Soviet citizenship, which was why the KGB hated them most of all the politicals. The Ukrainians and the other prisoners helped me adjust quickly. Pidgorodetsky and Verkholyak—two old Banderists serving twenty-five-year sentences—resewed my black camp uniform and cap so that they looked human, not humiliating. They did that only for their friends.

I stayed in this camp only a month, but it was enough to verify with my own eyes our Helsinki Group documents about prisoners. To establish this fact and to report on sides of prison and camp life that the group had not previously covered, I conceived the idea of a document on the situation of prisoners that would be composed by prisoners themselves and sent to the upcoming Madrid Conference on Security and Cooperation in Europe.

We did it. The Ukrainians Marchenko, Antonuk, and Marinovich, the Lithuanian Plumpa, the Estonian Kiirend, and I divided up the subjects. Each part of the document carried the signature of the person who had written it. The preamble, which I wrote, analyzed the reasons for the large number—3–5 million—of all types of prisoners in the USSR, including those not imprisoned but doing forced labor. The labor of these millions of slaves, I wrote, seemed to be cheap and profitable, feeding the huge staff of the Ministry of the Interior. But the state was actually losing by it because this sort of approach preserved obsolete technology and organization of labor.

To draw up such a document in camp is a major undertaking. One person writes while three or four do sentry duty in different locations to warn against a raid by an officer or stool pigeon. The draft of the document must be hidden, ideally in the ground. Then the text must be neatly copied onto cigarette papers; an even more vigilant guard must be mounted over this phase of the operation. The finished text must be made into a "candy," that is, wrapped in something that will remain undigested in the stomach, and hidden until one of the zeks[6] gets a chance to have a private visit. There are other methods as well which the KGB still does not know about and which I am not going to tell them about either. It took my friends a

---

[6]*Zek* is prison slang for "prisoner."

whole year to send our document, piece by piece, from Camp 35 out into freedom.

Irina came for a private visit three weeks after I arrived. Soviet strict-regime camps, at best, give only three days of private visits every year. For political prisoners they usually give zero days. But in any case, according to the law, the very first visit cannot be refused. The camp authorities scheduled a date with Irina. When she arrived after traveling nearly a thousand miles, they said they were having repairs, why not come another time? Irina refused and told them she would go home and report at a press conference how they illegally canceled her first visit. They offered her a room in another camp, but only for two days. "The law says three," she reminded them. "I'm going back and will report at a press conference—"

The situation with the Nobel Prize was still indefinite. And so they gave her the private visit.

The guard came up to my lathe.

"Get ready to be off."

"Where to?"

"Don't know."

He led me away. To the isolator? No, we had turned toward the exit. A prisoner transport? Why were they taking me without my things? In a paddy wagon, sitting inside an upright coffin of a cell measuring 2 by 2 by 4 feet, I was brought to some other camp, to a barrack. A visit!

"Strip. Bend over. So . . . Show it. So . . . Spread it. So . . . Again. So . . . Squat down. So . . . Show it. So . . . Get dressed. Not those, these. No, wait a minute. Bend over. Yes, yes, again. Don't talk! So . . . Show it. So . . ."

This exploration goes on for more than an hour, and the time for the visit is passing, your time. Meanwhile they are searching your wife. Finally you put on some sort of humiliating garments with short pant legs and sleeves and two buttons missing, which have been specially chosen for you as a political. Coming from the lathe, you are tired, unwashed, your head shaved bare. They lock the two of you up together. Your wife embraces you, maybe she still loves you, but you are not the person she remembers.

Irina told me that they had searched our apartment twice more, and that the Helsinki Watch groups continued to work;

new members tried to fill the places of the many who had been arrested or had emigrated. She admiringly described the work of the new Moscow members—Tatiana Osipova, a computer operator, Victor Nekipelov, a poet, and Sergei Polikanov, a physicist and corresponding member of the Soviet Academy. I asked her to declare publicly that even in camp I remained a member of the Moscow group as an observer. And I gave her the "candy" that my fellow zeks had prepared weeks ago, hoping that someone would get a visit.

Soon after, I was transferred to Camp 37. This camp had two living zones, big and little. Mine (No. 2) was the little one: fifty by a hundred yards surrounded by five rows of barbed wire, some electrified, two high wooden fences, a watchtower at each corner, an ultrasound signal system, and dogs barking behind the wooden fences. Inside all this was a single living barrack, a small wooden privy we called the White House, and a small toolshed. The barrack housed thirty to forty men, mainly war criminals—ex-Polizei and others who had collaborated with the Nazis during the war. Mostly simple peasants who had been put inside for war crimes, they were now collaborating with the KGB. Only one person other than myself in this small zone was here for Article 70 (propaganda): Kuzma Dasiv, a Ukrainian engineer. The moment that Dasiv learned from one of the former war criminals, who had heard it from the guard, that I was being brought into the camp, he set up a brief meeting with Paruir Airikyan. Airikyan was just about to be taken out of the camp to a prisoner transport. As soon as I arrived, Dasiv literally pushed me into a small storeroom. Inside waited Airikyan. It was too dark to see whether he had changed since his trial in Yerevan four years ago. "Dasiv is one of us," he whispered. "All the war criminals work for the KGB. But don't be afraid of the Latvians—they were really partisans, not war criminals." Three minutes later a guard flung open the door and pulled him away.

They put me to work again on the lathe. My old experience during the war years helped me, but the labor was exhausting. Unless you were an ex-Nazi, you were forbidden to rest during work and, after work, to rest lying down or even to close your eyes while sitting up. During the first months I did not manage to fulfill the production norm, so they gave me only a one-day meeting with my family the next year; after that we were never permitted to meet in camp again. At least I still had the right to walk around inside the living zone. The sight of forest beyond the fence, the sky, birds, the grass inside the zone—it was beautiful. Sometimes I picked grass for vitamins and gathered a few of what I called "edible nonedible mushrooms," which I boiled carefully. Later, alas, much of our little grassy zone was converted to a rabbit farm surrounded by barbed wire. The war criminals were in charge of it. Every Saturday the camp Chekist, Gadeyev, would go there carrying a big, skinny briefcase and leave with a fat one. The officer for political education went on Fridays.

Even after the 1978 Nobel Prize went to Sadat and Begin, the camp officers continued to handle me with a certain caution. I was still a corresponding member of the Armenian Academy. Although they always took away the notes on physics or logic I made during my free time, they sometimes gave them back. And they did not even punish me for two political hunger strikes. The first, which lasted a couple of days, began on October 30, the Day of the Political Prisoners of the Soviet Union, when the political prisoners in Camp 37 traditionally went on hunger strike. Several weeks before, I had secretly sent Irina —for transmission to Soviet dissidents and the West—an announcement of the strike and a demand that all arrested members of the Helsinki Watch groups be freed. On December 10, International Human Rights Day, another traditional strike day, I began a five-day strike. Again, I had asked Irina in advance to transmit an announcement of the strike, along with an appeal to the Soviet leaders, in which I said that "striving for a growth of influence in the world would be reasonable if it were based on the concepts of democratic socialism. But you are helping the development of totalitarian systems. This is a risky game, dangerous for the country and the world. . . ." Soon afterward the Soviets invaded Afghanistan.

In February 1979, I felt that some sort of decisive reversal had occurred. Two years later, Irina discovered that the Armenian Academy had expelled me at this very time. The camp authorities stopped returning my notes and forbade *any* scientific words or symbols, on even a high school level, to be used in letters to and from me.

It was a major blow. I declared a work and hunger strike and got immediately slapped into an isolator for five days. A guard escorted me into an old wooden barrack enclosed by barbed wire and gave me other clothes—the same black uniform as in the usual zone but absolutely worn out; the same cold underwear (wool underwear is not permitted in camp), also dilapidated; and one-hundred-year-old dirty slippers. My own pair of socks, handkerchief, and metal mug. That was all you were allowed to have in the isolator. That and a latrine bucket, rusty and full of microscopic holes.

The cell measured 3.75 by 10 feet, with a small outside window and two concrete posts like tree stumps. A naked shelf of planks for sleeping rested on them at night; it was raised and lowered from outside. I sat down on a post. Chinks in the walls let in drafts. Outside, the temperature was 40 below. I began to shiver. Much later I learned various prison skills for getting a little warmer, such as hiding a newspaper from the guard and slipping it under the back of your shirt. It felt cold even then. You couldn't warm yourself with food because there was hardly any of it, and the so-called "hot" food came only every second day.

The cell had no washbasin. In order to empty the latrine pail and wash up, I was taken out of the cell once or twice a day. But you couldn't keep yourself clean. That, said the camp doctor, was part of the punishment.

I would shout, "Chief, give me a piece of newspaper!"

"What for?"

"What do you mean, 'what for?' To wipe, of course."

"Just a second, I'll phone the duty officer. . . . Just a second. . . . No, the duty officer won't permit it."

"How am I supposed to wipe myself?"

"Your finger."

"In that case give me paper and a pen. I'm going to write a complaint." (You had the right to make complaints.)

"Just a second."

He would hand over a sheet of notebook paper. You could tear it in half and use half to wipe and the other half to write a complaint.

The most difficult thing was sleep. At night I would rub the wood of the plank bed, then lie down for ten minutes until the planks grew cold again, then rub the wood, then lie down, and so on throughout the entire night. Usually I put my slippers under the back of my shirt, and if the guard was kind, I could cover my head with my handkerchief. In daytime the plank bed rested flat against the wall; it was forbidden to sleep, even standing. For violations they could increase your punishment.

After my five days in the isolator were up, they returned my papers and I went back to the lathe. Now I could do scientific work only in secret. My cover turned out to be a prisoner named Alexander Nilov, a physicist from the Lumumba Institute in Moscow—which almost certainly meant he collaborated with the KGB. He was a double agent in temperament, and a very nice, educated, sociable adventurer. The KGB caught him preparing to spy for the CIA, and gave him ten years for it. After tossing all night, sure that I had found him out, Nilov confessed to me one morning in the camp that the Chekists had instructed him to spy on Orlov. I nodded knowingly, although the thought had never crossed my mind. He began to help. The war criminals and stoolies believed that Nilov was not a prisoner but a KGB officer dispatched to spy on Orlov. So when he was near me, which was conveniently often, the fools left us alone in order not to interfere with his job. He kept watch while I rewrote my latest calculations (or latest declarations) on cigarette paper, to send secretly to Irina.

I used every opportunity for reaching her. Our living zone included a small library, attached to which was a librarian—a young, unmarried woman with a child. We became friends, although that was forbidden to the staff. She intended to marry a young *zek* scheduled to be released soon. One day a stoolie saw them together, the KGB pulled her in for questioning, and she got fired. I asked her to transmit my logic calculations to Irina when she left the camp. But two ex-Polizei in the kitchen behind the thin wall of the library overheard our conversation, the KGB immediately interrogated her, and she gave them the first page of my calculations. She brought the rest to Irina a week later. I was thrown into the camp prison for six months "for attempting an illegal anti-Soviet correspondence."

It was the same cell I had inhabited before, but now the regime was different—in some ways easier, in some ways harder. At night they gave me a mattress, blanket, and pillow, and during the day a one-hour walk. Papers and books were permitted. The "hot food" came every day, because they took me out for work every day but Sunday to a work cell next door. I had to turn the handle of a machine that produced steel mesh. It was much harder even than my factory work on the lathe, and I did not manage to fulfill the production norm. During one such stretch in the camp prison I was rescued by Anatoly Koryagin, who worked another shift. A psychiatrist with a Ph.D. in medical sciences, Koryagin had been sentenced to seven years strict regime and five years of exile because of his struggle against using psychiatry for political purposes. He secretly put mesh from his own pile into mine. And when I once started coughing blood, he somehow got the medicine I needed, smuggling it to me at great personal risk. Yet we had never met each other face to face, and never did during camp.

Three quarters of my term was spent in cells like this— and more than half a year altogether under the isolator regime. The rest of the time I was in the ordinary zone. But wherever I was, the idea of escape was never far from my mind. I cooked up schemes with Marzpet Arutyunyan, my best friend, the leader of an Armenian nationalist youth organization who had been sentenced to "7 + 5" for propaganda. His brother, Shagen, was at the same time in another camp for his participation in organizing the Armenian Helsinki Watch Group. We discussed digging a tunnel from the barrack to outside the camp—about fifty yards; or escaping hidden in a truck that hauled metal filings from our lathes; or even in the camp jeep, which had once been repaired in our factory. (A jeep is small, but so were we.) Had I been in the ordinary zone just once for at least six consecutive months, we'd have done it.

EIGHTEEN

Letters from Irina

Several dissidents' wives had already been arrested for helping their husbands, and Irina knew these women very well. Moreover, she hated politics. But she still continued to struggle for me. I secretly sent her information and political appeals, which she secretly sent abroad, utterly disregarding the danger to herself. And through letters to Valya Turchin and Lyuda Alexeeva, who were now living in the United States, she also sent her own information and appeals—to journalists, scientists, human-rights organizations, and governments in the West. Ten years later Valya gave me an enormous file containing her letters. Here are some extracts from them:

August 27, 1979
On August 21, 1979, I was permitted to have a visit with my husband . . . Instead of the legally prescribed three days . . . I and his son Alexander were given one day. "Your husband is not fulfilling his norm at the lathe."

My husband looked extremely exhausted and thin. Because of work in two shifts, one following on the heels of the other, his sleep has been completely destroyed . . . My husband has declared a hunger strike three times.

241

[H]e was put twice in an isolator. In the isolator he could not sleep because of the cold . . . [H]e rubbed the bare boards of the plank bed with his hands in order to warm the boards up a bit . . . [H]e has been forbidden to conduct scientific correspondence. . . .

He asks that scientists try to secure the liberation of Sergei Kovalyov.

On May 12 [1979], he made an appeal: "On the Anniversary of the Helsinki Watch Group: I believe that our sacrifices are not in vain. . . ."

My husband has asked me to communicate the fact that he favors the signing of the SALT II Treaty.

November 30, 1979

I want to report how our authorities are killing my husband as a scientist . . . [T]he administration forbids him . . . in his letters even to mention anything about his scientific ideas . . . On October 22 [1979], because of an attempt to transmit a scientific article outside to freedom he was put in the internal camp prison, where he will be kept for half a year . . . The authorities hate my husband and at the same time fear him . . . because they are unable to compel him to keep silent.

I appeal to the scientific world—to intervene in the fate of my husband, not to let him perish before the end of his term. The suppression of his intellect, his gradual physical destruction—this is the sentence being carried out against Orlov.

May 15, 1980

The founder of the Moscow Helsinki Watch Group . . . today, May 15, 1980 . . . declares a two-day hunger strike. He is demanding: Amnesty for all political prisoners. A stop to repressions against public organizations that speak out in defense of human rights.

Orlov's appeal to the Madrid Conference [on Security and Cooperation in Europe] is this: "[A]ll of us who fight in defense of human rights are interested in détente, but in that version where public control of governments is recognized as an important factor for peace . . . If a state declares its model of society to be a real model for others, then it should not interpret international criticism of that model as interference in its internal affairs."

September 5, 1980

Declaration: I, the wife of Yuri Orlov, again and yet again appeal to you, scientists, the public, the participants in the coming Madrid Conference—do not let my husband perish in camp. From October 1979 to April 1980 Orlov was punished by imprisonment in the camp prison and deprived of all visits. Soon after leaving the prison in the summer . . . he was once again punished, by being deprived of visits . . . [access to] the camp shop, and a food parcel that was the only parcel [permitted him by law] for three and a half years . . . In August Orlov was punished once again [by detention] in the camp prison for six months and . . . for yet another year he is deprived of visits with family.

The authorities have announced to my husband once already: "Forget you are a scientist, Orlov. You'll never leave camp!"

I am in a state of desperation.

January 17, 1981

I beg of you to transmit my information . . . There are persistent rumors that Yuri has been deprived of his rank as a corresponding member of the Armenian Academy of Sciences. To find out exactly is absolutely impossible. The academy refuses to answer me. Perhaps the Defense Committee can inquire of the academy? Do try. . . .

To the Madrid Conference:

On the day the conference reconvenes, as he did on its opening day, Yuri Orlov is declaring a hunger strike. He once again issues an appeal . . . to take a decision on amnesty for political prisoners in all countries that have signed the Helsinki Accords . . .

Yuri Orlov considers that genuine détente and trust among peoples require great openness and sharing of information in all areas of public life—social, economic, military . . .

He repeats the proposal he advanced four years ago to

begin preparations for an international conference on declassifying state secrets . . .

I once again appeal to the conference with a call to save
my husband from barbarous treatment . . . [W]hen he sat resting, he was forbidden to put his head on his arms. On October
15, [1980], Orlov had a bitter argument over this with the officer
Salakhov. On October 25 my husband fell ill and was laid up
with a high temperature. On October 30, for this conversation
with the officer . . . he was dragged out ill and thrown into an
isolator. . . .

January 8, 1983
There is a genuine threat of a new sentence. Yura has been
deprived of the right to ANY correspondence and since the
end of October or the beginning of November 1982 has been
in the camp prison . . . I am writing a complaint to the Perm
prosecutor and I am asking him to inform me why there are
no letters from my husband . . . I am going to inquire further
somewhere around the beginning of January . . . There simply
is no reply . . . I have written to Madrid to Mr. Kampelman[1]
on Yuri's situation.

I can now add this. In the camp prison they forced Yuri
to perform hard labor . . . They raised his production norm
. . . And while [Yuri was] still in the zone the common criminal
Tarasenko [Mongol], who had already beaten up two prisoners,
threatened to cut off Orlov's nose and ears . . .

The complaints of the prisoners never get beyond the bounds
of the institution . . . There is total surveillance. For sending
information out [the prisoners are] cruelly punished . . .

If Yura receives an additional sentence he will never get
out alive. After all, he is already 58 years old . . . The prison
regime is on the way to being more and more cruel. I am
desperate, I do not know what to do. . . .

---

[1]Max Kampelman, U.S. ambassador to the 1981–83 Madrid Conference on Security and Cooperation in Europe.

NINETEEN

Hard Days

Losing your sense of humor is the most dangerous thing of all.

In March of '83, off my head with hunger, cold, and lack of sleep in the isolator, I concluded that I had endangered my friends on the outside through a piece of carelessness and must kill myself to save them. My internal equilibrium broke and I made a serious mistake. Those were hard days.

But I have to start earlier, with the summer of '82. Just then, two years before the end of my term, the KGB decided that it was time to concoct a new case against me and that I had to be worn down morally at any price. They hadn't been able to shut me up in the usual ways—hard labor and punishments. So they turned our zone into a madhouse.

Camp had been difficult before that, but familiar. Every autumn when the officers got back from vacation and tackled their work with fresh zeal, they simply locked me up on some excuse or other in a separate cell. Altogether I would put in up to eight months' solitary every year. I was ready for it. As far back as my first days in the camps, Nilov had warned me it was planned that way. "Right in front of me, KGB were debating where was the best place to keep Orlov," he recounted in his businesslike manner. "And they decided solitary was best. Two were from here, the third came from Moscow." True, I had not been sentenced to solitary, so their decision was illegal, which Nilov says he daringly hinted to them. This interesting notion gave the KGB men a terrific laugh.

"But why solitary?" I asked a little stupidly.

"You have a big influence on people," Nilov replied. "They can't keep an eye on you in the zone. You'll set up a correspondence with outside."

"The KGB exaggerates," I said after a pause.

The KGB did exaggerate, not my abilities but its own. They forbade me to write in my letters about life in camp, about science, about politics. I wrote secretly, and my secret correspondence never got broken off. The Chekists could not imagine that it was easier to do it in solitary, where there was just me and the guard. The guard was not guarded. And then, if he was sympathetic to a dissident . . .

Even in the zone things did not go exactly to KGB plan. Although some of the ex-Polizei worked for the Chekists as they once had for the Nazis—not out of fear but love, not all were sadistic by nature; they had been through the terrible mill first of the Stalinists and then the Nazis. They lacked diligence. The young stool pigeons were even less diligent. Many were tormented by doubts, and passionately wanted to remain at least outwardly innocent. And sometimes there were men like Nilov, who confessed to their comrade *zek*s and even helped them, playing both sides. The KGB net was full of holes.

And so they kept me in solitary confinement much of the time. When I came back into the zone from a stretch of solitary in 1982, May was ending. It was my sixth spring in captivity. One old *zek* had warned me: five years is bearable, but after five everything will be too much, your soul will start smoking. My soul wasn't smoking. The living space seemed enormous, one hundred paces from barbed wire to barbed wire instead of two paces from wall to wall in my cell; clouds overhead instead of patches on the ceiling; day and night instead of a perpetually burning forty-watt bulb. Freedom. But the joy of liberation was gone. Everything seemed a bit familiar, predictable. Rather boring. That's dangerous in here, I thought. It's just an illusion.

The traditional tea to celebrate getting out was pleasant as always. Among the many new people I found half-deaf, half-dead Morozov, who felt certain that he would not live to see freedom (and he did die in prison, in 1986). Of my old friends in the zone, only Marzpet Arutyunyan, Karpenok, and Chitava were left. The four of us sat at one table in the mess and shared all our food equally, whatever we had. Misha Karpenok was a cheerful, witty Cossack who did not go into the army but across the Turkish border. The Turks brought him back because they couldn't believe it was possible, just like that, to sail through the paranoid multilayered Soviet barriers. "But it was a holiday, Border Guard Day," Misha told us, laughing. "The guards were drunk. The alarms weren't working either." Vakhtang Chitava was a journalist who had criticized Russification in Georgia.

After tea Chitava took me aside, a bit further away from the stoolies. "Nilov asked me to tell you urgently," he whispered, "that a KGB man came from Moscow and tried to persuade him to act against you. He refused, and they transferred him to another zone."

"I don't understand," I said. "Nilov was working for them anyway."

"That's something else. He sounded very agitated. This is some other operation. You should have seen how he looked! This is something else," Chitava insisted. What did it all mean? What had Nilov left unsaid? What had he refused to do?

We learned very soon what it all meant. From the criminal depths they dredged up two wild young men—a gangster and a thief—and shoved them in with us. This was something new; criminals weren't kept in our zone. The KGB invented political cover stories for them, but they weren't literate enough and got them confused. The gangster wasn't literate at all. He was the famous "Mongol"[1] from the famous Moscow gang that liked to take peaceable fat men with large, unearned incomes, nail them into coffins, and then, of course, start sawing these coffins with two-man saws. If a man confessed where he kept his riches, fine, you have your life, we have ours, each to his own. If he didn't, they went on sawing, the work wasn't dusty. A simple racket, and it went without a hitch. But I heard later on a prisoner-transport train that when they were caught, Mongol told a bit too much to the citizen interrogator. He saved his own skin and the rest of his pals got the firing squad. It followed

---

[1]Mongol's real name is Victor Tarasenko. According to a Soviet journal, he was released after fourteen years in camp and began laundering his money by investing it in cooperatives (*Chelovek i Zakon*, No. 3, 1989).

that he might have only a tiny bit of time left to live. Apparently that's why he and the KGB made a deal. Who would try to even old scores with him in a political zone? The Chekists hid him here. He worked latrine duty. The zone was small, the people clean, not much trouble. Cleaning toilets being a problem of sanitation, it was logical for them not to put his cot in our barrack but apart from us, in the infirmary, among the clean test tubes. Mongol bathed on major holidays.

One day Marzpet Arutyunyan was lying there in the infirmary, still recovering from a savage beating he had been given by officers in Rostov Prison because his two cell mates had escaped. The duty officer, neat and severe, came in and irritably asked Mongol, "Why aren't you at roll call?"

"I'm waiting for them to bring me Orlov," the gangster confided.

"Orlov? What for?"

"I'm going to make him a queer!"

The officer roared with laughter, sat down on a cot, looked over at Marzpet. He asked the gangster, "That means you have hopes?"

"And how!"

This didn't alarm me much at first. But the scenario unfolded. They brought someone brand new into the zone, also with a political cover, this time a homosexual. I didn't have anything to do with him because a secret note had come from another zone, saying that he worked for the KGB. But what did they need a homosexual for?

In the Soviet Union homosexuality is illegal and earns camp terms of up to five years. This is one issue where the national morality sides with the law. So it would be a KGB triumph if they could manage to portray a well-known dissident as a homosexual. Personally I had never heard of homosexuality in political zones. It is, however, a common occurrence in the criminal ones. Both officially and unofficially only the "female" side of the pair is considered a "queer." The situation of the "females" is horrible. They are officially segregated from the other zeks, who do not speak to them as to human beings; they are the lowest caste, slaves of the slaves. People end up like that in various ways. For example, a man will lose at cards and not pay his debts—so he'll be "queered." It is impossible after that to return to respectable society. Criminals are merciless. What would be the situation of a political *zek* in a criminal zone if they shoved him in there after branding him a "queer"!

When this *zek* appeared in our zone, the authorities put him at a separate table in the mess hall and scratched his initials into a crude aluminum bowl. That marked bowl, the "queer's bowl," was his personal dish; everybody else ate out of the communal supply. I preferred not to speak with him because of his KGB connection, but they had their timetable. The homosexual would try to talk to me, the officers paired us on work details, the stoolies sent notes around the zones, saying, "Orlov is kissing a queer." We all knew how difficult that was, how risky, sending notes to the other zones. Yet for them it was easy—an officer would summon a *zek* from another zone and give him the note from his "friend" in ours.

Things were getting harder and harder. Every single day now, the gangster yelled, "Queer!" It was being repeated more and more frequently, and the stoolies and ex-Polizei were sniggering in an organized way that reminded me of a dog chorus. Long ago, just after the war, I had heard a German record of such a chorus; each dog barked its own note. (Several years later I learned that they were barking the Christmas song "Jingle Bells.") For the time being I held on, even believed that I was calm. What more? What next?

Next came theft—an unprecedented thing in the camps. Long underwear and toothbrushes began to disappear from the ex-Polizei, and turned up among my belongings, sometimes in my chest, sometimes under my pillow. The KGB were pushing to the limit. They had a couple of defamatory articles of the Criminal Code up their sleeves, a dozen "witnesses" would testify that I "associated" with a homosexual, and the same dozen would testify that I was stealing long underwear. Professors don't steal long underwear? You're funny, Yuri Fyodorovich. You have theories, but we have—facts.

"Queer!" brayed the ex-Polizei. "You're stirring up the zone, rights defender!"

"They're all fags," shouted Mongol. "Chief! Give them marked bowls!"

In the criminal zone you have to kill for words like that. Otherwise, according to the criminals' code, you're admitting that you are a "queer" and will be treated as one. But how should a political defend himself? I could have killed him.

("Everyone thinks you're infinitely kind," Irina used to laugh. "But I know.") I could have killed him out of sheer exhaustion. However, that would have been a gift for the KGB.

Once, coming into the mess hall from the factory, we saw that the homosexual's table had been moved right next to ours. We four dissident friends were separated from the others together with the homosexual! Loathing and anger seized us. That's how—I've seen it with my own eyes—peaceful people suddenly start counting whether there are enough telephone poles between Moscow and Vladivostok to string up all the Communists. Vileness begets vileness. We weren't counting poles, of course. But all the same, what were we to do? Our table in the mess had been the closest to the political officer's rostrum. Now the table nearest the rostrum turned out to be the homosexual's. "Citizen Major," I said to the political officer, "you made the right political decision, putting the homosexual's table right under your rostrum! You're separated together with him."

"What?"

They put his table back. The initiative, for the moment, was in our hands. When there were no guards nearby, we laughed and laughed, even though we did not feel like laughing. The stoolies did not know how to respond, the unanticipated problem was intellectually beyond the camp Chekist, Gadeyev, and for a while we had derailed the KGB's program.

A year later, when they read out to me the official warning of the KGB at the end of my term, they cited "reports by prisoners." It seemed that with the "aim of inciting riots"—there's a stiff criminal article covering that—"Orlov moved tables, organized theft of personal articles and fights." Homosexuality and long underwear were not referred to directly.

Fights! Fights, that is, beating up the politicals, also figured in the plans of the KGB, as we ourselves had expected. The criminals were to beat us up, and we were to be put in the camp prison for it. The weakest of us was Mark Morozov, who looked as if a puff of wind would literally knock him down. They began with him. Mongol worked him over while we were in the factory, just like that, for no reason. Then he did a job with a chair on the Marxist Anatoly Churganov. A war veteran, Churganov had fought corruption in Krasnodar Province. Naturally he had been accused of slander and in 1982 given five years of strict regime, not counting exile. Then, in 1983, the secretary of the Krasnodar Party Committee got demoted for corruption. (Naturally this did not affect Anatoly's fate. He served his full term and was "rehabilitated" only in 1989.)

When the higher-ups weren't around, I called a meeting of the *zeks*. "Listen!" I said to Mongol. "We're going to write a petition. They'll send you back to the criminals. Apparently it's too safe for you here."

"Ha!" responded the gangster confidently. "If I want to, I can kill whoever I want, and nothing will happen to me. I have a certificate. I'm crazy, got it?" That was a more than logical answer. In real life textbook logic doesn't work.

"There are lots of crazy people everywhere," I remarked enigmatically. He decided we had something in mind that we weren't mentioning, and for a while was quiet. Until now Gadeyev had been briefing him only on Saturdays, when he picked up his rabbit from the ex-Polizei. Now they discussed their common project every day.

We, too, convened frequently. "They're preparing a new term for you," said Chitava. "A criminal charge at any price They don't want a second political trial for you, they got burned on the first one. I see only one way out: to catch the thief. Then we'll control the situation."

And Chitava did catch the thief. It was the second criminal, who had been keeping quiet, as if above the fray. He was shifting long underwear from one chest into another—mine—when Chitava caught him red-handed. "Let's have a talk," Chitava said softly. He always spoke softly. Marzpet and Morozov came up as witnesses. Misha Karpenok wasn't there—he was finishing up his seven years, and they were keeping him in the isolator so that we couldn't send anything out with him. (It didn't help. I was able to get my work in logic to him.) Chitava shook the criminal by the shoulders, looking into his eyes. "What's with you, scum! Why are you doing this? Who instructed you? Who's directing you? KGB? The KGB?" The criminal's eyeglasses fell off. A Georgian intellectual, Chitava bent over to pick them up, and the criminal grabbed a heavy ceramic teapot, swung, and smashed it down on his skull. . . .

I was outside when one of the ex-Polizei burst from the barrack, howling hysterically, "They're beating our guys!" Mongol rushed at once to the barrack with a tremendous, freshly whittled club. (Clubs are forbidden, I managed to think.) "What are you standing there for, you blockhead?" an ex-Polizei shouted to the Tatar on the watchtower. "Phone the duty officer! Murder!" I flew to the barrack and found Mongol furiously pounding away at Morozov and the homosexual. As I jumped in, Mongol turned his club on me. Next to him stood a silent sergeant, attentively watching. (Don't raise your arms! I said to myself.) There was a cry of "Get the rights defenders!", and the second criminal, the thief, suddenly appeared alongside the sergeant and Mongol. Just then I saw Chitava.

I ran to him. Marzpet and I moved him to a safe place and covered him with a padded jacket. Officers were coming in by then—"Morozov to the isolator!"—For what?—They picked him up, but he pulled out a razor blade from somewhere, slashed himself, and fell. "Arutyunyan—to the isolator!"—For what?—Marzpet did not resist. All the time, higher-ups kept coming and coming into the barrack. Chitava was moved to the infirmary. The "investigation" began at once.

Actually they were planning just to draw up false affidavits for a new criminal case on "fighting and riots committed by a group of prisoners," consisting of Chitava, Arutyunyan, Morozov, and the homosexual, "organized and led by the prisoner Orlov." All were dictated that same day to the ex-Polizei and the two criminals. In order not to create unnecessary confusion in the affidavits, so to speak, they did not send for anyone from the "group" except, of course, their agent, the homosexual.

But the Chekists felt that something was missing. They needed direct proof of my "leadership" of the riots. Where was Orlov when he was "leading" the fight? What was he doing? And here things backfired. The old Latvians who were doing time for various war-related incidents and on whom the KGB had counted to have been reeducated long ago and to understand without guidance what was true and what was not—"every Soviet person knows that"—refused to lie, and testified that Orlov had been talking to them outside during the fight and had not taken part in it.

"What did you talk about with Orlov?"

"Just this and that. Mushrooms," the old men replied.

Kodors, a former anti-Soviet partisan, added, "And we went into the barrack together. Then, for no reason at all, they beat Orlov with a club."

"Who beat Orlov? What club? Did you *personally* see it?"

"Why only me? I'm a prisoner. You go ask your own man, the sergeant."

"No one laid a finger on Orlov. It just seemed that way. You didn't take part in the fight, did you? Or did you, eh? Go now." The KGB had to exclude the Latvians from the case, which was left incomplete for the moment.

It seemed to me that I had been beaten, so I went to the doctors. "You're imagining something again, Orlo-o-v!" they sang in duet. One was the wife of the special department officer and the other was the wife of a Chekist. "There are no welts on your back, don't exaggerate. You have the flu. You'll get a work release." The whole zone had seen the bloody welts on my back.

They wouldn't let us visit Chitava. He was being guarded, in effect, by Mongol, who was also lying down—to rest his nerves. The second criminal, the thief, was strolling about the compound.

I went on a hunger strike. "Kick out the gangsters," I wrote in my declaration. "Punish the provocateurs." The doctors, of course, immediately canceled my work release, and I was locked up in the isolator "for calling for a hunger strike and for insulting the prisoners." Thus, by the end of the summer of 1982 I found myself back in solitary, on the isolator regime for two weeks and then on the usual prison regime. Everything was normal. A cell 3.75 by 10 feet. Sparrow rations. Perpetual forty-watt bulb. Wind in the cracks. Ice-cold nights. Nevertheless, the hunt had been interrupted. There were no stoolies, no gangsters, no ex-Polizei. Just myself and a guard and a peephole between us. I could finally catch my breath.

While camp is hard physically, psychologically it is harder, because the KGB doesn't leave anyone in peace for a minute. If you don't change your opinions, which is noted right in your personnel file, then they will try to break you as a person. You don't trust most of the people around you, and every moment have to look out for provocations. In this respect solitary is easier than the zone.

* * *

Chitava lay for a month in the prison hospital and then was removed to the isolator for the "fight." After that, they released him into another zone. Marzpet was in and out of the isolator. Morozov was taken to Chistopol Prison. We never did learn how he got hold of that razor. They apparently decided to use the criminals and the homosexual elsewhere and transferred them. One way or another Chitava had ruined the Chekists' plan for our zone; new ones were needed. Meanwhile they starved me in the camp prison. But I lived, and did science.

What does it mean to do science in camp? Thinking is good, thinking is a delight, even if you want to lie down on the floor with exhaustion after work in the cell next door—which is forbidden. If, however, you decide to write your ideas down and get them outside because it is uncertain whether you will live to see that outside, then you will curse yourself! You write furtively on cigarette paper in a microscopic hand, "Wave function F is equal to . . ." and every second you expect: now they're going to catch me, punish me, the work will be lost. Then your friend literally swallows your work rolled into a little ball and wrapped in plastic. He is hoping for a private meeting with his wife. During their meeting his wife will wash that little ball, swallow it, and bring it outside. Your friend waits for the meeting. They always grant visits unexpectedly. . . . He swallows, washes, swallows, washes, and keeps on swallowing your work. And—they don't give him the visit, just as they haven't given you one for five whole years.

You start all over again. Nearly everything is ready. Where's the plastic? But someone comes over and you rashly destroy it all. Then start again from the beginning, and place your work into, alas, untrustworthy hands. Still perhaps you'll be lucky. The untrustworthy hands send it to the KGB, and you get sent to the isolator. In solitary you go back to your thoughts. . . . It turns out that you had been hasty, hoping for a chance to send your work out. Wave function F does not equal what you had written!

Around the New Year 1983 they began a new hunt. As it was, we in the camp prison were doing the very hardest work, and in three shifts. All of a sudden they exactly doubled our production norm to make it absolutely impossible to fulfill. Why a factor of 2 and not 1.8 or, say, 2.3? "Systematic major non-fulfillment of the norm," declared the political officer, "is a malicious violation of the regime." To be upset was pointless, so I was not—at least that's how it seemed to me. But precisely this disturbed their plans, so they removed from the work cell everything I might be able to sit down on. "Orlov, you're not at a spa. You'll have to work standing up all eight hours, six days a week. You'll sit on the floor? You do know that's a violation!" I thought about it. What was the sense of going to work? Punishment in either case. I went on a work strike. Father Gleb Yakunin, who was working a different shift—he had been arrested several months after me—also went on strike. The political prisoners had already been on strike in the zones for many weeks, demanding a stop to the terror at the hands of the camp criminals. The isolators were overflowing, but the strikers were standing firm. Father Gleb and I were glad to join them.

I was put back on the isolator regime for a fifteen-day stretch, which they kept renewing because I refused to work. The weeks passed by, the spring of 1983 began. With less than a year left to the end of my seven-year term, I conceived the stupid idea of keeping up my work strike and staying in the isolator until then. I thought I could last. But by now I had acquired the dangerous habit of obsessively meditating on escape. From my coming exile. From camp, if they added to my sentence. Even from the isolator. Those sweet, narcotic dreams took the edge off my hunger, sleeplessness, and perpetual headache. I overrated my strength. Finally I came unstuck.

I had opened the transom of my little window to air out the cell, and a chickadee flew in. I froze with happiness. Soon we became friends. She would fly in to get warm and have a chat, perch on my shoulder and hop about there. It couldn't last.

One day she flew into the corridor toward the guards. "Get it out, it's against regulations," said the senior guard, and they chased the chickadee. Absolutely terrified, she flew at a window and smashed herself up against the glass. Just then they were bringing me back to my cell. The bird was thrashing on the floor, wings spread, lying on her back. I picked her up. The guards were silent, embarrassed. Back in the cell I took off my undershirt and laid the chickadee on it. There was no blood.

By evening she flew, sat down on my shoulder, chirped hello. But she would not eat any crumbs, just had a drink from my mug. The next day she would not even drink, would not fly outside. I gathered her up in my hands—she chattered like a magpie in fright—and tossed her through the transom into the air. She returned at once and sat down, offended, a little away from me. That night she huddled in a corner, under the shirt, where no one saw her and she saw no one and could die quietly alone with herself. I began to weep for the first time in all those years. The tears poured and poured.

In the isolator they gave you only a pound of bread a day, and if you aren't working, the rest of the food comes every other day—three servings, about thirty spoonfuls, of watery soup; one serving, about eight spoonfuls, of kasha at midday; and a thumb-sized piece of herring in the evening. No meat, no fats, no sugar, no tea. I started to leave the evening soup from food day over for the even emptier mornings. A day or two after the bird died, I returned to my cell from dumping out my latrine bucket and did not see the mug of precious soup.

"You are obliged to take food at the prescribed time. Secondly it is forbidden to keep food for long. The doctor has said three hours, no more," declared the senior guard. They were worrying about my health.

"Fascists," I said—calmly, I thought. "Fascists, give back the soup."

"Right away, on the double," replied another guard, the same sergeant who was standing next to Mongol when he beat me. "And you'll pay for that 'fascists.' " He locked the cell, let down my plank bed, and left.

I shouted. Pounded my fists and my latrine bucket against the iron door. Smashed the forty-watt bulb. Shouted again . . . Finally I dropped onto the planks. The unaccustomed darkness was pleasant. Not a single sound could be heard in the barrack. The strikers had obtained some concessions, and the isolator cells were empty for the moment. Depression finally gripped me. How could I have become unstuck like that? They got what they wanted and I had helped them myself! I was tormented by shame.

Five days later I was called in to interrogation for a new— and criminal—case. "You are being charged under Articles . . ." read the interrogator in a bored voice. "Resistance with the use of force . . . Inflicting heavy insults on the authorities . . . Damage to the electrical system . . . First question: . . ." It was useless to try to prove that there had been no "resistance," that smashing a light bulb was not "damaging the electrical system." The witnesses were my guards. "In the course of the summer of 1982," their report said, "Orlov organized three thefts . . . three fights . . . repeatedly . . . despite multiple warnings . . ."

Three weeks of this passed. "Orlov, sign here." The censor, who was also deputy director of the special department, peeped through the tiny food hatch of my cell door. I had once petitioned them to send the academy a scientific article I had written in camp and the guards had seized. Their answer had come, I now had to sign it: the article had been forwarded to the KGB and was being reviewed. In fact, I had not expected otherwise. I only wanted to test the official reaction. My friends outside had already received that same article from me.

I had mentioned in my petition that it was impossible to stop my thoughts, that two articles I had written in camp had already been published in Western scientific journals. . . . "For whom are you writing your articles, Orlov?" the censor asked sweetly through the hatch.

"For the CIA," replied the officer escorting her, and they laughed.

That night I lay on the bare planks in the isolator and thought, What have you done? You actually wrote with your own hand that your scientific articles were being sent to the West. Soviet "experts" will declare your work secret. It will be intercepted on its way to a Western journal. No scientist will ever see it to prove that the "expert" evaluation is monstrously absurd. And even in the West, some journalists will write, "The possibility cannot be ruled out that Orlov really . . ." Everyone involved will be charged with high treason. The criminal case they're building against you now is only against you. But that is only the beginning. The next one will be on transmitting a scientific article, and will be a case against other people. You sacrificed them for your own sake!

Later, analyzing the details, I understood that the KGB had not been planning any such thing. They would have had to acknowledge that I was a scientist, when as far back as six years ago they had declared that I had not been a scientist for a long time. But I worked this out only later. At the time there seemed to be just one exit. The case had to be stopped. They needed me. If I didn't exist, there wouldn't be any case at all. Tomorrow was shower day. After the shower they gave us the big scissors, so that we could cut our nails. There was no other way. All night, lying on the planks, I practiced the stab in the chest, the stab in the heart. If I missed, didn't kill myself, I would destroy the others. I couldn't miss.

In the morning it turned out that the scissors in the duty room had got lost.

So that's how it happened. I wrote a statement: stop the legal prosecution and I'll go to work, I'll avoid violations of camp regime until the end of my term, if—if, I stipulated—there are no provocations or violations on the part of the camp administration itself.

Soviet dissidents should not write such statements. Even the weak promise I made was a mistake. Not because compromises are inadmissible, absolutely not, but because the KGB will immediately try to use a statement like mine to break apart the human-rights movement. And that was revealed right away. A mere three days later a Chekist flew in from Moscow. "Your statement gives us nothing," he said. "Even without it you are obliged to observe the regime. Write an open letter to Yelena Bonner in Moscow and your friends in the West so that they will not mention your name anymore."

"No," I replied. For so many years I had looked through them as if they didn't exist, and now I was listening to this sort of thing! I should have foreseen it.

"But you do understand," said the man from Moscow.

"I do."

"We'll take steps."

"So will we."

"Oh no! No, no," exclaimed the chief of the regional KGB, who had shown up, too. "We'll do it differently."

They closed the case, and I knew that they would not return to it. Bureaucrats don't like that sort of thing. If need be, they would cook up a new one. But why had they closed it? That quickly became clear. A week before my return to the zone, while I was still in the isolator and could not refute it at once, they lined up the zeks and solemnly read out a typewritten forgery: allegedly I had "renounced any further political activities!" Even Orlov, they said, had given up this hopeless work; follow his example . . .

No one believed them, even though they had closed the case. When I came back to the zone in early July 1983, Marzpet Arutyunyan, Oles Sherchenko, and my other dissident friends embraced me. I explained to them what had happened and how. On July 10, after recovering a little, I went on a hunger strike. My strike declaration demanded, as we had often demanded, a general amnesty for political prisoners. From solitary I had already alerted the outside to the strike.

They force-fed me on the twelfth and sixteenth day. I got diarrhea, and my rectum swelled, but my soul was clean once more. A sense of inner freedom never deserted me again.

On the eighteenth day I was transferred to the hospital.

TWENTY

In Transit

In the isolation of the hospital my hunger strike would achieve nothing, so I decided to break it off, recover my strength, and think. Obviously I had been doing too much for my fifty-nine years. The constant struggle with the KGB, the physical regime, the secret writing and rewriting of scientific papers and appeals every single day had come to be beyond my strength. Now I understood how people sometimes commit suicide not out of love, not out of grief, but simply because they have reached the limits of fatigue.

After two weeks they moved me back to camp and then, in September, out of the zone as usual—first to an isolator and then to the prison. Evidently they hoped to use the new Article 188–3, introduced by Andropov, about criminal accountability for violating the camp prison regime. Even a hunger strike was considered a "violation." The new law permitted the endless imposition of additional prison terms in camp, just as under Stalin, since according to this law the camp administration was both plaintiff and witness.

In November Gadeyev summoned me to the duty office in the camp prison. I stood in front of his desk. Behind me was a guard.

"You twisted us around your little finger," Gadeyev said.

"We dropped the case, but you went right back to your own thing again. Real men don't act like that."

"The train has left the station."

"The train has left the station, but we'll catch up with it!"

"Are you finished?" I asked.

Gadeyev froze like an adder, searching for a response. I looked out the window with sincere indifference. I could see the tiny exercise court—a barbed-wire cage for human beings. On the far side of the cage, old men with picks and shovels were hacking out a pit for a new privy of boards. It ought to have been made earlier. The old one had long since overflowed. The winter before, a mountain of frozen excrement mingled with the food garbage of the guards had piled up over the brim. No doubt this sort of thing would surround me the rest of my life. Well, let it.

"Take him out."

The duty guard returned me to the cell. The bolts rumbled shut.

On December 10, International Human Rights Day, the political prisoners always declared a hunger strike, demanding one thing: a universal political amnesty. This time Oles Shevchenko, a Ukrainian democrat and nationalist, Marzpet Arutyunyan, and others proposed not holding the strike. Oles deliberately committed an infraction to get into an isolator and let us know.

"Yuri Fyodorovich!" he shouted when the guard had gone outside. The guards usually urinated in the snow of our exercise court. "Please don't strike, and we won't. Otherwise they're going to accuse you of leading a hunger strike and set up a new case against you before you're released. These are dangerous days for you right now. Father Gleb, did you hear me?"

We muttered, "Yes," the outer door creaked, and we fell silent. It was absolutely forbidden to talk between cells.

This was a sacrifice for my sake. Not to go on a hunger strike on the tenth was indecent.

On December 11 Gadeyev summoned Yakunin: "Who organized the 'non-strike' on December 10?" Only a supreme idiot with rabbits in his briefcase could have posed such a question.

"No one," Yakunin innocently said. "According to the regulations, no hunger strike was stipulated for December 10."

* * *

My channel of communication with the world of freedom
had long worked only in one direction—outward. I did not
know about Irina's courageous appeals from the heart of Moscow, or the tremendous efforts of Valya Turchin and Lyuda
Alexeeva in America. I knew nothing of the determination with
which hundreds of other people in the West were defending
me, particularly scientists. I was reconciled to the idea that the
West had forgotten about me, indeed, about all of us. The hell
with them.

But probably because that was not so, and perhaps because
a change of power was already brewing inside the Kremlin, and
perhaps because it had become clear to the Chekists that I had
turned to stone and they would not have some new and glorious
case against me right now, they released me from camp at the
end of my term and sent me off to Siberia.

Late in the evening on February 6, 1984, I was led from
the work cell to the duty room of the camp prison. For two
hours they searched me, plucked at me, and looked me over.
Finally they finished up and I shouted "Farewell!" to Gleb and
Marzpet, who had once again landed in the isolator next door.
"Till we meet again!" they shouted back. ("I'll write an infraction
report on you!" the duty guard snarled at them.)

I was led out of the zone to the storehouse where my books
had been kept in my other suitcase. They turned the suitcase
over to me along with a new camp uniform, in case I had
managed to sew into my old one some information about the
camp, or some appeals, or something else very awful—never
giving the least thought to the fact that I could find room for
all of this inside my head. Then they put me in a paddy wagon
and took me off somewhere, and then we went further on foot:
an officer with a pistol, two soldiers with tommy guns, a German
shepherd straining at the leash, and me lugging two heavy
suitcases full of books. All these years my son Sasha had kept
sending me useful scientific books. Some had been put in my
hands at the start, before my expulsion from the academy. But
afterward all of them had piled up at the storehouse, because
we did not have the right to receive books from friends and
relatives. Inside the camp we were permitted to have only five
books, and the officers for political education threw themselves

on any books above this number as if they were enemy pillboxes. It was, of course, forbidden to send books to anyone anywhere.

I dragged along my suitcases, panting, while my escorts moved rapidly ahead. Evidently we were about to be late for the train. The officer said to a soldier, "Take a suitcase," and I was grateful.

The train approached in the stormy night, barely visible through the dense, slanting snow. The commander of the convoy of the Stolypin car took the packet with my case record, I was locked up in a narrow one-man cell, and the train pulled out. At last! But where were they taking me? The convoy commander, an elderly officer, seemed a decent person, not vicious. So I asked him. "Right now to Sverdlovsk. Further on to Krasnoyarsk. You can ask again there," he replied, and moved away from the grating. Every cell in a Stolypin car has a grating on the corridor side instead of a wall; there are no windows. In the corridor where the soldiers walk, there are windows without grating, frosted with white paint. The common cell of a Stolypin has two benches on the lowest level. Up above are plank bunks that can be lowered to form a complete second level; you reach them by climbing through a small hole cut in the planks. A foot and a half above that, running along two sides of the cell, are two sleeping shelves one foot from the ceiling.

The convoy commander sets the tone of the whole convoy. For the first and only time in my life I had a calm convoy that begrudged you neither water nor a trip to the toilet. This was an anomaly. In Sverdlovsk things became normal. In the cell of the transit and interrogation prison where they dumped me for a week—when formally I was already supposed to be in exile—the windows had double gratings but no glass. Outside was a Siberian February. And all the way further on, right to the end of my four-week journey of almost four thousand miles, I could forget about any glass in the windows. Wooden panels that totally shut out the light but let in the air and the cold helped protect only against a direct wind. The common criminals broke the glass, shouting and transmitting secret letters from window to window; windows were their chief avenue of communication. They also exploited the plumbing system, using the toilet bowls as megaphones. And then there were the walls. Sitting in some tiny waiting cell that measures 3 by 2 feet and stinks of urine, locked up in there for one, two, three, or four hours, you can gather for Amnesty International enough material for a whole year of work—material it will probably never learn about. There are inscriptions, inscriptions, inscriptions: "Shot. Vanya Petrov. Date." "Shot. Pyotr Ivanov. Date." "A tenner for Sorokin. Date." "Pike was here from Camp #22." "Pass the word: Kholopov is a fairy named Masha."

The guards could not struggle against information like this. Many tens of thousands of prisoners passed through each big transit prison in a year, and each transit prison was an interrogation prison as well. Even angels would turn into savage beasts from such floods of prisoners; and prison guards are no angels. They are trapped in the same cities and towns, the same discomfort, that all Soviet people are, and they have learned in the cradle that everything in the world is a fraud except the fact that two hundred rubles, no matter the source, are better than one. . . .

I have already been pounding for a whole hour on the door and shouting "Guard!" from the Sverdlovsk waiting cell I was shoved into five hours before, at three o'clock in the morning. The cell has no water or toilet. Finally a woman's voice: "Why are you banging? Do you want a punishment cell?"

"A toilet! To pee!" She goes away. I bang on the door and shout again.

In another hour's time, the same voice: "What?"

"To pee."

"Pee in your boot." She goes away. Only idiots like me suffer on such a scale. There are four corners in the cell, so what other toilet do you need? In one of the corners are some bloody rags: women have been in here, too.

Half an hour later I hear the familiar sound of food distribution, and breakfast is handed through the door—a piece of bread, barley porridge in a crumpled tin bowl, and a spoon with a thick, smooth handle half a finger long so you can't shove it up your own or someone else's throat.

Finally they lead me out to the toilet and from there to a big hall full of prisoners and soldiers. It is a search before boarding the prisoner-transport train. Actually the soldiers are seeking things that might be useful. The captain, who has been holding my case file in his hands, points me out from a distance, and a sergeant approaches: "You anti-Sovietchik whore! Just look at what lovely suitcases you have! Rewards for espionage? Open up!" Without waiting, he tugs with all his might at the top of the second suitcase, and books and papers that haven't already been taken away from me—everything—pour out on the floor.

"Books! You whore, don't you know? Five books—no more!"

"That was camp. But this is a prisoner transport. I am going into exile."

"You don't know where you're going. Five books!"

I call for the captain and explain the law to him. He leaves in silence.

"Well, you bitch, just wait!" the sergeant hisses as he pockets my mirror and gathers in his arms the precious personal letters that have gone through the camp censor, as well as a packet with scarce glue powders for plastic dental crowns. Irina had sent the glue to camp in an attempt to save my teeth. It had been lying at the storehouse; I have taken it for exile.

"Get out! Faster!"

I hurriedly throw everything into my suitcases, get a loaf of bread, a little bag of sugar, and a pile of salted sprats in my newspaper. Knowing about prisoner-transport trains, I have brought newspapers.

They ram us into paddy wagons, men into one compartment and women into another. The two women with us simply cannot fit into their 2 by 2 by 4 foot box. The soldiers shove them in one after the other, then push the door shut and padlock it. We men are in a big box, 4.5 by 6 feet. Some are lucky enough to get a seat on a side bench; the rest of us fall on them, trying to grab hold of the walls; the center is packed like neutrons in white dwarf stars, so there is nowhere to fall. They lock us in. Between us and the driver's cabin are guards with tommy guns and a German shepherd. One of the common criminals asks them for a butt, and a soldier gives him one. Knocking us against each other from side to side as it lurches over the ruts, the paddy wagon takes us to the freight station. At the station the passengers in the ordinary passenger cars will not see us. Their doors will be shut while we are being loaded into the Stolypin car.

"Get out! Sit down!" In a big column, four in a row, we

squat with hands clasped behind our heads. All around us are
tommy guns. The German shepherds bark in excitement.

"Get going! Don't fall behind! On the double! Don't fall
behind, you motherfuckers!"

A soldier swats me on the neck. I fall, get up. The dogs
are barking. Puffing and wheezing, I try not to lag behind with
my suitcases. The column is running along the rails. Evidently
we are late for the train again.

"Sit down!" Gasping for air, I squat. What a mistake, bringing the books. But how can I do without books?

They pack the cells of the Stolypin car as they did the paddy
wagon. This convoy is normal. It is already midnight, and there
is no water, no toilet. The kidneys and bladders of all the *zeks*
are chilled. From the cells come the shouts of people demanding
to go to the john.

"Up yours!" a soldier answers indifferently.

"Rock the car!" the *zeks* finally decide. It seems they are on
the point of turning it over; there will be a catastrophe. The
convoy commander comes out of the guards' section of the car,
and the guards take water around in a tank, then lead us in
turns to the toilet.

I have fallen ill. My nose is running, I am racked by a
cough and feel as if I have a high temperature. My cell mates
take pity on me and give me the very highest shelf; the others
stand and sit for two days, taking turns. Some twenty-five prisoners have been crammed into an ordinary compartment intended for four persons.

The city of Krasnoyarsk. Once again a week's wait in an
enormous transit and interrogation prison. The usual "Faster,
you whores!" from the Stolypin to the paddy wagon, then the
crush in the paddy wagon, then endless verifications, searches,
waiting, and then a shower: it is a humane rule that each prisoner must have one at each transit prison. Generally speaking,
the showers are not too bad. The *zeks* do not try to sidestep
them; as far as possible they keep themselves clean. Knowing
about the shower rule, I have set aside a stock of newspapers
so that I won't have to lay my things on the slime of the cement
floors. This shower has several sprays in one room. In the ves-
tibule to the room, under the supervision of a guard, they are

clipping everyone bare one after another at top speed with the very same set of clippers, while tucking under everyone's collar the very same sheet, gray with dirt and covered with hair.

"I am not supposed to be clipped," I tell them. "I am being transported to exile."

"I don't know anything about that. The duty officer ordered me to clip everyone."

"I have completed my term, completed it!"

"If you're here in prison, that means you haven't completed it."

Finally, after all the processing, they take me to a big cell. Two-level iron bunks with twenty-six places on each level and without any bedding take up almost all the floor space. Instead of springs they have iron bands, and on them are sitting or lying about 120 men. But this already seems a paradise. In the corner is an open toilet with a drain; the cement floor is not dirty. By the wall, prisoners are playing with homemade cards at a large table. There are almost no young people. Repeaters, I note to myself. They are always tidier.

On one bunk lies a boy of no more than twenty-five, with a smashed-in face and, they tell me, broken ribs. He has just been kicked to a pulp by the guards for talking back to them. They dragged him out in the corridor, fell upon him in a heap, and then tossed him back into the cell. That will teach him! He is still bleeding, and his comrades are helping him. The walls are covered with *zek* blood, too—from crushed bedbugs. As usual, being a newcomer, I am met by questions. Under what article was I convicted? For what? How long was I imprisoned and where? My article is a respected one, my sentence good and long. They accept me into their company and, because I am ill, let me lie down and even spread a padded jacket on my bunk. Prisoners look favorably upon "anti-Soviet propaganda."

Another week passes. The lawful term of my imprisonment ended on February 10, 1984, and on that day my period of exile ought to have begun, but here I am still being dragged about from prison to prison. Now they haul me off to Irkutsk. In the Stolypin I lie up on the second level. As usual, for many, many hours in a row they have given out no water. I still have a fever, and my throat is parched. The other prisoners, who have eaten salty herring—on prisoner transports they always give out only herring—can't bear to wait, and begin, as usual, to set up a shout.

"Who shouted?" A sergeant approaches.

"What are we supposed to do? Croak without water?" protests a young fellow.

"You'll croak right now," says the blue-eyed sergeant firmly. He summons a soldier. They unlock the door and haul the fellow out; the soldier leads him off to the guards' section of the car. I never see him again and do not know what they did with him.

"Now," says the sergeant, "who else was shouting? No one? That means everyone. So be it. When I say, 'Up!,' everyone climbs up, one after another. When I say 'Down!,' everyone down. Whoever is too slow, I'm going to hurry along with my mallet. Clear? Up!"

He has a hefty wooden mallet in his hand, the same kind they use to knock on the bunks—why, I never figured out. Through the open cell door, he hits someone's back with the mallet until the *zek* has clambered up through the hole. Scrambling, the *zek*s roll away head over heels so as not to hinder the ascent of the next person, who is now being beaten with the mallet.

"Down!"

"Up!"

"Down!"

"Up!"

For the time being I have to forget the fact that I am sick. I have to get moving. We are totally in the sergeant's hands. I look into his eyes: there is nothing there, just a sky-blue emptiness. However, he does not beat me.

He chases us up and down nineteen times.

"That's how it is! So now get your water."

In Irkutsk, the captain who accepts our group warns us gaily, "Just keep this in mind. You are in the Irkutsk transit prison—there's none worse. Clear?"

"For now we don't have any place for you," a lieutenant politely informs me after I have gone through all the usual processing. "We are going to put you up temporarily in the isolator. Okay? Just till morning. A bed there? It's the dead of night and the warehouse is shut. Not a chance. I don't have a bed myself," he laughs. "After all, you do have a padded jacket. And you'll have everything tomorrow."

He leads me into a deep basement, down to the isolator. There is a cement floor, plank bunks upholstered with tin plate, of course no glass in the window. But I am lucky to have at least a toilet with water.

"Cold?" the lieutenant asks with curiosity. "It doesn't seem cold to me. My house is even colder," he laughs again. "Well, have a good night. Tomorrow morning we'll transfer you out of here."

Naturally, they don't transfer me out of there either the next morning or the evening of the day after. The entire week they keep me, I must fight for the usual daily prison ration instead of the every-other-day isolator ration, and bang on the door for an hour and a half until the guard comes. He threatens to beat me for making a disturbance, and then for the tenth time looks with astonishment at all the things still left with me—suitcases, padded jacket, boots, cap—none usually permitted in the isolator. After going off somewhere to phone, he finally brings me something to eat. . . .

At the end of my week in Irkutsk they handcuffed me to another prisoner, and put us along with six other such pairs and a couple of militiamen in an ordinary civilian airplane flying to Yakutsk. The regular passengers tried not to see our handcuffs. I stared at these "ordinary" people with greedy curiosity, not having seen any for seven years. The flight attendant politely offered us water.

In the Yakutsk prison, after body searches, waiting, and all the usual, I was finally examined by a doctor because this was almost the end of the journey. Diagnosing pneumonia, she put me in the TB section of the prison clinic. In my ward for four, there was of course no glass in the window, but my neighbors had glued newspapers over the window hole, using a homemade paste from black bread. All of them were under investigation. The sports trainer from Mirny, a member of a countrywide network engaged in the theft and sale of uncut diamonds, he had only two possible courses of action: either betray some of the rest of the gang and be rubbed out by his comrades, or else not betray any of them and be shot himself after trial. He chose the first course. The journalist alleged that a criminal case had been cooked up against him because he criticized the higher-ups. The reindeer-breeder, a member of the Even tribe, had for the umpteenth time killed a Yakut in a local vendetta.

The doctor did everything she could, keeping me in the prison clinic for several days, and I recovered a bit.

"They are sending you to Kobyai District," she said casually one day. "It's a good district, with better food than in Yakutsk." To be sure, I had no idea how things were with food in Yakutsk.

On March 6 they handcuffed me again, put me in an airplane, and after a one-hour flight to the north, unloaded me in some settlement.

"Well, here you are," said the militiaman, taking off the handcuffs. "This is your place. Sangar, center of Kobyai District. From here you can spit on the Arctic Circle."

"It's still not his place," an official in civilian clothes corrected him. "He should go on to Kobyai Village."

The official took me first to the district militia and then to a local construction office, where he left me all alone. I walked about the office. No one was guarding me!

TWENTY-ONE

Exile

They gave me an advance on my pay, work clothes, and five woolen blankets. I climbed into the body of a canvas-covered truck, wrapped myself in the blankets, and leaned against the back of the cab. It was 4:00 P.M. and rather dark, but not so cold, about −30 degrees Fahrenheit. Only half a month ago, the driver said, the temperature went down to −80 and your nose fell off at once if you poked it out. "But yours is in its place," I remarked. "Yes, but I drink a liter of antifreeze every day." The chief construction engineer got in beside the driver, and we headed for the Yakut village of Kobyai, my place of exile. It was only sixty miles away, the first fifteen across the frozen Lena River and its branches. However, this was a Yakut road. The engine howled as our truck slammed through snow-drifts and jolted over frozen ruts, backside swinging, wheels screaming for a grip, melting the ice, getting deeper and deeper, so that the driver had to stop and cut young larch trees to shove under the wheels for traction. Around 4:00 A.M. we finally arrived. "Just on time," wheezed the driver, and winked at me with his left eye, which, to be sure, had been winking even before.

The engineer took me to a trailer—a bedroom with three

271

4-man bunks, and a kitchen with a stove, table, and benches—
that housed the carpenters of the Sangar Mobile Mechanized
Column. They were building a nursery school across the street.
My job was to guard the construction site against theft of materials and, especially, arson by drunk Yakut youths. "Here,
guys, is your watchman," the engineer announced to the sleepy
workers. "We wouldn't mind having something hot to eat."
Immediately hot tea appeared, along with bread and butter,
buckwheat porridge, canned meat, and vodka.

It was March 6, 1984. My life in exile had begun.

The nursery school, no bigger than the average American
private home, had been started two years ago, before General
Secretary Andropov died, so it definitely needed guarding.
(They raised the walls when General Secretary Chernenko
died, and successfully covered it with a roof only when Gorbachev's *perestroika* was born.) In violation of the law I was held
responsible for the construction site around the clock. During
the day the site had to be watched only when the carpenters
left Kobyai for lack of materials, which happened constantly;
otherwise I slept a few hours and then worked spasmodically
on physics and a paper on wave logic I had begun thinking
about in camp. But all night every night, dressed in felt boots,
a cap of wolf fur, and a sheepskin coat Irina had sent from
Moscow with Sasha Barabanov, my friend and former pupil,
I circled carefully about the incompleted building. Any theft
or arson would have been a good excuse to send me back to
prison.

For the first two weeks, my head spun and my legs buckled,
but little by little I revived from work in the fresh air, a full
stomach, and a landscape without guards, barbed wire, and
fences. True, the local militiaman, Sergeant Okhlopkov, who
was as thick as thieves with the KGB, had unlawfully forbidden
my walking beyond the village limits. Yet at the start this village
of three thousand inhabitants appeared to be a tremendous
space. The former district center, Kobyai had everything:
shops, a bakery, a telephone exchange, two movie houses, a
ten-year ordinary school, a boarding school for children from
small neighboring taiga villages, and even a music school. In
any case, how could you define the limits of a village that
sprawled like a big octopus, its tentacles interspersed with lakes

and forest and big barns with permanently starving sovkhoz[1] cattle? The very ends of the tentacles crawled into the vast taiga—whortleberry swamps and larch forests with saplings so dense that you could not squeeze your leg between them; during a storm hundreds came unscrewed at the roots from the peaty soil and fell all together like soldiers before a firing squad.

Along the tentacles, bumpy streets meandered past clean, spacious wood houses with woodpiles and blocks of ice stored outside them. Several dozen privately owned cows and horses wandered around the village, lovely Yakut horses, plush-coated and rather small, throats fringed with delicate hairs like old ladies' beards. From my nursery school I could watch the cows sedately walk across the lakes to watering holes cut in the ice, while bands of horses tore past them, long tails streaming. I liked being alone, I had tired of people, I felt free.

All the same, it was a mine field.

Several days after my arrival two friendly young Yakut loggers confided that the District Party Committee had sent a couple of lecturers to warn everyone that the Orlov about to be delivered was an American spy; that the bookstore was displaying Nikolai Yakovlev's book *CIA Target—The USSR,* which depicted Sakharov and myself as CIA agents; and that some of the schoolteachers had explained to their smaller pupils who I was. Soon a detachment of eight- and nine-year-old girls and boys, commanded by a brave eleven-year-old girl, began a campaign against the spy. Nearly every day, keeping under what they imagined was good cover, the children conspicuously bounded and crawled from hill to hill and tree to tree toward the nursery school until I was encircled. Then, at a cry from their commander, they all popped up, threw a shower of stones at me, and silently ran off. I usually remembered to position myself out of range when they were due to arrive. They were not dangerous, of course; only, once in the distance a not-so-small schoolboy gestured with a knife. But there were things worse than a knife.

The Sangar Mobile Mechanized Column carpenters were friendly from the start, and one told me that the chief engineer had been interrogating his workers as to whether I was spread-

---

[1] A sovkhoz is a state farm.

ing anti-Soviet propaganda. An investigator from Sangar had
then pressured two of them to speak against me, seeking material for a new case. When I asked the militia why people were
being coerced into giving false testimony, they threatened to
open up a new case against me for slandering the state. But I
named my friend as a witness, with his consent. "We'll see about
that," Sergeant Okhlopkov grumbled. After that I heard nothing about it. My friend had left Kobyai—to be on the safe side.

These games by the authorities produced an unexpected
effect: the carpenters began approaching me with political questions. I carefully scrutinized their faces and listened to their
voices, trying to read who they really were. A single careless
conversation, and a new case would be prepared. The young
Yakut men from the village, whose faces I never learned to
read, always wanted to discuss politics with me. Usually drunk,
sometimes violent, they worked as truck drivers, hunters, sovkhoz fishermen, and loggers. Their political views were rather
sophisticated, perhaps because many of them had been in criminal camps for hooliganism (but never theft) and had met both
political and religious prisoners inside. The fishermen could
hear foreign radio broadcasts once they got further from the
powerful jamming station in Sangar, and knew a bit about the
dissidents. They talked interestingly about their lives—and
about mine as well, revealing that before I arrived in Kobyai,
a Chekist had come "from Moscow" to arrange the conditions
of my exile, and part of the arrangement was that after this
exile I would get pasted with another one. Unfortunately the
young Yakuts often wanted to drink with me; once they settled
down for a visit in the trailer, it was difficult to dislodge them
and dangerous to try. It was even more dangerous to ask the
carpenters to help.

Although friendly to me, a fellow ex-con, the young Yakut
workers were generally hostile to Russians and violently disliked
the Russian workers from Sangar. The love was mutual. Late
one night as I headed for the trailer kitchen to warm up, a
couple of attractive and dead-drunk Yakut schoolgirls followed
me in. One immediately flopped onto the floor, the other
swayed against me and asked where the men were. "Asleep," I
replied. "Good. I need guys!" she announced, "lots of them!,"
and lurched off to the bedroom. Shouting and cursing, the
workers jumped out of their bunks, lifted the girl up by her

arms and legs, and flung her outside. Her girlfriend landed beside her. The next day, when the carpenters went to the trailer for lunch, the young Yakut men tried to pick a fight with them. But the carpenters had axes.

"Better get lost, Fyodorovich," they advised. It was important to avoid all conflicts, so I got lost and headed for the militia. They required me to report there every other day instead of once a week, and I had to keep getting their written permission to pick up registered mail, because they managed never to give me identity papers. This was illegal, too. At least the post office handed over my unregistered mail, and some arrived every day, though none from abroad—that channel had been blocked.

I was sitting in the militia station with smug Sergeant Okhlopkov, who was lecturing me about how it was a mistake to spread rumors that I was a professor—look out, Orlov, we'll ship you off to a booby hatch—when he got a telephone report that the young Yakuts, armed with axes and hunting knives, had surrounded the trailer. The carpenters had just beaten them off with logs. "Lucky you weren't there, Orlov," Okhlopkov said, putting down the phone with a nasty grin. "Pro-fessor. So you think you're smarter than me? I'll get to the bottom of just who provoked this fight."

Sergeant Okhlopkov was a persistent and inventive man. Soon after his threat he tried to frame me for dereliction of duty, with the help of a former gangster and exile whom the chief engineer had asked to check on my work—in other words, my unofficial boss. This ex-gangster's tractor-trailer had been stolen not very far from my nursery school, and both he and Okhlopkov claimed to have found me absent from my post on the night of the theft. The new case was almost ready. But I could prove Okhlopkov was absent himself that night, and the carpenters testified that they had seen me on duty every night. I wrote a complaint to Moscow, and Okhlopkov's scheme collapsed. Of course, it turned out that the tractor-trailer had not been stolen at all.

Things were going badly. The authorities' violations of the law were unpleasant, but the entrepreneurial Okhlopkov—a lieutenant now—was positively dangerous. So were some of the young Yakuts. After their defeat at the hands of the carpenters, they had begun to eat, drink, and defecate inside my nursery school in my absence. Cleaning up their mess was nothing beside the constant anxiety that sooner or later they would toss a lighted cigarette onto some trash, and then . . .

For the first time I seriously considered escape from exile. It was the middle of April. The roads would not become a sea of mud until May, so I could try to thumb a ride right to Yakutsk, switch to another truck, and go further south down the big road to the Baikal-Amur railway. The newspapers said that this sector of the railway was operating, and perhaps in this wonderful case they were telling the truth. If they were, I could hop a freight train west, and after that cross the Afghan border. But the probability of success seemed to be zero or almost zero; better to wait until that arrest was clearly imminent. For the present I would make alternative plans and prepare myself.

So I stayed on, fighting the labor-law violations and also secretly taking long forest walks to build up my endurance and reconnoiter possible escape routes. That was my son Sasha's idea, to train myself in the forest. Meanwhile, alarmed by the workers' support for me in the tractor-trailer adventure, my bosses temporarily moved me into a good individual apartment near the airport until the finishing touches were put on a new dormitory for construction workers. I quickly wrote to Irina about the apartment, and at the very end of April she came for a week's visit with Zhenya Tarasov and another physicist friend, Lev Ponomaryov. It was a happy reunion, but the news they brought about what had happened in the past five years was awful.

Nearly all the old and new members of all the Helsinki groups, the members of Amnesty, the editors of *The Chronicle of Current Events*, the administrators of the Russian Social Fund, and some one thousand other dissidents had either been forced to emigrate or were in prisons, camps, psychiatric hospitals, or exile. Many of my closest friends—Tanya Velikhanova and Sergei Kovalyov, Sergei's son Ivan and Tanya Osipova (who was now Ivan's wife), Victor Nekipelov and Tolya Shcharansky, Vladimir Albrecht and Sergei Khodorovich, Father Gleb Yakunin and Malva Landa, Yelena Georgyevna Bonner and even Andrei Dmitriyevich Sakharov himself—some of the best people of this generation—had been crucified.

"The situation is terribly oppressive," Irina said. "A year and a half ago Yelena Georgyevna disbanded the Moscow Helsinki Group because the KGB threatened to arrest Sofia Kalistratova. Only three members were still free by then, the two of them and Naum Meiman. But an International Helsinki Federation has been formed, imagine that! You started it all. For many years, Valya Turchin has been campaigning for you among scientists in America. Thousands of friends and strangers all over the world are still fighting. Amnesty. The SOS Committee—that's Sakharov, Orlov, Shcharansky—in the United States. Special committees in Toronto and Paris and Geneva. In CERN people are even wearing T-shirts with your name on them. Many scientists are still boycotting contacts with the academy because of your case and Sakharov's exile. Some Nobel laureates, too.[2] And the director of DESY Laboratory in Hamburg has invited you to work there. Didn't you once study German?"

So I had not been forgotten. We had not been forgotten. Although the Soviet authorities were still like a brick wall to everyone, sooner or later the pressure from the West would help, if not myself, then at least the future of our idiotic country.

"And do you really believe that this country will ever change?" Irina asked.

"Not in my lifetime. But I'm sure it has a future. If I weren't sure, I wouldn't have done anything."

"You're an optimist! Nobody believes that. Anyway, if the KGB doesn't gobble you up completely, it will be just because of scientists."

Soon after Irina, Tarasov, and Ponomaryov left for home, I was moved to the workers' dormitory. It was noisy, but at least they gave me a separate bedroom—to limit my chance of conducting propaganda among the residents. I could do scientific work there and put up my son Sasha, who visited me for a couple of weeks. The slim, smooth-faced graduate student I had last seen five years ago had been transformed into a robust, bearded scientist. Yet he was still the charmingly absentminded

---

[2]We did not know at the time that Pyotr Kapitsa had written a long letter to Andropov defending Sakharov and myself.

boy I remembered. For years he had been urging foreign scientists he met in the USSR to press for my release by boycotting Soviet contacts. Now, just in case I was never released, he trained me in clandestine marches through the taiga. Starting at six in the morning, we silently walked miles and miles along dirt roads until I could go no further. Soon after Sasha left, I gave up this regime. It was too exhausting.

Thanks to Irina's appeals and the pressure of my scientist and émigré friends abroad, the Kobyai authorities more or less ceased their open violations of the law early in the summer of 1984. And so I was permitted to fly to Sangar to see a dentist. Back in camp my teeth had been ground down to stumps under the pretext of preparing them for crowns, which had quickly cracked. The whole operation had been repeated, and now the remnants of teeth and crowns cut my mouth so that it bled. In Sangar my dentist ruined the teeth even more. My dental technician was interrogated by the KGB, the woman who helped me find the technician was interrogated by the KGB, and her husband beat her up because she had been interrogated by the KGB. But I met Misha Gornostayev.

Misha, an independent-minded Byelorussian who had gone to Siberia for a while, hunted me up in the hotel.

"How did you know I was here?" I asked him.

"Very simple. The wife of one of the KGB chiefs told her girlfriends at work, in strictest confidence, 'Orlov is in Sangar.' " Misha and his family became my first close friends in exile.

At about the same time a Yakut stopped me on the street in Kobyai and delivered an impassioned, tipsy speech:

"Where is Sakharov? Where is Orlov? Where is Tverdokhlebov? Don't ever forget!"

"No, I'll not forget where I am," I replied, smiling. It was astonishing to hear this in a remote Yakut village. He introduced himself, and after that would point at me and tell selected acquaintances in Kobyai, "You have to help him." Everybody knew what he was talking about. I had been trying to rent or buy separate housing, yet whenever I found a place, the very next day the owner would back out of our deal with embarrassment and one excuse or another. Some Yakut owners had already confessed that after we had reached an agreement, a Chekist or a militiaman visited them and said that the local prosecutor had absolutely forbidden it—but that I should not be told.

In response to the lobbying of my tipsy acquaintance, one Russian couple who worked for the state gas pipeline decided to help. Ignoring a clear threat from Lieutenant Okhlopkov, they turned over to me a small house: one room with a couple of beds and a portrait of Stalin, and a tiny kitchen with an iron stove and a table. A greenhouse, privy, and animal shed were close by. The landlord, Yuri Pavlovich, a kind blue-eyed fellow when sober and rather terrifyingly white-eyed when drunk, had been inside camps many times—twenty years altogether—at the start for almost nothing and after that for murders. The first murder was self-defense in camp, and then he got into the habit. By his reckoning he had committed seven murders, but I think there were only five. While he was still in camp, Tamara Alexeyevna, a divorced gas technician with three children, had married him from a photo. She was a brave woman, perhaps because she had grown up in an orphanage during the war; and perhaps for this reason, too, Lieutenant Okhlopkov's warning had gone in one ear and out the other. Neither Tamara nor Yuri was greatly in love with the militia.

Yuri categorically refused to accept any rent. In return for their kindness I took care of their plastic-covered greenhouse, two pigs, eighteen chickens, and two roosters. In return they presented me with a young dog, Dina, and allotted six hens and Petka, a haughty rooster, for my personal use, as well as cucumbers and tomatoes from the greenhouse. In return I undertook to fix up the house, which they had built themselves from low-grade planks, roofing slates, and tar paper. And in return for all this, the authorities confiscated their house and drove Tamara out of Kobyai. But that happened later.

Finally I had a place to receive guests. Alas, a trip to me was a grueling and expensive operation: nearly four thousand miles by plane from Moscow to Yakutsk, then two hundred from Yakutsk to Sangar, then sixty from Sangar to Kobyai, in three stages, often lasting a week; sometimes searches at the airports; and most difficult for Irina, the horror of the outdoor toilets—mountains of filth worse than any I had seen in the camps. Nevertheless, I was rarely alone. Throughout that happy summer of '84, Irina lived in the house along with one

or another of my sons and friends, among them the physicist
Yuri Golfand, the only enthusiastic supporter of my ideas on
wave logic.

I now had a relief worker with whom I took turns guarding
our perpetually uncompleted nursery school twelve hours at a
stretch. I had chosen to work the quiet night shift. From home
to school was only a fifteen-minute walk along the bank of one
of the lakes. Arriving at 6:00 P.M., I checked for missing construction materials and for smoke where a cigarette butt had
been tossed on the peaty ground. If you don't spot that, the
ground will catch fire in a day or two; my privy had once almost
burned down that way. A little bit later, Irina and whoever else
was visiting would lug a water-filled kettle, frying pan, and food
to the carpenters' trailer, where I had a hot plate. Once dinner
was finished, I circled around the nursery school for hours and
hours with my guests, discussing physics and logic, politics and
psychology. After seven years of isolation, after the stench of
the cells and loutishness of the guards, these discussions were
like mouthfuls of oxygen. They revived hope—but of what? I
pushed aside that question for now. When my friends went
home to sleep, I lay down to rest on a pile of planks, buried in
my sheepskin coat. But mostly I read: my Sasha and Sasha
Barabanov had brought me a vast quantity of books, all that I
had asked for, and in summer here, the sunrise arrived with
the sunset at around 2:00 A.M.

At 6:00 A.M, my workday ended, I went home for a big
breakfast and slept until lunch. Our landlords, Tamara and
Yuri, often joined us then, and sometimes my new, kindhearted
friends from across the street—Nina Ivanovna, who taught
needlework and home economics, and her Yakut husband, a
bookkeeper on the sovkhoz. Work around the house began
after lunch. A tremendous lot had to be done: covering the
roof and installing gutters to catch rainwater for drinking and
cooking, insulating the house, preparing firewood for nine
months of winter. (And even when stacking firewood, we did
not stop talking science.) Tarasov had brought an incredible
number of tools from Moscow, even a scarce electric saw, as
well as special nails and a hand cart for transporting heavy
objects; I had bought some tools in the local store. Everyone
took turns lugging pails of water to the greenhouse and feeding
the animals. At night I went off to work again, and my youngest

son, Lev, when he was there, headed for the music school to practice the piano. Lev was all grown up now, a jazz musician, and so extraordinarily handsome that a young Yakut woman once spent half a day reverently staring at him from a distance as he helped me fix the roof.

In the middle of August I reached the age of sixty and retired with a pension of only sixty-seven rubles a month because I had been classified as "unemployed" for the past ten years—hard labor in camp does not count as labor! Food and money provided by innumerable friends in the Soviet Union and abroad made it possible to live. Retirement was a tremendous relief, releasing me from constant anxieties about arson in the nursery school and giving me a little more time for sleep, science, forest walks, and the precious company of my guests. By now the general atmosphere in the village had become considerably friendlier than it was at the start of my exile. I think that only the old teacher of the youngest children still believed I was an American spy. Even the young commander had called off her stone-throwing troops during my last weeks at the nursery school. Everybody saw that I worked long and hard, and this they respected. But what really broke their suspicious, hostile attitude toward me were the visits of my wife, children, and friends that summer. The whole village knew exactly who they were: they had been required to register with both the village Soviet[3] and the militia, where their documents were thoroughly examined and checked. No, you couldn't say anything, doctor-professors, scientific workers—respectable. Perhaps he isn't such an enemy of the people? So most of the locals were no longer afraid of me. A young Yakut woman even confided that she and some girlfriends had read an "article on religion" of mine (she must have meant Helsinki Group *Document No. 5*) in a toilet when she was in Irkutsk studying at a technical school.

Nina, Tamara, and their husbands remained my closest friends. Since I had moved in too late to plant a garden, they showered me with fresh produce from the fair-sized allotment each family had near its home. Without these allotments they could not have survived. To be sure, by Soviet standards people did not live badly in Kobyai. Because of the wage supplement for work in the north, they earned two and a half times more

---

[3]The popularly elected local assembly, controlled by the Party.

than people on "the mainland," everyone had a television, and
many had motorcycles. But the shops issued only six eggs per
person twice a year and a little more than two pounds of meat
per month per person—which was not surprising, since the
sovkhoz had more petty bureaucrats than milk cows. The sovkhoz calves often starved to death, or were killed by the wild
local dogs, or became stuck in the swamps and died there. The
only vegetables you could buy at the sovkhoz were cabbages,
and then only for a few days in the autumn.

Around Christmastime, which is January in Russia, someone somewhere woke up, and a Chekist visited the head office
of Tamara Alexeyevna's employers, demanding that she be removed from Kobyai because she was helping enemy of the
people Orlov to live. Tamara heroically decided to fight and
refused to evict me. I could not volunteer to leave, because
there was absolutely no available place to go. The forces in this
battle were unequal. Tamara was promptly and falsely charged
with embezzlements, one more serious than the other, and with
allowing me to live in her house without the approval of the
village Soviet. Awful, incessant investigations began. Some of
the locals, seeing that Tamara was being trampled on, began
to write ever more fantastic denunciations. She and Yuri Pavlovich had buried in their garden a portable radio transmitter
for communicating with the CIA, and they had too many pigs.
Pig audits began. I hastily helped Tamara sell her piglets, which
had been born in September. One local bureaucrat actually said
to me, "If everyone is going to be in love with their pigs as she
is, we'll never manage to build any Communism." That meant
Kobyai was really far from Communism, because our monthly
meat ration was higher than the ration in most other parts of
the country. The psychological warfare lasted all spring. The
authorities charged that the house I was living in had been built
illegally and even made out of stolen construction materials.
Finally they announced that it would be destroyed to make way
for a war memorial.

Obviously as part of this operation I was badly beaten up
that spring, at the end of April 1985. My son Sasha had to leave
for Novosibirsk, and both the Kobyai and Sangar airports,
which had dirt runways, could be closed at any moment for the
mushy spring season. However, in defiance of all orders some

heavy truck rigs were carrying freight to Yakutsk across the thawing marshes and rivers. Yuri Pavlovich arranged for a truck driver to give Sasha a lift. Sasha climbed into the cab of the truck, laden with a bag of buckwheat meal for his Novosibirsk friends and *pirozhki* baked by Tamara for himself. I said good-bye and set out for home. At midnight, not far from the militia station, three men ran after me while a fourth stood off to the side. They asked me who I was, knocked me down with a punch in the face, and began kicking my head and ribs. I covered my head with my hands, and briefly lost consciousness a couple of times. Finally they ran off and I staggered home, my head seriously knocked about for the third time in my life; two months later I still had problems with my eyesight.

Who had beaten me, and why?

Lieutenant Okhlopkov had been promoted and transferred to Sangar in January. His successor pointed out one of the men who had beaten me, but carefully covered up for the other participants. They were evidently the principals, probably some of the ten or so spruce young men in the village who worked for the KGB and hardly bothered to conceal their identity, hanging about the airport on days when my guests arrived or departed, and always ostentatious in their surveillance. As for this fellow, it quickly turned out that he had been misled. Truly distressed, he lamented that he would not have beaten up a "friend of Sakharov," had he known.

In the summer of 1985, one year after she and her husband had invited me to live in their house, Tamara was forced to leave Kobyai. That was the KGB punishment for her too cherished friendship with me and my sophisticated friends. All the terrible accusations against her were immediately dropped, and the authorities generously gave her a new job somewhere south of Yakutsk. Tamara now went to live there with her boyfriend; her marriage with Yuri, no fortress even before, had also been destroyed. The boyfriend was a ship captain on the Lena River. Two months after Tamara's expulsion from Kobyai a KGB captain called him in for questioning: "You once worked on ocean liners abroad. Now you are living with Tamara. But Tamara was once a friend of Orlov. And Orlov is—you know who he is. You understand the connection, don't you?" Two years later Tamara's ship captain was murdered on the street, nobody knows why.

* * *

The beating and Tamara's tragedy showed me how uncertain my own future was. With my Moscow friends I began new preparations for a summer escape. Longer and longer walks on the taiga to build my strength ... mapping possible routes from Kobyai to Yakutsk ... compass ... flippers for swimming through lakes ... stored protein concentrate, salt, and matches ... telephone numbers and codes for reaching some Moscow friends not known to the KGB. I was ready in case of a crisis. The taiga was almost impenetrable for me, but it was better to give up the ghost in the forest than surrender to them for another term in camp.

My immediate problem was to find a new home—an apparently impossible task, because people were afraid. Then, unexpectedly, in the autumn of 1985 the businesslike chief engineer of the sovkhoz, a friend of Nina Ivanovna, arranged for me to rent a house from his relatives at a rather high price. It was a decent Yakut log house near the forest, two little rooms and a kitchen with a smallish brick stove, set in a plot of good land. The landlord allotted a piece of ground for my own garden. My chickens went to Nina Ivanovna because the new house had no animal shed; she would keep me supplied with eggs from them, and with much other food as well. Irina and Sasha Barabanov helped me move, plug the cracks between the logs, haul enormous logs for the thirty to forty cubic yards of firewood needed for the winter, and furnish the interior. It took us all summer. From the old house we carted over planks for future repairs, firewood, and even rich soil from the now-broken-up greenhouse. I built a bookcase to hold my scientific books and Russian classics bought in the good local bookshop. Irina covered the windows, the two iron beds, and the two tables in the kitchen with beautiful material. Getting ice for water in the winter I took care of myself, after my guests went home.

There are innumerable lakes around Kobyai, but wells are impossible because of the permafrost, and the sovkhoz could not seem to manage a piped-in water system. As a result, water was delivered throughout the village all day long in tank trucks during the summer—an expensive operation. In winter we locals stocked up on ice cut from the lakes in October, while it was still no more than a foot and a half thick. The previous winter Tamara had provided me with ice. This winter Nina Ivanovna's husband and their engineer friend took me along with them to cut it. We drove in a truck to the lake that seemed most pure, then marked out a section with a *peshnya*, which is like a pike but with a hook near the end, and used it to hack out a hole large enough for a hand-powered ice saw. Then we sawed out rectangles one yard across, hauled them out of the water with the *peshnyas*, and loaded them onto the truck. It was heavy labor. I stacked these big pieces of ice outside my house and chipped off small pieces throughout the winter, putting them in three big barrels inside the house to thaw for cooking and drinking. For washing and bathing, I gathered snow and melted it on the stove. In warm weather I could use the shower that Tarasov had made for me out of a pail with a sieve in the bottom, and had brought all the way from Moscow; otherwise I bathed myself in a large trough close to the stove so as not to wet the wooden floor, under which my potatoes were stored. Melting enough water for a bath took a fair amount of time, but the public bath was unspeakable.

Once the ice was prepared, I could concentrate on scientific work, with frequent interruptions to saw and split logs throughout the day, chip ice, shop, and cook. Although it was all rather tiring, at least there were no longer numerous animals to feed: just Dina, my dog, and Barakhlo, a kitten I had acquired. I bought a sack of small frozen carp for each of us and cooked the fish on the stove. When there were no carp, Dina and I would go about the village collecting bones for her, which I then broke up with an ax. Barakhlo could get along on kasha and mice in the cellar. Dina, being a Yakut dog, did not understand kasha. She understood meat. Occasionally she supplied her own, killing small animals in the forest, yet for some strange reason refused to eat them unless I cut them up for her.

One day in November a telegram arrived from Marat Veksler, saying that the American biochemist George Wald had pressed Gorbachev for my release.[3] Marat learned about it from

---

[3]Wald had come to Moscow to present Gorbachev with a peace statement signed by more than fifty other Nobel laureates.

Wald's press conference in Moscow; it had not been reported
in the newspapers. When I displayed his telegram to the militia
and the village Soviet, they were gratifyingly paralyzed by shock.
"I hope the Wald business will help," Irina said when she arrived
for her winter visit. But, as usual, I decided not to get my hopes
up. So I devoted myself to work and, after narrowly escaping
asphyxiation by stove fumes, finished my article on logic, sent
it to the USSR Academy of Sciences, and immediately began
work on a new one. Spring was coming soon. I would then have
to spend hours in the garden and the little plastic-covered
greenhouse Tarasov and I had built, planting potatoes, tomatoes, cucumbers, dill, parsley, and lettuce in preparation for
the new summer. Summer in Yakutia lasts just two months, but
it is very hot and there is light nearly twenty-four hours a day.
If you prepare properly and work hard, and there are no summer frosts, you can harvest many vegetables for the rest of the
year.

That summer of 1986 started out well. The house was full
of guests—Irina and my son Sasha, Sasha Barabanov, and Katya
Veksler, who had grown into a lovely beauty since the days she
delighted in spotting our Chekists behind the birch trees. There
was no pressure from the militia, Lieutenant Okhlopkov's re-
placement having turned out to be a nice drunk who liked to
have philosophical discussions with me about whether platonic
love existed ("It does," I assured him). General secretaries had
died one after another, and had finally been replaced by Mikhail
Gorbachev. There were glimmers of *glasnost* and *perestroika* in
the papers; the decay of our brilliant totalitarian "scientific society" seemed to be starting much earlier than I expected.
"Maybe Gorbachev will ask me to be his adviser," I joked to
Nina Ivanovna's husband, a very kind man but a Stalinist, as
many Yakutians are. Irina had secretly accepted an invitation
for me to lecture at the Swedish Academy. Academicians Yevgeny Velikhov and Moisei Markov were trying to get my wave-
logic article published in a Soviet scientific journal. And a large
group of accelerator physicists from CERN, headed by Pierre
Lefèvre, Dieter Möhl, and Nobel laureate Simon Van der Meer,
had refused to attend a conference at Novosibirsk because I
was not invited. Many other distinguished physicists, like An-

drew Sessler of the Lawrence Radiation Laboratory in California, also boycotted it.

On August 14, the day after my birthday, Irina and I were summoned to the village Soviet for a chat with a sleek, sharp-nosed KGB man from Moscow and the chief of the Kobyai District KGB, who looked rather like a samurai. Moscow began with a shrill attack on Irina.

"You are sending slanderous materials to the West alleging that Orlov was beaten to the point of brain concussion. We are going to charge you under Article 64 of the Criminal Code for being an accessory to subversive activity." Article 64 covered treason.

"Are you trying to tell me that you personally witnessed my husband being beaten up—but not to the point of brain concussion? Or are you trying to tell me that he was not beaten up at all?" she asked very calmly. "All of Kobyai saw his mashed-up face in the course of a month. Do you deny that?" she added. En route to the meeting we had agreed that she would be utterly calm and deliberate; it would drive them out of their minds. And in fact her questioner wilted at once and switched to me. I could be transferred to a city, that would be better for my scientific work. To what city? Well, for example, Yakutsk. In Kobyai you have a house, a vegetable garden? Of course, you would be living in a dormitory there, we have no apartments. You also won't get a garden. But you can make use of the library. Of course, you will have to promise not to engage in anything illegal. . . .

"I do not want to leave Kobyai," I said.

Irina and I became anxious. I had set down roots in the village, everyone treated me well. Now, deeply disappointed, the KGB was going to smash it all.

TWENTY-TWO

The Last Sunday in September

On the last Sunday in September 1986, I sat at home alone writing my first political appeal from exile, a plea to the Vienna Conference on Security and Cooperation for an amnesty of political prisoners in the countries that had signed the Helsinki Accords. My guests had returned to Moscow. I had harvested a fine crop of vegetables. The house was protected against the cold. Forty cubic yards of firewood were prepared, the stove was in working order, my health was good. All was ready for winter.

At midday, exactly noon, the locked door was violently yanked, feet began hammering against the jamb, then the door was yanked again. I shoved my notes in a pocket—the best place during a house search—went to the door, and opened it. Two men came inside, a Yakut of about forty with a vaguely familiar face, and a young Russian, a sturdy fellow straight off the cover of a Soviet book on the CIA or perhaps an American one on the KGB.

"Who are you?" I inquired.

"Can it be you have forgotten?" said the Yakut, hurt. "I am chief of the Kobyai District KGB." Ah, yes. The samurai.

"Well, and you?"

"He is with me." The Russian silently stationed himself by

the door. "Get your things together! You have an hour to pack.
The plane is waiting."

So, they had come. My soul disconnected itself. I felt
nothing.

"What should I take? For the north, south, west? The east?"
"I do not know."

I decided to expect the worst and pack as for a prisoner
transport—mug, spoon, pens, warm clothes, photographs of
my family, the most important papers and books.

"How many books? Five?" Perhaps I would learn something. You were allowed five books in camp.

"What do you need books for?"

That sounded like prison. I began sorting out the scores
of books and stacks of scientific notes and calculations that had
accumulated during the past two and a half years. What should
I take? Too much would be heavy; too little, and something
crucial might get left behind. And better put on an ordinary
padded jacket, a cheap hat: one way or another criminals would
seize better clothes during transport. Everything went into a
suitcase and rucksack. Once again I would be dragged down.

The appeal! The appeal in my pocket!

"A visit to the toilet—before the journey. Just a minute."
The district chief frowned, hesitated a second, then nodded.
Dina and Barakhlo were waiting for me in the garden. The
Chekists watched through the window. After getting rid of the
appeal, I stood for a long time in my small wooden privy. Two
weeks earlier, when I was digging up potatoes in the garden,
a couple of unfamiliar men in black suits, a Yakut and a Russian,
had appeared on the front steps of the house next door, and
one pointed me out to the other. When I straightened up, they
turned away and vanished in a hurry around a corner. That
same afternoon I loosened one of the back boards of my privy
in case of emergency. Now the emergency had arrived. I could
push the board aside, crawl through, and race unseen along
the line of sight from window to privy, then turn right into the
woods, the taiga. It would take them a while to fetch their dogs.
I had thought about it a thousand times, how to lose the dogs.
By water, of course, this time of year; not everywhere was frozen
yet. Hell! Dina would follow me. I should have thought to lock
her up before leaving the house.

I went back through the door. Barakhlo jumped from the privy roof and trotted along the fence railing after me. Idiot, I should have escaped just as soon as those two men appeared! Had I not resolved to escape at the very first sign of impending arrest? But when it came down to it, I had lacked the will to understand. The sign appeared, you glimpsed it by chance, so don't hang about for confirmation, run! Instead, you loosen a board, idiot, fooling yourself.

"Let's go?"

"Let's go." I gathered up my things and left without looking back. The district chief locked the door, dropped the key in his pocket, and walked through the little gate onto the street. The Russian marched behind me. In front of the house two motorcycles waited, a familiar Yakut informer sitting on the one with a sidecar. How silently the scum had crept up to the house! The Chekists ordered me to climb into the sidecar, then took off at high speed. The informer followed with me, and Dina rushed alongside, her tongue hanging out, still panting from the distemper she had suffered that summer. The streets were absolutely dead, deserted, although it was a Sunday. Could they possibly have forbidden people to go outside their homes?

A plane really was waiting for us on the dirt airfield, a ten-seat biplane. The motorcycles drove right up to it, past the decrepit airport building. No one was outside the building, but faces were pressed against the windows. Just then I discovered that my suitcase was gone. All those books and papers! Lost. To my amazement, the district chief ordered the informer to drive back and look for it. He returned after fifteen minutes with the suitcase; it had fallen overboard near the start of our ride. "Now *you* wait a moment," the district chief said, jogged into the airport building, evidently to ban peering through the windows, and jogged back. "No one wants to go on this trip!" he exclaimed, grinning at his own joke. The informer and the Russian did not smile. I heaved my things into the empty plane and climbed up the small ladder, the Chekists behind me. The informer stayed put. Dina jumped in, and the Russian flung her out with a kick. She did not yelp, just stood there, not taking her eyes off me in the doorway. She'll perish, I thought. She's a Yakutian dog, she'll die waiting at the airport. And the cat will perish, too, with winter coming and the house locked up. Our pilot came aboard, shut the door, and we took off. Dina did not move.

The larch trees had already shed their delicate needles and the taiga was turning black, but the swamps were still green. Thin, transparent ice covered the lakes. Gradually they turned into still-unfrozen channels, the channels into branches, the branches into streams, and finally the tremendous Lena River. We were approaching Sangar. The dirt airfield was empty. I collected my suitcase and rucksack, and they led me into a barrack for repairmen at the end of the airfield, then left. A worker was fixing a hot plate to boil water for afternoon tea. Should I try to make a run for it? I went outside. The Russian was lounging by the door. I went back. Other workers came in and took off their coats. The heating coil had been repaired, tea was ready. "Sit yourself down!" No one asked what I was doing there. They brought him, it's their business. I drank tea with them and looked through the window. A green two-engine military plane gracefully landed. The Russian came into the barrack. "Let's go!" He led me to the front of the plane, watched me board, and disappeared.

Already sitting in the small officers' section were the district chief and another Yakut. "Chief of the Yakutia KGB," he cordially announced in answer to my question. As soon as I was seated opposite them, the plane took off and headed south. The face of the district chief was gloomy. We flew in total silence. Why a military plane? *And where are we going?* It would be pointless to ask. Half an hour later we landed at the Yakutsk airport. They had threatened to transfer my exile here. Or had they really meant prison? I was asked to take my things along, and we stood on the airfield for a while. Not one single living soul could be seen. "It would be nice to have some lunch," I suggested. Always best to eat sooner rather than later. They silently led me to the administration building some distance away. At the entrance stood a quartet of Chekists, and Moscow Chekists at that, immediately recognizable by their faces. They did not look at us. We went to the second floor into some office, the Yakutia chief gave an order, and a middle-aged woman brought all three of us very good food. She was pointedly at-

tentive to me; a shadow of scorn, light as air, touched her
treatment of them. Perhaps she had been told that I was being
taken to prison again?

Over the herring, the district chief started to discuss the
beating that I had received more than a year before. "The KGB
had nothing to do with it," he repeated over and over, meanwhile betraying with his eyes that it had. His boss, the Yakutia
chief, leaned back in his chair as if he had nothing whatsoever
to do with all that. It was strange, as if I had some power to
hurt them. I wondered why they seemed so eager to establish
their innocence. Perhaps, like Khrushchev, Gorbachev was
cleaning out the stables and calling the KGB to account?

Over the steak, the district chief jumped to the subject of
Misha Gornostayev, my Sangar friend: "What do you think,
why did Gornostayev make a show of resigning his position as
chief engineer in order to become an ordinary electrician?"

"It was not done for effect. He got fed up with doing
bureaucratic work instead of real work," I explained. "He feels
that as an electrician he is producing benefits for people, not
just paper. And he earns much more, too. He's master of his
trade, first class."

"Orlov, you always twist things to suit yourself!" He looked
nervous. It was obvious that he had started to build a case
against Misha. How was that going to look to his bosses now, a
case against someone struggling against the bureaucracy, just
like the general secretary himself?

In the middle of dessert, the Moscow quartet entered: "It's
time." *So it's not going to be Yakutsk.* I stood up. They suddenly
materialized in front, behind, and on either side of me—also
masters of their trade. We left the district chief and his boss to
their tea and cookies, and went out to the same military plane.
Boarding this time by a ramp under the tail, I now realized
that the plane was designed for landing troops in border-guard
operations. Inside we passed a bench for soldiers and a huge
fuel tank; I dumped my suitcase and rucksack next to the bench
and was led to the officers' section. I sat down by a window,
the Chekists sat around me. Some officer was there already—
a border guard. The five of them started to chat. It was rapidly
getting dark outside the window when we took off. The pilot
headed north.

We touched down in thick darkness and a depressing landscape: skeletons of scorched or perhaps storm-beaten firs, black against the deep mauve sky. The airport building was new and, to my surprise by now, had people in it. They acted as if it were normal for someone to walk around with a suitcase, rucksack, and four men obviously guarding him. But then, the passengers on my flight to Yakutsk and exile had pretended that my handcuffs did not exist. I looked for the flight-information board. So, we were in Polyarny. *Polyarny?* According to the mosaic murals on the walls, gold and diamonds were mined here. A happy worker, arm raised like the Statue of Liberty, held aloft a diamond flashing a sunburst of rays. "Where is this place?" I asked one of my guards.

"Arctic Circle." It must have been a brand-new city; I had never seen it on a map.

The Chekists got hold of a local KGB jeep and driver, and we rode down long streets flanked by the usual five-story buildings, then past enormous dredges, ending up in a two-room apartment, which they opened with their own key. It was a kind of dormitory, three beds to a room.

"That's your bed," they told me. "Make yourself comfortable." One of them was going to a store to get everybody food; I gave him money for mine. He brought back some canned fish and bread, and they politely invited me to join them.

"Where are you taking me?"

"Yuri Fyodorovich! It's you who are taking us, though where, by God, we don't know."

We lay down to sleep, two of them in my room, a third in the other room; the fourth sat guarding the entryway. I could not change anything, and my conscience was clear. I slept well.

In the morning we returned to our plane. The border-guard officer joined us, and we flew west to Norilsk, once infamous for its camps. I stood around the terminal with my suitcase and rucksack while my guards engaged the local authorities in lengthy, mysterious conversations. *This must be the last stop.* Here in this big city between the Arctic Circle and the Arctic Ocean, there would be no private house, no garden, and almost no possibility for visitors to reach me. The ideal place for exile. But after two hours we were off again, flying up to the Arctic Ocean itself and turning west along the coast. *Where the hell are we going?* I could not tear myself away from the window. The tundra, frozen but almost free of snow, shimmered like lovely brown silk, and the black-green waves of the ocean seemed motionless, a photograph. I stared and stared, trying to see them move, sure they were moving. At last it dawned on me that they had been suddenly frozen.

"Where are we flying to?" one of the Chekists asked the border-guard officer.

"Is it Spitsbergen?" the archipelago held jointly by Norway and the USSR. Perhaps they were going to give me to Norway. I listened carefully, but the officer did not reply. Now the taiga lay below us again, with gigantically long, wide cuttings that ran from north to south. Logging country. And the country of camps.

At midday we landed at a city 250 miles south of the Arctic Ocean—"Pechora," announced one of the guards. We left the plane, discovered a civilized lavatory in a building of its own, and then walked around for a while.

"Petrov-Agatov is serving time right over there in that camp," chatted another guard, pointing to the barbed wire two hundred yards away, just where the city streets began. "Remember him?"

"I remember. I see you're right at home in camp country. What's he in for this time?"

"Same as always—swindling."

"The perfect coauthor for the KGB and the Central Committee. The committee revised that *Literary Gazette* article against Ginzburg and me ten times."

"How do you know that?"

"So then, we're flying to Spitsbergen?"

From Pechora, however, we flew not northwest to Spitsbergen but southwest. *It's Moscow. It's prison.*

By late afternoon we reached Sheremetyevo Airport. Two black Volgas and four new Chekists in black suits met us. They raced ahead in their car. ("What Russian doesn't love a fast ride?" Gogol once asked.) Leningrad Prospect. Gorky Street. The building where perhaps right now Irina was visiting her mother. *Forget about that.* Red Barracks Street. But today no black Volgas were stationed like dreadnoughts along my route to prison. He was right, the head of Lefortovo. We were meeting again. They opened the steel gates, the cars drove into a small courtyard, the gates closed immediately behind us. All the Chekists left. I sat for two hours unattended in the car. Finally they led me inside to a special room, searched me, inventoried my things, took them away, and had me dress in prison clothes. The new system was that you were forbidden to wear your own. A familiar guard, no longer young, silently led me into a cell and slammed the iron door with a crash. That had not changed in nine and a half years. Neither had the cell: two made-up iron beds, one stripped bed, another person. I immediately demanded paper to write a complaint. On what basis had they switched my regime from exile to prison? After an hour I was led away to interrogation. It was already late evening.

"Yuri Fyodorovich," began the same interrogator who had questioned me nine years before about the Shcharansky case, "you have been brought here for now as a witness in the criminal case concerning the anti-Soviet activity of the so-called Russian Social Fund to Aid Political Prisoners and Their Families, which falls under Article Seventy, Part Two, of the Criminal Code. What can you tell us about this activity? An irregular beginning? Very well, let us begin correctly. Your last name? First name? Patronymic?" He read out some testimony to the effect that the Moscow Helsinki Watch Group had been involved in the work of the fund. Such activity had always been punished, and under Andropov had been made officially illegal. The case file already looked rather plump. There was nothing for me to say and no reason to say anything except that I didn't know anything and didn't remember anything, but they'd better remember that they couldn't legally hold someone as a witness longer than three days.

And so I was interrogated a few hours every day for three days—easy compared with my last visit to this place.

"Who helped you in camp?"

"No one."

"Who helped your family?"

"I don't know."

"Who helped you in exile?"

"Only scientists."

"Who?"

"I won't tell you. But why is it a crime to help prisoners and exiles?"

"Because, for one thing, any information about them is a state secret."

On the fourth day, when I had already announced my refusal to participate in further interrogation because I was being illegally detained, and when I expected them to reclassify me for the next ten days as a "suspect," and then as a "defendant"—the usual game—the guards led me into a room furnished with soft carpet, good imitation antiques, and golden wallpaper. It seemed beautiful, after the cell. Sitting there were two high KGB officials in civilian clothes, faces puffy and noses violet from the sweet life. I was invited to sit opposite them on a delicate gilded chair in the center of the room. They introduced themselves, and I immediately forgot their names. The one at the table tonelessly read out a decree of the Presidium of the Supreme Soviet that deprived me of Soviet citizenship. "You will be sent to the United States on the next available plane," he tonelessly added. "Your wife will travel with you. But until then, according to regulations, you will have to wait here." *I may not see the children for the rest of my life. And where were those regulations written down?*

Being stripped of citizenship before deportation was supposed to be the most horrible punishment. So far only Trotsky and Solzhenitsyn had suffered it. Yet the bloodshot eyes of the elderly Chekists expressed unconcealed envy, then clouded over, perhaps with visions of unattainable Mediterranean seas, naked maidens along the shores. . . . They roused themselves and began to chat. "Don't be in a hurry to make anti-Soviet statements abroad, Yuri Fyodorovich," said the one on the couch in a friendly way. "We realize, of course, that anti-Soviet organizations will immediately get you in their clutches. But know that changes are being prepared in our country such as you yourself once dreamed of."

I demanded a visit with my children.

That evening they took my measurements, and by morning a well-tailored suit and a shirt were ready. I was also issued a necktie and shoes that fit perfectly. After having lived sixty-two years, I had finally discovered how to acquire decent clothing in the Soviet Union. Wearing the new suit, I was led into a room to await my sons. The authorities were allowing the visit. They arranged it in their usual style—a telephone call summoning the children not to Lefortovo but OVIR, the department for emigration, and without explaining why. Dima, afraid they would detain him and send him abroad, too, declined to go. When Sasha and Lev arrived at OVIR, they were put in a Volga and driven to the prison. Our brief meeting took place in the presence of two vigilant officers. We simply said farewell. As we hugged for the last time, Sasha whispered, "Don't be afraid for us. Just keep fighting for people."

The next morning three members of the Moscow Chekist quartet hurriedly packed me and my suitcase into a Volga. The rucksack, they said, was too old to take. So, apparently, were my two address books and some photographs of Sakharov, but I only found out about that later. As the car raced to the airport, I peered over the shoulders of the guards. Byelorussia Station. Here my father and mother first met, here they took the train to visit me in our village. Now I would never see what had become of the desolate, empty place where Gniloye once stood. My whole life, I had kept delaying that trip. . . On the left, behind the fences, Aviation Factory No. 22, where my father had been a metal worker. How many factories there were in Moscow! Yet my stepfather, too, once worked here, and Galya . . .

Carrying my suitcase, the Chekists escorted me onto an Aeroflot plane directly from the airfield. The plane was empty. They gestured to several rows near the front, "Sit somewhere there," stowed my suitcase, and left. What about Irina? Had they deceived me? Would they ship me off alone? I sat down by a window.

After half an hour Irina suddenly appeared, followed by Richard Combs, deputy chief of mission at the U.S. embassy, and the other passengers. Irina looked sad and tired. "So, they finally liberated you." We kissed, and she sat down beside me. People slowly filed past us, strangers, more strangers, then a familiar face. The young theoretician from ITEP smiled, put out his hand, loudly said hello. "In the airport a lot of people saw me off," Irina said, "hoping to get a glimpse of you." Two more familiar faces, physicists from Serpukhov. They said hello stiffly and looked away. "If only I'd known that customs wouldn't check my things. How many photos I left behind! And I gave most everything else away. Now I'm left with just one suitcase, like after a fire."

"This isn't liberation," I said. "It's deportation. Why?"

"But didn't they tell you? The swine! A Soviet spy, Zakharov, was arrested in America. To rescue him, Moscow set up a provocation and arrested the American journalist Nicholas Daniloff."

"So?"

"Reagan refused to trade a spy for a hostage. Then they started to talk about adding someone else to the hostage. And finally they, quote, came to an agreement on the release of some person called Orlov, unquote. That's what Shevardnadze said at the press conference. It was in the newspaper on Sunday."

The plane was taking off. I did not want to look out of the window. Sunday? The Kobyai Post Office, where our newspapers came, was closed on Sundays, and I had been under guard since Sunday noon. So for five whole days everyone else had known. For two days they had flown me all over the map lugging that damn suitcase and rucksack, letting me think I was being sent back to prison or a new place of exile. Then for three days in Lefortovo they had acted as if a new case were being prepared against me. And all along the district chief, his boss, the guards, the interrogator—everyone—had known that I was to be released.

Typical.

Irina dozed. The long flight passed quickly. Serge Schmemann, a *New York Times* correspondent on his way home, had arranged to be on my flight. We had a two-hour interview, and then I chatted about physics with the friendly young theoretician from ITEP.

Science. To begin everything from the very beginning one more time. A new language. No matter, we will manage. After all, my head is still on its usual place.

TWENTY-THREE

Falling from the Moon

Still thinking about everything and nothing, I sleepily walked off the plane at Kennedy Airport into the arms of four tremendous black security men carrying tremendous pistols and clothed top-to-toe in black. They immediately surrounded us, drove a path through an enormous crowd of journalists and friends, swept us into a room for a brief reunion with Lyuda Alexeeva and Valya Turchin, swept us out into another room packed with more journalists and friends, deposited us at a table, and planted their bodies between us and the surging crowd. It suddenly dawned on me that I had to make a decision.

Science would have to wait.

For the next four months I campaigned for those left behind, using every press conference, every meeting, every interview, to mention names: Sakharov, still exiled in Gorky; Koryagin, still in our old camp; members of the Helsinki groups in camp or exile; and especially Marchenko in the Chistopol Prison, who had declared many weeks ago a hunger strike to the death for a general amnesty of political prisoners in the USSR. This man—if he said it—would do it, no matter that the authorities answered, "Die! There are no political prisoners in the USSR!" We must hurry to help him. Lyuda and I talked about him everywhere. Helsinki Watch in New York prepared for me two big photo placards of Nelson Mandela and Anatoly Marchenko. People knew Mandela. Let them know Marchenko and defend both men.

I worked with the same intensity as in Moscow before my arrest. Days and days of interviews with journalists, meetings in the White House, meetings with members of Congress, speeches to academies of science, visits to scientific colleagues and defense committees, more speeches, more interviews—it was physically easier than camp but harder than exile. For the first time in my life I had to take sleeping pills, take them night after night, week after week, in order to overcome fatigue enough to get some sleep. The pills disgusted me.

A few days after arriving in the West, I met with President Reagan and Secretary of State Shultz, who were about to go to Reykjavík for negotiations with Gorbachev. I inquired what was being done to save Sakharov. Sakharov, thank goodness, was known to everyone, and had even become a special concern of Western governments.

"When we ask the Soviets to let Sakharov and his wife go abroad to her family in Boston," Reagan said, "they reply that it is impossible because he knows too many state secrets. Obviously it's a game, but we can't prove otherwise. What's the best way to proceed?"

The president's question slightly embarrassed me. So far as I knew, Sakharov had not asked to leave the country. But that was exactly what the Soviets wanted: to keep discussion of human rights focused on emigration to relatives. The official line was that neither political prisoners nor political opposition existed at all in the Soviet Union. Maybe refuseniks existed, but this, they said, was a completely artificial Jewish problem, nothing whatever to do with human rights. As to human rights, they would look candidly into your eyes and insist that they had never violated them and that anyway it was their internal affair, so don't interfere.

"The best approach in Sakharov's case," I advised Reagan, "is not to demand his emigration but simply his release, with freedom to live in Moscow or anywhere he likes. Sakharov has publicly stated that he does know secrets, and that he considers it a serious insult to suppose he would ever divulge any of them." When Gorbachev's famous telephone call to Gorky released him at last from exile later that December, Sakharov returned like a homing pigeon to his Moscow apartment.

In late October I left the Turchins' pleasant house in New Jersey and headed for Europe with Catherine Fitzpatrick, research director of U.S. Helsinki Watch. A superb translator, Katya knew more about Soviet political prisoners than anyone else in the world except Lyuda in New York and Kronid Lubarsky in Munich. During the next six weeks I traveled to the capitals of nearly every European country to meet with leaders of the political right and the political left—Margaret Thatcher, Willi Brandt, Helmut Kohl, and Petra Kelly, members of parliaments, heads of trade unions—Orlov defense committees, and scientific laboratories. In London I finally shook the hand of my remarkable lawyer, John Macdonald. And in Vienna I was elected honorary chairman of the International Helsinki Federation, umbrella organization for the movement our Moscow Helsinki Watch Group had started ten years before.

Lyuda joined us at the 1986 Vienna Conference on Security and Cooperation in Europe, which had just begun. The faces of the Western delegates seemed an undifferentiated blur, like all non-Russian faces in those days, but the Soviet delegates were immediately recognizable even before they opened their mouths: they all looked like watchtower guards from the camps. And when they opened their mouths . . .

"You're being used by the State Department, Yuri Fyodorovich!" This Soviet specialist in (naturally) humanitarian relations had just heard Secretary of State Shultz make a speech in which he demanded the release of Sakharov, Marchenko, Koryagin, and all members of the Soviet Helsinki groups, and it was no secret that Orlov had asked him to do that. And here was Orlov himself in his natty KGB suit, fraternizing with the Western delegations—clearly, a Shultz agent.

"Perhaps *you* will help release our prisoners?" I proposed. He stared at me as if I had just fallen from the moon.

I was actually beginning to feel that way after weeks of discussions with sympathizers in America and Europe who, unlike Reagan and Shultz, believed that strong human-rights pressure on the USSR could create instabilities endangering international peace, or who saw no connection at all between international security and human rights. A little more than ten years had gone by since the 1975 Helsinki Accords had formally established that connection and our Moscow group had begun to act on it, but many people still did not understand. My campaign for political prisoners also had to be a campaign for ideas. Therefore, across two continents, I tried to make the case for what we members of Helsinki groups had always regarded as elementary truths. Russia could not have turned into such an armed camp, I argued, pouring its wealth and talent into the bottomless pit of the military, without the unprecedented restrictions on free movement and exchange of information that regimes after 1917 had imposed within Russia herself and between Russia and the outside world. The resulting barriers to any democratic control of the military, and to mutual knowledge and understanding between Russians and other peoples —these were the menaces to international peace and security, not pressure by governments or citizens on behalf of human rights. In general such pressures united peoples, made them feel part of the same world family of human beings. And that feeling, I insisted, was more important for future international peace and security than any amicable relations among rulers. Good official relations between two governments meant nothing when even one of the two was totalitarian. Good relations with Nazi Germany during the shameful Munich period gave England and France zero security, and relations between Nazi Germany and the Soviet Union were extrasuperexcellent just before the start of the bloodiest war between them.

Predicting that democracy and demilitarization in the USSR would be strongly correlated, I urged that the West use all legal channels to push the Soviet government toward radical democratic reform in the interests of its own security. That meant determined opposition to human rights violations, because suppression of human rights was sufficient to protect the system in a strongly consistent totalitarian country. Sakharov and other dissidents could, if released, do more for peace, security, and stable disarmament through changing the political system than all the official and unofficial East-West negotiators put together.

Few people took these arguments seriously. The idea of human rights was still somewhat vague, whereas security was concretely defined in terms of counterforces or mutual disarmament, and to some people the very idea of pressing the Soviets for reform smacked of reactionary Kremlin-bashing. The most serious and common objection I met was that Russians were not ready for democracy. History, people told me, showed that Russians were submissive by nature and lacked the democratic mentality that comes from experience in democracy; therefore, pressure for radical democratic reform was pointless. Or, they said, history showed that Russians were violent by nature and lacked the democratic mentality that comes from experience in democracy; therefore pressure for radical democratic reform was dangerous. We must, everyone agreed, be grateful to Gorbachev and encourage him.

This kindly, well-meaning conclusion was poorly supported by such inconsistent claims about inheritance and experience, and selective, inaccurate appeals to Russian history. Did a naturally submissive people make three revolutions and one civil war in our century? Did a naturally violent people suffer the destruction of more than 60 million peaceful fellow citizens in the course of three decades at the hands of their rulers? Was the survivors' silence so obviously the silence of natural slaves? History showed that Russia did, in fact, have democratic experience from the 1860s until October 1917[1]—not a great deal, certainly, but still something. History also showed that democratic experience did not guarantee democracy. For all their democratic experience, the Italians had their Mussolini, the Germans their Hitler, the French their Pétain, the Norwegians their Quisling, and the Americans their McCarthy. . . .

And thus, on the basis of bad logic and worse history, many ardent democrats ardently opposed strong pressure for fundamental democratic reform in the USSR. I was astounded. Russians were indeed ready for democracy. But the West was not ready for democracy in Russia.

Few Western participants in the Vienna Conference considered gratitude the obvious perspective from which to view the Soviets—as the Soviet delegation discovered when it pro-

---

[1]The slaves were freed in Russia in 1861, a little bit earlier than in the United States, and for about sixty years after that Russia experienced tremendous pressure of radical democratic public opinion. She had independent juries from 1861 until October 1917; a parliament, no censorship, free political parties, and trade unions from 1905 until October 1917; and from February until October 1917, a non-monarchist government and even elected army commanders.

posed convening a special CSCE human rights meeting in Moscow in 1987. What nonsense, the very idea of such a meeting in a country that still kept thousands of political prisoners, some in special psychiatric hospitals, still held one of the greatest living scientists under virtual house arrest in exile, and still persecuted unofficial peace groups! It was like Nazi Germany proposing to host an international conference on genetics.

Although most Western delegates seemed disconcerted by the Soviet proposal, and the English, Canadians, and Americans considered it absolutely farcical, I felt that most heads of state would not be receptive to a simple appeal to boycott the proposed meeting. With Gorbachev's recent decree of *glasnost*, the curious phenomenon of Western Gorbamania had begun, and millions of people were riveted by the man they saw as the liberal czar of a backward nation. Western governments might, however, accept the idea of placing conditions on the meeting, *and the conditions might be met.* For it seemed to me that despite its usual bravado, the Soviet regime must be facing some grave general crisis in its position to have entered the novel and unpredictable process of *glasnost.* True, the state monopoly on information had already been broken by Solzhenitsyn, Sakharov, and the dissidents, who had been exercising their own *glasnost* for at least a quarter of a century. But when I had remarked years ago in a private letter to Congresswoman Millicent Fenwick that we had thrown ourselves on barbed wire so that others could walk over our bodies, it had never occurred to me that those "others" would be the Politburo itself! Obviously the Soviets were now in desperate need of Western support. Well, if they badly wanted it, and for that reason were concerned with the image of the USSR as a civilized country, let them meet conditions that would be absolutely normal in any civilized state. The main condition, of course, had to be the release of all political prisoners. Other conditions would include free access to the meeting by unofficial East European and Soviet journalists and human rights organizations, as well as freedom for ordinary Soviet citizens to bring complaints to CSCE delegates without reprisals. By the time I left Vienna at the beginning of December, after having met with nearly all the Western delegations, the idea of a Moscow human rights meeting with conditions had taken hold. But Margaret

Thatcher unequivocally rejected the Soviet proposal in any form. When I met with her on my way home, I urged her to consider a Moscow meeting with strong conditions attached to it, adding that if the West lacked the strength to insist on them, then, yes, it would be better not to attend.

On December 8, while the Soviet delegation was still cheerfully offering Moscow hospitality, Anatoly Marchenko perished. The hunger strike of that brilliant writer, industrial worker, and nonviolent opponent of state violence had indeed been to the end. The delegates at Vienna already knew his appeal to them, smuggled out of the Chistopol Prison with the help of his wife, Larisa Bogoraz, a famous dissident herself. Now Vienna discussed his death—and the Moscow human rights meeting. Two months later the Soviets announced that they would begin releasing people imprisoned under Article 70 ("anti-Soviet agitation and propaganda"), because of "troubles these prisoners are creating for our international relations." Month after month prisoners would be released in small numbers, like drops of blood squeezed from a stone; month after month the Western delegates at Vienna did not settle the question of a Moscow meeting, and more prisoners would be let out. Finally, in December 1988, when most of the prisoners were free, the American delegation agreed to the Soviet proposal under State Department pressure to end the conference before the new administration took office. A reluctant England and an even more reluctant Canada then agreed, and the controversial Moscow human rights meeting was officially scheduled for 1991.

At the start of February 1987, the very month that the political prisoners who did not officially exist began to be released, I returned to scientific work after thirteen years of forced interruption. The beautiful hilly countryside around Cornell University in Ithaca, New York, reminded me of estates near Moscow, and my research position as senior scientist in the university's Laboratory of Nuclear Studies seemed ideal. What was not ideal at all was going to Ithaca alone. It turned out that Irina had traveled with me from Moscow only because she feared to complicate my rescue from Siberia. Desperately unhappy at being apart from my old friend Sasha Barabanov,

she returned to Moscow shortly before I left for Ithaca. To be
sure, it is better when it happens with your friend than with
your enemy.

And so I began what I hoped would be the last start of a
new life. Kurt Gottfried, a brilliant physicist and longtime member of the SOS Committee, helped settle me in. I had felt immediately drawn to him when we first met, and had accepted
Cornell's invitation partly because of him. Kurt was on the point
of finding someone to teach me English when Slava Paperno,
a specialist in linguistics, recommended one—an extremely
smart humanities lecturer who had begun studying Russian
with him, and conveniently lived in an apartment below mine.
I went downstairs for my first one-hour lesson and stayed for
six hours of fierce debate on Chekhov in my twenty words of
English and her two hundred words of Russian. Day by day my
English got better and her Russian got worse. So we bought a
house in the country and married shortly after my divorce from
Irina.

Being free to do physics was one thing, actually doing it
was another. My exquisitely patient colleagues made no demands on me, but during that first winter at Cornell my mind
for physics seemed frozen. Faces were still a blur, everyone
muttered in a language which seemed to be English but which
I still could barely understand, and scores of letters from all
over the world kept arriving and piled up in boxes. It came as
a relief to make two human rights trips to Europe in three
weeks that spring—at least translators always materialized. On
the second trip I met again with Margaret Thatcher, who
wanted to talk with me before her trip to Gorbachev in Moscow.
After criticizing Gorbachev's self-contradictory efforts to save
both his country and his party, I gave her a big list of religious
prisoners prepared by Helsinki Watch in New York, and she
promised to help them. Then she asked for something positive
to take to her discussions with Gorbachev. "Well, you both have
your *perestroika*s in economics," I suggested, "compare your
troubles."

Following my rule to meet representatives of all parts of
the political spectrum, I arranged to talk with David Owen while
I was in London. He found the developments in the Soviet
Union both fascinating and puzzling. "But why did Gorbachev

begin *perestroika?*" he asked. "An obvious economic crisis," I answered. He seemed not to understand my reply at all. Perhaps, like many people I had been speaking with, he simply could not conceive of a crisis in that planned system. The economic catastrophe in the Soviet Union, obvious to Soviet dissidents, took a long time to register abroad, even when Gorbachev finally conceded in public that a major problem existed. After years of promulgating fantasy statistics that were not only believed but sometimes actually inflated by the West, the Kremlin found itself in the position of the boy who cried wolf.

The humanitarian fantasy, however, was still not playing well at the Vienna Conference when I revisited it in October, 1987. By now the French delegation had suggested dividing the controversial Moscow human rights meeting into three parts—Paris, 1989, Copenhagen, 1990, Moscow, 1991—as a diplomatic way to set a standard for the Soviets. However, despite their release of political prisoners, the Soviets had not yet officially offered to meet a single condition under discussion. A little crack finally appeared in the wall during my visit, when Yuri Kashlev, head of the Soviet delegation, declared that the Moscow meeting would be free and open to the public. Yet this formulation was too unclear, as I pointed out to the delegates. My trial in 1978, similarly declared "free and open to the public," had been free and open to the specially chosen public with which the KGB packed the courtroom. As for the rest: "Sorry, no more space!"

My second winter in the West, an envelope arrived in the mail from Vernon Hughes of Yale University, head of a large international group proposing to make a precise measurement of the anomalous magnetic moment of the muon. Hughes had sent some materials from the project proposal, an invitation to attend the next meeting of the group, and a copy of a letter I had written him from Yerevan twenty years before, when he was heading a similar experiment. Reading through the materials, I began some calculations, and without even realizing it plunged back into physics. The pattern of my life in the West was established—an equilibrium between work in science and work in human rights. Now I began to attend sessions of Hughes's group in Brookhaven, combining these trips with meetings in New York with Helsinki Watch leaders Bob Bernstein, Aryeh Neier, and Jeri Laber, and started experiments on some of my old ideas about wave logic. In May 1988 I met privately with Secretary Shultz, and then joined several other dissidents in a meeting with President Reagan before the Moscow summit trip in June. This time Shultz was chiefly interested in the current political and economic situation, and the possible future structure of the Soviet Union ("It will be a confederation," I predicted). Nevertheless, I asked him and later asked the president to meet separately with dissidents and refuseniks when they were in Moscow—which they did. Separate meetings would strengthen the dissidents' prestige and safety, sharpen their identity in the West (where refuseniks and dissidents were often considered identical), and remind everyone that there existed a whole range of human rights problems worth fighting for.

Two months later we transferred four suitcases of books and a few clothes for a year to a little town in France just across the border from Switzerland. My old friend Pierre Lefèvre, and new friends Dieter Möhl and Simon Van der Meer, had invited me to do accelerator research at CERN in Geneva. Our house and the neighboring villages and fields, cow and sheep pastures, roads and streams, were right in the center of an amazing underground doughnut, LEP—CERN's almost-completed electron-positron collider, 18 miles in circumference and 150 feet deep. Carlo Rubbia, director-elect of CERN, told me that LEP was in some ways the realization of a twenty-year-old proposal of mine; some physicists had considered it rather lunatic at the time. I was glad to contribute to CERN, now, by helping to improve antiproton intensity 1.5 times through a method that became known as "shaking." Unfortunately, not all my ideas could be realized. I proposed to Emilio Picasso, head of LEP, that we run our own experiment on "cold fusion"—a controversial scientific fiction much in the news that year—using heavy Russian vodka instead of the usual heavy water, and then publish the results. "We will have lots of heating and neutrons and gammas and everything," I assured him. But Emilio wouldn't play.

Ten years of various kinds of imprisonment had left me a prisoner of time, with too few years left for science, and too few hours in a day for my research, for human rights, for writing this book. So I really did not see much of the miraculous mountains surrounding CERN, and not much of anything else except my office, the control room of CERN's antiproton accumulator, and my study at home. But the warmth of the friendship around us compensated for everything. Pierre and Dieter watched over me like grandmothers over a boy whose high fever has just broken; Georges Charpak delicately tempted me into relaxation, driving us in his French-speaking car to his house, where he poured us wines from the year of my arrest, the year of my imprisonment, and the year of my liberation; and Max and Anya Reinharz were the kind of new friends you feel certain will become old ones.

It was moving to work among fellow scientists who had fought so hard, so long, and so influentially for my freedom. Scores of CERN physicists had boycotted Soviet scientific meetings on my account, and others had protested and worn "Free Y. Orlov" T-shirts during them. Posters with my picture and a call for my release still decorated office doors and laboratories, many people still kept their T-shirts, and the "Yuri Orlov Committee," now concerned with persecuted scientists everywhere, even retained its old name until I persuaded them to change it. When I privately received an appeal for help from the wives of some of the arrested members of the Armenian "Karabakh Committee"—mostly scientists, including friends of mine—I was able to turn to the CERN committee, and they mounted a strong campaign.

Toward the end of November 1988 I flew for the last time to the Vienna Conference, invited to discuss the Moscow human-rights meeting with the head of the American delegation, Warren Zimmerman, and other delegates. I explained my view yet again ("Agree, but attach strong conditions") and also took some part in unofficial discussions of the proposed concluding document of the conference. A statement exclusively about "openness and access" to CSCE meetings, formulated with the specificity of a legal contract between parties who know each other well enough not to trust one another, had been diplomatically relegated to a chairman's statement in an appendix on the last page. It named no names, but did not have to. The document itself was much more concrete and detailed on the subject of human rights than the original 1975 Final Act, and included specific remedies for victims of human rights violations as well as guarantees for monitors. But owing to strong Soviet objections, the word *monitors*—on which I had insisted —was completely absent. Nevertheless, Moscow had agreed to a great deal, and certainly that was due to Western pressure, which was much stronger in Vienna than at the 1982 Madrid Conference and much much stronger than at Belgrade in 1978. Western diplomats told me many times that this pressure had been created by the dissidents, especially the Soviet Helsinki movement. We had showed, they said, that it was possible to use the human rights provisions of the Helsinki Accords, demonstrated how to use them, and provided a moral example impossible for the West to ignore. Hearing this gave me a sense of satisfaction, but not of victory. Russia was still too small for the two of us—myself and the KGB—and they had no plans to move out.

TWENTY-FOUR

What Is to Be Done?

Being in Russia again was like seeing a mad, unkind woman you once passionately loved and for whose sake you suffered pain, humiliation, and despair. Of that old, damned love there remains—love. But now it is detached and mingled with pity, revulsion.

On June 3, 1989, I found myself in Moscow.

During one of his trips to CERN, my old friend Alexander Skrinsky, chairman of the Nuclear Physics Department of the USSR Academy of Sciences and director of the Novosibirsk Institute of Nuclear Physics in Siberia, had invited me to a workshop at the institute. His institute was a distinguished one, and the academy itself would sponsor the trip; I might never get another such chance to see the children. My son Sasha, a mathematical physicist, had already been refused permission to visit me in France on the grounds that he knew state secrets— Sasha, who had never been near a state secret in his life. I applied for a visa.

Just before the start of the workshop, the Soviet authorities turned down my application. But some creative artist issued the most impressive Soviet visa in all of Europe to my humanist wife, identifying her as a scientist-technologist, listing as her

sponsor the State Committee for Atomic Energy, which she had
never heard of, and permitting her to visit a special scientific
institute she had never heard of either. The U.S. State Department, Helsinki Watch groups, scientists in CERN, DESY in
Hamburg, and the Soviet Union—including my friends Lev
Okun, Andrei Sakharov, and Yevgeny Tarasov—all tried to
help. A week passed, the workshop was ending. The hell with
it, I thought, and we left for the CSCE human-rights conference
in Paris. When we arrived, we learned that a ten-day visa limited
to Moscow had suddenly appeared in Geneva, Washington, and
Bern. Despite *perestroika*, members of the Soviet Academy had
needed to go as high up as Politburo member and former KGB
chief Chebrikov to get approval for my trip. My wife went to
Geneva and back that same day for the visa and clothing we
had bought my sons, and the next morning we left Paris for
Moscow.

Suitcases crammed with scientific papers, the clothing, and
a bottle of Moscovskaya vodka from Paris, we were met at the
airport by a black Volga sent by the academy, and delivered to
Zhenya Tarasov's familiar apartment. How many cups of tea
he and I had drunk there together! Dima and Sasha still lived
with Galya in the same building as Zhenya, in the apartment
ITEP had given us long ago. Next door was ITEP itself, where
I would give seminars on my research at CERN and Cornell—
and where the assembly of scientific and technical staff had
recently voted to petition the Supreme Court to review my trial
and conviction, despite objections from the institute's Party secretary.[1]

All that week, from morning until late at night, Zhenya's
apartment was under siege by Uniate priests from the Western
Ukraine with a petition for the Paris human-rights conference;
a journalist from the liberal magazine *Ogonyok* with a plan for
an interview that its editor might or might not publish;[2] a pho-
tographer with pictures he had secretly taken of Sakharov outside the courthouse during my trial in 1978; and Moscow
friends and acquaintances who arrived at all hours, crowded

---

[1] On June 19, 1989, shortly after Article 70 was cut from the Criminal Code, the
petition was denied on the grounds that my guilt had been confirmed by the evidence,
and that my activities had been judged "in accordance with legislation [Article 70] then
in effect."

[2] It was published in September (issue #35).

around the dining-room table, overflowed into the living room and kitchen, and when I was out, held discussions among themselves or watched political news on TV. Sasha Podrabinek, now released from exile, brought his wife and children from a town near Moscow, and Zhenya's brother came from Tula with greetings and cakes from their old mother, Zinaida Afanasyevna, who had once hidden me in her house. My Sangar friend Misha Gornostayev flew in from Minsk, where he and his family now lived. And at last, from distant Kaliningrad, appeared my son Lev. I had hoped to see my Kobyai friends Tamara and Nina Ivanovna, but Tamara could not be located, and Nina Ivanovna said on the telephone that she probably could not reach Moscow in time. Dina and Barakhlo? They had disappeared without a trace.

Dr. Tarasov calmly orchestrated my schedule and ferried me around Moscow in his twenty-seven-year-old car, a molting masterpiece he personally kept in perfect working order. Lev played us a recording of his music, demonstrated the synthesizer I had sent him, and took us off to a Western-style crafts market. Nearly every morning and evening I strolled with Dima or Sasha around the little park outside our building, then up and down the street past ITEP next door. It was bittersweet to walk there. In this institute, thirty-six years earlier, I had begun my career, and three years later the Politburo had expelled me from this very place, crippling my scientific and family life.

Moscow struck me with its poverty and air of neglect. More garbage sat uncollected than twelve years ago, and I even recognized familiar rails and pipes dumped among the buildings. Many of the people on the street, in trams, in offices, appeared exhausted and sullen. Now they had much less food, and longer lines for it. Sugar and soap were being rationed; Mila Tarasov had spent a week assembling enough meat to feed us. And Moscow was a showcase. Everywhere were signs of impending economic catastrophe, the inevitable one, because the Soviet system had not been working for a very long time—a fact hitherto unknown only to Sovietologists and to that large part of the isolated Soviet population which ladled meat soup not from real saucepans but from mirages in official newspapers. After the experiment with private ownership under NEP in the twenties, our economic development had been artificially sustained by a combination of state terrorism, blind public enthusiasm, and self-cannibalism—scientists working in *sharaga*s, roads built by slave labor, machinery bought with grain snatched from the people's mouths. For the sake of the purity of our experiment, we systematically destroyed the most productive parts of our population.[3] Half a century after the Revolution we had squeezed all the juice out of ourselves, and the inevitable swift collapse began: corruption unprecedented in history, nearly total loss of interest in production, undeveloped high technology except in military and related areas, and a shocking lack of development in the social sphere, especially food and housing. Hardly any ordinary people still believed in comprehensive, centralized "scientific planning," that ineffective, inhumane, profoundly unscientific fantasia of goals arbitrarily set from above and coercive methods for trying to achieve them. Seventy years after the Revolution the Soviet people had less meat than they did under the czar. They were forty-fifth in the world in per capita income, thirtieth in life expectancy, fiftieth or worse in infant mortality.

Was it for this that tens of millions of lives were ruined in the camps?

Why were people carried away into the abyss of a radical social experiment? Why not first test that brilliant theory on rats? From the very start two ideas intertwined in our modern history—one a pure and lovely dream of a paradise on this earth, to be built not in eternity but in the lifetime of our children, or our grandchildren, or our great-grandchildren; the other, a nightmarish faith that to build this paradise we had to annihilate all who did not believe in the dream, who were not of the heavenly tribe, who resisted. Twentieth-century Russia was like a handsome, brilliant young man who resolved to dedicate himself to the good, constructed a perfect blueprint of universal happiness, and in its name—temporarily, of course, temporarily—tied his fate to murderers. He went along with them in all manner of crimes, acquired all their vices. Life was a rough draft, the fair copy always postponed until a tomorrow that never arrived. Finally a moral ruin, nothing learned, all beliefs gone, his youth, health, and talent wasted, he suddenly

---

[3]The current estimate in the Soviet press is that 65 million people were killed, or died from camp or famine, in the Soviet Union during the post–Civil War period up to Khrushchev.

comes to his senses, takes a look at himself, and is horrified. All life lost! What is to be done?

Confronting the bankruptcy of the Party and the future of the country as a world power, the Party apparatus looked for a savior, and that savior was Gorbachev. They did not simply permit him to begin reforms, did not simply entrust themselves to him, but held on to his coattails with both hands in the hope that he would haul both them and the country out of the abyss. Their loyal son offered *perestroika* and *glasnost* as the tactical solution to the problem. *Perestroika* meant some as yet undefined economic restructuring, and *glasnost* some officially regulated freedom to get and impart information, and to criticize the bureaucracy; conceived as a limited tool for achieving *perestroika*, *glasnost* was chiefly a way to struggle against corruption and inefficiency, and to generate constructive new ideas.

Was it not clear to the Politburo beforehand that not even a single brick could be pulled from the Leninist-Stalinist structure without bringing the whole thing down? They surely sensed the danger of reform. Khrushchev did, and backed off; his successors did, and dragged their heels until the construction began to crack under its own weight. The vagueness of Gorbachev's *perestroika* bore the stamp of fear and doomed it to failure, quite apart from the fact that any kind of *perestroika* was bound to be too little, too late without fundamental reform of the political structure. What Gorbachev should really have feared was *glasnost*. With his confident announcement of *glasnost*, he unwittingly broke the global lie underpinning the entire system, and thus set in motion one of the greatest dramas of the twentieth century: the agonizing collapse of the last supreme empire of the world, and the crash of the great dream of entire peoples.

The country was prepared for it. After twenty-five years of secretly reading and discussing the ideas of Sakharov, Solzhenitsyn, and the dissidents, Soviet citizens began to emerge from their samizdat-filled kitchens and, step by step, in increasing numbers, inexorably and peacefully push the boundaries of Gorbachev's *glasnost* toward the dissidents' conception of it: freedom of expression in the Western sense, a fundamental human right. It was the people themselves who created the *glasnost* that history textbooks will forever associate with Gorbachev's name.

Perestroika had left the workers cold from the start, and by
the time I arrived in Moscow, the once-hopeful intelligentsia
had become pessimistic about it. But *glasnost* was still making
everyone bubble with a giddy kind of self-excitation that you
could feel in the atmosphere. Just during my visit, the Congress
of People's Deputies was holding its first session, broadcast on
television and radio at Gorbachev's insistence. He created the
Congress as a kind of clearinghouse of information and democratic marketplace of ideas judiciously regulated by the presence of Party loyalists among the deputies. Not understanding
that democracy and freedom of expression cannot be doled out
like doses of medicine, Gorbachev got far more than he expected. Apartments and courtyards and streets and even black
Volgas throughout the country resonated with the voices of
Moscow deputy Yuri Vlasov bluntly criticizing the KGB; Baltic
deputies speaking in favor of full economic independence from
Moscow; and Uzbekistan delegate Adil Yakubov poignantly describing Uzbekistan village children, so destroyed by malnutri-
tion, pesticides, and picking cotton twelve hours a day, every
day, with absolutely no days off, no holidays, no leave, that the
army refused to accept them. Everyone heard Andrei Sakharov,
a delegate from the academy, propose transferring all Party
power to the Congress and the regional Soviets, and giving the
land directly back to the peasants. When an organized claque
in the visitors' gallery drowned him out, or Gorbachev cut him
short with a rude remark and, indeed, once even cut off his
microphone, the entire country knew. The Congress gave millions their first glimpse of real civic life.

And every evening while the Congress was in session, the
democratic association "Memorial" held massive meetings in the
Luzhniki sports complex. Gorbachev had approved them under
some pressure from the Moscow deputies. I attended several
of those extraordinary meetings presided over by my physicist
friend Lev Ponomaryov. One evening the square in Luzhniki
was jammed with forty thousand people of all ages. Overhead
fluttered flags of various unions, fronts, and parties—the tri-
color of the Democratic Union; the black with red stars of the
Anarcho-Syndicalists; the white with sky-blue cross of the Russian National Front, and goodness knows how many others—
and banners with slogans in support of the democratic deputies
of the Congress; in support of Sakharov; in support of Boris

Yeltsin; in support of the democrats of Georgia, Armenia, and the Baltics; against the party apparatus and the conservative majority in the Congress; against Gorbachev for his support of the Party apparatus. Only the red flags of the Communists were absent. No, we did not sacrifice ourselves in vain, I thought, struggling to squeeze my way through the resisting mass of the crowd. It took half an hour to reach the barrier near the speakers' platform.

I managed it just in time to hear a political speech by Father Gleb Yakunin, my old friend from camp. After Father Gleb, several democratic deputies of the Congress reported on the day's session. Then Boris Yeltsin—opponent of Gorbachev, popular hero, and congressional deputy—arrived like an American presidential candidate in a swirl of grim-faced escorts. They rushed him onto the platform, where he addressed the wildly cheering crowd with a speech supporting Sakharov and attacking the conservatives in the Congress, who had attacked Sakharov that very day. The figure of Yeltsin keenly interested me. Was he a populist, as many Moscow intellectuals said? Apparently not. A populist facing thousands of ordinary people would not devote his speech to defending the most famous intellectual in all of Russia.

When Yeltsin was done, Lev Ponomaryov asked me to speak. I congratulated the crowd for standing before me as internally free people, strikingly different from what they had been twelve years ago. Mentioning my recent talks with Lech Walesa in Strasbourg, Adam Michnik, Jacek Kuron, and other Solidarity leaders in Warsaw, I urged them to follow Solidarity's example and seek mutual support between workers and liberal intelligentsia in the struggle for both democracy and a better material standard of living. I ended by declaring the urgent need to form a broadly based, peaceful second party to compete with the Communist Party and provide a constructive framework for any future mass worker movement. (Yeltsin would make a good head of that party, I thought to myself, and not for the first time. I had even written about that somewhere.) Then the gathering passed Lev Ponomaryov's resolution calling for citizenship to be restored to Solzhenitsyn, Vladimir Bukovsky, and myself.

Afterward, activists from various groups rushed up to talk with me, and little slips of paper got passed hand over hand—

greetings, requests for help, even a message for my son Lev. By the time I left, the two militiamen atop the railway embankment along the far side of the square were still at their post. Silhouetted against the pale evening sky, they seemed to loom threateningly over the crowd. But it was just a sinister effect of the light, for only twenty or so militiamen were at the meeting, and their instructions had obviously been to protect, not menace.

On our last day in Moscow my wife and I went with Galya and Dima to the crematorium to see my mother's grave. We entered by the Donskoy Monastery next door, where I used to walk among the ancient gravestones as a little boy. The factory was gone now, and the building surrounded by scaffolding; the old cemetery had become a jungle of weeds, bushes, and trees. But on the other side of the monastery wall my mother's little patch of ground was tidy, the photograph I had selected long ago still fixed to the stone. Mother looked beautiful, just as she had wished. She looked like Carmen.

That evening, the Bryksins gave a farewell party. "You're alive and have your health, that's the main thing," Yekaterina Mikhailovna said briskly, hugging me tight. She had become nearly blind. Anya, Nona, their husbands, and their children were all there, along with my sons and the Tarasovs. The Sakharovs needed to rest up from the Congress, but Anichka and Nona had managed to assemble other dissident friends still in Moscow. Larisa Bogoraz brought the son born to her and Anatoly Marchenko. Pasha had his father's face, brave and handsome.

Everyone looked older, and perhaps a little sad. Father Gleb was still defending the rights of religious believers, and Sergei Kovalyov and Larisa continued their human rights activities in an international organization now. But Tanya Velikhanova had withdrawn from human rights work, because, she said, it had become too political and politics did not suit her temperament or talent. Sofia Kalistratova had been allowed to have a legal practice again; her criminal file, opened on account of her membership in the Moscow Helsinki Group, had been closed.

Under a photograph of Ivan Yemelyanovich high on the wall, we ate, proposed toasts, traded jokes as in the old days.

Someone began to play the piano, and Yekaterina Mikhailovna sang Russian romances in a pure, steady voice. Then the piano burst into a fox-trot, and I danced with her until we both dropped from exhaustion.

Back in Paris as a member of the American delegation, I reported to the CSCE human rights meeting about my Moscow trip, and then returned to Geneva. It was time to think of going home. Just before we left for Ithaca, I saw Andrei Dmitriyevich Sakharov for the last time. Our reunion the previous December had been all too brief and formal—at a huge human rights celebration given by President Mitterrand, and a small gathering of French scientists and mathematicians who had fought for us both. Now Sakharov and Yelena Bonner spent nearly half a day with our CERN human rights committee and two Chinese students involved in the democratic movement. The Tiananmen Square massacre had occurred less than two months before, and we all wanted to understand how to help the scientists and students being persecuted in China. Sakharov favored, as I did, boycotts of official scientific meetings in China, and I am sure he would have joined the campaign that Asia Watch, the Robert F. Kennedy Memorial Center for Human Rights, and I organized next spring to help the persecuted Chinese scientists, especially astrophysicist Fang Lizhi, "the Chinese Sakharov."

We had supper that evening under the grape arbor of a private house, enjoying a rare moment of peace. Sakharov said he liked my speech in Luzhniki, which gladdened me because he had not yet made much contact with workers, and an alliance between intellectuals and workers was, I believed, necessary to defeat the regime. Toward the end of the evening he and Yelena reminisced about their encounters with the militia outside the courtroom at my trial. That is my last image of him— wrapped in my wife's tiger-patterned shawl against the evening chill, joking about the militia and sipping tea. Five months later he died suddenly at home on the eve of what he had said to Yelena would be a battle in the Congress. Sakharov had already transformed Russian history. Had he lived, he would have transformed it again. For near the end of his life, almost overnight, he developed into a brilliant, committed politician, not only leading tough battles in the Congress, but meeting with industrial workers, and drafting a new constitution that I would call a "constitution of human rights." The only public figure acceptable to all parts of his too vast country, Sakharov had become just the person to lead a decaying nation exhausted with itself, yet still capable of responding to great honesty, great professional achievement, great suffering, and great precision of thought.

After Sakharov's death I decided that it would be useful to express my views about the political structure of the USSR at some meetings of the Interregional Group of People's Deputies, which Sakharov had led in the Congress. Everything was arranged. But the Soviet Consulate in Washington, D.C., played their usual game until departure time ("We are waiting for permission from Moscow"), and then confided to the travel agency arranging my trip that they had a standing list of people to be denied visas, and Orlov was on it. At least they were not impolite, as the Czech Consulate in Washington had been the previous month when first refusing me a visa to visit their newly elected president. Told that Orlov had received an invitation from Vaclav Havel, they sneered, "So who is Havel, anyway?"

I presumed that the official blacklist would be modified for the 1990 annual meeting of the International Helsinki Federation, which had been scheduled for Moscow at the end of May, just before the Copenhagen CSCE human rights meeting— partly to test conditions for the famous Moscow human rights meeting of 1991. Well aware of it, the Foreign Ministry had assured the IHF that all its members, including the honorary chairman, would be permitted to attend. My plan was to go first to Uppsala, where the university was giving me an honorary degree for work in physics and human rights, then to Moscow for our IHF meeting, and then on to Copenhagen.

A few weeks before I had to leave for Uppsala, our travel agency, which was also handling arrangements for Helsinki Watch in New York, informed me that the Soviet authorities had refused to grant me a visa. Since Rosalynn Carter planned to attend our meeting, I telephoned her office for help and also called Kerry Kennedy, with whom I had been working on the Fang Lizhi campaign, to see if Senator Kennedy could do something. A week later, our travel agency telephoned me to say that they had my visa and would send it express with my tickets to Scandinavia. Days passed, nothing arrived, time was getting short. I telephoned. "We'll send them tomorrow," they promised. My wife telephoned the next day. "We've sent them." Still nothing arrived. The visa and tickets needed to be sent that very afternoon to reach me in time. She telephoned again, and was told that they had been mistaken, nothing had been sent. "What exactly are you planning to send?" she asked with a flash of inspiration. "Your husband's tickets and your visa." But she had canceled her trip long ago! What about my visa? "According to the Soviet Consulate, none will be issued." "But you told my husband on the telephone that you had his visa!" she protested. "You know your husband's English, he must have misunderstood." They promised to send my tickets and her visa that afternoon, but when someone from the Washington office of Helsinki Watch went there to check, nothing had been sent; on my instructions she commandeered them. Meanwhile, in New York, the Danish Consulate refused me a visa to Copenhagen because I had none for Moscow. Considering all this extremely odd, my wife decided to escort me on my trip.

As I strolled through the gardens of Linnaeus next to our hotel in Uppsala, met with colleagues, and gave talks on iontrapping and on human rights, the boring farce unfolded itself across three continents. Helsinki Watch in New York kept us up to date. The Soviet Foreign Ministry insisted to a scandalized IHF in Moscow that I had of course been granted a visa, but they would check. The key people at our travel agency were conveniently out of town—in Moscow; the person left behind declared to Helsinki Watch that everything was "Orlov's own fault for causing the Soviets so much trouble." The Foreign Ministry reported back to the IHF that a four-day visa was waiting for me in Washington, and one in Stockholm that the Soviet ambassador in Sweden refused to release. A physics colleague in Uppsala called the Soviet Consulate, and reported that the ambassador was not even in the country.

A Soviet visa was indeed sitting in Washington. We decided that the safest thing would be for Helsinki Watch to send it express to Uppsala. Amid the booming of real cannon, the piece of paper arrived at the great hall of the university just as a laurel wreath was being placed upon my head. After the ceremony we raced back to the hotel, where I changed out of my evening dress in the cloakroom, and reached the airport just in time for our flight to Moscow. On the plane I hurriedly drafted the speech that I was scheduled to give the next morning but no one expected me to deliver.

Sheremetyevo Airport at 2:00 A.M. was deserted. The young KGB border guard looked sleepy in his glass booth. He leafed through my U.S. reentry permit and unlocked the waist-high barrier—how few formalities! It automatically locked behind me. The guard glanced at my wife's American passport, at her, at a computer display, and picked up the telephone. Another KGB guard squeezed like a sardine into his booth, then another, and another. They anxiously conferred, looked at me, made telephone calls, looked at me, conferred some more. After ten minutes of this a KGB officer appeared on my side of the barrier, asked for my reentry permit, and genially invited me for a little chat. "No, I will not. We can fly back, and then to Copenhagen for the international human rights conference." The sardines froze in their booth. The officer disappeared, then reappeared with two more guards: "Please follow me." At that moment my wife gathered her entire store of Russian words into one handful and contemptuously threw it into his face. The KGB officer vanished, the barrier clicked open, and I passed through it again. We were asked to sit and wait, while half a dozen guards milled around, keeping an eye on us. Forty minutes later our passports were returned as if nothing had happened, and we were cheerfully waved into Moscow.

Luckily the Bryksins were in town. We arrived at 5:00 A.M. to find everyone but the children wide awake and dressed, the table laid with supper. On three hours' sleep we headed for the other side of Moscow and the House of Tourists, a kind of convention center containing a hall for meetings, a hotel, and a butcher shop selling rooster combs and feet. Downstairs in the meeting hall youngsters from the new Moscow Helsinki Watch Group tended a registration table and handed out name tags and earphones for people wanting English translations of the mostly Russian proceedings. It looked just like a Western physics conference. The big auditorium upstairs was filled with human rights activists from all over the Soviet Union, Helsinki monitors from America, Europe, Eastern Europe, and the Soviet Union, political activists, journalists, Rosalynn Carter with her guard of Secret Service men, and assorted "contact people"

from the Soviet Foreign Ministry. Karl Johannes von Schwartzenberg, chairman of the IHF, opened the meeting and introduced my speech.

I began by asking why the current Russian revolution—
the fourth one—was proceeding so peacefully in the Russian
Republic itself, and why it would very probably continue to be
peaceful. One of the main reasons, I suggested, was that the
transformations now occurring had been prepared by dissidents
who were strongly against violence in principle; in this respect,
they were *anti-revolutionary revolutionaries.* Many years ago Sakharov and I had discussed our approach to future political movements and parties in Russia, and had concluded that human
rights movements with a very high level of morality and commitment to nonviolent struggle must precede any political
struggle for power, in order to give future politicians a moral
example and educate them to respect internationally recognized
human rights. Otherwise there would be a new round of bloody
history in Russia. For a quarter of a century the entire Russian
intelligentsia and some workers had privately discussed and
rediscussed the powerful current of "samizdat" and information
created by such dissidents, meeting there many ideas about
human rights and democracy long before the official *glasnost*
and *perestroika.* That was why a huge number of peaceful political movements and politicians appeared in Russia almost immediately after some freedom had been granted from the top.
And that was why almost every "front" and party in Russia now
wanted to show that it respected human rights. It had even
become a kind of fashion in Russia, sometimes on the very
surface of people's mentality, but a good beginning nonetheless.
And all of it had been prepared in the course of that twenty-
five years of underwater development.

I ended by noting that many former human rights activists
were now politicians and influential deputies of parliaments.
This was not a bad transition, I said, and indeed I would like
any future Russian politician to have some practical experience
with human rights work. In a totalitarian country it was impossible to separate human rights and politics, but ideally there
must be permanent groups exclusively devoted to human
rights, separate from any politics. There must be individuals
with special sensitivities and talents, ready to help and suffer
for all people persecuted on account of their views or peaceful

struggle for rights—individual or collective, religious or political, social or economic—no matter whether they are right or left, top or bottom, Communists included. In other words, we must struggle to the end of this world for civilized methods of human relations.

It was the first officially permitted nongovernmental international human rights conference ever held in the Soviet Union. "Are you proud? What are you feeling?" asked a local journalist. "No, it is your business to feel, not mine," I replied too bluntly. "I simply have no time to feel anything for more than one second. My business is to listen and work." And what I listened to from early morning until late at night during our two days of hearings on the human rights situation in the USSR was terrible. All the reports, especially from the Soviet provinces, painted a detailed picture of unspeakable destruction affecting millions: dead infants, infants with AIDS, no child care, no maternity care, dead rivers, dead lakes, dead seas—simply without water—fields poisoned by radiation, people poisoned by radiation, poisoned by industrial smoke, young soldiers beaten, raped, insulted in the army, old invalids near starvation, without medical help, and on and on and on.

Western human rights activists were shocked. I was not, but the freedom and anger of the reports did surprise me. In Luzhniki the previous year, I had forgotten that you must take into account not only what people are saying but even more what they are *not* saying. Despite the mood of exhilaration produced by *glasnost,* long habits of self-censorship had not completely died in 1989. Now, in 1990, people were placing no limits on what they discussed, and the mood was heavy with accusation. Perhaps, I hoped, listening to condemnations of the Communist Party and Marx, Lenin, Communism, socialism, for genocide, for genocide, for genocide!—perhaps, I hoped, because every Russian is now afraid of civil war, it will not break out here, in Russia itself. It seemed that people had finally understood only this year what had been done to them, their lives, and their country during our revolutionary seventy years, and had begun to hate. You could feel that hatred—sometimes hot, sometimes cold, always intense—running through nearly every report. In our much more terrible day, I thought, we dissidents did not feel so much hatred, probably because we had the time to organize our emotions. But will these people have it? I had written a long time ago that if reforms began too late, they would not dampen but, instead, release public hatred. . . .

Yet all the speakers, with the exception of one retired colonel and some nationalist reporters from the Caucasus, condemned violence. And conversations with people on the street and old friends like Sergei Kovalyov, Father Gleb, and Lev Ponomaryov—all deputies to the Russian Parliament now—calmed me. The public mood had turned to optimism about the future again, they said, because Boris Yeltsin had become president of the Russian Republic. Workers supported him, and many ordinary people had visibly revived after his election. So he had some time for reforms, as long as people trusted him and still had hope because of him. Since Sakharov's death they trusted practically no one else. "Nobody believes in Gorbachev now," I was told. "He began well, but did things for his own purposes, not for the people. That's why he stopped at the halfway point. Yeltsin is a different sort of man. He'll move quickly. We believe him."

It became clear to me that the fate of Russia and all the other republics of the Soviet Union depended on the success of the Russian democrats, especially Yeltsin. But they did have to move quickly. Yeltsin confirmed this idea twice during our one-hour conversation on June 4. Joining us in his presidential office were Rosalynn Carter, Jeri Laber, Katya Fitzpatrick, Jonathan Fanton, and my wife.

"I know our people and I know their mood," he said with intensity. "Either we will be able to change their lives in two years, or it will be Romania here." Yeltsin was alluding to the fate of Ceaucescu.

If it comes here, I thought to myself, if it really does come, it will be much worse than in Romania. "When we hang all the Communists—All! Understand?—we'll hang you first, you Communist scum!" My neighbor in a nearby punishment cell had shouted that to the camp officers. Was he a fascist? A criminal? No, a Soviet Marxist, arrested in 1982 in the huge city of Kuibyshev for attempting to organize an alternative Marxist-Leninist Worker Party. The bell had in fact begun ringing from all sides years ago. Now the critical question was what would come first: rampant murderous hatred for Communism, or full dismantling of the system. Gorbachev had still utterly failed to realize it. That seemed to be the main difference between him and the president of the Russian Republic. Yeltsin, a man of common sense, quickly assimilated the new reality—the decay of the Soviet empire and the crash of the socialist economic system together with the state ideology, while Gorbachev remained a prisoner of ideas.

Russians have always been a deeply ideological people; life, for them, must have a special meaning. Through most of this century, the Communist ideology gave one to the lives of millions. How terrible to discover your worldview is shit and blood! The dissidents had discovered that a long time ago, and now, with the revelations under *glasnost,* so had virtually the entire nation. But there remained Russians like Gorbachev, unable to confront the total bankruptcy of their old faith and unable really to understand the democratic alternative. Desperately confused by the developments around them, they still clung to the mirage of a unified Soviet Union, to belief in strong central power as the only protection against anarchy—and even to belief in the nation's messianic role. On July 27, 1990, despite *perestroika's* complete lack of success and almost complete lack of content, Gorbachev would declare to a group of Soviet journalists and scholars: "Let us not be overmodest. Our *perestroika* is bound to change the world, if we first make it through these one and a half months, and then for some time beyond that."[4]

All of this explained very well Gorbachev's deep uncertainty in domestic affairs, and his failure to grasp the obvious contradiction in trying to salvage both the nation and the standard-bearer of Communist ideology, the Party. Forced to retreat by circumstances and pressure from below, Gorbachev stumbled, clumsily redefining socialism every step of the way. By the time his Central Committee formally repealed the one-party system—while continuing to insist on the leading ideological role of the Communists—the entire nation had begun to hate the Communist Party. By the time he formally accepted the necessity of a free-market economy—but without any certain deadline and with the contradictory qualification of a socialist orientation—people had begun to loathe the very word

---

[4]Reported in *Russkaya Missel,* No. 3840, 10 August 1990, p. 8.

socialism. And by the time he finally agreed to form a free confederation of Soviet republics—with almost all power remaining
in Moscow's hands—several republics had formally rejected the
idea of a Soviet Union in any form as being equivalent to empire. I seriously expected him to declare: "Capitalism, comrades, is just what real Leninism is!" at the very moment when
the last statue of Lenin in Russia was smashed or sold to the
city of Boston.

Tacking between old dreams and current realities, Gorbachev had always accepted too late the recommendations of
the dissidents and new democrats. However, as president of
the USSR he had not been slow to concentrate in his hands
more formal power than any Soviet leader since Stalin. He had
yet to exercise any of it over the KGB, the organ of totalitarian
control, the cancerous tumor on Russian society. To be sure,
even after several years of *perestroika* nobody in Russia knew
how to remove that tumor without a knife. But no Russian had
failed to recognize the friendly delicacy of Gorbachev's relations
with the KGB. (Those relations had largely excaped many an-
alysts in the West, who calculated how many days, weeks, or
months the KGB would continue to tolerate the unbelievable
democrat Gorbachev.)

Of course, the KGB generals and top military generals—
those lovers of law and order—knew all along how to seize
power at any moment. Their problem was that, with the full
set of great Communist ideas widely discredited, moral ruin
behind them and lack of public support ahead, they did not
know what to do after seizing it. So despite all their troops,
tanks, missiles, guns, camps, prisons, and guards, they had been
in a kind of semiparalysis, watching the hemorrhage of central
power. In the absence of mass armed revolts in the Russian
Republic, the probability of a coup by the KGB and the
military—with or without Gorbachev—seemed to me small.

Concerned about just such revolts, Yeltsin had moved
swiftly to construct a plan for changing the political structure
of the Russian Republic. He sketched it for us that afternoon
in his office. All power, on his plan, however much they wanted,
would go to the local elected bodies; the highest authorities and
the president of the Republic himself would have only those
powers delegated to them from below. This seemed to me a
very sensible idea. Yeltsin's proposed structure would construc-

tively channel the potentially volatile nationalist ambitions developing within Russia. And it would help restore Russia's infrastructure by focusing people's attention on their concrete interests, and stimulating individual and local initiative in spheres like economics, culture, and the enviroment. The hierarchical structure of our central planning had automatically excluded millions of people from decision-making and responsibility; the result had been a fantastic degradation of that infrastructure, with catastrophic consequences for people's everyday lives.

On the subject of independence movements in other Soviet republics, Yeltsin made the startling declaration that he would resist efforts to use soldiers from the Russian Republic to suppress them. He said little about economics—only that he had a "team" at work, and that he would sell factories and land to the people. The famous Yeltsin-Shatalin "500-day plan" was unveiled a few months later. Originally formulated by Grigory Yavlinsky, one of Yeltsin's ministers, and worked out by academician Shatalin, one of Gorbachev's own economists, it was a plan for rapid transition to a modern market economy.

In November, after receiving the 1990 Nobel Peace Prize, Gorbachev blocked the plan and transition. His delay of fundamental economic and social reform had already lost the nation crucial time: after five years of *perestroika*, the USSR had moved much closer to catastrophe. To delay once again, when all the old economic connections everywhere in the country were cracked, smashed, broken to bits—plainly this man did not understand what was going on around him!

The following month, the smell of a creeping Stalinist coup led by Gorbachev himself became unmistakable. He seemed finally to have realized the complete illogic of attempting to save the country through "bourgeois freedoms" and still keep it fundamentally under Communist control. (Pontecorvo, not to mention Stalin, understood this long ago.) *Glasnost* and the other freedoms with which Gorbachev tried to shore up the collapsing structure of empire and ideology had only inspired people to flee it and start building something new on their own. By now, scores of independent publications had sprung up, hundreds of independent political and social groups. Republics and subrepublics announced they would seek independence;

the Russian parliament granted more and more regions in Russia the status of free-enterprise zones (exactly what I proposed in my letter to Brezhnev seventeen years before), and introduced some private ownership of land; workers formed their own non-Communist trade unions. Entire city governments and governments of republics conversed with one another over the heads of the Kremlin, acting as if they really did inhabit a genuinely free world. And they did more than converse. The city of Leningrad signed bilateral agreements with the republic of Estonia, and the giant republic of Russia, under the leadership of Yeltsin, entered into a partnership with the little Baltics that amounted to an embryonic confederation of independent republics, a union against the Union.

The accelerating and apparently inexorable momentum of these developments swept Gorbachev to a critical decision point. He had only two choices, now: to break with the Party and lead the nation forward into history together with the democrats, or retreat into history together with the Party apparatus and top generals. Gorbachev chose to turn back.

For the first time he made explicitly clear his opposition to private ownership and full independence for the Soviet republics, ideas he had always resisted in practice. Then he removed all the moderates from his government and surrounded himself with hard-liners. Obviously given carte blanche, his new team began a campaign of hyperbolic lie and accusation, an insane rehash of Stalinist motifs. KGB chief Kryuchkov, a "liberal professional" only weeks before, accused the West of sending Russia poisoned food in the guise of humanitarian assistance. Defense Minister Yazov falsely accused insurgent Soviet republics of planning to commandeer the nuclear weapons on their territory, and at the same time criticized their decision to be nuclear-free zones. Finally, on January 13, 1991, following an old Leninist scenario familiar to every child in Budapest and Prague, the Gorbachev team took a decisive bloody step into an empty nowhere.

Anonymous committees of "national salvation" had mysteriously sprung up in the Baltics; challenging the legitimacy of democratically elected Baltic governments and charging them with creating "disorder" and "terror," the committees appealed to Moscow for protection. At 1:30 A.M. on January 13, the eve of war in the Gulf, the military garrison in Vilnius, Lithuania, attacked the local television studios and broadcasting tower, crushing unarmed citizens under their tanks, firing on unarmed crowds. Fifteen people died, including a child; more than one hundred were wounded. Western, Baltic, and Soviet journalists saw it all. That evening on television, Interior Minister Pugo declared that the operations had been defensive, the Lithuanians had fired against the tanks; later, a television film even claimed that the victims had perished from heart attacks and traffic accidents. With the publication of eyewitness reports contradicting the official story, Gorbachev unsuccessfully sought to suspend the freedom of the press guaranteed by law.

Had the Nobel laureate lost his mind? Had the democrat been outmaneuvered by reactionary forces? Had the opportunist bowed to pressure from the right? Or had the convinced Leninist made one of the sharp turns for which he praised Lenin in speeches to audiences at home? Were his *glasnost* and *perestroika* like Lenin's NEP, simply a calculated tactic of temporary liberalization that had served its purpose?

The response by Russian democrats was immediate. On January 13, thousands of Muscovites demonstrated against the state violence. Boris Yeltsin urged Russian soldiers and officers serving in the Baltics to resist orders to attack "legally formed state bodies" and "peaceful civilians who are protecting their democratic achievements." Six days later, *hundreds of thousands* of people demonstrated in Moscow and several other cities in Russia. (And twenty-three years ago, only seven people had demonstrated in Moscow against the Soviet invasion of Czechoslovakia!) These mass demonstrations surprised me: so many people had suddenly understood the connection between democratic life elsewhere and their own life, their own security.

Yet there still are Western observers who fail to understand the connection, want stability in the Soviet Union at all costs, and think they can find it in a government that guns down unarmed democrats and children. They should think again. The Soviet Empire is finished and the Party is finished, whatever happens. If Gorbachev and his associates follow their current course, they will end by pushing the nation into civil war. And that would be the last crime ever committed by Communist power.

EPILOGUE

Let us at least learn from experience. The greatest and most tragic human experiment has almost ended. The society of "scientific socialism," built to serve the eternal human desires of community and equality, degraded its members and left many with no desires at all. But the spirit of collectivism inside each of us lives together with the spirit of individualism. Therefore, some people, somewhere, in some future century, may try to build a society of individual interests alone, and may be prepared to annihilate those who wish otherwise. And after this "scientific capitalism" or "scientific anarchy," the pendulum will swing again in the other direction. We cannot stop the pendulum any more than we can eradicate human nature. We can, however, moderate its swings by remembering that all people have the same right to express their opinions, no matter which ones, and have the same right to live in their own way, no matter which way, provided that they do not use force or violence. *Means are more important than ends in the civilized struggle for ideas.* Our dreams may be the loveliest on earth, but if we wade through blood and terror to achieve them, we will arrive to find ourselves destroyed.

Don't kill.

Appendix One
Letter to Brezhnev

Much-esteemed Leonid Ilyich!

These questions have been prompted by the campaign against A. D. Sakharov.

1. Our scientists have received approximately only one thirtieth of the Nobel prizes in the basic sciences. We have both remarkable researchers and remarkable results, but you must realistically evaluate the situation as a whole. The gap with respect to the number and quality of discoveries has not been decreasing. Do you not think that this means our nation is intellectually lagging dangerously behind other developed nations?

2. It is a historical fact that a new scientific and industrial revolution has begun and continues intensively in the West, and that our state philosophy was long at odds with all principal directions of modern thought: the theory of relativity, quantum theory, genetics, cybernetics. Today it is preferred not to recall these failures. However, the scientific revolution is still far from over, and the exact sciences continue to invade fields of knowledge that our ideology still considers "scientific-Marxist philosophy," not subject to revision. Attempts at objective analysis in these fields are considered an encroachment upon the state. On the whole, such ideological intolerance limits our capacities for complex thought and unbiased evaluation of experience. Do you not think that because of this our intellectual lag will continue even in the future?

This does not mean there should be no state ideology whatsoever. I am deeply convinced that both the people and the state should profess certain moral principles drawn up long ago in human experience: love for one's native land, and human conscience. Ethics common to all humanity, they were created and preached by the best representatives of generations. There is yet another principle whose importance we must understand if we wish to be stopped at the brink of the final cataclysm of history. It consists in this, namely, that the fanatic adherence to principles betrays the principles themselves; that in human relations, any principle is bound to have a certain indeterminacy of interpretation and permit significant freedom of choice.

But our ideology has an entirely different character. It calls itself "scientific," which is dangerous for any ideology because scientific truth can undergo radical changes. It is harmful even for the science that the ideology is striving to preserve. As for the state, by supporting such an ideology with all its resources, it finds itself in a very foolish position.

Does it not follow that the repressive apparatus of the state must be detached from this ideology; that from kindergarten to the Academy of Sciences we must be released from *compulsory* education in, and from obedience to, principles which are so unreliable from both the scientific point of view and even the point of view of historical experience?

3. We need not renounce our own path of evolution, at the foundation of which lies the condemnation of private ownership. But we should recognize that there exist yet other, parallel paths, which have their own virtues. Thus, for example, Western experience has shown that the problem of the "absolute impoverishment of the masses" is effectively solved even within the framework of modern capitalism—by scientific and technological methods and by additional factors: partial control by the state side; pressure of trade-union struggle carried out in the framework of bourgeois freedoms; pressure of the public conscience; and fear of explosions of violence. We further see that the capitalistic economy has learned to use "regulating rods" for averting dangerously explosive situations, and operates in the sort of oscillating mode that we can consider normal. Finally, it is necessary to recognize that the very complex problems entailed by the concentration of power in a few hands are softened and muted in a beneficial way by bourgeois freedoms, and this is by no means a defect, whereas for us the same problems arise blatantly in all their magnitude.

At the same time, it is evident that if we were to live absolutely isolated from the outside world, we would not know that other stable historical paths existed. Moreover, the most important scientific truths would be unknown to us for a very long time, since they would lie beyond the bounds of the ideological barrier, protected by all the power of the state. And, incidentally, by virtue of that our ideology would turn out to be "proven"—essentially just as it was until 1953.

Learning these historical facts, must we not regard with extreme caution absolutely all "theories" and "laws" of social development? In the region of state management, should we not turn to a careful but active *experimental* search for the optimal paths, taking into account our own historically formed ideas and characteristics? That search is now being held back by the absence of *glasnost* and the absence of freedom of discussion on any questions about the economic and political structure of our society.

4. It seems correct to say that the variant of a severely regulated socialism becomes advantageous as an alternative to wasteful, free capitalism only when there is a basic scarcity of energy and other resources. However, today one can consider it proven that humanity will manage to provide itself with energy in the course of the next hundreds of years. Do you not think that for this reason severe regulations are already unnecessary, and we can pass to almost complete freedom in the sphere of ideas, excluding from this sphere only ideologies of violence and revolt? Do you not think, further, that for the same reason we might fearlessly be able to pass to much greater freedom of expression of personal initiative also in the sphere of production?

5. The biggest error of the Marxist theory of social development is that the innate spiritual needs and qualities of man do not enter into the theory. In effect, Marxism denies them a presence in the nature of man. However, this assumption is not proven scientifically, that is, by the methods of experimental biology, biochemistry, biophysics. Science is only just edging up to these questions. But by observing the "large-scale" disparity between practice and Marxist theory, one can already point to the most critical blunders.

First of all, human ethics—conscience—exists and is one of the powerful and eternal driving forces of history. This quality springs up in a person together with imagination, and thanks to a capacity to feel pain not just from actual but even from imagined sufferings. A person is therefore able to suffer when he knows about the suffering of others. Marx himself was just such a person, although he created an oversimplified scheme that does not take this quality into account.

As for violence, to which such importance is attached in Marxism, it also is a driving force of history. However, here is an important and subtle point. Human violence is by no means always a strictly determined consequence of external conditions, as it is among animals, but can apparently spring up spontaneously and then "go critical." The problem of violence therefore demands *eternal* vigilance by its principal opponents, regardless of their social system and level of civilization.

Further, the need for free and sometimes spontaneous choice is an innate quality of human beings. Precisely free choice, but not "freedom as knowledge of necessity," is true freedom. It is senseless to struggle against this need. A modern state must be able to satisfy it, while at the same time limiting it within a reasonable framework of law.

The need to express his very own individual opinion to others is, also, the most important innate need of a human being, especially when his stomach is full.

Does it not seem to you that the approach we have taken to man and his place in society is primitive and objectively does not really conform to human qualities and needs?

6. Do you agree that true culture is indivisible and continuous, and that our intellectual lag can be explained to a considerable extent by those devastating breaks that we ourselves made in our delicate cultural fabric in the course of history; that a scholar's intellect is cultivated by the scientific tradition, and not just the scientific but indeed the entire cultural milieu; and that the limits placed on imagination in art influence imagination in science?

7. Do you agree that we do not seriously study the problem of stimulating large-scale economic activity; that while truly keeping within the framework of state ownership, we might be able—advantageously for business—to intensify stimuli sharply by imitating Western experience? Perhaps, for example, it is necessary to introduce a regime of free initiative into some branches of the economy, from time to time, while simultaneously linking managers' salaries to their profits—determining the economic sphere to be brought under such a regime with reference to the current state of the market. However, it is clear that the most important thing is to have the opportunity to discuss *any* ideas in this area freely. Do you agree with this?

8. Various claims about "partial capitalism without private ownership" or something of that kind will possibly shock some dogmatists. But, first, our chief principle—absence of private ownership—will remain; and, second, I am forced to note that in our country, socialism has in practice taken on the characteristics not even of "feudalism without private ownership," but—under Stalin—of slaveholding without private ownership. Indeed, what were the millions of inmates of the camps, or the scientists in *sharagas*, if not slaves of the state? And how does the *kolkhoznik* without a passport differ from the communal peasant [under the czars] as regards his rights? What sort of thing is our current system of local residence permits, if not a feudal restriction of free movement around the territory of the country? The impression will arise that up to now our people have not learned to think in unfeudal categories in the sphere of legal relations. Is it not time for us to pass to another, more modern plane of freer relations?

9. One of the most effective opportunities to equalize intellectual potential among countries is to abolish the ban on free travel abroad. I am talking about trips taken whenever and for as long as is necessary to a scholar, engineer, student, writer, artist, and any citizen. What is the sense of this prohibition, which does not benefit the state and humiliates citizens?

10. One of the survivals of history in our consciousness is the fact that we will not permit anyone any criticism of the Central Committee. In these circumstances it must be recognized that the only legal channel of "feedback" for internal policy is the transmission of works of criticism abroad, so that by a complicated path back they reach the ears of the government. Does no one on the Central Committee understand the utter absurdity of this situation?

11. Our method of political administration is a typical regime without feedback. In essence, we compete with capitalism while having placed ourselves in the most disadvantageous conditions; we do not exploit *all* possible stimuli and all channels of feedback; and we do not trust our own fellow citizens. We would avoid many blunders and calamities if the people were granted as a first step at least a consultative voice, not formally but in practice, and if we turned, for example, to the well-tried method of feedback—freedom of the press, that is, a press without political and ideological censorship, with the proviso mentioned above. Does it not seem to you that some tensions have arisen in the country today which might be easily and painlessly removed by abolishing censorship, assuming it were done in time?

12. Any criticism of the Central Committee is regarded as a crime. Therefore people either "vacillate together with the Party" or are hurled against the barricade of a brutal struggle. You know, of course, that today there has appeared a small but growing number of people being hurled against that barricade. This "logic of struggle" is imposed by the government itself. I ask, what is the point of it? Would it not be more intelligent for us, at the end of the twentieth century and sixty years after the Revolution, finally to establish normal, intermediate forms of mutual relations between citizen and state? I mean again and primarily, as the first step—abolition of censorship of the press, free exchange of information, *glasnost*.

13. You obviously understand that to imprison opponents in psychiatric hospitals and to cripple them there by injections—this measure is like sterilization of political opponents in the Nazi Reich. Here, basically, there is nothing to ask about.

Yours sincerely,
Y. ORLOV
Professor, Doctor of Physical and
Mathematical Sciences, Corresponding
Member, Armenian Academy of Sciences

September 16, 1973

Appendix Two
On the Founding of the Public Group to Support Compliance with the Helsinki Accords in the USSR

The Public Group to Support Compliance with the Helsinki Accords in the USSR has been founded, May 12, 1976, in Moscow. The Group's aim is to support observance of the humanitarian articles of the Final Act of the Conference on Security and Cooperation in Europe. This means the following articles of the Final Act:

1. Declaration on Principles Guiding Relations between Participating States. Section VII. Respect for human rights and fundamental freedoms, including the freedom of thought, conscience, religion, or belief.

2. Cooperation in Humanitarian and Other Fields. 1) Human Contacts (in particular, sub-section (b) Reunification of Families) 2) Information 3) Cooperation and Exchanges in the Field of Culture 4) Cooperation and Exchanges in the Field of Education.

The Group considers its immediate aim to be that of informing all Heads of State signatory to the Final Act of August 1, 1975, and the public as well, of direct violations of the articles mentioned above. Given this aim, the Group:

1) will accept directly from Soviet citizens *written* complaints that concern them personally and relate to violation of the articles mentioned above, and will forward such complaints in condensed form to all Heads of States signatory to the Final Act, as well as to the public. The Group will retain the original complaint signed by the author;

2) will gather, with the assistance of the public, other information about violations of the articles mentioned above, organize it, and forward it along with our appraisal of its reliability to the appropriate Heads of States and to the public.

In some cases, when the Group encounters specific information about extreme acts of inhumanity such as:

- removing children from the custody of religious parents who wish to raise their children in their own faith;
- compulsory psychiatric treatment aimed at altering a person's ideas, conscience, religion, beliefs;
- the most dramatic cases of division of families;
- extreme inhumanity in treating prisoners of conscience,

the Group intends to ask Heads of States and the public to form International Commissions for verifying such information on the spot, since the Group itself will not always be able to verify such crucial information directly.

The Group hopes that its information will be taken into account at all the official meetings stipulated by the Final Act in the section, "Follow-up to the Conference."

In their activities, the members of the Support Group are proceeding from the conviction that problems of humaneness and openness of information directly relate to problems of international security, and we call upon the public of the other states participating in the Helsinki Conference to form their own national Support Groups to promote full implementation of the Helsinki Accords by their respective Governments.

We hope that in future a corresponding International Support Committee will also be formed.

The members of the Public Group to Support Compliance with the Helsinki Accords in the USSR are:

> Ludmilla Alexeeva
> Mikhail Bernshtam
> Yelena Bonner
> Alexander Ginzburg
> Pyotr Grigorenko
> Dr. Alexander Korchak
> Malva Landa

Anatoly Marchenko
Prof. Yuri Orlov, leader of the group
Prof. Vitaly Rubin
Anatoly Shcharansky

May [12], 1976
Moscow

INDEX

Abrikosov, Alexei, 162
Agursky, Mikhail, 175
Agursky, Venya, 175
Airikyan, Paruir, 178, 179, 236
Albrecht, Vladimir, 186, 207, 276
Aleksanyan, Akop, 153, 159
Alexander Gerasimovich, 134–135
Alexeeva, Ludmilla "Lyuda," 162, 299–
    300, 301
  author's arrest and, 205, 213, 214,
    215
  campaign for author's release by,
    227n, 241, 262
  Helsinki Watch and, 189, 190, 196,
    201, 204
Alikhanov, Abram Isakovich, 101, 117,
    118–119, 121, 128, 130, 136, 141,
    143–144, 149–151
Alikhanyan, Artemii Isakovich, 136,
    140, 141, 142, 144, 146–147, 149,
    156, 157, 158, 221
Amalrik, Andrei, 186–187, 188–189,
    198, 207
Ambartsumyan, Victor, 171
Amnesty International, 168, 171–172,
    176, 185–186, 207
Amundsen, Roald, 46
Andropov, Yuri, 260, 272, 277n, 295
anti-revolutionary revolutionaries, 323
Armand, Yelena, 162
arrestometer, 114–115
Arutyunyan, Marzpet, 240, 247, 248,
    251, 252, 254, 259, 261, 262

Arutyunyan, Shagen, 240
Avalov, Robert, 119
Azbel, Mark, 174

Bagritsky, Eduard, 52
Baier, Vladimir, 147
Baltic republics, 317, 329, 330
Bandera, Stepan, 81
Barabanov, Alexander "Sasha," 56, 272,
    280, 284, 286, 305–306
Baragin, Pyotr (author's stepfather), 50,
    61, 64, 68, 90, 297
Baragin, Vasily "Vasya," 61, 62
Barakhlo, 285, 290–291, 313
Begin, Menachem, 237
Belotserkovsky, Vadim, 221
Bely, Andrei, 205
Berdnyk, Oles, 204
Berestetsky, Vladimir Borisovich, 110,
    112, 114–115, 116, 143, 207
Bernstein, Robert, 308
besprizornik, 34, 141
Blokhina, V. P., 184, 229
Bogolyubov, N. N., 188
Bogomolov, Yevgeny "Zhenya," 106–
    107, 116, 131–132
Bogoraz, Larisa, 153, 189, 190, 305, 318
Bohr, Niels, 100n, 113
Böll, Heinrich, 173
Bonner, Yelena, 161, 173, 187, 191,
    231n, 258, 276–277, 319
Brandt, Willi, 301

Brezhnev, Leonid, 164–165, 166, 185,
194–195, 203, 226, 329, 331–336
Britansky Soyuznik, 79
Brodsky, Joseph, 174
Bryksin, Ivan Yemelyanovich, 105, 166,
167, 182, 318
Bryksina, Anna Ivanovna "Anya," 165–
168, 175, 179, 182, 186, 318, 322
Bryksina, Nona, 166, 318
Bryksina, Yekaterina Mikhailovna, 166,
167, 172, 318, 319, 322
Budker, Gersh Itskovich (Andrei
Mikhailovich), 106, 114, 117, 133,
147, 163, 173, 221
Bukharin, Nikolai, 54, 79
Bukovsky, Vladimir, 183, 204, 317
Burlakov, 149

capitalism, 115–116, 119, 135, 153
Carter, Jimmy, 228
Carter, Rosalynn, 320, 322, 325
Cavendish Laboratory, 100n
Ceaucescu, Nicolae, 325
CEC (Central Executive Committee), 35
central planning, 83, 186, 314, 328
CERN, 122, 277, 286–287, 308–309,
312
Charpak, Georges, 309
Charter 77, 203n
Chebrikov, Victor, 312
Cheka:
creator of, 131
"prophylaxis" program of, 84
secret police called, 40n, 82n
Chekists, *see* KGB.
Chernenko, Konstantin, 272
children, removal of, 200
China, human rights abuses in, 319
Chirikov, Boris, 130
Chitava, Vakhtang, 247, 251–254
Christian Committee for the Defense of
Believers' Rights, 203
Chronicle of Current Events, 178–179,
187, 205
Churganov, Anatoly, 250–251
Chuvilo, I. V., 150
CIA Target—The USSR (Yakovlev), 273
Code of Criminal Procedure, 223, 228
collective farms, 63–64, 77
collectivization, 23–24, 31–32, 73, 81,
140–141
Combs, Richard, 297
Communism, 53, 83, 99, 200, 282, 324
Communist Party of the Soviet Union,
315, 317, 324, 326, 329, 330
Conference on Security and
Cooperation in Europe, human
rights meetings of:
in Copenhagen, 307, 320
in Paris, 307, 312, 319
in Moscow, 304–305, 307, 309, 310,
320

Conference on Security and
Cooperation in Europe, review
conferences of:
in Belgrade, 310
in Madrid, 198, 234–235, 242–243,
244n, 310
in Vienna, 288, 301–305, 307, 309–
310
Congress of Peace-Loving Forces, 168
Congress of People's Deputies, 316, 317,
319, 320
Cornell University, 305–306
Corvalán, Luis, 204
Criminal Code, 312n
Czechoslovakia, Soviet invasion of, 152–
153, 330

Daniel, Yuli, 153
Daniloff, Nicholas, 298
Dasiv, Kuzma, 236
denunciations, 56–57, 81–82, 105–106,
131–132, 141, 163, 282
DESY, 277, 312
détente, 194–195
Dickens, Charles, 130
Dina, 279, 285, 289, 290–291, 313
Dubov, 199
Dzerzhinsky, Felix, 52, 131, 216
Dzhemilyev, Mustafa, 196
Dzhrbashyan, 171

"Economic Problems of Socialism"
(Stalin), 115
Einstein, Albert, 113
"enemies of the people," 55, 62–63
Engels, Friedrich, 84
environmental reeducation, 107–108
Esenin-Volpin, Alexander, 149
Estonia, 329

Fang Lizhi, 319, 320
Fascell, Dante B., 219
Fedotov, Ivan, 177–178
Fenwick, Millicent, 188, 219, 304
Finland, Soviet invasion of, 60–61
First Circle, The (Solzhenitsyn), 166, 167
Fitzpatrick, Catherine "Katya," 301, 325
"500-day plan," 328, 329
Fock, Vladimir Alexandrovich, 113
food rationing, 31, 73–74, 96, 282

Gadeyev, 237, 250, 251, 260–261
Gamow, George, 79, 113
Garick, *see* Nagorsky, Garik
genetics, 79, 107–108
Ginzburg, Alexander, 162, 189, 190,
196, 201, 202, 204, 207–208, 211,
212, 213, 214, 294
Ginzburg, V. L., 188
glasnost, 286, 304, 315–316, 323, 324,
326, 328, 330
Gluzman, Semyon, 183

Gogol, Nikolai, 294
Golfand, Yuri, 280
Gorbachev, Mikhail Sergeyevich, 165,
    173, 180, 285, 300, 316, 317, 325,
    326–330
  coup by, 327, 328
  difference between Yeltsin and, 326
  KGB and, 327
  reforms of, 326–327
  Sakharov and, 300–301, 316
  as savior of Party, 315
  self-contradictory goals of, 306, 326
  violence in Lithuania and, 329–330
  Western attitudes toward, 303, 304
Gorky, Maxim, 46, 52, 54
Gornostayev, Misha, 278, 292, 313
Gottfried, Kurt, 306
Grigorenko, Pyotr, 183, 191, 196
Grigorenko, Zinaida Mikhailovna, 183
Gulag Archipelago, The (Solzhenitsyn),
    172, 173, 205
Gurfinkel, Rosa, 34, 35–46, 63

Havel, Vaclav, 320
Helsinki Accords (1975), 188–189, 302,
    310
Helsinki Watch (U.S.), 301, 306, 307,
    320, 321
Helsinki Watch Group (Moscow)
  author's trial and, 225, 227, 231
  democratization in USSR and, 195
  disbanding of, 277
  documents produced by, 195–197,
    200–201, 203–204
  founding of, 188–192, 225, 337–339
  on international security, 302
  KGB searches and, 204–205
  new members of, 236
  publicity on, 192–193, 194–195, 213–
    214
  rebirth of, 322
  Russian Social Fund and, 295
  Shcharansky case and, 218–219
  support for other groups, 203
  Working Commission on psychiatric
    abuse and, 206
Helsinki Watch movement
    (international), 203, 277, 301
Helsinki Watch movement (Soviet
    Union):
  beginnings, 203
  declaration on terrorism, 207
  on international security, 302
  KGB searches and, 204
  Moscow group and, 203
  Nobel Prize nomination for, 223, 232,
    233
  persecution of members of, 276, 299
  Shultz appeal and, 301
  Western praise of, 310
Home Guard, 59, 66
homosexuality, 248

Hughes, Vernon, 307
human rights, international security
    and, 301–303
Hungary, postwar elections in, 77–78

individualism, 43, 99, 102, 330
Initiative Group for the Defense of
    Human Rights, 183
Institute for Physical Problems, 136
Institute of Nuclear Physics,
    Novosibirsk, 147, 287, 311
Institute of Nuclear Research, Dubna,
    112, 134
Institute of Terrestrial Magnetism and
    Dissemination of Radio Waves,
    162
Institute of Theoretical and
    Experimental Physics (ITEP),
    112, 117, 118–122
International Helsinki Federation (IHF),
    277, 301, 320
  Moscow meeting (1990), 320, 322–325
International Human Rights Day, 180,
    261
"Is a Nontotalitarian Socialism Possible?"
    (Orlov), 186
isolators, 233, 238, 242, 256
ITEP, see Institute of Theoretical and
    Experimental Physics

Jews, Soviet, 79, 104–105, 111, 125,
    125n, 201, 300

Kalistratova, Sofia, 277, 318
Kampelman, Max, 244
Kandyba, Ivan, 202
Kapayev, 223
Kapitsa, Pyotr Leonidovich, 98, 99–100,
    101, 112, 113, 114, 136, 164,
    277n
Karabakh Committee, 309
Karpenok, Mikhail "Misha," 247, 251
Kashlev, Yuri, 307
Katalikov, 223
Katyn, Polish officers murdered at, 80
Kelly, Petra, 301
Kennedy, Kerry, 320
KGB:
  coup by, 327
  Gorbachev's relations with, 327
  information leaks from, 231–232
  informers of, 131–132, 141, 215–216,
    236, 239, 290
  pedigree of, 40n
  perestroika and, 327
  provocateurs of, 199, 247–248
  psychiatric incarceration by, 183
  searches by, 185–186, 204–205
  secret agents of, 163, 197–198
  surveillance by, 141–142, 165, 174–
    175, 179–182, 198–199, 207, 239
Kheifets, Semyon, 142

Khodorovich, Sergei, 180, 276
Khodorovich, Tatiana Sergeyevna
    "Tanya," 178–179, 180, 183,
    189–190
Khrushchev, Nikita Sergeyevich, 65,
    118, 121, 128, 131, 139, 140,
    143–145, 146, 178, 315
    in Armenia, 143–145
    author's dismissal and, 121, 128
    Hitler's invasion and, 65
    reforms instituted under, 131, 139,
        146, 315
    religious persecution under, 178
    "thaw" under, 131
    Twentieth Party Congress speech of,
        118, 139, 140
Kirov, Sergei, 40
Klava, 111, 119, 120
Klebanov, Vladimir, 199–200
Kobyai, Siberia, 270, 271–273, 281–282,
    284–285
Kobzarev, Igor, 188
Kodors, 253
Kohl, Helmut, 301
kolkhoz, 23–24
Kolomensky, Andrei, 170, 171–172
Komsomol, 40, 53, 66, 107, 167, 168
Kopelev, Lev, 172
Korchak, Alexander, 190, 193
Korolyov, Sergei Pavlovich, 113, 215
Koryagin, Anatoly, 240, 299, 301
Kostya, 159–160
Kovalyov, Ivan, 276
Kovalyov, Sergei, 181, 208, 276, 318,
    325
    trial of, 187–188
Kronrod, Alexander, 149–150
Kryuchkov, Vladimir, 329
kulaks, 23, 24, 31
Kurchatov, Igor Vasilyevich, 112, 113–
    114
Kuron, Jacek, 317
Kuzmitchov, Yuri, 59
Kuznetsov, Yevgeny "Zhenya," 106–107,
    132

Laber, Jeri, 308, 325
labor camps, classifications of, 178n
Lake Sevan, 144–145
Landa, Malva, 190, 193, 195, 201, 205,
    276
Landau, Lev Davidovich, 98, 100, 101,
    112, 113, 133
Lebedev, Andrei, 170, 171–172
Lebedev, Pyotr (grandfather), 34
Le Corbusier, 118
Lefèvre, Pierre, 286, 308, 309
Lefortovo Prison, 215–216, 294–295
Lenin, V. I., 62, 70, 114, 119, 162, 195,
    324, 327, 330
Leningrad, 329
Leningrad University, 114

Lenin Library, 60
Leontovich, Mikhail, 221
LEP, 308
Levich, Veniamin, 174, 188
Lipavsky, Sanya, 197–198, 201
Literary Gazette, 207, 294
Litvinov, Maxim, 176
Litvinova, Tatiana, 176
London, Jack, 58
Louis, Victor, 206
Lubarsky, Kronid, 301
Lubentsova, V. G., 226, 227, 229, 230
Lubyanka Prison, 40, 103
Lukyanenko, Levko, 202
Lumumba Institute, 239
Lysenko, Trofim Denisovich, 107–108

MacBride, Sean, 168, 176
Macdonald, John, 227, 301
Makarov-Zemlyansky, 157, 158, 181
Mandela, Nelson, 300
Marchais, Georges, 185
Marchenko, Anatoly, 190, 195, 202,
    299–300, 301, 305, 318
Marchenko, Valery, 233–234
Markov, Moisei, 286
Marx, Karl, 83, 84, 99, 115, 324
Marxism, 84, 89, 98, 99, 107–108, 115
Maslyansky, 102, 103–105, 126
Mayakovsky, Vladimir, 52
Medvedev, Roy, 162
Meiman, Naum, 277
Memorial Society meetings, 316–318
Mendel, Gregor, 108
Mensheviks, 121–122
Metalnikov, 54–55
Mezentsev, 120, 121, 122, 157
MGB, 40n, 82n, 103
Michnik, Adam, 317
Migulin, Vladimir, 221
Mikolashka, 56–57
Mikoyan, Anastas, 156
Military-Industrial Committee, 149
Ministry of Middle Machine Building,
    156–157
Möhl, Dieter, 286, 308, 309
Molotov, V. M., 61, 66
Molotov-Ribbentrop Pact (1939), 66
Mongol, see Tarasenko, Victor "Mongol"
Morgan, Thomas Hunt, 108
Morozov, Georgy, 184
Morozov, Mark, 210, 231, 232, 246, 250,
    251, 252, 254
Morozov, Pavlik, 223
Moscow Committee for Human Rights,
    168
Moscow Industrial Institute, 81
Moscow University, Physico-Technical
    Department of, 92, 96–101, 111,
    114
Muller, Hermann, 79
My Testimony (Marchenko), 190

Nagorsky, Garik, 159, 179–180
Natalya Nikolayevna, 46
Neier, Aryeh, 308
Nekipelov, Victor, 236, 276
NEP (New Economic Policy), 35, 118, 313, 330
Nesterov, Vadim, 120
Nicholas II, czar of Russia, 46, 116–117
Nikolayev, 126, 127, 128
Nilov, Alexander, 239, 245, 246, 247
Nina Ivanovna, 280, 281, 284, 285, 286, 313
Nina Sergeyevna, 161
Nixon, Richard, 174
Nizhny Tagil, 72
NKVD, 40, 80n
nonlinear oscillations, theory of, 117
Novocherkassk, 154–156
NTS, 205

October Revolution, 46, 150
Okhlopkov, Lieutenant, 272, 274, 275, 279, 283, 286
Okun, Lev, 132, 207, 221, 312
Order of Lenin, 150
Orekhov, Victor, 210, 231–232
Orlov, Alexander "Sasha" (son), 117, 143, 157, 159, 202, 209, 212, 221, 262, 297, 311, 312, 313, 318
  labor camp visited by, 241
  Siberian exile and, 276, 277–278, 280, 282–283, 286
  trial attended by, 226, 228, 231
Orlov, Dmitry "Dima" (son), 110–111, 118, 143, 157, 159, 209, 221, 297, 313, 318
  trial attended by, 226, 228, 230–231
Orlov, Dmitry "Mitya" (uncle), 21, 30, 32, 33, 37–39, 41, 49, 95
  collectivization and, 23, 24
  on wolves, 17–20
Orlov, Fyodor Pavlovich "Fedya" (father), 22, 30–36, 59, 110, 297
  death of, 37–38, 39
  as father, 31, 35
Orlov, Lev (son), 147, 148, 150, 221, 281, 297, 313, 318
Orlov, Pavel (grandfather), 16, 18, 19, 126
Orlov, Pyotr Pavlovich "Petya" (uncle), 17–18, 20, 21, 30, 32, 33, 37, 41, 49, 69, 70, 71, 72, 90, 94–95, 135
  collectivization and, 23
  ironic attitude of, 55–57, 70
  political beliefs of, 97
Orlov, Vladimir "Vovka" (cousin), 71, 90
Orlov, Yuri Fyodorovich:
  activism vs. scientific work of, 97, 112, 130, 154, 156, 181, 307
  Amnesty International and, 168, 176
  Armenian Academy of Sciences and,

154, 156–157, 162, 170–171, 179, 233, 237, 243
  arrests of, 174–175, 207, 208, 213, 214–215, 220, 231
  baptismal name of, 16
  campaign for, 241, 262, 277, 286–287, 309
  campaign to free Soviet political prisoners, 298–302, 304
  Chekist effort to recruit, 85–88
  country childhood of, 15–29, 41–42
  deportation of, 296–298
  economic ideas of, 115–116, 119, 135, 164–165, 186
  education of, 27, 44, 45–48, 51, 59–60, 62, 71, 76, 81, 88, 89, 91–92, 96–102
  factory work of, 69–75, 92
  family village of, 20–21, 24, 297
  as father, 110–111, 117, 143, 147–148, 157, 159, 181, 221, 281, 296, 297, 311, 313
  finances of, 50–51, 100, 101, 117, 130, 133, 162, 173, 174, 281
  girlfriends of, 44–45, 84–85
  health of, 17, 20, 22, 39, 42, 58, 75, 148–149, 233, 240, 244, 253, 259, 267, 269, 272, 278
  hunger strikes by, 237, 238, 241, 242, 243, 253, 259–260, 261
  in hiding, 192–193, 208–214
  interrogations of, 82, 85–88, 103–105, 126–128, 205–206, 207, 216–222, 256–257, 295–296
  ITEP dismissal of, 121, 123–125, 133, 143–144, 313
  as janitor, 96
  KGB prosecution of, 153, 220, 222–224
  KGB surveillance of, 132, 141–142, 165, 174–175, 179–182, 198–199, 207, 329
  in labor camps, 232–262
  Lysenko's genetics investigated by, 107–109
  marriages of, 110, 147–148, 149, 161, 214, 235, 305–306
  on means vs. ends, 62, 131, 206, 330
  military service and, 66, 75–78, 80–81, 89
  Moscow boyhood of, 29–65
  Moscow revisited by, 311–319, 320–325
  on nonviolence, 8, 53, 140, 323, 330
  Party membership and, 77, 82, 86, 107, 118–119, 122, 150–151, 162
  philosophy studied by, 51, 59, 89
  political beliefs developed by, 53, 81–84, 88, 89, 97, 102, 115–116, 118, 119–120, 131, 134–135, 140, 153–154, 164–165, 180–181, 300

Orlov, Yuri Fyodorovich (*cont.*)
  political doubts of, 51–52, 62–64, 70,
      73, 79, 89, 97
  in prison, 215–217, 220, 232, 295
  as private tutor, 133, 162, 174, 181
  pseudonym used by, 173
  refusal to emigrate by, 207
  release of, 288–298
  samizdat essay by, 186
  scientific articles by, 117, 122, 173,
      181, 221, 232, 242, 254, 257, 286
  scientific career of, 88, 89, 110, 111–
      112, 117, 121, 122, 128, 130, 136,
      142–143, 146, 147, 149, 154,
      156–158, 170–171, 239, 305–
      308, 311, 312, 320–321
  second case against, 245, 250, 251,
      252, 256–258, 274, 275
  in Siberian exile, 271–291
  Soviet citizenship of, 296, 317
  trial of, 185, 225–231, 233, 307, 312
Orlova, Elizaveta "Liza" (wife of Petya),
      41, 68, 71, 90
Orlova, Irina "Ira" (wife), 147, 148, 149,
      150, 154, 221
Orlova, Klavdiya Petrovna (mother), 22,
      30, 32, 40–42, 48, 90, 96
  background of, 34–36, 91, 130
  death of, 129, 135
  first marriage of, 35–38
  ill health of, 90–92, 101, 128–129
  jobs of, 33, 39–40, 50, 72, 92, 135
  as mother, 22, 41–44, 45, 51, 59, 65,
      68
  protectiveness of, 49, 53–54, 55
  remarriage of, 42, 48, 50
Orlova, Pelageya (grandmother):
  attitude to hardship of, 24, 27–28
  attitude to violence of, 18, 20, 22
  author raised by, 16–17, 20, 22, 24,
      26–28, 39
  background of, 27, 117
  death of, 95
  Fyodor Orlov's death and, 37, 38
  living earned by, 15–16, 24, 25, 33,
      48, 65
  Mitya Orlov's abuse of, 38–39
  wolves and, 16–17
  World War II and, 66–67, 95
Orlova, Zinaida "Zina" (aunt), 27, 51, 91
Orzhonikidze, Sergo, 69–70
Osipov, Mikhail, 70
Osipova, Tatiana, 236, 276
Owen, David, 306–307

Paperno, Vyacheslav "Slava," 306
Papkevich, Galina "Galya" (wife), 110,
      111, 117, 118, 129, 130–131, 136,
      143, 147, 148, 157, 312, 318
  interrogation of, 221
Pasteur, Louis, 46
Pentecostals, 177–178, 200, 202, 208

perestroika, 272, 286, 306–307, 312, 315,
      316, 323, 326–327, 328, 330
Petersburg (Bely), 205
Petrov, 53
Petrov-Agatov, 208, 294
Picasso, Emilio, 308
Plyushch, Leonid, 180, 183, 184–185,
      188, 222, 229
Plyushch, Tatiana "Tanya," 180,
      183–185
Podgorny, Nikolai, 186
Podrabinek, Alexander, 204, 206, 231,
      313
Poland, 60, 80, 203*n*, 317
Polikanov, Sergei, 236
Pomeranchuk, Isaac, 112, 117, 149
Ponomaryov, Lev, 276, 277, 316, 317,
      325
Pontecorvo, Bruno, 133–134, 328
"Prague Spring," 152
Pravda, 63, 121–122, 163
psychiatry, political abuse of, 183–185,
      199–200, 206, 240
Pugo, Boris K., 330
Pushkin, Alexander, 46, 81, 161, 224
Pypin, Alexander, 147

Reagan, Ronald, 298, 300, 308
refuseniks, 174, 197, 300, 308
Reinharz, Anya, 309
Reinharz, Max, 309
Resurrection (Tolstoi), 62
Ribbentrop, Joachim von, 61, 66
Rubbia, Carlo, 308
Rubin, Vitaly, 189, 190, 197, 198
Rudenko, Mikola, 186, 204, 213
Rumer, Yuli Borisovich, 113
Russian parliament, 325, 329
Russian Republic, 323, 325, 326, 327,
      328, 329
Russian Social Fund to Aid Political
      Prisoners and Their Families,
      201, 208, 276, 295
Rutherford, Ernest, 100*n*

Sadat, Anwar as-, 237
Sagdeyev, Roald Z., 162, 164, 221
Sakharov, Andrei Dmitriyevich, 160,
      161, 162, 168, 170, 171, 173, 181,
      183, 185, 187, 196, 208, 225, 273,
      277, 299, 300–301, 302, 312, 316,
      317, 318, 319, 320
  author's friendship with, 160–161,
      164, 170, 173, 283, 297, 312, 319
  author's trial and, 231*n*, 319
  commitment to nonviolence of, 323
  death of, 319–320, 325
  Moscow Helsinki Watch Group and,
      191, 195
  persecution of, 163–164, 276, 277
  reform judged impossible by, 190
  samizdat, 153, 162, 178, 315, 323

Schmemann, Serge, 298
Schwartzenberg, Karl Johannes von, 323
science, Marxism and, 89, 98, 107–108, 115
Sergo Ordzhonikidze Lathe Factory, 69–72, 135
Sessler, Andrew, 287
Seventh-Day Adventists, 195, 200
Shafarevich, Igor, 170, 183
Shalman, Yevgeny, 223–224, 226, 228, 232
Shaposhnikov, Matvei Kuzmich, 155n
sharagas, 113, 113n, 172, 314
Shatalin, Stanislav, 328
Shcharansky, Anatoly "Tolya," 187, 197–198, 201, 217, 218–219, 276, 277, 295
    author's arrest and, 213, 214
    Helsinki Watch and, 188, 189, 190, 191, 197, 201, 202
Shcholokov, Nikolai, 226
Shelkov, Vladimir, 195
Shevardnadze, Eduard, 298
Shevchenko, Oles, 259, 261
shock-workers, 51
Shostakovich, Dmitry, 140
Shostakovich, Nina, 140
Shultz, George, 300, 301, 308
Skrinsky, Alexander, 311
Slepak, Alexander, 197, 201, 202
Snezhnevsky, Andrei V., 184–185
socialism:
    capitalism and, 135, 186, 119–120
    communism vs., 83
    in Czechoslovakia, 152, 153
    democracy and, 119–120, 134–135, 164
    failure of, 8, 324
    as idée fixe, 139
Socialist Revolutionaries, 121–122
Solidarity, 317
Solzhenitsyn, Alexander Isayevich, 136, 165–166, 167, 168, 172, 173, 182, 201, 205, 208, 295, 296, 317
    author's meetings with, 165–166, 172–173
    as political prisoner, 136
SOS Committee, 277
Sources of Fast Neutrons, The (Orlov), 173
Soviet Union:
    absurdity commonplace in, 7
    central planning in, 83, 314, 328
    détente policy and, 194–195
    as dictatorship of bureaucracy, 84
    dissidents' existence denied by, 300
    economic crisis of, 306–307, 313–314, 328
    education under Stalin in, 47n, 51–52, 59
    as empire, 330
    environmental catastrophe in, 324
    German invasion of, 65–66, 67, 71

Jews in, 59, 104–105, 111, 125, 125n, 201, 300
    mass political murder in, 8, 314, 314n, 324
    official corruption in, 226
    one-party system in, 83, 326
    political opposition denied by, 300
    postrevolutionary culture of, 51–53
    self-cannibalism of, 314
    "Winter War" with Finland of, 60–61
sovkhoz, 273n, 282
Stakhanov, Alexei, 55–56
Stalin, Joseph, 47, 65–66, 78, 80, 81, 155
    agricultural success claimed by, 115
    Armenian deportations under, 138–139
    attack on science under, 112–115
    death of, 116–117
    Gorky's poisoning ordered by, 54
    Khrushchev and, 118, 139, 146
    Lenin and, 62, 114
    nuclear weapons development and, 98, 114
    Russians' support for, 139
    Soviet constitution and, 82
Steel, David, 227n
Stolypin, Pyotr, 233n
Stolypin cars, 233, 263
Sudakov, Vladimir "Volodya," 112, 120
Supreme Soviet, Presidium of, 35n

Talochka, 49
Tamara Alexeyevna, 279, 280, 281, 282, 283–284, 285, 313
tamizdat, 167
Tarasenko, Victor "Mongol," 244, 247–248, 249, 250, 251, 252, 253, 256
Tarasov, Yevgeny Kuprianovich:
    author aided by, 173, 207, 209
    author's friendship with, 131, 211, 312, 313, 318
    scientific career of, 122, 142, 173
    visits to Siberia by, 276, 277, 280, 285, 286
Tarasova, Mila, 212, 313
Tarasova, Zinaida Afanasyevna, 210, 211, 212, 313
Thatcher, Margaret, 301, 304–305, 306
"Thirteen Questions to Brezhnev" (Orlov), 164–165, 186, 331–336
Tikhonov, A. I., 204, 205, 206, 214
Tikhy, Oleksy, 204, 213
Tolstoi, Alexei, 80
Tolstoi, Lev, 44, 46, 62, 73, 147, 200
Tolstoi Children's Library, 45–46
Tretyakov, Yevgeny, 122
Trofimov, 220
Trostnikov, Victor, 101–102
Trotsky, Leon, 54, 131, 296
Tsvigun, Semyon Kuzmich, 226, 227
T-34 tanks, 7, 72

Tupolev, Andrei Nikolayevich, 113, 215
Turchin, Valentin "Valya," 131, 162,
    175–176, 181, 185, 299, 301
  Amnesty International Group begun
    by, 168, 176
  author's arrest and, 207, 212, 213,
    214, 231
  campaign for author's release by, 241,
    262, 277
  Helsinki Watch and, 188–189, 202,
    205
  on "inertia of fear," 152
Tverdokhlebov, Andrei, 168, 176,
    185–186
Twentieth Party Congress, 118, 139

Ukraine, author's trip to, 202

Valitova, Irina (wife):
  author's arrest and, 208, 214, 220,
    221, 226, 227n
  author's deportation and, 297–298,
    305
  author's Siberian exile and, 272, 276–
    277, 278, 279, 284, 286, 287
  author's trial and, 226, 228, 230, 231
  background of, 156
  campaign for author by, 241–244,
    262, 278
  dissident friends of, 187, 197
  as founding member of Amnesty
    group, 168
  information from author transmitted
    by, 235–236, 237, 239, 241–244,
    262
  KGB and, 174–175, 181, 186, 192,
    198–199, 204, 205, 287
  labor camp visited by, 235–236, 241
  on living among dissidents, 162
  marriage of, 156, 161, 221–222, 250,
    305–306
  prison visited by, 232
  travels of, 159, 202
Van der Meer, Simon, 286, 308
Vaska, 21–22
Vassilev, Yevgeny, 58
Vavilov, Nikolai Ivanovich, 79, 113

Vavilov, Sergei, 113
Veksler, Marat, 198, 208, 285
Veksler, Yekaterina "Katya," 198, 286
Velikhanova, Tatiana "Tanya," 179, 276,
    318
Velikhov, Yevgeny, 286
Vilnius, Lithuania, 329
Virko, Igor, 173
Vishinsky, Andrei, 227
Vlasov, Anatoly, 200, 208
Vlasov, Yuri, 316
Voitsekhovsky, Bogdan, 102, 103
Voronel, Alexander, 174
Voronina, Lidiya, 201, 204, 205

Wald, George, 285–286
Walesa, Lech, 317
wave logic, 164, 181, 232, 280, 308
Weisskopf, Victor, 157–158
wheat, Lysenko's experiments on, 108
"Why Did I Leave the Soviet Union?"
    (Gamow), 79
"Will the Soviet Union Survive Until
    1984?" (Amalrik), 186–187
workers, 64, 84, 134, 154

Yakovlev, Nikolai, 273
Yakovlev, Yuri Sergeyevich, 216, 218,
    219, 220, 221, 222
Yakubov, Adil, 316
Yakunin, Gleb, 203, 255, 261, 262, 276,
    317, 318, 325
Yavlinsky, Gregory, 328
Yazov, Dmitry T., 329
Yeltsin, Boris, 317, 325, 327–328, 329,
    330
Yemelyanov, S. A., 226, 229–230
Yerevan Physics Institute, 136, 142, 150,
    158
Yesin, Sergei, 150
Young Pioneers, 47, 53
Yuri Pavlovich, 279, 280, 282, 283

Zakharov, G. F., 298
zatirukha, 73
Zimmerman, Warren, 309
Zyuzya, 19, 24, 27, 28–29